ADMINISTRATIVE BEHAVIOR

A Study of Decision-Making Processes
in Administrative Organizations

HERBERT A. SIMON

FOURTH EDITION

fP

THE FREE PRESS

THE FREE PRESS
A Division of Simon & Schuster Inc.
1230 Avenue of the Americas
New York, NY 10020

THE FREE PRESS and colophon are trademarks
of Simon & Schuster Inc.

Designed by Michael Mendelsohn of MM Design 2000, Inc.

Manufactured in the United States of America

printing number

20 19 18 17

Library of Congress Cataloging-in-Publication Data

Simon, Herbert Alexander, 1916–
    Administrative behavior: a study of decision-making processes in
administrative organizations / Herbert A. Simon.—4th ed.
        p. cm.
    Includes index.
    ISBN 0–684–83582–7 (alk. paper)
    1. Management.   2. Decision-making.   3. Organizational behavior.
I. Title.
HD31.S55   1997
658.4—dc20   96–34148
                                                         CIP

To D. P. S.

CONTENTS

INTRODUCTION TO THE FOURTH EDITION

WITH THIS FOURTH EDITION, *Administrative Behavior* marks its fiftieth birthday. As we are made constantly aware of the lightning speed of change in our world, we might well ask whether anything that was written before mid-century could still be true as the second millennium approaches. If our topic were electronic computers or molecular genetics, little in a 1997 edition might survive from 1947. However, our topic is organizations. Human organizations, quite large ones, have been with us for at least four thousand years. Although the physical technology a modern army employs is wholly different from the technology employed by the armies of Nineveh or Egypt or X'ian, the processes people used in these ancient armies to make decisions or to manage people appear quite familiar to us and largely unchanged over the centuries. Basic organizational processes have not yet undergone a deep revolution. At most, they have just begun, in our own era, to confront major change, both social and technological.

So the task of this book, in its fourth appearance, is twofold. The first task is to describe clearly those processes—decision-making and management of people—that have been central to the effective operation of human organizations since their first appearance. The second task is to examine how modern technology—both changes in social values and practices, and the new technologies of electronic communication and information processing—are now changing management and decision-making. For the first task, we can rely mainly upon the original text of *Administrative Behavior*. To fill gaps in that text, modify some emphases, and address the new knowledge we have gained and the new problems and opportunities that confront organizations, we shall have to amplify it in considerable measure.

THE BOOK'S AIMS

Administrative Behavior is basically a book for organization watchers and organization designers. As the preface to the original edition explains, the book's aim is to show how organizations can be understood in terms of their decision processes. Almost all of us qualify as organization watchers, as we spend most of our waking lives in organizational environments.

Many of us qualify also as organization designers, as we have managerial responsibilities of greater or lesser scope for maintaining and modifying organizations.

We are organization watchers, too, all of us, in our role as citizens. Increasing attention (and criticism) has been fixed in recent years upon the functioning of our society's largest organizations: its large corporations and its governmental agencies. Hence, this could also be described as a book for Everyperson—for it proposes a way of thinking constructively about organizational issues that concern all of us. Somewhat in contrast to current public cynicism, *Administrative Behavior* is generally upbeat about organizations, and although mindful of their shortcomings, it focuses on how they operate, and particularly on the conditions that enable them to operate well.

STRUCTURE OF THE BOOK

In this fourth edition, as in the previous ones, the text of the original work is kept intact, for there is essentially nothing in it that I wish to retract. *Administrative Behavior* has served me as a useful and reliable port of embarkation for voyages of discovery into human decision-making: the relation of organization structure to decision-making, the formalized decision-making of operations research and management science, and in more recent years, the thinking and problem-solving activities of individual human beings. Evidently, it has served a similar function for many other persons, for it continues to be widely read and cited.

But although I have no urge to recant, I do wish to augment the text considerably. In order both to develop and illustrate some of its important themes and to introduce the new issues that are of current interest and concern, extensive commentaries on these old and new themes have been appended to each of the chapters of the first edition. I think readers will find this format more coherent than the tripartite organization (lengthy introduction, original text, reprints of recent articles) of the previous edition. Anyone who wishes to stick to the "basics" of the first edition can read the eleven chapters and ignore the commentaries. Those who wish to confront some of the gaps in that treatment and the new topics and issues created by a rapidly changing world can include some or all of the commentaries in their reading. Many of the commentaries are drawn from articles that I have published over the years, but they have been wholly rewritten and rearranged for this new edition to give coherence to the text.

The basic organization of the book, then, may be outlined quite simply. After the general introduction and summary of Chapter I and its commentary, it builds up five strata of topics, each of which provides a basis for dealing with the next.

(1) Chapters II and III (and the Appendix following Chapter XI) lay out some conceptual issues that are basic to the structure of human choice.

(2) Chapters IV and V construct a theory that describes and explains the realities of human decision-making, essential for understanding the influences that come to bear upon decision-making in an organizational environment.

(3) Chapter VI provides a motivational link between the individual and the organization—explaining why organizational influences, and particularly the influence of authority, are such effective forces in molding human behavior.

(4) Chapters VII through X examine the main organizational influence processes—authority, communication, efficiency, and organizational loyalty—in detail in order to explain how organization affects the decision-making process.

(5) Chapter XI applies the analysis to questions of organization structure.

Although I have emphasized the basic continuity in human organizational behavior over the centuries, the formal study of organizations is relatively new. *Administrative Behavior* belongs to perhaps the second generation of modern studies of organizations, following the so-called "classical" theory represented by Frederick Taylor, Fayol, and Gulick and Urwick. Since the first edition appeared, there has been a great outpouring of writing and research on human relations and a persistent questioning of earlier views (of both first and second generations) about the exercise of authority in organizations.

During these same years, the study of human thinking and decision processes has also been pursued vigorously, with the result that the theory of bounded rationality that is developed here now rests, much more solidly than fifty years ago, on firm empirical foundations. Moreover, the computer has appeared and multiplied in the world of business, introducing new systems for communication and information processing. Finally, the dependence of organization structure and processes upon environment and technology is now understood with increased clarity. These are some of the new topics that are treated in the expanded text.

Administrative Behavior was written on the assumption that decision-making processes hold the key to understanding organizations. The developments noted above make decision-making even more central to organizations today than it was twenty-five years ago. It is my hope that the book, augmented by the commentaries, will continue to help those who would like to understand better and manage more effectively these complex social systems, the organizations in which we do our work.

An apology: The original text of *Administrative Behavior* was written, of course, long before the norm of gender-neutral writing was established, and its sins egregiously in its almost exclusive use of masculine pronouns. I can only apologize for this historical fact and have tried to make atonement by preserving symmetry of the genders in all of the new materials— the commentaries to the original chapters.

PREFACE TO THE FIRST EDITION

THIS STUDY REPRESENTS AN ATTEMPT to construct tools useful in my own research in the field of public administration. It derived from my conviction that we do not yet have, in this field, adequate linguistic and conceptual tools for realistically and significantly describing even a simple administrative organization—describing it, that is, in a way that will provide the basis for scientific analysis of the effectiveness of its structure and operation. Among the studies of administrative organizations that I have read, few have caught and set down in words the real flesh and bones of an organization; even fewer have convinced me that their conclusions as to the effectiveness of the organization or the recommendations for its improvement could properly be deduced from the evidence presented.

The response to the preliminary edition of this book and to several published articles drawn from it shows that these doubts are not peculiar to me but are shared by many practitioners and researchers in the field of administration. This state of affairs constitutes a serious indictment of our science, and of ourselves as scientists. An experiment in chemistry derives its validity—its scientific authority—from its reproducibility; and unless it is described in sufficient detail to be repeated it is useless. In administration we have as yet only a very imperfect ability to tell what has happened in our administrative "experiments"—much less to insure their reproducibility.

Before we can establish any immutable "principles" of administration, we must be able to describe, in words, exactly how an administrative organization looks and exactly how it works. As a basis for my own studies in administration, I have attempted to construct a vocabulary which will permit such description; and this volume records the conclusions I have reached. These conclusions do not constitute a "theory" of administration, for except for a few dicta offered by way of hypothesis, no principles of administration are laid down. If any "theory" is involved, it is that decision-making is the heart of administration, and that the vocabulary of administrative theory must be derived from the logic and psychology of human choice.

I hope that this volume may be of some use to three groups of persons: first, to individuals concerned with the science of administration, who may find in it some applicable methods of description and analysis of organization; second, to practical administrators who may find it helpful sometimes to think of administration at that third level of generalization of which Mr. Barnard speaks in his Foreword; third, to graduate and undergraduate students who may wish to supplement their textbooks with a closer study of the behavioral processes that go to make the real warp and woof of administration.

HERBERT A. SIMON
December, 1946

ACKNOWLEDGMENTS

"And certainly there were many others ... from whom I had
assimilated a word, a glance, but of whom as individual beings
I remembered nothing; a book is a great cemetery in which,
for the most part, the names upon the tombs are effaced."
Marcel Proust, *Time Regained*

OVER THE MANY YEARS THAT THIS BOOK, or revisions of it, have been
in preparation, the list of persons to whom I am indebted for assistance, criticism, and encouragement has grown to unmanageable proportions. I hope I will be pardoned for singling out a few upon whom I have
called most frequently for help, and failing to name many others who
have aided me.

First Edition:

I am indebted, first, to the Faculty of the University of Chicago which
made of its campus when I studied there a nettle-field of intellectual stimu-
lation, but in particular to Mr. Clarence E. Ridley, the late Professor Henry
Schultz, and Professor Leonard D. White. Among colleagues and others
who have read and criticized earlier drafts or the published preliminary edi-
tion of the book, I must mention Messrs. Lyndon E. Abbott, Herbert
Bohnert, Milton Chernin, William R. Divine, Herbert Emmerich, Victor
Jones, Albert Lepawsky, Lyman S. Moore, Richard O. Niehoff, Charner
Marquis Perry, C. Herman Pritchett, Kenneth J. Seigworth, Edwin O.
Stene, John A. Vieg, William L. C. Wheaton, and the members of the
Public Administration Discussion Group. Mr. Harold Guetzkow proved,
as always, my exceptionally severe and helpful critic.

To the late Chester I. Barnard I owe a special debt: first, for his book,
The Functions of the Executive, which exerted a major influence on my
thinking about administration; secondly, for the extremely careful critical
review he gave the preliminary version of this book; and finally for his
Foreword to the first edition.

Later Editions:

A number of chapters of this book, and important portions of the commentaries, have been adapted from published articles. References to the sources will be found where these materials appear.

Over fifty years, numerous colleagues have contributed to my continuing education on matters administrative and organizational. Many are identified in footnotes, but I should like to single out some with whom I was most closely associated and who therefore are most responsible for what I learned. At Illinois Institute of Technology, there were Victor Thompson and the late Donald Smithburg, with whom I collaborated in writing *Public Administration*. In the 1950s, at what was then Carnegie Institute of Technology, my main partners in organizational studies were, at first, Harold Guetzkow, George Kozmetsky, and Gordon Tyndall; subsequently, Richard Cyert, James March, and William Dill. During the 1950s and into the '60s we carried out a wide range of empirical studies that carried us deep into business organizations and their decision processes. I thank DeWitt C. Dearborn for his permission to use our joint work on identification in the commentary to Chapter X. I am deeply indebted to all of these colleagues, as well as to at least two dozen other faculty colleagues and able graduate students who populated the halls of the Graduate School of Industrial Administration at Carnegie Institute of Technology in this period.

Of course organizational research was not the only source of my education. It came also from extensive observation of the organizations I have lived in and worked in, and in whose management I have participated in a variety of roles: research project director, department head, associate dean, consultant, and trustee. These include four universities (Chicago, Berkeley, Illinois Tech, and Carnegie Mellon), the Economic Cooperation Administration (Marshall Plan organization), a number of corporations and government agencies with which I have had consulting relations, and the Board of Trustees of Carnegie Mellon, on which I have held membership for nearly twenty-five years. In particular, I want to mention my pleasure in working with the late Lee Bach, the first dean of the Graduate School of Industrial Administration, and Jake Warner, Dick Cyert, and Robert Mehrabian, the presidents of Carnegie Mellon University during most of my tenure there.

A book is much work in the making, and in the making of this fourth edition, I have had the friendly and skillful aid of my assistant, Janet Hilf, who has helped at every stage of the process, not the least support being her protection of my time from other demands, and of

Beth Anderson and Philip Rappaport of The Free Press, who served as editors of this project.

As I reread the names of those whose help with the first edition I acknowledged, I find two people whose lifelong friendship I count among my special blessings. No young man could have been more fortunate than I in his first boss. I marvel, in retrospect, at Clarence E. Ridley's combination of theoretical insight and practical astuteness, at his ability both to plan and to see that the plans happened, and at his talent for causing his associates to play way over their heads. I am especially grateful to him for his tolerance of youthful brashness, his almost reckless willingness to delegate responsibility to the young, and his warm friendship.

My friendship with Harold Guetzkow began on a train that carried us both to Chicago in 1933 to become freshmen at the University. It was Harold who first interested me in cognitive psychology when we were still undergraduates. Although that interest incubated for two decades, it has been my major preoccupation, if not obsession, since the middle 1950s. I owe to Harold, among many other things, much of the deep intellectual pleasure that these years have brought me.

And what shall I say of my wife, Dorothea, to whom this edition of *Administrative Behavior*, as well as the three previous editions, is dedicated? Claude Bernard once said, "If I had to define life in a word, it would be: Life is creation." Ten years before *Administrative Behavior* appeared, Dorothea and I decided to share that life of creation; and so we have done: while the book was germinating, while it was being written and published, and during the fifty ensuing years.

CHAPTER I

Decision-Making and Administrative Organization

ADMINISTRATION IS ORDINARILY DISCUSSED as the art of "getting things done." Emphasis is placed upon processes and methods for insuring incisive action. Principles are set forth for securing concerted action from groups of men. In all this discussion, however, not very much attention is paid to the choice which prefaces all action—to the determining of what is to be done rather than to the actual doing. It is with this problem—the process of choice which leads to action—that the present study is concerned. In this introductory chapter the problem will be posed and a survey made of the topics to be taken up in the remaining chapters.

Although any practical activity involves both "deciding" and "doing," it has not commonly been recognized that a theory of administration should be concerned with the processes of decision as well as with the processes of action.[1] This neglect perhaps stems from the notion that decision-making is confined to the formulation of over-all policy. On the contrary, the process of decision does not come to an end when the general purpose of an organization has been determined. The task of "deciding" pervades the entire administrative organization quite as much as does the task of "doing"—indeed, it is integrally tied up with the latter. A general theory of administration must include principles of organization that will insure correct decision-making, just as it must include principles that will insure effective action.

DECISION-MAKING AND THE EXECUTION OF DECISIONS

It is clear that the actual physical task of carrying out an organization's objectives falls to the persons at the lowest level of the administrative

---

[1]For two notable exceptions to the general neglect of decision-making see C. I. Barnard, *The Functions of the Executive* (Cambridge: Harvard University Press, 1938), and Edwin O. Stene, "An Approach to a Science of Administration," *American Political Science Review*, 34:1124–1137 (Dec., 1940).

hierarchy. The automobile, as a physical object, is built not by the engineer or the executive, but by the mechanic on the assembly line. The fire is extinguished, not by the fire chief or the captain, but by the team of firemen who play a hose on the blaze.

It is equally clear that the persons above this lowest or operative level in the administrative hierarchy are not mere surplus baggage, and that they too must have an essential role to play in the accomplishment of the agency's objectives. Even though, as far as physical cause and effect are concerned, it is the machine gunner and not the major who fights battles, the major is likely to have a greater influence upon the outcome of a battle than any single machine gunner.

How, then, do the administrative and supervisory staff of an organization affect that organization's work? The nonoperative staff of an administrative organization participate in the accomplishment of the objectives of that organization to the extent that they influence the decisions of the operatives—the persons at the lowest level of the administrative hierarchy. The major can influence the battle to the extent that his head is able to direct the machine gunner's hand. By deploying his forces in the battle area and assigning specific tasks to subordinate units he determines for the machine gunner where he will take his stand and what his objective will be. In very small organizations the influence of all supervisory employees upon the operative employees may be direct, but in units of any size there are interposed between the top supervisors and the operative employees several levels of intermediate supervisors who are themselves subject to influences from above, and who transmit, elaborate, and modify these influences before they reach the operatives.

If this is a correct description of the administrative process, then the construction of an efficient administrative organization is a problem in social psychology. It is a task of setting up an operative staff and superimposing on that staff a supervisory staff capable of influencing the operative group toward a pattern of coordinated and effective behavior. The term "influencing" rather than "directing" is used here, for direction—that is, the use of administrative authority—is only one of several ways in which the administrative staff may affect the decisions of the operative staff; and, consequently, the construction of an administrative organization involves more than a mere assignment of functions and allocation of authority.

In the study of organization, the operative employee must be at the focus of attention, for the success of the structure will be judged by his performance within it. Insight into the structure and function of an organization can best be gained by analyzing the manner in which the decisions and behavior of such employees are influenced within and by the organization.

CHOICE AND BEHAVIOR

All behavior involves conscious or unconscious selection of particular actions out of all those which are physically possible to the actor and to those persons over whom he exercises influence and authority. The term "selection" is used here without any implication of a conscious or deliberate process. It refers simply to the fact that, if the individual follows one particular course of action, there are other courses of action that he thereby forgoes. In many cases the selection process consists simply in an established reflex action—a typist hits a particular key with a finger because a reflex has been established between a letter on a printed page and this particular key. Here the action is, in some sense at least, rational (i.e. goal-oriented), yet no element of consciousness or deliberation is involved.

In other cases the selection is itself the product of a complex chain of activities called "planning" or "design" activities. An engineer, for example, may decide upon the basis of extensive analysis that a particular bridge should be of cantilever design. His design, further implemented by detailed plans for the structure, will lead to a whole chain of behaviors by the individuals constructing the bridge.

In this volume many examples will be given of all varieties of selection process. All these examples have in common the following characteristics: At any moment there are a multitude of alternative (physically) possible actions, any one of which a given individual may undertake; by some process these numerous alternatives are narrowed down to that one which is in fact acted out. The words "choice" and "decision" will be used interchangeably in this study to refer to this process. Since these terms as ordinarily used carry connotations of self-conscious, deliberate, rational selection, it should be emphasized that as used here they include any process of selection, regardless of whether the above elements are present to any degree.

VALUE AND FACT IN DECISION

A great deal of behavior, and particularly the behavior of individuals within administrative organizations, is purposive—oriented toward goals or objectives. This purposiveness brings about an integration in the pattern of behavior, in the absence of which administration would be meaningless; for, if administration consists in "getting things done" by groups of people, purpose provides a principal criterion in determining what things are to be done.

The minute decisions that govern specific actions are inevitably instances of the application of broader decisions relative to purpose and to method. The walker contracts his leg muscles in order to take a step; he takes a step in order to proceed toward his destination; he is going to the destination, a mail box, in order to mail a letter; he is sending a letter in order to transmit certain information to another person, and so forth. Each decision involves the selection of a goal, and a behavior relevant to it; this goal may in turn be mediate to a somewhat more distant goal; and so on, until a relatively final aim is reached.[2] In so far as decisions lead toward the selection of final goals, they will be called "value judgments"; so far as they involve the implementation of such goals they will be called "factual judgments."[3]

Unfortunately, problems do not come to the administrator carefully wrapped in bundles with the value elements and the factual elements neatly sorted. For one thing, goals or final objectives of governmental organization and activity are usually formulated in very general and ambiguous terms—"justice," "the general welfare," or "liberty." Then, too, the objectives as defined may be merely intermediate to the attainment of more final aims. For example, in certain spheres of action, the behavior of men is generally oriented around the "economic motive." Yet, for most men, economic gain is not usually an end in itself, but a means for attaining more final ends: security, comfort, and prestige.

Finally, the value and factual elements may be combined, in some cases, in a single objective. The apprehension of criminals is commonly set up as an objective of a municipal police department. To a certain extent this objective is conceived as an end in itself, that is, as aimed toward the apprehension and punishment of offenders against the law; but from another point of view apprehension is considered a means for protecting citizens, for rehabilitating offenders, and for discouraging potential offenders.

The Hierarchy of Decisions. The concept of *purposiveness* involves a notion of a hierarchy of decisions—each step downward in the hierarchy consisting in an implementation of the goals set forth in the step immediately above. Behavior is purposive in so far as it is guided by general goals or objectives; it is rational in so far as it selects alternatives which are conducive to the achievement of the previously selected goals.[4]

---

[2] In chap. iv, this distinction between mediate and final goals will be elaborated, and its necessity shown.

[3] The word "factual," though possibly misleading, is used for lack of a better term. It is clear that the "facts" on which practical decisions are based are usually estimates or judgments, rather than positive and certain items of fact. To add to the confusion, the term "valuation" is often applied by writers to refer to this process of judging or estimating facts. The reader will avoid confusion if he remembers that "value" in this study refers to *ought*'s, however certain, "fact" to *is*'s, however conjectural.

[4] This definition of "rational" is not exact, and will be further elaborated in chap. iv.

It should not be inferred that this hierarchy or pyramid of goals is perfectly organized or integrated in any actual behavior. A governmental agency, for instance, may be directed simultaneously toward several distinct objectives: a recreation department may seek to improve the health of children, to provide them with good uses for their leisure time, and to prevent juvenile delinquency, as well as to achieve similar goals for the adults in the community.

Even when no conscious or deliberate integration of these goals takes place in decision, it should be noted that an integration generally takes place in fact. Although in making decisions for his agency, the recreation administrator may fail to weigh the diverse and sometimes conflicting objectives against one another in terms of their relative importance, yet his actual decisions, and the direction which he gives to the policy of his agency will amount in practice to a particular set of weights for these objectives. If the program emphasizes athletics for adolescent boys, then this objective is given an actual weight in practice which it may, or may not, have had in the consciousness of the administrator planning the program. Hence, although the administrator may refuse the task, or be unable to perform it, of consciously and deliberately integrating his system of objectives, he cannot avoid the implications of his actual decisions, which achieve such a synthesis in fact.

The Relative Element in Decision. In an important sense, all decision is a matter of compromise. The alternative that is finally selected never permits a complete or perfect achievement of objectives, but is merely the best solution that is available under the circumstances. The environmental situation inevitably limits the alternatives that are available, and hence sets a maximum to the level of attainment of purpose that is possible.

This relative element in achievement—this element of compromise—makes even more inescapable the necessity of finding a common denominator when behavior is aimed simultaneously at several objectives. For instance, if experience showed that an organization like the Work Projects Administration could at one and the same time dispense relief and construct public works without handicapping either objective, then the agency might attempt to attain at the same time both of these objectives. If, on the other hand, experience showed that the accomplishment of either of these objectives through the organization seriously impeded the accomplishment of the other, one would have to be selected as the objective of the agency, and the other sacrificed. In balancing the one aim against the other, and in attempting to find a common denominator, it would be necessary to cease thinking of the two aims as ends in themselves, and instead to conceive them as means to some more general end.[5]

An Illustration of the Process of Decision. In order to understand more clearly the intimate relationships that exist in any practical administrative problem between judgments of value and fact, it will be helpful to study an example from the field of municipal government.

What questions of value and fact arise in the opening and improvement of a new street? It is necessary to determine: (1) the design of the street, (2) the proper relationship of the street to the master plan, (3) means of financing the project, (4) whether the project should be let on contract or done by force account, (5) the relation of this project to construction that may be required subsequent to the improvement (e.g., utility cuts in this particular street), and (6) numerous other questions of like nature. These are questions for which answers must be found—each one combining value and factual elements. A partial separation of the two elements can be achieved by distinguishing the purposes of the project from its procedures.

On the one hand, decisions regarding these questions must be based upon the purposes for which the street is intended, and the social values affected by its construction—among them, (1) speed and convenience in transportation, (2) traffic safety, (3) effect of street layout on property values, (4) construction costs, and (5) distribution of cost among taxpayers.

On the other hand, the decisions must be made in the light of scientific and practical knowledge as to the effect particular measures will have in realizing these values. Included here are (1) the relative smoothness, permanence, and cost of each type of pavement, (2) relative advantages of alternate routes from the standpoint of cost and convenience to traffic, and (3) the total cost and distribution of cost for alternative methods of financing.

The final decision, then, will depend both on the relative weight that is given to the different objectives and on judgment as to the extent to which any given plan will attain each objective.

This brief account will serve to indicate some of the basic features of the process of decision—features that will be further elaborated in this study.

[5]From the description by MacMahon, Millett, and Ogden of the WPA during its planning stage, it would appear that thinking about this integration was at a rather primitive level in the organization at the time the basic decisions were made. Arthur W. MacMahon, John D. Millett, and Gladys Ogden, *The Administration of Federal Work Relief* (Chicago: Public Administration Service, 1941), pp. 17–42.

DECISION-MAKING IN THE ADMINISTRATIVE PROCESS

Administrative activity is group activity. Simple situations are familiar where a man plans and executes his own work; but as soon as a task grows to the point where the efforts of several persons are required to accomplish it this is no longer possible, and it becomes necessary to develop processes for the application of organized effort to the group task. The techniques which facilitate this application are the administrative processes.

It should be noted that the administrative processes are decisional processes: they consist in segregating certain elements in the decisions of members of the organization, and establishing regular organizational procedures to select and determine these elements and to communicate them to the members concerned. If the task of the group is to build a ship, a design for the ship is drawn and adopted by the organization, and this design limits and guides the activities of the persons who actually construct the ship.

The organization, then, takes from the individual some of his decisional autonomy, and substitutes for it an organization decision-making process. The decisions which the organization makes for the individual ordinarily (1) specify his function, that is, the general scope and nature of his duties; (2) allocate authority, that is, determine who in the organization is to have power to make further decisions for the individual; and (3) set such other limits to his choice as are needed to coordinate the activities of several individuals in the organization.

The administrative organization is characterized by specialization— particular tasks are delegated to particular parts of the organization. It has already been noted above that this specialization may take the form of "vertical" division of labor. A pyramid or hierarchy of authority may be established, with greater or less formality, and decision-making functions may be specialized among the members of this hierarchy.

Most analyses of organization have emphasized "horizontal" specialization—the division of work—as the basic characteristic of organized activity. Luther Gulick, for example, in his "Notes on the Theory of Organization," says: "Work division is the foundation of organization; indeed, the reason for organization."[6] In this study we shall be primarily concerned with "vertical" specialization—the division of decision-making duties between operative and supervisory personnel. One inquiry will be into the reasons why the operative employees are deprived of a por-

---

[6] Luther Gulick and L. Urwick, eds., *Papers on the Science of Administration* (New York: Institute of Public Administration, 1937), p. 3.

tion of their autonomy in the making of decisions and subjected to the authority and influence of supervisors.

There would seem to be at least three reasons for vertical specialization in organization. First, if there is any horizontal specialization, vertical specialization is absolutely essential to achieve coordination among the operative employees. Second, just as horizontal specialization permits greater skill and expertise to be developed by the operative group in the performance of their tasks, so vertical specialization permits greater expertise in the making of decisions. Third, vertical specialization permits the operative personnel to be held accountable for their decisions: to the board of directors in the case of a business organization; to the legislative body in the case of a public agency.

Coordination. Group behavior requires not only the adoption of correct decisions, but also the adoption by all members of the group of the same decisions. Suppose ten persons decide to cooperate in building a boat. If each has his own plan, and they do not communicate their plans, the chances are that the resulting craft will not be very seaworthy; they would probably meet with better success if they adopted even a very mediocre design, and if then all followed this same design.

By the exercise of authority or other forms of influence, it is possible to centralize the function of deciding so that a general plan of operations will govern the activities of all members of the organization. This coordination may be either procedural or substantive in nature: by procedural coordination is meant the specification of the organization itself—that is, the generalized description of the behaviors and relationships of the members of the organization. Procedural coordination establishes the lines of authority and outlines the sphere of activity of each organization member, while substantive coordination specifies the content of his work. In an automobile factory, an organization chart is an aspect of procedural coordination; blueprints for the engine block of the car being manufactured are an aspect of substantive coordination.

Expertise. To gain the advantages of specialized skill at the operative level, the work of an organization must be so subdivided that all processes requiring a particular skill can be performed by persons possessing that skill. Likewise, to gain the advantages of expertise in decision-making, the responsibility for decisions must be so allocated that all decisions requiring a particular skill can be made by persons possessing that skill.

To subdivide decisions is rather more complicated than to subdivide performance; for, while it is not usually possible to combine the sharp eye of one workman with the steady hand of another to secure greater precision in a particular operation, it is often possible to add the knowledge of a lawyer to that of an engineer in order to improve the quality of a particular decision.

Responsibility. Writers on the political and legal aspects of authority have emphasized that a primary function of organization is to enforce the conformity of the individual to norms laid down by the group, or by its authority-wielding members. The discretion of subordinate personnel is limited by policies determined near the top of the administrative hierarchy. When the maintenance of responsibility is a central concern, the purpose of vertical specialization is to assure legislative control over the administrator, leaving to the administrative staff adequate discretion to deal with technical matters which a legislative body composed of laymen would not be competent to decide.

MODES OF ORGANIZATIONAL INFLUENCE

Decisions reached in the higher ranks of the organization hierarchy will have no effect upon the activities of operative employees unless they are communicated downward. Consideration of the process requires an examination of the ways in which the behavior of the operative employee can be influenced. These influences fall roughly into two categories: (1) establishing in the operative employee *himself* attitudes, habits, and a state of mind which lead him to reach that decision which is advantageous to the organization, and (2) imposing on the operative employee decisions reached elsewhere in the organization. The first type of influence operates by inculcating in the employee organizational loyalties and a concern with efficiency, and more generally by training him. The second type of influence depends primarily upon authority and upon advisory and informational services. It is not insisted that these categories are either exhaustive or mutually exclusive, but they will serve the purposes of this introductory discussion.

As a matter of fact, the present discussion is somewhat more general than the preceding paragraph suggests, for it is concerned with organizational influences not only upon operative employees but upon all individuals making decisions within the organization.

Authority. The concept of authority has been analyzed at length by students of administration. We shall employ here a definition substantially equivalent to that put forth by C. I. Barnard.[7] A subordinate is said to

[7]Chester I. Barnard, *The Functions of the Executive* (Cambridge: Harvard University Press, 1938), pp. 163 ff.

accept authority whenever he permits his behavior to be guided by the decision of a superior, without independently examining the merits of that decision. When exercising authority, the superior does not seek to convince the subordinate, but only to obtain his acquiescence. In actual practice, of course, authority is usually liberally admixed with suggestion and persuasion.

Although it is an important function of authority to permit a decision to be made and carried out even when agreement cannot be reached, perhaps this arbitrary aspect of authority has been overemphasized. In any event, if it is attempted to carry authority beyond a certain point, which may be described as the subordinate's "zone of acceptance," disobedience will follow.[8] The magnitude of the zone of acceptance depends upon the sanctions which authority has available to enforce its commands. The term "sanctions" must be interpreted broadly in this connection, for positive and neutral stimuli—such as community of purpose, habit, and leadership—are at least as important in securing acceptance of authority as the threat of physical or economic punishment.

It follows that authority, in the sense here defined, can operate "upward" and "sidewise" as well as "downward" in the organization. If an executive delegates to his secretary a decision about file cabinets and accepts her recommendation without reexamination of its merits, he is accepting her authority. The "lines of authority" represented on organization charts do have a special significance, however, for they are commonly resorted to in order to terminate debate when it proves impossible to reach a consensus on a particular decision. Since this appellate use of authority generally requires sanctions to be effective, the structure of formal authority in an organization usually is related to the appointment, disciplining, and dismissal of personnel. These formal lines of authority are commonly supplemented by informal authority relations in the day-to-day work of the organization, while the formal hierarchy is largely reserved for the settlement of disputes.

Organizational Loyalties. It is a prevalent characteristic of human behavior that members of an organized group tend to identify with that group. In making decisions their organizational loyalty leads them to evaluate alternative courses of action in terms of the consequences of their action for the group. When a person prefers a particular course of action because it is "good for America," he identifies himself with Americans; when he prefers it because it will "boost business in Berkeley," he identifies himself with

---

[8]Barnard (*op. cit.*, p. 169) calls this the "zone of indifference"; but I prefer the term "acceptance."

Berkeleyans. National and class loyalties are examples of identifications which are of fundamental importance in the structure of modern society.

The loyalties that are of particular interest in the study of administration are those which attach to administrative organizations or segments of such organizations. The regimental battle flag is the traditional symbol of this identification in military administration; in civil administration, a frequently encountered evidence of loyalty is the cry, "Our Bureau needs more funds!"

This phenomenon of identification, or organizational loyalty, performs one very important function in administration. If an administrator, each time he is faced with a decision, must perforce evaluate that decision in terms of the whole range of human values, rationality in administration is impossible. If he need consider the decision only in the light of limited organizational aims, his task is more nearly within the range of human powers. The fireman can concentrate on the problem of fires, the health officer on problems of disease, without irrelevant considerations entering in.

Furthermore, this concentration on a limited range of values is almost essential if the administrator is to be held accountable for his decisions. When the organization's objectives are specified by some higher authority, the major value-premise of the administrator's decisions is thereby given him, leaving to him only the implementation of these objectives. If the fire chief were permitted to roam over the whole field of human values—to decide that parks were more important than fire trucks, and consequently to remake his fire department into a recreation department—chaos would displace organization, and responsibility would disappear.

Organizational loyalties lead also, however, to certain difficulties which should not be underestimated. The principal undesirable effect of identification is that it prevents the institutionalized individual from making correct decisions in cases where the restricted area of values with which he identifies himself must be weighed against other values outside that area. This is a principal cause of the interbureau competition and wrangling which characterize any large administrative organization. The organization members, identifying themselves with the bureau instead of with the over-all organization, believe the bureau's welfare more important than the general welfare when the two conflict. This problem is frequently evident in the case of "housekeeping" agencies, where the facilitative and auxiliary nature of the agency is lost sight of in the effort to force the line agencies to follow standard procedures.

Organizational loyalties also result in incapacitating almost any department head for the task of balancing the financial needs of his department against the financial needs of other departments—whence the need for a centrally located budget agency that is free from these psychological biases. The higher we go in the administrative hierarchy, and the broader becomes the range of social values that must come within the administrator's purview, the more harmful is the effect of valuational bias, and the more important is it that the administrator be freed from his narrower identifications.

The Criterion of Efficiency. We have seen that the exercise of authority and the development of organizational loyalties are two principal means whereby the individual's value-premises are influenced by the organization. What about the issues of fact that underlie his decisions? These are largely determined by a principle that is implied in all rational behavior: the criterion of efficiency. In its broadest sense, to be efficient simply means to take the shortest path, the cheapest means, toward the attainment of the desired goals. The efficiency criterion is completely neutral as to what goals are to be attained. The commandment, "Be efficient!" is a major organizational influence over the decisions of the members of any administrative agency; and a determination whether this commandment has been obeyed is a major function of the review process.[9]

Advice and Information. Many of the influences the organization exercises over its members are of a less formal nature than those we have been discussing. These influences are perhaps most realistically viewed as a form of internal public relations, for there is nothing to guarantee that advice produced at one point in an organization will have any effect at another point in the organization unless the lines of communication are adequate to its transmission, and unless it is transmitted in such form as to be persuasive. It is a prevalent misconception in headquarters offices that the internal advisory function consists in preparing precisely worded explanatory bulletins and making certain that the proper number of these are prepared, and that they are placed in the proper compartment of the "router." No plague has produced a rate of mortality higher than the rate that customarily afflicts central-office communications between the time they leave the issuing office and the moment when they are assumed to be effected in the revised practice of the operative employees.

Information and advice flow in all directions through the organization—not merely from the top downward. Many of the facts that are rel-

---

[9]For further discussion of the efficiency concept, see Clarence E. Ridley and Herbert A. Simon, *Measuring Municipal Activities* (Chicago: International City Managers' Association, 1943).

evant to decision are of a rapidly changing nature, ascertainable only at the moment of decision, and often ascertainable only by operative employees. For instance, in military operations knowledge of the disposition of the enemy's forces is of crucial importance, and military organization has developed elaborate procedures for transmitting to a person who is to make a decision all relevant facts that he is not in a position to ascertain personally.

Training. Like organizational loyalties and the efficiency criterion, and unlike the other modes of influence we have been discussing, training influences decisions "from the inside out." That is, training prepares the organization member to reach satisfactory decisions himself, without the need for the constant exercise of authority or advice. In this sense, training procedures are alternatives to the exercise of authority or advice as means of control over the subordinate's decisions.

Training may be of an in-service or a pre-service nature. When persons with particular educational qualifications are recruited for certain jobs, the organization is depending upon this pre-training as a principal means of assuring correct decisions in their work. The mutual relation between training and the range of discretion that may be permitted an employee is an important factor to be taken into consideration in designing the administrative organization. That is, it may often be possible to minimize, or even dispense with, certain review processes by giving the subordinates training that enables them to perform their work with less supervision. Similarly, in drafting the qualifications required of applicants for particular positions, the possibility should be considered of lowering personnel costs by drafting semi-skilled employees and training them for particular jobs.

Training is applicable to the process of decision whenever the same elements are involved in a large number of decisions. Training may supply the trainee with the facts necessary in dealing with these decisions; it may provide him a frame of reference for his thinking; it may teach him "approved" solutions; or it may indoctrinate him with the values in terms of which his decisions are to be made.

THE EQUILIBRIUM OF THE ORGANIZATION

The question may next be raised why the individual *accepts* these organizational influences—why he accommodates his behavior to the demands the organization makes upon him. To understand how the behavior of the individual becomes a part of the system of behavior of the organization, it is necessary to study the relation between the personal motivation of the individual and the objectives toward which the activity of the organization is oriented.

If a business organization be taken, for the moment, as the type, three kinds of participants can be distinguished: entrepreneurs, employees, and customers.[10] Entrepreneurs are distinguished by the fact that their decisions ultimately control the activities of employees; employees, by the fact that they contribute their (undifferentiated) time and efforts to the organization in return for wages; customers, by the fact that they contribute money to the organization in return for its products. (Any actual human being can, of course, stand in more than one of these relations to an organization, e.g. a Red Cross volunteer, who is really a composite customer and employee.)

Each of these participants has his own personal motives for engaging in these organizational activities. Simplifying the motives and adopting the standpoint of economic theory, we may say that the entrepreneur seeks profit (i.e. an excess of revenues over expenditures), the employees seek wages, and the customers find (at certain prices) the exchange of money for products attractive. The entrepreneur gains the right to dispose of the employees' time by entering into employment contracts with them; he obtains funds to pay wages by entering into sales contracts with the customers. If these two sets of contracts are sufficiently advantageous, the entrepreneur makes a profit and, what is perhaps more important for our purposes, the organization remains in existence. If the contracts are not sufficiently advantageous, the entrepreneur becomes unable to maintain inducements to keep others in organized activity with him, and may even lose his own inducement to continue his organizational efforts. In either event, the organization disappears unless an equilibrium can be reached at some level of activity. In any actual organization, of course, the entrepreneur will depend upon many inducements other than the purely economic ones mentioned above: prestige, "good will," loyalty, and others.

In an organization such as that just described, there appears, in addition to the personal aims of the participants, an *organization* objective, or objectives. If the organization is a shoe factory, for example, it assumes the objective of making shoes. Whose objective is this—the entrepreneur's, the customers', or the employees'? To deny that it belongs to any

---

[10]We follow Barnard (*op. cit.*) here in insisting that customers are an integral part of the system of organization behavior. Whether they are "members" or not is a terminological question of no particular importance. Suppliers of materials might have been added, above, as a fourth class of participants; but they would not add any essentially new element to the picture.

of these would seem to posit some "group mind," some organismic entity which is over and above its human components. The true explanation is simpler: the organization objective is, indirectly, a personal objective of *all* the participants. It is the means whereby their organizational activity is bound together to achieve a satisfaction of their own diverse personal motives. It is by employing workers to make shoes and by selling them that the entrepreneur makes his profit; it is by accepting the direction of the entrepreneur in the making of shoes that the employee earns his wage; and it is by buying the finished shoes that the customer obtains his satisfaction from the organization. Since the entrepreneur wishes a profit, and since he controls the behavior of the employees (within their respective areas of acceptance), it behooves him to guide the behavior of the employees by the criterion of "making shoes as efficiently as possible." In so far, then, as he can control behavior in the organization, he establishes this as the objective of the behavior.

It is to be noted that the objectives of the customer are very closely, and rather directly, related to the *objectives* of the organization; the objectives of the entrepreneur are closely related to the *survival* of the organization; while the objectives of the employee are directly related to neither of these, but are brought into the organization scheme by the existence of his area of acceptance. Granted that pure "entrepreneurs," "customers," and "employees" do not exist; granted further that this scheme needs to be modified somewhat to fit voluntary, religious, and governmental organizations, still it is the existence of these three type roles which gives behavior in administrative organizations the particular character that we recognize.

ORGANIZATION OF THIS VOLUME

The framework of the investigation that is to be undertaken in subsequent chapters has now been set forth. We may conclude the present chapter by outlining briefly the order in which the various topics will be taken up.

Chapter II is also, in a sense, prefatory. The present work was undertaken partly as a result of the author's dissatisfaction with the so-called "principles of administration" that are to be found in the current literature of administrative theory. In Chapter II these principles are subjected to critical analysis with a view to showing their inadequacy and the need for their development along the lines suggested here.

In Chapter III, the exposition, properly speaking, begins with an analysis of the role played by value questions and questions of fact in administrative decision. This is followed, in Chapter IV, by a description of the conceptual apparatus that will be used throughout the volume for the description and analysis of social behavior systems, including behavior in administrative organizations.

Chapter V will consider the psychology of the individual in the organization and the ways in which the organization modifies his behavior. In Chapter VI the organization will be viewed as a system of individuals whose behavior maintains some sort of equilibrium—along lines suggested above. Chapter VII will analyze in detail the role of authority and vertical specialization in organization, and the organizational processes through which such specialization is effectuated. Chapter VIII is concerned with the process of communication whereby organizational influences are transmitted. In Chapter IX the concept of efficiency will be examined in detail, and in Chapter X, organizational loyalty, or identifications.

Chapter XI brings the volume to a close with a survey of the structure of administrative organizations and a discussion of the problems faced by research in administrative theory.

DECISION-MAKING AND
ADMINISTRATIVE ORGANIZATION

THIS COMMENTARY ON CHAPTER I enlarges on several of the topics discussed there. It says a little more about the nature of the organizations in which decision-making is embedded. It discusses the respective roles of organizations and markets in coordinating behavior in a modern industrial society. It introduces the topic, to be developed in later chapters, of the impact that computers have had and are having upon organizations. Then, it elaborates further on the "vertical" specialization of decision-making introduced in the chapter. Finally, it comments briefly on lines of organizational research and theory, especially those related to the decision-making process, that have emerged since *Administrative Behavior* was first published.

ORGANIZATION AND PERSONALITY

In recent years, organizations have not had a good press. Large organizations, especially large corporations and Big Government, have been blamed for all manner of social ills, including widespread "alienation" of both workers and executives from their work and from society, with resulting "bureaucracy" and organizational inefficiency. As we shall see later, the empirical evidence that alienation or inefficiency are more widespread than they have been in previous ages and in other societies is nonexistent, as is any evidence that alienation is to be attributed to organizations. However, this kind of criticism has one merit: It takes organizations seriously and recognizes that they do influence the behavior of the people who inhabit them.

A rather different skeptical view of organizations, often expressed by managers, is that it is the person who matters, not the organization. I am sure you have heard it many times: "I used to think that organization was important, but now I think it is much more a matter of personality. The important thing is the person in the office. Someone who has drive, ability, imagination can work in almost any organization." To be sure, "personality" is a useful concept. But that personal characteristics are impor-

17

tant for organizational performance does not imply that organizational characteristics are unimportant. The complex world of human affairs does not operate in such simpleminded single-variable ways.

Moreover, personality is not formed in a vacuum. One's language is not independent of the language of one's parents, nor are one's attitudes divorced from those of associates and teachers. One does not live for months or years in a particular position in an organization, exposed to some streams of communication, shielded from others, without the most profound effects upon what one knows, believes, attends to, hopes, wishes, emphasizes, fears, and proposes.

If organization is inessential, if all we need is the person, why do we insist on creating a position for the person? Why not let all create their own positions, appropriate to their personal abilities and qualities? Why does the boss have to be called the boss before his or her creative energies can be amplified by the organization? And finally, if we have to give managers some measure of authority before their personal qualities can be transformed into effective influence, in what ways may this effectiveness depend on the manner in which others are organized?

The answer is simple. Organization is important, first, because it provides the environments that mold and develop personal qualities and habits (see especially Chapters V and X). Organization is important, second, because it provides those in responsible positions with the means for exercising authority and influence over others (see especially Chapter VII). Organization is important, third, because, by structuring communications, it determines the environments of information in which decisions are taken (see especially Chapter VIII). We cannot understand either the "inputs" or the "outputs" of executives without understanding the organizations in which they work. Their behavior and its effects on others are functions of their organizational situations.

MEANING OF THE TERM "ORGANIZATION"

The tendency to downplay organizational factors in executive behavior stems from misunderstanding of the term "organization." To many persons, an organization is embodied in charts or elaborate manuals of job descriptions and formal procedures. In such charts and manuals the organization takes on more the appearance of a series of orderly cubicles following an abstract architectural logic than a house inhabited by human beings. And the charting and manual-writing activities of the Departments of Organization that one finds in large corporations and governmental agencies more often reinforce than dispel this stereotype.

In this book, the term *organization* refers to the pattern of communications and relations among a group of human beings, including the processes for making and implementing decisions. This pattern provides to organization members much of the information and many of the assumptions, goals, and attitudes that enter into their decisions, and provides also a set of stable and comprehensible expectations as to what the other members of the group are doing and how they will react to what one says and does. The sociologist calls this pattern a "role system"; we are concerned with the form of role system known as an "organization."

Much of what an executive does has its principal short-run effect on day-to-day operations. The executive makes a decision about a product price, a contract for materials, the location of a plant, or an employee's grievance. Each decision has the immediate effect of settling the specific question at hand. But the most important cumulative effect of this stream of decisions and refusals to decide—like the erosion caused by a steady trickle of water—is upon the *patterns* of action in the organization surrounding the executive. How will the next contract be made? Will it be brought to the executive at all, or handled by subordinates? What preparatory work will have been done before it reaches the executive, and what policies will guide those who handle it? And after the next contract, what about the next ten and the next hundred?

Every executive makes decisions and takes actions with one eye on the matter at hand and one eye on the effect of *this* decision upon the future pattern—that is to say, upon its organizational consequences.

ORGANIZATIONS AND MARKETS[11]

One cannot discuss organizations as coordinators of human action without referring to another powerful coordinating mechanism in modern societies: markets. In fact, the currently popular denigration of organizations is the obverse face to the acclamation of markets as the ideal mechanism for economic and social integration. The dissolution of the Soviet Union was widely hailed as a clear demonstration of the superiority of the market over centralized planning as a social organizer. Subsequent events have taught us that the matter is a good deal more complex than that. Markets do indeed seem to work, in modern industrial economies, more effectively than central plans. But as the Russian, and even our own, experience shows, markets only work effectively in the presence of a healthy infrastructure, and in particular, in an environment of effi-

---

[11]The topic of this section is discussed at greater length in "Organizations and Markets," *Journal of Economic Perspectives*, vol. 5, no. 2, Spring 1991, pp. 25–44, reprinted in *Models of Bounded Rationality*, vol. 3 (Cambridge: MIT Press, 1996).

ciently managed business firms and other organizations. Markets comple-
ment organizations; they do not replace them.

Visitors from another planet might be surprised to hear our society
described as a market economy. They might ask why we don't call it an
organizational economy. After all, they observe large agglomerations of
people working in organizations. They encounter large business firms, public agencies, universities. They have learned that 80 percent or more of the
people who work in an industrialized society work inside the skins of organizations, most of them having very little direct contact, as employees,
with markets. Consumers make frequent use of markets; most producers are
embedded in large organizations. Our visitors might well suggest that, at
the least, we should call our society an organization-and-market society.

In neoclassical economics, organizations are dealt with in "the theory of the firm." But the business firm of economic theory is a pitifully
skeletonized abstraction. It consists of little more than an "entrepreneur"
who seeks to maximize the firm's profits by selecting a manufacturing
volume and price, and to do so, uses a production function (which relates
outputs to inputs) and a cost function (which prices these outputs and
inputs as a function of volume). The theory says nothing about the technology that underlies the firm's production function, the motivations
that govern the decisions of managers and employees, or the processes
that lead to the maximizing decisions. In particular, it does not ask how
the actors acquire the information required for these decisions, how they
make the necessary calculations, or even, and this is the crux of the matter—whether they are capable of making the kinds of decisions postulated by utility-maximizing or profit-maximizing theory. The "entrepreneur" of economic theory makes static decisions in a fixed framework,
bearing little resemblance to the active innovator who launches new
enterprises and explores new paths.

Much of this book is devoted to filling out (and correcting) this
impoverished description of organizations. Major attention will be given
(beginning in Chapters IV and V) to the ways in which people actually
make decisions, and how their decision-making processes are molded by
limits on their knowledge and computational capabilities (bounded rationality). Other chapters (especially Chapters VI and IX) will seek to
explain how the members of organizations are motivated to act in support
of the organizations' goals, and how they acquire organizational loyalties.

In recent years, there has been some attempt, under the label of the
"new institutional economics," to find a place in economic theory for real
organizations. The key idea is to regard most organizational phenomena as
simply another kind of market behavior, of market interaction between
employees and their employers. This view focuses on the employment

contract. The new institutional economics tries to explain how organizations operate by analyzing the employment contract and other explicit or implied contracts that individuals have with organizations.

Although this approach represents an improvement over the skeleton it replaces, it also has grave limitations. In actual fact, all of us who are employees of organizations are governed in our actions not only by our immediate personal gain but (to an important extent) by an intent to contribute to the accomplishment of the goals of the organization. It is only possible for organizations to operate successfully if, for much of the time, most of their employees, when dealing with problems and making decisions, are thinking not just of their own personal goals but of the goals of the organization. Whatever their ultimate motivations, organizational goals must bulk large in employees' and managers' thinking about what is to be done.

The new institutional economics tries to explain these motivations as produced by enforcement of the employment contract through authority and rewards for good performance. But it is well known that a system of sanctions and rewards can produce, by itself, only minimally productive performance. Hence a realistic theory of organizations must explain the other sources of motivation to advance organizational goals. Succeeding chapters will have a great deal to say about these motivational issues, and especially about the nature and psychological roots of organizational loyalty.

DECISION-MAKING AND THE COMPUTER

The first edition of this book was published shortly after the first modern electronic computer came into the world and some years before it found even the most prosaic applications in management. In spite of the extensive use of computers in organizations today, we still live pretty much in the horseless carriage stage of computer development. That is, we use computers to perform more rapidly and cheaply than before the same functions that we formerly carried out with adding machines and typewriters. Apart from some areas of middle-management decision, where techniques like linear programming (from operations research) and expert systems (from artificial intelligence) are now widely employed, computers have changed executive decision-making processes and the shapes of organization designs only modestly.

We must be cautious, however, about extrapolating from past to future. The automobile, when it first appeared, also had a modest impact: It took over tasks formerly performed by horse and wagon. It gave few hints of its future enormous effects on our whole transportation system and, indeed, on our whole society—suburbanization, mobile homes, the long-distance family vacation, to mention just a few obvious examples.

We have learned by now that the computer, too, is something far different from an oversized adding machine, and far more significant for our society.[12] But its significance is only just beginning to emerge, the appearance of personal computers about a decade ago perhaps being a decisive turning point. One way to conjecture what important novel tasks computers may take on is to review the many metaphors that have been applied to them. First, the computer is an incredibly powerful number cruncher. We have already proceeded, especially in engineering and science, a considerable way toward discovering what can be done by number crunching, but we will find new uses as computer power continues to increase. Second, the computer is a large memory, and we are just now beginning to explore (for example, on the World Wide Web) how large data bases must be organized so that they can be accessed selectively and cheaply in order to extract the information they contain that is relevant to our specific tasks.

Third, the computer is an expert, capable of matching human professional-level performance in some areas of medical diagnosis, of engineering design, of chess playing, of legal search, and increasing numbers of others. Fourth, the computer is the core of a new worldwide network of communications, an "information superhighway." Everyone can now communicate with "everyone," almost instantaneously. Fifth, the computer is a "giant brain," capable of thinking, problem solving, and, yes, making decisions. We are continually finding new areas of decision— evaluating credit risks, investing funds, scheduling factories, diagnosing corporate financial problems—where computers can play an important role or sometimes do the whole task.

From the capabilities of computers for pouring out large volumes of information, it has been easy to draw the wrong conclusion: that the main condition for exploiting the computer more fully is to enhance its powers of information storage and information diffusion. On the contrary, the central lesson that the computer should teach is that information is no longer scarce or in dire need of enhanced distribution. In contrast with past ages, we now live in an information-rich world.

In our enthusiasm for global networks of unlimited information, we sometimes lose sight of the fact that a new scarcity has been created: the scarcity of human time for attending to the information that flows in on

---

[12]Elsewhere, in *The New Science of Management Decision* (New York: Englewood Cliffs, N.J.: Prentice-Hall, revised edition, 1977), I have examined these developments in the computer and in operations research, as well as their implications—both present and prospective—for management and organization. Although *New Science* is now twenty years old, it continues to give a realistic picture of the impact of the new technology on decision-making. The commentary on chap. viii of the present book examines the continuing developments in this domain that are taking us into the future.

us. The information revolution has multiplied the amount of information that a single person can scatter around an organization, or around the world; it has not increased the number of hours a day that each person has available for digesting information. The main requirement in the design of organizational communication systems is not to reduce scarcity of information but to combat the glut of information, so that we may find time to attend to that information which is most relevant to our tasks—something that is possible only if we can find our way expeditiously through the morass of irrelevancies that our information systems contain.

Chapter VIII and its commentary explore the problems of communication and organization design in a world where information is not scarce, but time to attend to it is. The commentary explains why the first, and even second, generations of management information systems and management decision aids have generally been something less than a great success, and sketches the forms that more effective information systems may be expected to take in the future.

"VERTICAL" DECISION-MAKING: THE ANATOMY OF THE DECISION PROCESS

Chapter I refers to "vertical" specialization: the division of decision-making duties between operative and supervisory personnel. The chapter also notes that the subdivision of decision-making into components goes much farther than this. Any important decision is based on numerous facts (or suppositions of fact) as well as numerous values, side conditions, and constraints. We can think of all of these facts and values as the *premises* of the final decision—the raw material inputs, so to speak, to an assembly process that ends with the decision itself.

The manufacture of a physical product can be carried out in a large number of specialized departments: for converting the raw materials, fabricating them into components of the final product, assembling the components, and finishing the product. In the same way, a decision can be divided into components, each fabricated by specialists and specialized groups, and finally brought together into a coordinated picture. Thus, reaching a decision to put a new product on the market may require contributions of facts and goals from design engineers (improving the product or lowering its cost), manufacturing engineers (simplifying the manufacturing process by redesign), marketing specialists (predicting the size and nature of the prospective market), financial specialists (designing alternative methods of financing a new factory), legal specialists (identifying prospective patent problems, product liability), and so on. Throughout this book, we will use the term *decision premises* to refer to the facts and values that enter into this decision-fabricating process, a process that involves fact-finding, design, analysis, reasoning, negotiation, all seasoned with large quantities of "intuition" and even guessing.

A major task in organizing is to determine, first, where the knowledge is located that can provide the various kinds of factual premises that decisions require, and, second, to what positions responsibility can reliably be assigned for specifying the goals to be realized and the constraints and side conditions a decision must satisfy. Designing effective processes for composing premises into decisions is as important as designing effective processes for fabricating and distributing the organization's products. A considerable part of this book will be concerned with identifying the origins of different kinds of decision premises and tracing their processes of assembly.

THE SOCIOLOGY AND PSYCHOLOGY OF ORGANIZATIONS

The question is sometimes asked whether an analysis of organizations in terms of decision-making processes is "sociological" or "psychological." The question is a bit odd; it is like asking whether molecular biology is biology or chemistry. The correct answer in either case is "both." This book analyzes organizations in terms of the decision-making behavior of their participants, but it is precisely the organizational *system* surrounding this behavior that gives it its special character. The roles of organization members are shaped by the goals with which they identify, and goal identifications, in turn, depend heavily upon location in the organization and the pattern of organizational communication.

The concept of *role* provides the standard sociological explanation of behavior—the captain goes down with his ship because he has accepted the role of captain, and that is what captains do in our culture. There is a reason, however, for describing behavior in organizations in terms of decision premises instead of roles. In its original connotation of dramatic part, "role" implies too specific a pattern of behavior. A mother does not speak set lines; her role behavior adapts to and depends upon the situation in which she finds herself. Moreover, there is room for all sorts of idiosyncratic variation in the enactment of a social role.

The difficulties in role theory drop away if we view social influence as influence upon decision *premises*. A role is a specification of some, but not all, of the premises that underlie an individual's decisions. Many other premises also enter into the same decision, including informational premises and idiosyncratic premises that are expressive of personality differences. For some purposes it may be enough to know the role premises to predict a choice. For other purposes, the informational premises or others may be the crucial ones.

Unless the premise is taken as the unit, role theory commits an error that is just the opposite of the one committed by economic theory—it does not leave any room for rationality. If a role is a pattern of behavior, the role may be functional from a social standpoint, but the performer of the role cannot be a rational actor, or even an actor with volition—the performer simply acts his or her part. On the other hand, if a role consists in the specification of value and factual premises, then the enactor of the role will often have to think and solve problems in order to use these facts to attain these values. A role defined in terms of premises leaves room for calculation in behavior, and for the involvement of the actor's knowledge, wants, and emotions.

Of course, decision-making analysis is not the only approach to the study of organizations, any more than biochemistry is the only approach to the study of organisms. A number of investigators, especially sociologists, prefer to look at more global characteristics of organizations and to relate these to variables like organization size or organizational environment. Such studies have an important place in research on organizations; but ultimately, of course, we wish to find the connections between the various levels of inquiry. If organizations that operate in different industries (e.g., steel companies as compared with advertising agencies) typically take on different structural characteristics, we will want to explain these latter differences in terms of underlying differences in decision-making requirements. The differences in requirements will reflect, in turn, differences in the environments in which the organizations operate.

Decision-making in organizations does not go on in isolated human heads. Instead, one member's outputs become the inputs of another. At each step, the process draws upon the body of knowledge and skills that is stored both in the memories of employees and in the organization's data bases and computer programs. Because of this interrelatedness, supported by a rich network of partially formalized but partially informal communications, decision-making is an organized system of relations, and organizing is a problem in system design. Readers can decide for themselves, while they continue through the pages of this book, whether they are reading "psychology" or "sociology," or they can decide that it doesn't matter. I confess that I hold the latter view.

DEVELOPMENTS IN ORGANIZATIONS AND THEIR THEORY

A major function of the commentaries appended to the chapters of this edition is to discuss the changes in organizations and the changes in organization theory that have taken place since the first edition was published, and that are still taking place. Changes in theory are, of course, a different matter from changes in organizations, and the former might occur even if there were none of the latter (or vice versa). In any event, we need to distinguish the one from the other, and make clear which we are discussing at any given time.

"Schools" of Organization Theory

Surveys of organization theory frequently classify the writings on which they comment according to "schools." A recent collection[13] of writings on organization recognizes eight such "schools": classical; neoclassical; organizational behavior (a.k.a. human resources); "modern" structural; systems, contingency, and population ecology; multiple constituencies/market organization; power and politics; organizational culture and symbolic management. What are we to make of all of this?

The notion of "schools," applied to a field of science, is an old-fashioned idea that has worn out its usefulness in management and organization theory. In biology or geology, we do not have schools, but we do have specialized domains of knowledge and theory: for examples, molecular genetics, cell biology, developmental biology, and population genetics in biology; geophysics, paleontology, oceanography, and petroleum geology in geology. Unlike "schools," these domains are not competing theories but sets of phenomena and knowledge about them that are sufficiently separable that they can be examined, at least for many purposes, independently, then related and given their proper place in a larger structure.

Theories in a science do change gradually, but at any given point in time only a few of them are at the frontier of conjecture and controversy. Moreover, only rarely do the advances of science involve the overthrow of major theories. What we normally see is steady accumulation in which theories, confronted with new bodies of fact and new phenomena, are strengthened, augmented, and modified. Even the great "revolutions" of relativity and quantum mechanics did not displace Newtonian mechanics and Maxwell's equations from key positions in physical theory.

In the developments of organization theory represented by the "schools" listed above, I do not see any conceptual earthquakes, but I do see substantial and continuing progress, triggered by careful observation and sometimes experimentation. The so-called neoclassical theory, of which this book is supposed by Shafritz and Ott to be an example, did question some of the overgeneralized "laws" of the classical theory, and did

---

[13]Jay M. Shafritz and J. Steven Ott, eds., *Classics of Organization Theory* (Pacific Grove, Calif.: Brooks/Cole, 1992).

propose carrying out organizational analysis in terms of decision-making, a somewhat novel, but not unprecedented, idea. But when we compare *Administrative Behavior* with the theory that preceded and followed it, we see that the hierarchy of authority and the modes of organizational departmentalization, to take two important examples, are still central concepts of organization theory. As the last half of Chapter II will make clear, these concepts continue to maintain this central role up to the present day.

For example, "modern" structural organization theory and contingency theory both continue to examine departmentalization. The former explores alternatives to pure hierarchy and unity of command (already questioned by the "neoclassicists"), proposing such forms as matrix organizations or organization by project. Contingency theory continues the exploration (initiated in the "proverbs" discussion of Chapter II of this book) of the way in which departmentalization depends on the technological, market, and other environments of the organization.

In a similar way, the concepts of systems, multiple constituencies, power and politics, and organization culture all flow quite naturally from the concept of organizations as complex interactive structures held together by a balance of the inducements provided to various groups of participants and the contributions received from them—a concept that originated with Barnard and is further developed in Chapter VI of this book and by the other "neoclassicists." In particular, the notions of organizational culture and symbolic organization theory carry forward ideas that are discussed in this book in terms of the inducement-contribution network and the organizational identifications it generates.

Similar comparisons could be made with the other terms the recent literature introduces. I emphasize these continuities because the proliferation of terms in administrative theory, well beyond the numbers of new concepts these terms denote, has done a serious disservice to students, making complex and confusing what is perhaps rather straightforward. Confucius attached great importance to "the rectification of names"— putting the right label on things. We need to be less concerned with rectifying names than with avoiding the multiplication of names. We need to attach the same names to concepts wherever those concepts are used. If we do this, we find that we do not need separate representations for the eight "schools" of organization theory, but that they fit rather nicely as developments of a single conceptual framework. Of course, I have a certain partiality to the way in which that framework is described in *Administrative Behavior,* but it is more important that we learn to build our science in cumulative fashion than that any particular formulation of it survive.

Changes in Organizations

Earlier, I expressed the view that people inhabiting organizations today would not find either the organizations of two thousand years ago or those of the future wholly unfamiliar. However, this view has been challenged recently, particularly by those who see modern electronic computers and communication networks as harbingers of a great revolution in the nature of work and of organizations.[14] Many of the new ideas focus on the dissociation of work from a common workplace because of the possibilities of remote communication.

For example, to the extent that work is not tied to a common workplace for organization members, it becomes easier for people to accept part-time employment in several organizations simultaneously, operating in a mode that lies somewhere between employment and consultation, or that resembles the putting-out system which preceded the factory system in weaving and other industries. The available data seems to show some increase in this kind of work pattern, which would certainly appear to have important implications for organizational identification and loyalty.

A related idea is that with easy communication of each with all, regardless of location, there will be more group participation in making decisions and solving problems. This idea has already spawned new products in the form of "groupware"—electronic software that is supposed to make it easier for groups of people to work together and to collaborate in generating reports and similar products, or to share access to common data banks. Networks would not have to be limited, of course, to single organizations, so that interorganizational communication and collaboration (e.g., e-mail and the World Wide Web) could be facilitated.

Another related idea is that the new communication networks make the traditional organizational hierarchy less important: messages can flow in all directions, horizontally as well as vertically. Some observers have attributed the recent downsizings of middle management to the waning importance of maintaining a single hierarchy of authority and communication.

Not all of the predicted changes are consequences of networking. Some of them are attributed to changing attitudes in society toward authority, and the demand for democratization of traditional authority relations.

I will not try to comment on these developments and prospects at this point, but those mentioned and others will be taken up as appropriate in the commentaries to later chapters.

---

[14]Two excellent surveys of views about these prospective new developments are E. H. Bowman and B. M Kogut, eds., *Redesigning the Firm* (New York: Oxford University Press, 1995); and D. M. Rousseau, "Organizational Behavior in the New Organizational Era," *Annual Review of Psychology*, vol. 48 (1997), Palo Alto, Calif.: Annual Reviews Inc.

CHAPTER II

Some Problems of Administrative Theory

SINCE THE PRESENT VOLUME DEPARTS RATHER WIDELY from the usual presentation of the "principles of administration,"[1] some explanation should perhaps be given for this deviation, and some description of the defects in the current theory which made this deviation necessary. The present chapter will first undertake a critical examination of the "principles," and then will turn to a discussion of how a sound theory of administrative behavior can be constructed. It builds, therefore, the methodological foundations for the later chapters.

It is a fatal defect of the current principles of administration that, like proverbs, they occur in pairs. For almost every principle one can find an equally plausible and acceptable contradictory principle. Although the two principles of the pair will lead to exactly opposite organizational recommendations, there is nothing in the theory to indicate which is the proper one to apply. To substantiate this criticism, it is necessary to examine briefly some of the leading principles.

SOME ACCEPTED ADMINISTRATIVE PRINCIPLES

Among the more common "principles" that occur in the literature of administration are these:

1. Administrative efficiency is increased by a specialization of the task among the group.
2. Administrative efficiency is increased by arranging the members of the group in a determinate hierarchy of authority.
3. Administrative efficiency is increased by limiting the span of control at any point in the hierarchy to a small number.
4. Administrative efficiency is increased by grouping the workers, for

---

[1]For a systematic exposition of the currently accepted "principles" see Gulick and Urwick, *op. cit.*, or L. Urwick, *The Elements of Administration* (New York: Harper & Brothers, 1945).

purposes of control, according to (a) purpose, (b) process, (c) clientele, or (d) place. (This is really an elaboration of the first principle, but deserves separate discussion.)

Since these principles appear relatively simple and clear, it would seem that their application to concrete problems of administrative organization would be unambiguous, and that their validity would be easily submitted to empirical test. Such, however, seems not to be the case.

Specialization

Administrative efficiency is supposed to increase with an increase in specialization. But is this intended to mean that *any* increase in specialization will increase efficiency? If so, which of the following alternatives is the correct application of the principle?

(A) A plan of nursing should be put into effect by which nurses will be assigned to districts and do all nursing within that district, including school examinations, visits to homes or school children, and tuberculosis nursing.

(B) A functional plan of nursing should be put into effect by which different nurses will be assigned to school examinations, visits to homes of school children, and tuberculosis nursing. The present method of generalized nursing by districts impedes the development of specialized skills in the three very diverse programs.

Both of these administrative arrangements satisfy the requirement of specialization: the first provides specialization by place; the second, specialization by function. The principle of specialization is of no help at all in choosing between the two alternatives.

It appears that the simplicity of the principle of specialization is a deceptive simplicity—a simplicity that conceals fundamental ambiguities. For "specialization" is not a condition of efficient administration: it is an inevitable characteristic of all group effort, however efficient or inefficient that effort may be. Specialization merely means that different persons are doing different things—and since it is physically impossible for two persons to be doing the same thing in the same place at the same time two persons are always doing different things.

The real problem of administration, then, is not to "specialize," but to specialize in that particular manner, and along those particular lines, which will lead to administrative efficiency. But, in thus rephrasing this "principle" of administration, there has been brought clearly into the open its fundamental ambiguity: "Administrative efficiency is increased by a specialization of the task among the group in the direction that will lead to greater efficiency."

Further discussion of the choice between competing bases of specialization will be undertaken later, but must be postponed momentarily until two other principles of administration have been examined.

Unity of Command

Administrative efficiency is supposed to be enhanced by arranging the members of the organization in a determinate hierarchy of authority in order to preserve "unity of command."

Analysis of this "principle" requires a clear understanding of what is meant by the term "authority." A subordinate may be said to accept authority whenever he permits his behavior to be guided by a decision reached by another, irrespective of his own judgment as to the merits of that decision.

In one sense the principle of unity of command, like the principle of specialization, cannot be violated; for it is physically impossible for a man to obey two contradictory commands. Presumably, if unity of command is a principle of administration, it must assert something more than this physical impossibility. Perhaps it asserts this: that it is undesirable to place a member of an organization in a position where he receives orders from more than one superior. This is evidently the meaning that Gulick attaches to the principle when he says:

> The significance of this principle in the process of coordination and organization must not be lost sight of. In building a structure of coordination, it is often tempting to set up more than one boss for a man who is doing work which has more than one relationship. Even as great a philosopher of management as Taylor fell into this error in setting up separate foremen to deal with machinery, with materials, with speed, etc., each with the power of giving orders directly to the individual workman. The rigid adherence to the principle of unity of command may have its absurdities; these are, however, unimportant in comparison with the certainty of confusion, inefficiency and irresponsibility which arises from the violation of the principle.[2]

Certainly the principle of unity of command, thus interpreted, cannot be criticized for any lack of clarity or for ambiguity. The definition of

---

[2]Gulick, "Notes on the Theory of Organization," in Gulick and Urwick, *op. cit.*, p. 9.

"authority" given above should provide a clear test whether, in any concrete situation, the principle is observed. The real fault that must be found with this principle is that it is incompatible with the principle of specialization. One of the most important uses to which authority is put in organization is to bring about specialization in the work of making decisions, so that each decision is made at the point in the organization where it can be made most expertly. As a result, the use of authority permits a greater degree of expertness to be achieved in decision-making than would be possible if each operative employee had to make all the decisions upon which his activity is predicated. The individual fireman does not decide whether to use a two-inch hose or a fire extinguisher; that is decided for him by his officers, and the decision communicated to him in the form of a command.

However, if unity of command, in Gulick's sense, is observed, the decisions of a person at any point in the administrative hierarchy are subject to influence through only one channel of authority; and if his decisions are of a kind that requires expertise in more than one field of knowledge, then advisory and informational services must be relied upon to supply those premises which lie in a field not recognized by the mode of specialization in the organization. For example, if an accountant in a school department is subordinate to an educator, and if unity of command is observed, then the finance department cannot issue direct orders to him regarding the technical, accounting aspects of his work. Similarly, the director of motor vehicles in the public works department will be unable to issue direct orders on care of motor equipment to the fire-truck driver.[3]

Gulick, in the statement quoted above, clearly indicates the difficulties to be faced if unity of command is not observed. A certain amount of irresponsibility and confusion is almost certain to ensue. But perhaps this is not too great a price to pay for the increased expertise that can be applied to decisions. What is needed to decide the issue is a principle of administration that will enable one to weigh the relative advantages of the two courses of action. But neither the principle of unity of command nor the principle of specialization is helpful in adjudicating the controversy. They merely contradict each other without indicating any procedure for resolving the contradiction.

If this were merely an academic controversy—if it were generally agreed and had been generally demonstrated that unity of command must be preserved in all cases, even with a loss in expertise—one could assert that in case of conflict between the two principles, unity of com-

---

[3]This point is discussed by Herbert A. Simon in "Decision-Making and Administrative Organization," *Public Administration Review* 4:20–21 (Winter, 1944).

mand should prevail. But the issue is far from clear, and experts can be ranged on both sides of the controversy. On the side of unity of command there may be cited the dicta of Gulick and others.[4] On the side of specialization there are Taylor's theory of functional supervision, Mac-Mahon and Millett's idea of "dual supervision," and the practice of technical supervision in military organization.[5]

It may be, as Gulick asserts, that the notion of Taylor and these others is an "error." If so, the evidence that it is an error has never been marshaled or published—apart from loose heuristic arguments like that quoted above. One is left with a choice between equally eminent theorists of administration, and without any evidential basis for making that choice.

What evidence there is of actual administrative practice would seem to indicate that the need for specialization is to a very large degree given priority over the need for unity of command. As a matter of fact, it does not go too far to say that unity of command, in Gulick's sense, never has existed in any administrative organization. If a line officer accepts the regulations of an accounting department with regard to the procedure for making requisitions, can it be said that, in this sphere, he is not subject to the authority of the accounting department? In any actual administrative situation authority is zoned, and to maintain that this zoning does not contradict the principle of unity of command requires a very different definition of "authority" from that used here. This subjection of the line officer to the accounting department is no different, in principle, from Taylor's recommendation that a workman be subject in the matter of work programming to one foreman, in the matter of machine operation to another.

The principle of unity of command is perhaps more defensible if narrowed down to the following: In case two authoritative commands conflict, there should be a single determinate person whom the subordinate is expected to obey; and the sanctions of authority should be applied against the subordinate only to enforce his obedience to that one person.

If the principle of unity of command is more defensible when stated in this limited form it also solves fewer problems. In the first place, it no longer requires, except for settling conflicts of authority, a single hierarchy of authority. Consequently, it leaves unsettled the very important question of how authority should be zoned in a particular organization

[4]Gulick, "Notes on the Theory of Organization," p. 9; L. D. White, *Introduction to the Study of Public Administration* (New York: Macmillan, 1939), p. 45.

[5]Frederick W. Taylor, *Shop Management* (New York: Harper & Bros., 1911), p. 99; MacMahon, Millett, and Ogden, *The Administration of Federal Work Relief* (Chicago: Public Administration Service, 1941), pp. 265–268, and L. Urwick, who describes British army practice in "Organization as a Technical Problem," Gulick and Urwick, eds., *op. cit.*, pp. 67–69.

(i.e. the modes of specialization), and through what channels it should be exercised. Finally, even this narrower concept of unity of command conflicts with the principle of specialization, for whenever disagreement does occur and the organization members revert to the formal lines of authority, then only those types of specialization which are represented in the hierarchy of authority can impress themselves on decision. If the training officer of a city exercises only functional supervision over the police training officer, then in case of disagreement with the police chief specialized knowledge of police problems will determine the outcome while specialized knowledge of training problems will be subordinated or ignored. That this actually occurs is shown by the frustration so commonly expressed by functional supervisors at their lack of authority to apply sanctions.

Span of Control

Administrative efficiency is supposed to be enhanced by limiting the number of subordinates who report directly to any one administrator to a small number—say six. This notion that the "span of control" should be narrow is confidently asserted as a third incontrovertible principle of administration. The usual common-sense arguments for restricting the span of control are familiar and need not be repeated here. What is not so generally recognized is that a contradictory proverb of administration can be stated which, though it is not so familiar as the principle of span of control, can be supported by arguments of equal plausibility. The proverb in question is the following:

Administrative efficiency is enhanced by keeping at a minimum the number of organizational levels through which a matter must pass before it is acted upon.

This latter proverb is one of the fundamental criteria that guide administrative analysts in simplifying procedures. Yet in many situations the results to which this principle leads are in direct contradiction to the requirements of the principle of span of control, the principle of unity of command, and the principle of specialization. The present discussion is concerned with the first of these conflicts. To illustrate the difficulty, two alternative proposals for the organization of a small health department will be presented—one based on the restriction of span of control, the other on the limitation of number of organization levels:

(A) The present organization of the department places an administrative overload on the Health Officer by reason of the fact that all eleven employees of the department report directly to him and the further fact that some of the staff lack adequate technical training. Consequently, venereal disease clinic treatments and other details require an undue amount of the Health Officer's personal attention.

It has previously been recommended that the proposed Medical Officer be placed in charge of the venereal disease and chest clinics and all child hygiene work. It is further recommended that one of the inspectors be designated chief inspector and placed in charge of all the department's inspectional activities; and that one of the nurses be designated as head nurse. This will relieve the Health Commissioner of considerable detail and will leave him greater freedom to plan and supervise the health program as a whole, to conduct health education, and to coordinate the work of the department with that of other community agencies. If the department were thus organized, the effectiveness of all employees could be substantially increased.

(B) The present organization of the department leads to inefficiency and excessive red tape by reason of the fact that an unnecessary supervisory level intervenes between the Health Officer and the operative employees, and that those four of the twelve employees who are best trained technically are engaged largely in "overhead" administrative duties. Consequently, unnecessary delays occur in securing the approval of the Health Officer on matters requiring his attention, and too many matters require review and re-review.

The Medical Officer should be left in charge of the venereal disease and chest clinics and child hygiene work. It is recommended, however, that the position of chief inspector and head nurse be abolished, and that the employees now filling these positions perform regular inspectional and nursing duties. The details of work scheduling now handled by these two employees can be taken care of more economically by the Secretary to the Health Officer, and, since broader matters of policy have, in any event, always required the personal attention of the Health Officer, the abolition of these two positions will eliminate a wholly unnecessary step in review, will allow an expansion of inspectional and nursing services, and will permit at least a beginning to be made in the recommended program of health education. The number of persons reporting directly to the Health Officer will be increased to nine, but since there are few matters requiring the coordination of these employees, other than the work schedules and policy questions referred to above, this change will not materially increase his work load.

The dilemma is this: in a large organization with interrelations between members, a restricted span of control inevitably produces excessive red tape, for each contact between organization members must be carried upward until a common superior is found. If the organization is at all large, this will involve carrying all such matters upward through several levels of officials for decision, and then downward again in the form of orders and instructions—a cumbersome and time-consuming process.

The alternative is to increase the number of persons who are under the command of each officer, so that the pyramid will come more rapidly to a peak, with fewer intervening levels. But this, too, leads to difficulty, for if an officer is required to supervise too many employees, his control over them is weakened.[6]

Granted, then, that both the increase and the decrease in span of control have some undesirable consequences, what is the optimum point? Proponents of a restricted span of control have suggested three, five, even eleven, as suitable numbers, but nowhere have they explained the reasoning which led them to the particular number they selected. The principle as stated casts no light on this very crucial question.

Organization by Purpose, Process, Clientele, Place[7]

Administrative efficiency is supposed to be increased by grouping workers according to (a) purpose, (b) process, (c) clientele, or (d) place. But from the discussion of specialization it is clear that this principle is internally inconsistent; for purpose, process, clientele, and place are competing bases of organization, and at any given point of division the advantages of three must be sacrificed to secure the advantages of the fourth. If the major departments of a city, for example, are organized on the basis of major purpose, then it follows that all the physicians, all the lawyers, all the engineers, or all the statisticians will not be located in a single department exclusively composed of members of their profession, but will be distributed among the various city departments needing their services. The advantages of organization by process will thereby be partly lost.

Some of these advantages can be regained by organizing on the basis of process *within* the major departments. Thus there may be an engineering bureau within the public works department, or the board of education may have a school health service as a major division of its work. Similarly, within smaller units there may be division by area or by clientele; e.g., a fire department will have separate companies located throughout the city, while a welfare bureau will have intake and casework offices in various locations. Again, however, these major types of

---

[6]A typical justification for limiting the span of control is given by L. Urwick, *op. cit.*, pp. 52–54.

[7]Cf. Schuyler Wallace, *Federal Departmentalization* (New York: Columbia University Press, 1941), pp. 91–146.

specialization cannot be simultaneously achieved, for at any point in the organization it must be decided whether specialization at the next level will be accomplished by distinction of major purpose, major process, clientele, or area.

Competition Between Purpose and Clientele. The conflict may be illustrated by showing how the principle of specialization according to purpose would lead to a different result from specialization according to clientele in the organization of a health department.

(A) Public health administration consists of the following activities for the prevention of disease and the maintenance of healthful conditions: (1) vital statistics; (2) child hygiene—prenatal, maternity, postnatal, infant, pre-school, and school health programs; (3) communicable disease control; (4) inspection of milk, foods, and drugs; (5) sanitary inspection; (6) laboratory service; (7) health education.

One of the handicaps under which the health department labors is the fact that the department has no control over school health, which is an activity of the county board of education, and there is little or no coordination between that highly important part of the community health program and the rest of the program, which is conducted by the city-county health unit. It is recommended that the city and county open negotiations with the board of education for the transfer of all school health work and the appropriation therefor to the joint health unit.

(B) To the modern school department is entrusted the care of children during almost the entire period that they are absent from the parental home. It has three principal responsibilities toward them: (1) to provide for their education in useful skills and knowledge, and in character; (2) to provide them with wholesome play activities outside school hours; (3) to care for their health and to assure the attainment of minimum standards of nutrition.

One of the handicaps under which the school board labors is the fact that, except for school lunches, the board has no control over child health and nutrition, and there is little or no coordination between that highly important part of the child development program and the rest of the program, which is conducted by the board of education. It is recommended that the city and county open negotiations for the transfer of all health work for children of school age to the board of education.

Here again is posed the dilemma of choosing between alternative, equally plausible, administrative principles. But this is not the only difficulty in the present case, for a closer study of the situation shows there are fundamental ambiguities in the meanings of the key terms: "purpose," "process," "clientele," and "place."

Ambiguities in Key Terms. "Purpose" may be roughly defined as the objective or end for which an activity is carried on; "process," as a means of accomplishing a purpose. Processes, then, are carried on in order to achieve purposes. But purposes themselves may generally be arranged in some sort of hierarchy. A typist moves her fingers in order to type; types in order to reproduce a letter; reproduces a letter in order that an inquiry may be answered. Writing a letter is then the purpose for which the typing is performed; while writing a letter is also the process whereby the purpose of replying to an inquiry is achieved. It follows that the same activity may be described as purpose or as process.

This ambiguity is easily illustrated for the case of an administrative organization. A health department conceived as a unit whose task it is to care for the health of the community is a purpose organization; the same department conceived as a unit which makes use of the medical arts to carry on its work is a process organization. In the same way, an education department may be viewed as a purpose (to educate) organization, or a clientele (children) organization; the Forest Service as a purpose (forest conservation), process (forest management), clientele (lumbermen and cattlemen utilizing public forests), or area (publicly owned forest lands) organization. When concrete illustrations of this sort are selected, the lines of demarcation between these categories become very hazy and unclear indeed.

"Organization by major purpose," says Gulick,[8] "serves to bring together in a single large department all of those who are at work endeavoring to render a particular service." But what is a particular service? Is fire protection a single purpose, or is it merely a part of the purpose of public safety? Or is it a combination of purposes including fire prevention and fire fighting? It must be concluded that there is no such a thing as a purpose, or a *unifunctional* (single-purpose) organization. What is to be considered as *a* single function depends entirely on language and techniques.[9] If the English language has a comprehensive term which covers both of two sub-purposes it is natural to think of the two together as a single purpose. If such a term is lacking, the two sub-purposes become purposes in

---

[8]*Op. cit.*, p. 21.

[9]If this is correct, then any attempt to prove that certain activities belong in a single department because they relate to a single purpose is doomed to fail. See, for example, John M. Gaus and Leon Wolcott, *Public Administration and the U.S. Department of Agriculture* (Chicago: Public Administrative Service, 1941).

their own right. On the other hand, a single activity may contribute to several objectives; but since they are technically (procedurally) inseparable the activity is considered as a single function or purpose.

The fact mentioned previously that purposes form a hierarchy, each sub-purpose contributing to some more final and comprehensive end, helps to make clear the relation between purpose and process. "Organization by major process," says Gulick,[10] "... tends to bring together in a single department all of those who are at work making use of a given skill or technology, or are members of a given profession." Consider a simple skill of this kind—typing. Typing is a skill that brings about a means-end coordination of muscular movements, but brings it about at a very low level in the means-end hierarchy. The content of the typewritten letter is indifferent to the skill that produces it. The skill consists merely in the ability to hit the letter *t* quickly whenever *t* is required by the content, and to hit the letter *a* whenever *a* is required by the content.

There is, then, no essential difference between a "purpose" and a "process," but only a distinction of degree. A "process" is an activity whose immediate purpose is at a low level in the hierarchy of means and ends, while a "purpose" is a collection of activities whose orienting value or aim is at a high level in the means-end hierarchy.

Next consider "clientele" and "place" as bases of organization. These categories are really not separate from purpose, but a part of it. A complete statement of the purpose of a fire department would have to include the area served by it; "to reduce fire losses on property in the city of X." Objectives of an administrative organization are phrased in terms of a service to be provided and an area for which it is provided. Usually, the term "purpose" is meant to refer only to the first element; but the second is just as legitimately an aspect of purpose. Area of service, of course, may be a specified clientele quite as well as a geographical area. In the case of an agency which works on "shifts," time will be a third dimension of purpose—to provide a given service in a given area (or to a given clientele) during a given time period.

With this terminology, the next task is to reconsider the problem of specializing the work of an organization. It is no longer legitimate to speak of a "purpose" organization, or a "process" organization, a "clientele" organization, or an "area" organization. The same unit might fall into any one of these four categories, depending on the nature of the larger organizational unit of which it was a part. A unit providing public health and medical services for school-age children in Multnomah County might be considered as (1) an "area" organization if it were part

---

[10]*Op. cit.*, p. 23.

of a unit providing the same service for the state of Oregon; (2) a "clientele" organization if it were part of a unit providing similar services for children of all ages; (3) a "purpose" or a "process" organization (it would be impossible to say which) if it were part of an education department.

It is incorrect to say that Bureau A is a process bureau; the correct statement is that Bureau A is a process bureau *within* Department X.[11] This latter statement would mean that Bureau A incorporated all the processes of a certain kind in Department X, without reference to any special sub-purposes, sub-areas, or sub-clienteles of Department X. Now it is conceivable that a particular unit might incorporate all processes of a certain kind, but that these processes might relate only to certain particular sub-purposes of the department purpose. In this case, which corresponds to the health unit in an education department mentioned above, the unit would be specialized by both purpose and process. The health unit would be the only one in the education department using the medical art (process) and concerned with health (sub-purpose).

Lack of Criteria for Specialization. Even when the problem is solved of proper usage for the terms "purpose," "process," "clientele," and "area," the principles of administration give no guide as to which of these four competing bases of specialization is applicable in any particular situation. The British Machinery of Government Committee had no doubts about the matter. It considered purpose and clientele as the two possible bases of organization and put its faith entirely in the former. Others have had equal assurance in choosing between purpose and process. The reasoning which leads to these unequivocal conclusions leaves something to be desired. The Machinery of Government Committee gives this sole argument for its choice:

> Now the inevitable outcome of this method of organization [by clientele] is a tendency to Lilliputian administration. It is impossible that the specialized service which each Department has to render to the community can be of as high a standard when its work is at the same time limited to a particular class of persons and extended to every variety of provision for them, as when the Department concentrates itself on the provision of the particular service only, by whomsoever required, and looks beyond the interest of comparatively small classes.[12]

[11]It should be noted that this distinction is implicit in most of Gulick's analysis of specialization (*op. cit.*, pp. 15–30). However, since he cites as examples single departments within a city, and since he usually speaks of "grouping activities" rather than "dividing work," the relative character of these categories is not always apparent in this discussion.

[12]*Report of the Machinery of Government Committee* (London: His Majesty's Stationery Office, 1918), p. 7.

The faults in this analysis are clearly obvious. First, there is no attempt to determine how *a* service is to be recognized. Second, there is a bald assumption, absolutely without proof, that a child health unit, for example, in a department of child welfare could not offer services of "as high a standard" as the same unit if it were located in a department of health. Just how the shifting of the unit from one department to another would improve or damage the quality of its work is not explained. Third, no basis is set forth for adjudicating the competing claims of purpose and process—the two are merged in the ambiguous term "service." It is not necessary here to decide whether the committee was right or wrong in its recommendation; the important point is that the recommendation represented a choice, without any apparent logical or empirical grounds, between contradictory principles of administration.

Even more remarkable illustrations of illogic can be found in most discussions of purpose *vs.* process. They would be too ridiculous to cite if they were not commonly used in serious political and administrative debate.

> For instance, where should agricultural education come: in the Ministry of Education, or of Agriculture? That depends on whether we want to see the best farming taught, though possibly by old methods, or a possibly out-of-date style of farming, taught in the most modern and compelling manner. The question answers itself.[13]

But does the question really answer itself? Suppose a bureau of agricultural education were set up, headed, for example, by a man who had had extensive experience in agricultural research or as administrator of an agricultural school, and staffed by men of similarly appropriate background. What reason is there to believe that if attached to a Ministry of Education they would teach old-fashioned farming by new-fashioned methods, while if attached to a Ministry of Agriculture they would teach new-fashioned farming by old-fashioned methods? The administrative problem of such a bureau would be to teach new-fashioned farming by new-fashioned methods, and it is a little difficult to see how the departmental location of the unit would affect this result. "The question answers itself" only if one has a rather mystical faith in the potency of bureau shuffling as a means of redirecting the activities of an agency.

These contradictions and competitions have received increasing

[13]Sir Charles Harris, "Decentralization," *Journal of Public Administration*, 3:117–133 (Apr., 1925).

attention from students of administration during the past few years. For example, Gulick, Wallace, and Benson have stated certain advantages and disadvantages of the several modes of specialization, and have considered the conditions under which one or the other mode might best be adopted.[14] All this analysis has been at a theoretical level—in the sense that data have not been employed to demonstrate the superior effectiveness claimed for the different modes. But, though theoretical, the analysis has lacked a theory. Since no comprehensive framework has been constructed within which the discussion could take place, the analysis has tended either to the logical one-sidedness which characterizes the examples quoted above or to inconclusiveness.

The Impasse of Administrative Theory

The four "principles of administration" that were set forth at the beginning of this paper have now been subjected to critical analysis. None of the four survived in very good shape, for in each case there was found, instead of a univocal principle, a set of two or more mutually incompatible principles apparently equally applicable to the administrative situation.

Moreover, the reader will see that the very same objections can be urged against the customary discussions of "centralization" vs. "decentralization," which usually conclude, in effect, that "on the one hand, centralization of decision-making function is desirable; on the other hand, there are definite advantages in decentralization."

Can anything be salvaged which will be useful in the construction of an administrative theory? As a matter of fact, almost everything can be salvaged. The difficulty has arisen from treating as "principles of administration" what are really only criteria for describing and diagnosing administrative situations. Closet space is certainly an important item in the design of a successful house; yet, a house designed entirely with a view to securing a maximum of closet space—all other considerations being forgotten—would be considered, to say the least, as somewhat unbalanced. Similarly, unity of command, specialization by purpose, decentralization, all are items to be considered in the design of an efficient administrative organization. No single one of these items is of sufficient importance to suffice as a guiding principle for the administrative analyst. In the design of administrative organizations, as in their opera-

---

[14]Gulick, "Notes on the Theory of Organization," in Gulick and Urwick, op. cit., pp. 21–30; Schuyler Wallace, op. cit.; George C. S. Benson, "Internal Administrative Organization," Public Administration Review, 1:473–486 (Autumn, 1941).

tion, over-all efficiency must be the guiding criterion. Mutually incompatible advantages must be balanced against each other, just as an architect weighs the advantages of additional closet space against the advantages of a larger living room.

This position, if it is a valid one, constitutes an indictment of much current writing about administrative matters. As the examples cited in this chapter amply demonstrate, much administrative analysis proceeds by selecting a single criterion, and applying it to an administrative situation to reach a recommendation; while the fact that equally valid, but contradictory, criteria exist which could be applied with equal reason, but with a different result, is conveniently ignored. A valid approach to the study of administration requires that *all* the relevant diagnostic criteria be identified; that each administrative situation be analyzed in terms of the entire set of criteria; and that research be instituted to determine how weights can be assigned to the several criteria when they are, as they usually will be, mutually incompatible.

AN APPROACH TO ADMINISTRATIVE THEORY

This program needs to be considered step by step. First, what is included in the description of administrative situations for purposes of such an analysis? Second, how can weights be assigned to the various criteria to give them their proper place in the total picture?

The Description of Administrative Situations

Before a science can develop principles, it must possess concepts. Before a law of gravitation could be formulated, it was necessary to have the notions of "acceleration" and "weight." The first task of administrative theory is to develop a set of concepts that will permit the description, in terms relevant to the theory, of administrative situations. These concepts, to be scientifically useful, must be operational; that is, their meanings must correspond to empirically observable facts or situations. The definition of "authority" given earlier in this chapter is an example of an operational definition.

What is a scientifically relevant description of an organization? It is a description that, so far as possible, designates for each person in the organization what decisions that person makes, and the influences to which he is subject in making each of these decisions. Current descriptions of administrative organizations fall far short of this standard. For the most part, they confine themselves to the allocation of *functions*, and the formal structure of *authority*. They give little attention to the other types of organizational influence or to the system of communication.[15]

What does it mean, for example, to say: "The Department is made up of three Bureaus. The first has the function of————, the second the function of————, and the third the function of————"? What can be learned from such a description about the workability of the organizational arrangement? Very little, indeed. For, from the description, there is obtained no idea of the degree to which decisions are centralized at the bureau level or at the departmental level. No notion is given of the extent to which the (presumably unlimited) authority of the department over the bureau is actually exercised, nor by what mechanisms. There is no indication of the extent to which systems of communication assist the coordination of the three bureaus, nor, for that matter to what extent coordination is required by the nature of their work. There is no description of the kinds of training the members of the bureau have undergone, nor the extent to which this training permits decentralization at the bureau level. In sum, a description of administrative organizations in terms almost exclusively of functions and lines of authority is completely inadequate for purposes of administrative analysis.

Consider the term "centralization." How is it determined whether the operations of a particular organization are "centralized" or "decentralized"? Does the fact that field offices exist prove anything about decentralization? Might not the same decentralization take place in the bureaus of a centrally located office? A realistic analysis of centralization must include a study of the allocation of decisions in the organization, and the methods of influence that are employed by the higher levels to affect the decisions at the lower levels. Such an analysis would reveal a much more complex picture of the decision-making process than any enumeration of the geographical locations of organizational units at the different levels.

Administrative description suffers currently from superficiality, oversimplification, lack of realism. It has confined itself too closely to the mechanism of authority, and has failed to bring within its orbit the other, equally important, modes of influence on organizational behavior. It has refused to undertake the tiresome task of studying the actual allocations of decision-making functions. It has been satisfied to speak of "authority," "centralization," "span of control," "function," without seeking operational definitions of these terms. Until administrative description reaches

[15]The monograph by MacMahon, Millett, and Ogden (*op. cit.*) perhaps approaches nearer than any other published administrative study to the sophistication required in administrative description. See, for example, the discussion on pp. 233–236 of headquarters-field relationships.

a higher level of sophistication, there is little reason to hope that rapid progress will be made toward the identification and verification of valid administrative principles.

The Diagnosis of Administrative Situations

Before any positive suggestions can be made, it is necessary to digress a bit, and to consider more closely the exact nature of the propositions of administrative theory. The theory of administration is concerned with how an organization should be constructed and operated in order to accomplish its work efficiently. A fundamental principle of administration, which follows almost immediately from the rational character of "good" administration, is that among several alternatives involving the same expenditure the one should always be selected which leads to the greatest accomplishment of administrative objectives; and among several alternatives that lead to the same accomplishment the one should be selected which involves the least expenditure. Since this "principle of efficiency" is characteristic of any activity that attempts rationally to maximize the attainment of certain ends with the use of scarce means, it is as characteristic of economic theory as it is of administrative theory. The "administrative man" takes his place alongside the classical "economic man."[16]

Actually, the "principle" of efficiency should be considered as a definition rather than a principle: it is a definition of what is meant by "good" or "correct" administrative behavior. It does not tell *how* accomplishments are to be maximized, but merely states that this maximization is the aim of administrative activity, and that administrative theory must disclose under what conditions the maximization takes place.

Now what are the factors that determine the level of efficiency which is achieved by an administrative organization? It is not possible to make an exhaustive list of these, but the principal categories can be enumerated. Perhaps the simplest method of approach is to consider the single member of the administrative organization, and ask what the limits are to the quantity and quality of his output. These limits include (a) limits on his ability to *perform*, and (b) limits on his ability to *make correct decisions*. To the extent that these limits are removed, the administrative organization approaches its goal of high efficiency. Two persons, given the same skills, the same objectives and values, the same knowledge and information, can rationally decide only upon the same course of

[16]For an elaboration of the principle of efficiency and its place in administrative theory see Clarence E. Ridley and Herbert A. Simon, *Measuring Municipal Activities* (Chicago: International City Managers' Assn., 2nd ed., 1943), particularly chap. 1 and the preface to the second edition.

action. Hence, administrative theory must be interested in the factors that will determine with what skills, values, and knowledge the organization member undertakes his work. These are the "limits" to rationality with which the principles of administration must deal.

On one side, the individual is limited by those skills, habits, and reflexes which are no longer in the realm of the conscious. His performance, for example, may be limited by his manual dexterity or his reaction time or his strength. His decision-making processes may be limited by the speed of his mental processes, his skill in elementary arithmetic, and so forth. In this area, the principles of administration must be concerned with the physiology of the human body, the laws of skill-training, and of habit. This is the field that has been most successfully cultivated by the followers of Taylor, and in which has been developed time-and-motion study and the therblig.

On a second side, the individual is limited by his values and those conceptions of purpose which influence him in making his decisions. If his loyalty to the organization is high, his decisions may evidence sincere acceptance of the objectives set for the organization; if that loyalty is lacking, personal motives may interfere with his administrative efficiency. If his loyalties are attached to the bureau by which he is employed, he may sometimes make decisions that are inimical to the larger unit of which the bureau is a part. In this area the principles of administration must be concerned with the determinants of loyalty and morale, with leadership and initiative, and with the influences that determine where the individual's organizational loyalties will be attached.

On a third side, the individual is limited by the extent of his knowledge of things relevant to his job. This applies both to the basic knowledge required in decision-making—a bridge designer must know the fundamentals of mechanics—and to the information that is required to make his decisions appropriate to the given situation. In this area, administrative theory is concerned with such fundamental questions as these: what the limits are on the mass of knowledge that human minds can accumulate and apply; how rapidly knowledge can be assimilated; how specialization in the administrative organization is to be related to the specializations of knowledge that are prevalent in the community's occupational structure; how the system of communication is to channel knowledge and information to the appropriate decision-points; what types of knowledge can, and what types cannot, be easily transmitted; how the need for intercommunication of information is affected by the modes of specialization in the organization. This is perhaps the *terra incognita* of administrative theory, and undoubtedly its careful exploration will cast great light on the proper application of the proverbs of administration.

Perhaps this triangle of limits does not completely bound the area of rationality, and other sides need to be added to the figure In any case, the enumeration will serve to indicate the kinds of considerations that must go into the construction of valid and noncontradictory principles of administration.

An important fact to be kept in mind is that the limits of rationality are variable limits. Most important of all, consciousness of the limits may in itself alter them. Suppose it were discovered in a particular organization, for example, that organizational loyalties attached to small units had frequently led to a harmful degree of intra-organizational competition. Then, a program which trained members of the organization to be conscious of their loyalties, and to subordinate loyalties toward the smaller group to those toward the larger, might lead to a very considerable alteration of the limits in that organization.[17]

A related point is that the term "rational behavior," as employed here, refers to rationality when that behavior is evaluated in terms of the objectives of the larger organization; for, as it has just been pointed out, the difference in direction of the individual's aims from those of the larger organization is just one of those elements of nonrationality with which the theory must deal.

Assigning Weights to the Criteria

A first step, then, in the overhauling of the proverbs of administration is to develop a vocabulary, along the lines just suggested, for the description of administrative organization. A second step, which has also been outlined, is to study the limits of rationality in order to develop a complete and comprehensive enumeration of the criteria that must be weighed in evaluating an administrative organization. The current proverbs represent only a fragmentary and unsystematized portion of these criteria.

When these two tasks have been carried out, it remains to assign weights to the criteria. Since the criteria, or "proverbs," are often mutually competitive or contradictory, it is not sufficient merely to identify them. Merely to know, for example, that a specified change in organization will reduce the span of control is not enough to justify the change. This gain must be balanced against the possible resulting loss of contact between the higher and lower ranks of the hierarchy.

Hence, administrative theory must also be concerned with the question of the weights that are to be applied to these criteria—to the problems

[17]For an example of the use of such training, see Herbert A. Simon and William Divine, "Controlling Human Factors in an Administrative Experiment," *Public Administration Review*, 1:487–492 (Autumn, 1941).

of their relative importance in any concrete situation. This question is an empirical one, and its solution cannot even be attempted in a volume like this one. What is needed is empirical research and experimentation to determine the relative desirability of alternative administrative arrangements. The methodological framework for this research is already at hand in the principle of efficiency. If an administrative organization whose activities are susceptible to objective evaluation be studied, then the actual change in accomplishment that results from modifying administrative arrangements in these organizations can be observed and analyzed.

There are two indispensable conditions to successful research along these lines. First, it is necessary that the objectives of the administrative organization under study be defined in concrete terms so that results, expressed in terms of these objectives, may be accurately measured. Second, it is necessary that sufficient experimental control be exercised to make possible the isolation of the particular effect under study from other disturbing factors that might be operating on the organization at the same time.

These two conditions have seldom been even partially fulfilled in so-called "administrative experiments." The mere fact that a legislature passes a law creating an administrative agency, that the agency operates for five years, that it is finally abolished, and that an historical study is then made of its operations is not sufficient to make of that agency's history an "administrative experiment." Modern American legislation is full of such "experiments" which furnish orators in neighboring states with abundant ammunition when similar issues arise in their bailiwicks, but which provide the scientific investigator with little or nothing in the way of objective evidence, one way or the other.

In the literature of administration, only a handful of research studies satisfy these fundamental conditions of methodology—and they are, for the most part, on the periphery of the problem of organization. There are, first of all, the studies of the Taylor group which sought to determine the technological conditions of efficiency. Perhaps none of these is a better example of the painstaking methods of science than Taylor's own studies of the cutting of metals.[18]

Studies dealing with the human and social aspects of administration are even rarer than the technological studies. Among the more important are the whole series of studies on fatigue, starting in Great Britain during the First World War, and culminating in the Western Electric experiments.[19]

[18]F. W. Taylor, *On the Art of Cutting Metals* (New York: American Society of Mechanical Engineers, 1907).

[19]Great Britain, Ministry of Munitions, Health of Munitions Workers Committee, *Final Report* (London: H.M. Stationery Office, 1918); F. J. Roethlisberger and William J. Dickson, *Management and the Worker* (Cambridge: Harvard University Press, 1939).

In the field of public administration, almost the sole example of such experimentation is the series of studies that have been conducted in the public welfare field to determine the proper case loads for social workers.[20]

Because, apart from these scattered examples, studies of administrative agencies have been carried out without benefit of control or objective measurements of results, they have had to depend for their recommendations and conclusions upon *a priori* reasoning proceeding from "principles of administration." The reasons have already been stated in this chapter why the "principles" derived in this way cannot be more than "proverbs."

Perhaps the program outlined here will appear an ambitious or even a quixotic one. There should certainly be no illusions, in undertaking it, as to the length and deviousness of the path. It is hard to see, however, what alternative remains open. Certainly neither the practitioner of administration nor the theoretician can be satisfied with the poor analytic tools that the proverbs provide him. Nor is there any reason to believe that a less drastic reconversion than that outlined here will rebuild those tools to usefulness.

It may be objected that administration cannot aspire to be a "science," that by the nature of its subject it cannot be more than an "art." Whether true or false, this objection is irrelevant to the present discussion. The question of how "exact" the principles of administration can be made is one that only experience can answer. But as to whether they should be logical or illogical there can be no debate. Even an "art" cannot be founded on proverbs.

As already indicated, the present volume will attempt only the first step in the reconstruction of administrative theory—the construction of an adequate vocabulary and analytic scheme. In saying that other steps must follow, one must be careful not to underestimate the importance or necessity of this first one. To be sure, the literature of administration has not been lacking in "theory," any more than it has in descriptive and empirical studies. What has been lacking has been a bridge between these two, so that theory could provide a guide to the design of "critical" experiments and studies, while experimental studies could provide a sharp test and corrective of theory. If this volume is successful, it will contribute toward the construction of such a bridge.

[20]Ellery F. Reed, *An Experiment in Reducing the Cost of Relief* (Chicago: American Public Welfare Assn., 1937); Rebecca Staman, "What Is the Most Economical Case Load in Public Relief Administration?" *Social Work Technique*, 4:117–121 (May-June, 1938); Chicago Relief Administration, *Adequate Staff Brings Economy* (Chicago: American Public Welfare Assn., 1939); Constance Hastings and Saya S. Schwartz, *Size of Visitor's Caseload as a Factor in Efficient Administration of Public Assistance* (Philadelphia: Philadelphia County Board of Assistance, 1939); H. A. Simon et al., *Determining Work Loads for Professional Staff in a Public Welfare Agency* (Berkeley: University of California, Bureau of Public Administration, 1941).

SOME PROBLEMS OF ADMINISTRATIVE THEORY

ORGANIZATION THEORY CAN BE APPROACHED in two ways. On the one hand, we can try, as in any science, to build up a factually correct description of the entities called organizations together with an explanation of their behavior, including the circumstances under which they behave effectively or ineffectively and how the effectiveness or ineffectiveness of particular organizational designs relates to the environments to which they must adapt. It is this "basic science" approach to organization theory that is taken in Chapter II.

On the other hand, we can think of organization theory as providing a guide to designing organizations—in the same way that architecture provides a guide to designing buildings, and engineering a guide to designing machines and structures. There is no conflict between basic science and engineering, but a notable difference in points of view. Science is concerned with establishing the laws that govern the behavior of systems of various kinds. Engineering is concerned with designing systems that will accomplish desired objectives. In this commentary, we will take a second look at organization theory from an engineering or design standpoint.

THE "PROVERBS" AND ORGANIZATION DESIGN

Consider the "proverbs" that occupied much of our attention in Chapter II. Classical theory asserted that an organization would be effective in so far as its design satisfied the "proverbs." We have shown that these classical principles were mutually contradictory, hence did not provide a good base for a science unless we could determine, through research, under what circumstances and to what degree each should take precedence.

If we look at the same question, not as a matter of science but of engineering, it becomes less forbidding. From this new standpoint, the proverbs are not unbreakable laws but guidelines for design. For example: "When you are evaluating a scheme for specialization, consider to what extent activities aimed at the same goals are brought together, activities using the same processes, activities carried on at the same location, and so on."

For designers to use these guidelines intelligently, they still need the scientific knowledge called for in Chapter II: knowledge of the circumstances under which one or another guideline takes on special importance. The central difficulty in classical organization theory was its preoccupation with discovering categorical "principles" of organization, applicable unqualifiedly to all organizations at all times. The "principles of organization" still appear with great regularity in textbooks on organization, but they have gradually been relativized by a stream of criticism and empirical research that has shown that different organizational designs are needed for different functions in different environments.

CONTINGENCY THEORY: ADAPTING ORGANIZATIONS TO CIRCUMSTANCES

As William Dill showed in an early study of this kind, a company that manufactures a wide range of diverse products for customers in several industries is bound to organize differently, if it wishes to survive and prosper, from a company manufacturing a single line of products for a homogeneous group of customers.[21] Additional studies, which now provide a wealth of information about the adaptations of organization to environment, have been carried out by Joan Woodward, Tom Burns and George M. Stalker, Charles Perrow, James D. Thompson, Paul R. Lawrence and Jay W. Lorsch, and a number of others.[22]

Some of the research along these lines goes under the label of "contingency theory." The central idea is that what constitutes effective organization structure depends on goals and social and technical circumstances. This theme recurs throughout *Administrative Behavior*. For example, the commentary on Chapter XI addresses the relation of organizational form to environment and task. In the commentary, a case study of the Economic Cooperation Administration, the Federal agency organized in 1948 to administer the Marshall Plan of aid to Western European nations, provides a powerful illustration of how goals influence

---

[21]See W. R. Dill, "Environment as an Influence on Managerial Autonomy," *Administrative Science Quarterly*, 2:409–443 (1958).

[22]An excellent introduction to this literature is provided by W. H. Starbuck, ed., *Organizational Growth and Development* (Harmondsworth, Middlesex, England: Penguin Books, 1971), especially Starbuck's introductory essay, "Organizational Growth and Development," chap. 9 by D. S. Pugh, D. J. Hickson, C. R. Hinings, and C. Turner, "The Context of Organization Structures," and the bibliography at the end of Starbuck's volume.

organization structure and vice versa. I will make a few preliminary comments on it here.

The ECA study emphasizes that designing an organization, like solving any other problem, begins with finding an appropriate way to represent the problem situation. Unless the designers come to the problem with a ready-made representation (i.e., the problem is of a kind that they have faced before), their initial concern must be to find such a representation, and only then can their attention shift to problem-solving.[23] In the ECA, initial ambiguity of the agency's goals and conflict among alternative goals led to the formation of competing representations. Only as these competitors were tested against the requirements of the agency's task and a consensus was reached, did the organization take definite form. Stabilizing the decision process in an organization requires that most participants in the process share a common picture of the organization and its goals.

A second example discussed in the commentary to Chapter XI is the organization of a business school, where one representation of the task comes from the sciences that underlie and inform business practice (e.g., economics, sociology, operations research, psychology, computer science); while a quite different representation comes from the "real" world of organizations and management to which the scientific knowledge is to be applied. What a business school, or any professional school, requires is a task representation that maintains a high degree of congruence between the pictures of the enterprise that are brought to it by faculty drawn from the world of science and faculty drawn from the world of practice.

STRUCTURE AND PROCESS IN DESIGN

Just as anatomy and physiology provide complementary approaches to the study of organisms, so structure and process provide complementary approaches to the study of organizations. Much of the research that relates organization to environment emphasizes the stable structural characteristics of organizations. In this volume we look more closely at the mechanisms of adaptation: how the decision-making process and the system of communications mediate between the organization and its environment. Two brief examples will illustrate how this viewpoint can be used to approach organization design in business.

---

[23]Representation in problem-solving and other cognitive tasks is discussed in chap. 3 of *Human Problem Solving, op. cit.*, and in J. R. Hayes and H. A. Simon, "Understanding Written Problem Instructions," in L. W. Gregg, ed., *Knowledge and Cognition* (Potomac, Md.: Erlbaum Associates, 1974).

Accounting Organization[24]

Some years ago an extensive study sought to determine how companies' accounting systems should be organized in order to be of the greatest usefulness to executives in making their decisions and solving their problems. Answering this question required determining what important kinds of decisions were made by operating executives, how accounting data might be useful in making these decisions, and at what point in the decision-making process the data could most usefully be injected. By observing the actual decision-making process in detail, and in a number of corporations, specific data needs were identified at important organizational levels—the vice-presidential level, the level of the factory manager, and the level of the factory department head, for example—each posing distinct problems of communication for the accounting department.

Out of the analysis of data requirements at specific locations, a general pattern of accounting department organization was developed that would be effective in providing data for operating executives. For example, it was proposed to establish at the factory department level one or more accounting analysts, thoroughly conversant with operations, to help department heads interpret and trace costs through the monthly cost statements. At higher levels, on the other hand, it was proposed to create a small number of strategically placed groups of analysts largely occupied with special studies rather than periodic reports—analyzing the costs and savings associated with possible changes in operating methods and equipment.

Our present interest lies not so much in the study's findings as in its implications for the *technique* of organizational design and reorganization.

1. The foundation of the study was an examination of how decisions actually were made and where.
2. The recommended organizational pattern for accounting was built around its task of informing and influencing these operating decisions.
3. The recommendations for organizational change were to be implemented by bringing about changes in the patterns of who talks to whom, how often, about what—rather than by changes in organization charts.

---

[24]This discussion is based on the report of a study carried out in collaboration with Harold Guetzkow, George Kozmetsky, and Gordon Tyndall, *Centralization v. Decentralization in Organizing the Controller's Department* (New York: Controllership Foundation, 1954).

Product Development

Industries that are based initially on a radically new technology typically go through several stages of product development and improvement. In the first stage, the principal source of product improvement is usually in the new technology itself and the sciences underlying it. Thus, when the computer industry was at this stage, industry leadership depended heavily on basic technical improvements in computer memories and circuits, improvements that stemmed, in turn, from advances in solid state physics and fundamental inquiry into the organization of computer hardware systems. At a later stage, product improvement became considerably more a matter of adaptation to end use—for example, providing appropriate software for customer applications.

An analysis of new-idea sources in these two stages would show that different types of research and development skills were needed, as well as different communications patterns between the engineering departments and their environments. In the long run, events forced the appropriate organizational changes on most companies (those that survived), but systematic organizational analysis of the product development process could often have brought these changes about more promptly and profitably.

The main problems in organizing research and development lie in bringing together information from two distinct sources: from the scientific disciplines that underlie the basic technologies being used, and from the environments that define product requirements for the end use. But this brings us right back to the problem of organization mentioned in the previous section of this commentary: the organization of a professional school poses almost the same problem as does the organization of R&D: how to synthesize crucial information for decisions when it originates in different and remote sources.

As these examples suggest, the key method of analysis proposed in this book is to develop a careful and realistic picture of the decisions that are required for the organization's activity, and of the flow of premises that contribute to these decisions. To do this, one needs a vocabulary and concepts that deal with organizational problems in a more fundamental way than does the homely wisdom that has passed for organizational analysis in the past.

CHAPTER III

Fact and Value in Decision-Making

IN CHAPTER I IT WAS POINTED OUT that every decision involves elements of two kinds, which were called "factual" and "value" elements respectively. This distinction proves to be a very fundamental one for administration. It leads first of all to an understanding of what is meant by a "correct" administrative decision. Secondly, it clarifies the distinction, so often made in the literature of administration, between policy questions and questions of administration. These important issues will be the subject matter of the present chapter.

To ground an answer to these questions on first principles would require that this volume on administration be prefaced by an even longer philosophical treatise. The necessary ideas are already accessible in the literature of philosophy. Hence, the conclusions reached by a particular school of modern philosophy—logical positivism—will be accepted as a starting point, and their implications for the theory of decisions examined. The reader who is interested in examining the reasoning upon which these doctrines are based will find references to the literature in the footnotes to this chapter.

DISTINCTION BETWEEN FACTUAL AND ETHICAL MEANING

Factual propositions are statements about the observable world and the way in which it operates.[1] In principle, factual propositions may be tested to determine whether they are *true* or *false*—whether what they say about the world actually occurs, or whether it does not.

---

[1] The positivist theory as to the nature of scientific propositions is discussed at length by Charles W. Morris, *Foundations of the Theory of Signs*, and Rudolf Carnap, *Foundations of Logic and Mathematics*, in International Encyclopedia of Unified Science, vol. I, nos. 2 and 3 (Chicago: University of Chicago Press, 1937 and 1938); P. W. Bridgman, *The Logic of Modern Physics* (New York: Macmillan, 1937); Rudolf Carnap, "Testability and Meaning," *Philosophy of Science*, 3: 420–471 (Oct., 1936), and 4: 2–40 (Jan., 1937); Rudolf Carnap, *The Logical Syntax of Language* (New York: Harcourt, Brace, 1937); Alfred J. Ayer, *Language, Truth, and Logic* (London: Victor Gollancz, 1936).

Decisions are something more than factual propositions. To be sure, they are descriptive of a future state of affairs, and this description can be true or false in a strictly empirical sense; but they possess, in addition, an imperative quality—they select one future state of affairs in preference to another and direct behavior toward the chosen alternative. In short, they have an *ethical* as well as a factual content.

The question of whether decisions can be correct and incorrect resolves itself, then, into the question of whether ethical terms like "ought," "good," and "preferable" have a purely empirical meaning. It is a fundamental premise of this study that ethical terms are not completely reducible to factual terms. No attempt will be made here to demonstrate conclusively the correctness of this view toward ethical propositions; the justification has been set forth at length by logical positivists and others.[2]

The argument, briefly, runs as follows. To determine whether a proposition is correct, it must be compared directly with experience— with the facts—or it must lead by logical reasoning to other propositions that can be compared with experience. But factual propositions cannot be derived from ethical ones by any process of reasoning, nor can ethical propositions be compared directly with the facts—since they assert "oughts" rather than facts. Hence, there is no way in which the correctness of ethical propositions can be empirically or rationally tested.

From this viewpoint, if a sentence declares that some particular state of affairs "ought to be," or that it is "preferable" or "desirable," then the sentence performs an imperative function, and is neither true nor false, correct nor incorrect. Since decisions involve valuation of this kind, they too cannot be objectively described as correct or incorrect.

The search for the philosopher's stone and the squaring of the circle have not been more popular pursuits among philosophers than the attempt to derive ethical sentences, as consequences of purely factual ones. To mention a relatively modern example—Bentham defined the term "good" as equivalent with "conducive to happiness," defining "happiness" in psychological terms.[3]

He then considered whether or not particular states of affairs were conducive to happiness, and hence good. Of course, no logical objection can be raised against this procedure: it is here rejected because the word "good" thus defined by Bentham cannot perform the function required of the word "good" in ethics—that of expressing moral preference for one

---

[2]Two recent treatments are Ayer, *op. cit.*, and T. V. Smith, *Beyond Conscience* (New York: McGraw-Hill, 1934).

[3]Jeremy Bentham, *An Introduction to the Principles of Morals and Legislation* (Oxford: Clarendon Press, 1907), p. 1.

alternative over another. It may be possible by such a process to derive the conclusion that people will be happier under one set of circumstances than under another, but this does not prove that they *ought* to be happier. The Aristotelian definition—that something is good for man which makes him correspond more closely with his essential nature as a rational animal[4]—suffers from the same limitation.

Thus, by appropriate definitions of the word "good" it may be possible to construct sentences of the form: "Such a state of affairs *is good*." But from "good" defined in this way it is impossible to deduce "Such a state of affairs *ought to be*." The task of ethics is to select imperatives—ought-sentences; and this task cannot be accomplished if the term "good" is defined in such a way that it merely designates existents. In this study, therefore, words like "good" and "ought" will be reserved for their ethical functions, and will not be predicated of any state of affairs in a purely factual sense. It follows that decisions may be "good," but they cannot, in an unqualified sense, be "correct," or "true."

The Evaluation of Decisions

We see that, in a strict sense, the administrator's decisions cannot be evaluated by scientific means. Is there no scientific content, then, to administrative problems? Are they purely questions of ethics? Quite the contrary: to assert that there is an ethical element involved in every decision is not to assert that decisions involve only ethical elements.

Consider the following passage from the *Infantry Field Manual* of the United States Army:

> Surprise is an essential element of a successful attack. Its effects should be striven for in small as well as in large operations. Infantry effects surprise by concealment of the time and place of the attack, screening of its dispositions, rapidity of maneuver, deception, and the avoidance of stereotyped procedures.[5]

It is difficult to say to what extent these three sentences are meant as factual propositions, and to what extent they are intended as imperatives, that is, as decisions. The first may be read purely as a statement about the conditions for a successful attack; the third may be interpreted as a listing of the conditions under which a state of surprise is achieved.

---

[4]Aristotle, "Nicomachean Ethics," bk. I, chap. vii, 12–18, in *The Basic Works of Aristotle*, ed. by Richard McKeon (New York: Random House, 1941).

[5]*Complete Tactics, Infantry Rifle Battalion* (Washington: Infantry Journal, 1940), p. 20.

But binding together these factual sentences—providing them with connective tissue, so to speak—is a set of expressed and implied imperatives, which may be paraphrased thus: "Attack successfully!" "Employ surprise!" and "Conceal the time and place of attack, screen dispositions, move rapidly, deceive the enemy, and avoid stereotyped procedures!"

In fact, the paragraph can be rephrased in another way, separating it into three sentences, the first ethical, the others purely factual:

1.   Attack successfully!
2.   An attack is successful only when carried out under conditions of surprise.
3.   The conditions of surprise are concealment of the time and place of attack, etc.

It follows that the decisions that a military commander makes to screen the dispositions of his troops contain both factual and ethical elements, for he screens the dispositions *in order* to effect "surprise," and this *in order* to attack successfully. Hence, there is one sense in which the correctness of his decisions can be judged: it is a purely factual question whether the measures he takes *in order* to accomplish his aim are appropriate measures. It is not a factual question whether the aim itself is correct or not, except in so far as this aim is connected, by an "in order," to further aims.

Decisions can always be evaluated in this relative sense—it can be determined whether they are correct, given the objective at which they are aimed—but a change in objectives implies a change in evaluation. Strictly speaking, it is not the decision itself which is evaluated, but the purely factual relationship that is asserted between the decision and its aims.[6] The commander's decision to take particular measures in order to attain surprise is not evaluated; what is evaluated is his factual judgment that the measures he takes will, in fact, attain surprise.

This argument may be presented in a slightly different way. Consider the two sentences: "Achieve surprise!" and "The conditions of surprise are concealment of the time and place of attack, etc." While the first sentence contains an imperative, or ethical, element, and hence is neither true nor false, the second sentence is purely factual. If the notion of logical inference be extended so as to apply to the ethical as well as the factual element in sentences, then from these two sentences a third may be deduced: "Conceal the time and place of attack, etc.!" Thus, with the

---

[6]This point of view is developed by Jorgen Jorgensen in "Imperatives and Logic," *Erkenntnis*, 7:288–296 (1938).

mediation of a factual premise (the second sentence), one imperative can be deduced from another.[7]

The Mixed Character of Ethical Statements

It should be clear from the illustrations already put forth that most ethical propositions have admixed with them factual elements. Since most imperatives are not ends-in-themselves but intermediate ends, the question of their appropriateness to the more final ends at which they are aimed remains a factual question. Whether it is ever possible to trace the chain of implementation far enough to isolate a "pure" value—an end that is desired purely for itself—is a question that need not be settled here. The important point for the present discussion is that any statement that contains an ethical element, intermediate or final, cannot be described as correct or incorrect, and that the decision-making process must start with some ethical premise that is taken as "given." This ethical premise describes the objective of the organization in question.

In administration, the mixed character of the ethical "givens" is usually fairly obvious. A municipal department may take as its objective the providing of recreation to the city's inhabitants. This aim may then be further analyzed as a means toward "building healthier bodies," "using leisure time constructively," "preventing juvenile delinquency," and a host of others, until the chain of means and ends is traced into a vague realm labeled "the good life." At this point the means-ends connections become so conjectural (e.g. the relation between recreation and character), and the content of the values so ill defined (e.g. "happiness"), that the analysis becomes valueless for administrative purposes.[8]

The last point may be stated in a more positive way. In order for an ethical proposition to be useful for rational decision-making, (a) the values taken as organizational objectives must be definite, so that their degree of realization in any situation can be assessed, and (b) it must be

[7]In fact the usual laws of inference do not appear to hold strictly in deducing one imperative from another. For a number of discussions of the possibility of a logical calculus for imperatives and attempts to construct a rigorous calculus, see the following: Karl Menger, "A Logic of the Doubtful: On Optative and Imperative Logic," *Reports of a Mathematical Colloquium* (Notre Dame, Indiana, 1939), series 2, no. 1, pp. 53–64; K. Grue-Sörensen, "Imperativsätze und Logik: Begegnung einer Kritik," *Theoria*, 5:195–202 (1939); Albert Hofstadter and J. C. C. McKinsey, "On the Logic of Imperatives," *Philosophy of Science*, 6:446–457 (1939); Kurt Grelling, "Zur Logik der Sollsätze," *Unity of Science Forum*, Jan., 1939, pp. 44–47; K. Reach, "Some Comments on Grelling's Paper," *ibid.*, Apr., 1939, p. 72; Kalle Sorainen, "Der Modus und die Logik," *Theoria* 5:202–204 (1939); Rose Rand, "Logik der Forderungssätze," *Revue internationale de la Theoria du droit* (Zurich), New Series, 5:308–322 (1939).

[8]See the excellent discussion of this point by Wayne A. R. Leys in "Ethics and Administrative Discretion," *Public Administration Review*, 3:19 (Winter, 1943).

possible to form judgments as to the probability that particular actions will implement these objectives.

The Role of Judgment in Decision

The division of the premises of decision into those that are ethical and those that are factual might appear to leave no room for judgment in decision-making. This difficulty is avoided by the very broad meaning that has been given to the word "factual": a statement about the observable world is factual if, in principle, its truth or falsity may be tested. That is, if certain events occur, we say the statement was true; if other events occur, we say that it was false.

This does not by any means imply that we are able to determine in advance whether it is true or false. It is here that judgment enters. In making administrative decisions it is continually necessary to choose factual premises whose truth or falsehood is not definitely known and cannot be determined with certainty with the information and time available for reaching the decision.

It is a purely factual question whether a particular infantry attack will take its objective or fail. It is, nevertheless, a question involving judgment, since the success or failure will depend upon the disposition of the enemy, the accuracy and strength of artillery support, the topography, the morale of the attacking and defending troops, and a host of other factors that cannot be completely known or assessed by the commander who has to order the attack.

In ordinary speech there is often confusion between the element of judgment in decision and the ethical element. This confusion is enhanced by the fact that the further the means-end chain is followed, i.e. the greater the ethical element, the more doubtful are the steps in the chain, and the greater is the element of judgment involved in determining what means will contribute to what ends.[9]

The process by which judgments are formed has been very imperfectly studied. In practical administration it may be feared that confidence in the correctness of judgments sometimes takes the place of any serious attempt to evaluate them systematically on the basis of subsequent results. But further consideration of the psychology of decision-making will have to be postponed to a later chapter.[10]

[9]Leys, *op. cit.*, p. 18, points out that this confusion has been present in most of the literature on administrative discretion.

[10]Barnard, *op. cit.*, presents an interesting, but perhaps too optimistic, view of the "intuitive" element in administrative decision, in an Appendix, "Mind in Everyday Affairs," pp. 299–322.

Value Judgments in Private Management

The illustrations used thus far in this chapter have been drawn largely from the field of public administration. One reason for this is that the problem of value judgments has been more fully explored—particularly in relation to administrative discretion and administrative regulation—in the public than in the private field. There is, in fact, no essential difference on this topic between the two. Decisions in private management, like decisions in public management, must take as their ethical premises the objectives that have been set for the organization.

There are important differences between public and private management, of course, in the types of organizational objectives that are set up and in the procedures and mechanisms for establishing them. In public administration final responsibility for determining objectives rests with a legislative body; in private management, with the board of directors, and ultimately with the stockholders.[11] In both fields serious problems have arisen as to the means to be used in implementing the responsibility of these control bodies.[12] It is to this problem that we turn next—again directing our attention particularly to the field of public administration. A little translation of terms should suffice to make most of the discussion applicable to the stockholder-management relationship.

POLICY AND ADMINISTRATION

In practice, the separation between the ethical and the factual elements in judgment can usually be carried only a short distance. The values involved in administrative decisions are seldom final values in any psychological or philosophical sense. Most objectives and activities derive their value from the means-ends relationships which connect them with objectives or activities that are valued in themselves. By a process of anticipation, the value inhering in the desired end is transferred to the means. The product of a manufacturing process is valued by its producers for its convertibility into money (which in turn has value only in exchange) and by its purchasers for the values to be derived from its consumption. Just so, the activities of a fire department, or a school system, are valued ultimately for their contribution to human and social life, and they retain their value only so long as they serve those more final ends.

[11]In chap. vi arguments will be presented that the true analogue of the legislative body is the customer rather than the stockholder.

[12]The private-management literature on this topic, while for the most part relatively recent, is growing rapidly. See for example Beardsley Ruml, *Tomorrow's Business* (New York: Farrar & Rinehart, 1945); Robert A. Brady, *Business as a System of Power* (New York: Columbia University Press, 1943); or Robert Aaron Gordon, *Business Leadership in the Large Corporation* (Washington: Brookings Institution, 1945).

To the extent that these intermediate values are involved, valuation includes important factual as well as ethical elements. Since the results of administrative activity can be considered as ends only in an intermediate sense, the values that will be attached to these results depend on the empirical connections that are believed to exist between them and the more final goals. To weight properly these intermediate values, it is necessary to understand their objective consequences.

At best it might be hoped that the process of decision could be subdivided into two major segments. The first would involve the development of a system of intermediate values, and an appraisal of their relative weights. The second would consist in a comparison of the possible lines of action in terms of this value system. The first segment would obviously involve both ethical and factual considerations; the second segment could be pretty well restricted to factual problems.

As already pointed out, the reason for making a division of this sort lies in the different criteria of "correctness" that must be applied to the ethical and factual elements in a decision. "Correctness" as applied to imperatives has meaning only in terms of subjective human values. "Correctness" as applied to factual propositions means objective, empirical truth. If two persons give different answers to a factual problem, both cannot be right. Not so with ethical questions.

Vagueness of the "Policy and Administration" Distinction

Recognition of this distinction in the meanings of "correctness" would lend clarity to the distinction that is commonly made in the literature of political science between "policy questions" and "administrative questions." These latter terms were given currency by Goodnow's classical treatise, *Politics and Administration*,[13] published in 1900. Yet, neither in Goodnow's study nor in any of the innumerable discussions that have followed it have any clear-cut criteria or marks of identification been suggested that would enable one to recognize a "policy question" on sight, or to distinguish it from an "administrative question." Apparently, it has been assumed that the distinction is self-evident—so self-evident as hardly to require discussion.

In *The New Democracy and the New Despotism*, Charles E. Merriam sets forth as one of the five principal assumptions of democracy "the desirability of popular decision in the last analysis on basic questions of social direction and policy, and of recognized procedures for the expres-

---

[13]Frank J. Goodnow, *Politics and Administration* (New York: Macmillan, 1900).

sion of such decisions and their validation in policy."[14] As to the exact scope and nature of these "basic questions," he is less explicit:

> It may be asked, Who shall decide what are "basic questions," and who shall determine whether the ways and means of expressing the mass will are appropriate and effective? We cannot go farther back than the "general understandings" of the community, always the judge of the form and functioning of the legal order in which the system is set.[15]

Similarly, Goodnow, in the original statement of the roles of politics and administration in government, fails to draw a careful line between the two. In fact, he comes perilously close to identifying "policy" with "deciding," and "administration" with "doing." For example:

> ... political functions group themselves naturally under two heads, which are equally applicable to the mental operations and the actions of self-conscious personalities. That is, the action of the state as a political entity consists either in operations necessary to the expression of its will, or in operations necessary to the execution of that will.[16]

And again:

> These two functions of government may for purposes of convenience be designated respectively as Politics and Administration. Politics has to do with policies or expressions of the state will. Administration has to do with the execution of these policies.[17]

At a later point in his discussion, however, Goodnow retreats from this extreme position, and recognizes that certain decisional elements are included in the administrative function:

> The fact is, then, that there is a large part of administration which is unconnected with politics, which should therefore be relieved very largely, if not altogether, from the control of political bodies. It is unconnected with politics because it embraces fields of semi-scientific, *quasi*-judicial and *quasi*-business or commercial activity—work which has little if any influence on the expression of the true state will.[18]

Without embracing Goodnow's conclusion regarding the desirability of removing some portions of administration from political control, we

[14]Charles E. Merriam, *The New Democracy and the New Despotism* (New York: McGraw-Hill, 1939), p. 11.

[15]*Ibid.*, p. 39.

[16]Goodnow, *op. cit.*, p. 9.

[17]*Ibid.*, p. 18.

[18]*Ibid.*, p. 85.

may recognize in this third statement an attempt on his part to segregate a class of decisions which do not require external control because they possess an internal criterion of correctness. The epistemological position of the present volume leads us to identify this internal criterion with the criterion of factual correctness, and the group of decisions possessing this criterion with those that are factual in nature.

In discussions of administrative discretion from the point of view of administrative law there has sometimes been a tendency to deny that there exists any class of factual questions which possess a unique epistemological status. Neither Freund nor Dickinson is able to find a justification for administrative discretion except as an application of decisions to concrete instances, or as a transitory phenomenon confined to a sphere of uncertainty within which the rule of law has not yet penetrated.[19]

To be sure, the two men offer different suggestions for the gradual elimination of this area of uncertainty. Freund relies upon the legislature to restrict discretion by the exercise of its function of policy determination.[20] Dickinson thinks that administrative discretion can gradually be replaced by general rules to be formulated by the courts, as principles gradually emerge to view from a given set of problems.[21] Neither is willing to admit any fundamental difference between the factual and normative elements involved in law-finding, or to see in that difference a justification for discretionary action.

The courts have come somewhat closer to a recognition of this distinction, though their separation of "questions of fact" from "questions of law" places in the latter category a great many factual issues—especially when "jurisdictional facts" and "constitutional facts" become "questions of law."[22] This is not the place, however, to discuss the whole problem of judicial review. These brief comments serve merely to illustrate the lack of any general agreement as to the fundamental difference between factual and value questions in the field of administrative law.

Opposed to the view that discretion is inherently undesirable, is the equally extreme view that *all* administrative decisions can safely be guided by the internal criteria of correctness, and that legislative control can be supplanted by the control which is exercised by the fellowship of science.[23]

[19]Ernst Freund, *Administrative Powers over Persons and Property* (Chicago: University of Chicago Press, 1928), pp. 97–103; John Dickinson, *Administrative Justice and the Supremacy of Law in the United States* (Cambridge: Harvard University Press, 1927), *passim.*

[20]Freund, *op. cit.,* pp. 98–99.

[21]Dickinson, *op. cit.,* pp. 105–156.

[22] Freund, *op. cit.,* pp. 289–299; Dickinson, *op. cit.,* pp. 307–313.

[23]C. J. Friedrich stresses the value of the "fellowship of science" in enforcing responsibility. He does not propose, however, to dispense with the device of legislative control. See "Public Policy and the Nature of Administrative Responsibility," in *Public Policy, 1940* (Cambridge: Harvard University Press, 1940), pp. 3–24. Cf. John M. Gaus, "The Responsibility of Public Administration," in *The Frontiers of Public Administration,* ed. Gaus, White, and Dimock (Chicago: University of Chicago Press, 1936), pp. 26–44.

Our own analysis exposes the fallacy of an argument that declares decisions to be all factual as clearly as it refutes an argument that declares them to be all ethical.

The position to which the methodological assumptions of the present study lead us is this: The process of validating a factual proposition is quite distinct from the process of validating a value judgment. The former is validated by its agreement with the facts, the latter by human fiat.

Legislator and Administrator

Democratic institutions find their principal justification as a procedure for the validation of value judgments. There is no "scientific" or "expert" way of making such judgments, hence expertise of whatever kind is no qualification for the performance of this function. If the factual elements in decision could be strictly separated, in practice, from the ethical, the proper roles of representative and expert in a democratic decision-making process would be simple. For two reasons this not possible. First, as has already been noted, most value judgments are made in terms of intermediate values, which themselves involve factual questions. Second, if factual decisions are entrusted to the experts, sanctions must be available to guarantee that the experts will conform, in good faith, to the value judgments that have been democratically formulated.

Critics of existing procedures for enforcing responsibility point to the high degree of ineffectiveness of these procedures in practice.[24] But there is no reason to conclude that the procedures are inherently valueless. First, for the reasons already explained, self-responsibility of the administrator is no answer to the problem. Second, the fact that pressure of legislative work forbids the review of more than a few administrative decisions does not destroy the usefulness of sanctions that permit the legislative body to hold the administrator answerable for *any* of his decisions. The anticipation of possible legislative investigation and review will have a powerful controlling effect on the administrator, even if this potential review can be actualized only in a few cases. The *function* of deciding may be distributed very differently in the body politic from the *final authority* for resolving disputed decisions.

It would not be possible to lay down any final principles with regard to a subject so controversial, and so imperfectly explored.[25] Nevertheless,

---

[24]Cf. Friedrich, *op. cit.*, pp. 3–8. It should be pointed out again that Friedrich does not propose to dispense with democratic control, but to supplement it with other sanctions.

[25]I. G. Gibbon treats of this question in "The Official and His Authority," *Public Administration*, 4: 81–94 (Apr., 1926), arriving at conclusions substantially in agreement with those set forth here.

if the distinction of factual from ethical questions is a valid one, these conclusions would seem to follow:

(1) Responsibility to democratic institutions for value determination can be strengthened by the invention of procedural devices permitting a more effective separation of the factual and ethical elements in decisions. Some suggestions will be offered along these lines in later chapters.

(2) The allocation of a question to legislature or administrator for decision should depend on the relative importance of the factual and ethical issues involved, and the degree to which the former are controversial. A proper allocation will become increasingly possible, without overburdening the legislature, to the extent that Point 1 above is successfully carried out.

(3) Since the legislative body must of necessity make many factual judgments, it must have ready access to information and advice. However, this must take the form not merely of recommendations for action, but of factual information on the objective consequences of the alternatives that are before the legislative body.

(4) Since the administrative agency must of necessity make many value judgments, it must be responsive to community values, far beyond those that are explicitly enacted into law. Likewise, though the function of making value judgments may often be delegated to the administrator, especially where controversial issues are not involved, his complete answerability, in case of disagreement, must be retained.

If it is desired to retain the terms "policy" and "administration," they can best be applied to a division of the decisional functions that follows these suggested lines. While not identical with the separation of "value" from "fact," such a division would clearly be dependent upon that fundamental distinction.

It would be naïve to suggest that the division of work between legislature and administrator in any actual public agency will ever follow very closely the lines just suggested. In the first place the legislative body will often wish, for political reasons, to avoid making clear-cut policy decisions, and to pass these on to an administrative agency.[26] In the second place the administrator may be very different from the neutral, compliant individual pictured here. He may (and usually will) have his own very definite set of personal values that he would like to see implemented by his administrative organization, and he may resist attempts by the legislature to assume completely the function of policy determination, or he may sabotage their decisions by his manner of executing them.

[26]This point is ably discussed by Leys, *op. cit.*, pp. 20–22.

Nevertheless, it would probably be fair to say that the attainment of democratic responsibility in modern government will require an approximation to those lines of demarcation between legislature and administrator that were outlined above.

A Note on Terminology

Before concluding this chapter, it should be pointed out that the term "policy" is often used in a much broader and looser sense than the meaning given here. In private management literature, particularly, "policy" often means either (a) any general rule that has been laid down in an organization to limit the discretion of subordinates (e.g. it is "policy" in B department to file a carbon of all letters by subject), or (b) at least the more important of these rules, promulgated by top management (e.g. an employee is allowed two weeks' sick leave per year). In neither of these usages is it implied that policy has any ethical content. Serious ambiguity would be avoided if different terms were used for these three concepts— the one discussed in preceding paragraphs, and the two listed just above. Perhaps the ethical premises of management could be called "legislative policy"; the broad non-ethical rules laid down by top management, "management policy"; and other rules, "working policy."

In addition to these several kinds of policy, or authoritatively promulgated rules, there are to be found in almost every organization a large number of "practices" which have not been established as orders or regulations, and which are not enforced by sanctions, but which are nevertheless observed in the organization by force of custom or for other reasons. Often, the line between policy and practice is not sharp unless the organization follows the "practice" (or "policy") of putting all its policies in writing.

CONCLUSION

This chapter has been devoted to an explanation of the distinction between the value elements and the factual elements in decision-making. It has been shown, furthermore, that this distinction is the basis for the line that is commonly drawn between questions of policy and questions of administration.

In the next chapter, the anatomy of decision will be further examined, with special reference to the concept of "rationality" in decision-making. The emphasis will remain upon the logical rather than the psychological aspects of decision.

FACT AND VALUE IN DECISION-MAKING

THE FIRST HALF OF CHAPTER III is concerned with the fundamental logical distinction between "is" and "ought," the second half, largely with the implications of this distinction for the organization and operation of democratic governments. For this reason, the chapter is probably of greatest interest to readers concerned with public administration, where the debate of the relation of policy to administration has a long history in which the is-ought distinction plays a central role.

However, the fundamental question of who is to establish the basic goals—the basic "oughts"—of an organization arises in organizations of all kinds, private and non-profit as well as public. In public administration the discussion of goal-setting focuses upon the responsibility of administrators to legislatures and voters; in business management, it focuses upon the responsibility of employees and executives to stockholders; in the management of private non-profit organizations, it focuses upon the role of boards of trustees in their relations with management and with clients (e.g., in educational institutions, students, alumni, donors).

"IS'S" AND "OUGHTS"

My reference in the second paragraph of Chapter III to logical positivism as providing the philosophical foundation for a treatment of "is" and "ought" has proved to be a red herring that has confused some commentators. Logical positivism is today widely thought to be a discredited philosophical position, and its name is now more often applied as a disparaging epithet than as a term of description. I have no desire to defend logical positivism, but would simply observe that the chapter's entire argument goes forward just as well if we replace "logical positivism" by "empiricism," or if we simply refrain from labeling the argument as belonging to any particular philosophical school.

The fundamental point is that you can't get an "ought," by any manner of careful reasoning, solely from a set of pure "is's." To reach an "ought" in the conclusions, at least some "ought" must be lurking in the initial premises. No amassing of knowledge about how the world really is can, entirely by itself, tell us how the world ought to be. For the latter, we must be willing to say what kind of a world we would like to have; we must posit some values that go beyond the facts.

When we start a line of thinking with an "ought," say, an organizational objective or goal, then that "ought" infects all of the following conclusions, which become, in the language of Chapter III, "ethical statements admixed with factual elements." Moreover, the "ought" that constitutes an organizational objective is usually already thoroughly mixed with factual elements. "We ought to introduce a new, cheaper, product line" presumably means that *in fact* there is a good market for such a line, and if we introduce it, we will increase our profit (the organizational objective).

If an objective is challenged, it is defended by pointing to some more fundamental objective toward which it is directed, and to the belief (a supposed *fact* which may or may not be valid) that accomplishing the former objective will contribute toward reaching the latter one. The fire department fights fires *in order to* reduce fire losses (fire fighting does, in fact reduce losses), *in order to* conserve valuable assets (buildings are valuable and useful), and so on—ending the chain, perhaps with final values like virtue, truth, and beauty.

I hope these brief comments will dispel any remaining confusion about the is-ought distinction, and make it less controversial.

"FACTUAL" DOES NOT NECESSARILY MEAN "TRUE"

The term "factual premise" does not mean an empirically correct statement but a belief, that is, an assertion of fact. The assertion may or may not be supported by evidence, and such evidence as exists may be of greater or lesser validity. Human decision-making uses beliefs, which may or may not describe how the world really is. We call such beliefs, whether true or false, "factual premises."

TECHNOLOGY AND TECHNOCRACY

The rapidly growing role of technology in our world over the past century has made it more and more difficult for T. C. Pits—the common person in the street—to judge correctly the technical issues that are central to many, if not most, important decisions. One can pick examples almost at random from the daily press: What are the health effects of various levels of oxides of nitrogen in the atmosphere, and what is the cost of reducing those levels?

It is sometimes suggested that we turn the decisions over to "experts" who really know the facts and can calculate their implications. Of course the fallacy of this technocratic solution to the problem is obvious. Because most decision premises mingle facts with values, we cannot turn the decisions wholly over to the experts without delegating to them the choice of values as well as the calculation of consequences. Chapter III introduces this problem, especially in its application to public organizations.[27] I will make a few additional comments on the issue here as it applies to private organizations, both for-profit and non-profit. More will be said about this aspect of it in later chapters and their commentaries.

THE AUTONOMY OF PRIVATE ORGANIZATIONS

The fact-value distinction raises two questions for private organizations: first, who shall choose the basic values at which an organization will aim and how will the chooser enforce the choice; second, how can compatibility be maintained between the goals chosen and pursued by a private organization and the goals that might be desired by the society in which the organization operates?

The usual answer to the first question is that, subject to the limits laid down by law, the owners choose the basic values of private for-profit organizations, and the trustees choose those of non-profit organizations. This raises a new question: how do the owners and trustees enforce their choices? A substantial literature examines the extent to which stockholders actually can and do control corporate policies in the face of the temptations managers may have to reap personal advantages from their positions. The same question arises for non-profit organizations, but it has probably not been investigated as thoroughly. Beyond recognizing that the issues are important, a lengthy discussion of them is largely beyond the scope of this book.[28]

Neoclassical economics answers the second question, compatibility of the goals of a private organization with the goals of its society, with the claim that, in an environment of free competitive markets, the organization that wishes to maximize its profits, or even to survive, has no choice but to produce as efficiently as possible those goods and services

---

[27]And I have discussed it somewhat more fully in chap. 3 of *Reason in Human Affairs* (Stanford University Press, 1983).

[28]A classical reference is A. A. Berle, Jr. and Gardner C. Means, *The Modern Corporation and Private Property* (New York: Macmillan, 1934). For more recent discussions see H. Demsetz and K. Lehn, "The Structure of Corporate Ownership: Causes and Consequences," *Journal of Political Economy*, 93: 1155–1177 (1985), and O. E. Williamson, *The Economic Institutions of Capitalism* (New York: The Free Press, 1985).

that consumers in the society choose to buy. Free markets and perfect competition force responsiveness to social values as expressed in the behavior of consumers, weighted by the buying power of each. They leave little choice of values to the private organization.

Even putting aside questions of income distribution, and consequent differences in individual buying power, in any real society this answer requires considerable qualification. Any departure from perfect competition gives leeway to organizations to choose between different values, and drives a wedge between profit maximization and achievement of the values that are expressed in the market. Equally serious, the presence of "externalities"—consequences of organizational activities that are not reflected in market prices—also encourages activities that contribute to profits to the detriment of other social values. The classical case of a negative externality is the smoke that a factory disperses over its surroundings. Similarly, activities producing "positive externalities"—benefits conferred on the community that are not reflected in market prices—are discouraged by the market mechanism.

Of course, activities producing negative externalities can be banned by legislation, taxed, or otherwise regulated (and those producing positive externalities subsidized), but the presence of externalities undermines the simplicity of markets as a universal means for social control of private organizational activity. It remains a fact, however, that the ability of organizations, for-profit or non-profit, to exercise power over a society, and to substitute their own values for the values of others, is severely restricted if they must rest on their own financial bottoms—if they may spend only such funds as they can acquire by offering their goods and services to the members of the society, and, in doing so, must compete with other organizations in the same position.

The presence of imperfections in a system of intermixed competition and monopoly, together with the complications created by negative and positive externalities, guarantee that a modern society will be a composite system which includes markets, large and small organizations, and a wide variety of legal and other governmental regulations and interventions. The possibility of such interventions creates, in turn, typical new problems: for example, organizations may be relieved, by subsidies and bailouts, of the consequences of their own improvidence. That this is not an imaginary danger is clear when we recall the bailouts of the Chrysler Corporation and the building and loan associations, and the long-maintained agricultural subsidies in our own society. Social organization is neither a simple nor an exact science.

CHAPTER IV

Rationality in Administrative Behavior

IN CHAPTER III IT WAS CONCLUDED that the correctness of an administrative decision is a relative matter—it is correct if it selects appropriate means to reach designated ends. The rational administrator is concerned with the selection of these effective means. For the construction of an administrative theory it is necessary to examine further the notion of rationality and, in particular, to achieve perfect clarity as to what is meant by "the selection of effective means." The process of clarifying this idea will throw considerable light, in turn, upon the concepts of "efficiency" and "coordination"—both of central importance to administrative theory.

Little will be said in this chapter about what goes on in the mind of a person making decisions—treatment of the subject from a psychological standpoint will be reserved for Chapter V. The present chapter will be concerned with the objective environment of decision—with the actual consequences that follow on choice. Choice, in so far as it is rational and cognizant of its objective conditions, involves a selection of one alternative from among several. The alternatives differ with respect to the consequences that flow from them, and an analysis of decision-making in its objective aspects will refer primarily to these variable consequences of choice.

Although this emphasis upon consequences will give the present chapter a definitely "rationalistic" bias, concentration on the rational aspects of human behavior should not be construed as an assertion that human beings are always or generally rational. That misconception, which permeated utilitarian political theory and a large part of classical economic theory, has been decisively refuted by modern developments in psychology and sociology.[1]

---

[1]The naïve utilitarian view is nowhere more strikingly set forth than by Jeremy Bentham, *op. cit.*, pp. 1–7, *passim*. On the other hand, rationalism is implicit rather than explicit in Adam Smith. See *An Inquiry into the Nature and Causes of the Wealth of Nations* (New York: E. P. Dutton, 1914), pp. 12–15. The criticism of rationalism has perhaps been most strongly urged by the Freudians, but is a matter of general acceptance among almost all modern schools of sociology and psychology. See, for example, Harold D. Lasswell, *Psychopathology and Politics* (Chicago: University of Chicago Press, 1930), pp. 28–37; Sigmund Freud, "The Unconscious," *Collected Papers* (London: L. and V. Woolf, 1925), 4:98–136; Vilfredo Pareto, *The Mind and Society* (New York: Harcourt, Brace, 1935), *passim*.

Since "good" administration is behavior that is realistically adapted to its ends, just as "good" business is economic behavior accurately calculated to realize gain, a theory of administrative decisions will of necessity be somewhat preoccupied with the rational aspects of choice. Later chapters of this study will pay more attention to the actualities of administrative behavior. The present chapter bears the same relation to these realistic analyses that a discussion of business principles and theories bears to a description of economic institutions and actual market behaviors; that is, it is not a description of how administrators decide so much as a description of how *good* administrators decide.[2]

MEANS AND ENDS

Fact and value, as already noted in Chapter III, are related to means and ends. In the process of decision those alternatives are chosen which are considered to be appropriate means for reaching desired ends. Ends themselves, however, are often merely instrumental to more final objectives. We are thus led to the conception of a series, or hierarchy, of ends. Rationality has to do with the construction of means-ends chains of this kind.[3]

The Hierarchy of Ends

Even at the physiological level means-end relationships serve to integrate behavior. At this level muscular tensions are coordinated for (as a means of) the performance of simple physiological acts—walking, reaching and grasping an object, turning the eyes toward an object. In the adult, these simple movements are largely unconscious and automatic; but the child must with great difficulty learn them, and this learning, although not at a reflective level, is not at all unlike the learning of an adult in a means-end situation.

But the taking of a step, the grasping of an object, is usually itself a means to a broader end. The clearest way to determine which ends are sought for their own sake, and which for their usefulness as means to more distant ends, is to place the subject in situations where he must choose between conflicting ends.

The fact that goals may be dependent for their force on other more

---

[2]The Appendix discusses at greater length the distinction between a practical science of administration (the study of what administrators "ought") and a sociology of administration (the study of what administrators "do").

[3]Talcott Parsons analyzes social action systems with the help of these same terms in *The Structure of Social Action* (New York: McGraw-Hill, 1937), pp. 44, 49, 228–241.

distant ends leads to the arrangement of these goals in a hierarchy—each level to be considered as an end relative to the levels below it and as a means relative to the levels above it. Through the hierarchical structure of ends, behavior attains integration and consistency, for each member of a set of behavior alternatives is then weighed in terms of a comprehensive scale of values—the "ultimate" ends. In actual behavior, a high degree of conscious integration is seldom attained. Instead of a single branching hierarchy, the structure of conscious motives is usually a tangled web or, more precisely, a disconnected collection of elements only weakly and incompletely tied together; and the integration of these elements becomes progressively weaker as the higher levels of the hierarchy—the more final ends—are reached.

The hierarchy of means and ends is as characteristic of the behavior of organization as it is of individuals. As a matter of fact, the mode of specialization which in Chapter II was called "organization by purpose" is nothing other than the arrangement of the organization structure to parallel the system of means and ends involved in the accomplishment of its purposes. Thus, the fire department has as its purpose the reduction of fire losses; but the means to the attainment of this end are the prevention of fires and the extinguishment of fires. These two principal means are often represented in the organization structure by a fire prevention bureau and the fire fighting forces, respectively. Since the latter must, in order to accomplish their purpose, be dispersed over the city, we find at the next level organization units specialized by area.

It is also as true of organizational as of individual behavior that the means-end hierarchy is seldom an integrated, completely connected chain. Often the connections between organization activities and ultimate objectives is obscure, or these ultimate objectives are incompletely formulated, or there are internal conflicts and contradictions among the ultimate objectives, or among the means selected to attain them. Thus, decision-making in the Work Projects Administration was complicated by the competing claims of "pump-priming" and immediate relief to the unemployed as agency objectives. In War Production Board decision-making, it was necessary to balance war needs against civilian requirements.

Sometimes the lack of integration in an organization's means-end hierarchy is due to refusal of the policy-making body to decide a "hot" issue of policy—Congress's refusal, for example, to determine for Selective Service the relative weight to be given to family status and occupation in deferments from military service. Sometimes the means-end connections themselves are obscure. For example, to say that it is the objective of an army to defeat the enemy leaves a great deal of room for dispute and inconsistency as to the proper strategies for achieving this end. (The controversy in this country between the "Germany first" and "Japan first" factions comes to mind in this connection.)

Both organizations and individuals, then, fail to attain a complete integration of their behavior through consideration of these means-end relationships. Nevertheless, what remains of rationality in their behavior is precisely the incomplete, and sometimes inconsistent, hierarchy that has just been described.

Limitations of the Means-End Schema

This analysis of rational behavior in terms of a means-end hierarchy may lead to inaccurate conclusions unless certain cautions are observed.

First, the ends to be attained by the choice of a particular behavior alternative are often incompletely or incorrectly stated through failure to consider the alternative ends that could be reached by selection of another behavior. It is not enough, in selecting a cantilever design for a bridge across a particular river, to know that this design will serve the purpose of bridging the river. The wisdom of the choice depends on whether the cantilever design will bridge the river more effectively and more economically than a suspension bridge, or a viaduct, or some other design. Rational decision-making always requires the comparison of alternative means in terms of the respective ends to which they will lead. As will be seen in Chapter VIII, below, this means that "efficiency"—the attainment of maximum values with limited means—must be a guiding criterion in administrative decision.

Second, in actual situations a complete separation of means from ends is usually impossible, for the alternative means are not usually valuationally neutral. It is from this difficulty that so many futile arguments arise as to whether "the ends justify the means." In the case of the Prohibition Amendment, for example, the means employed involved so many value questions—questions of personal liberty, proper police methods, etc.—that these soon overshadowed in importance the "ultimate" objective of temperance. Hence it was fallacious to talk of prohibition as merely a means to the highly desirable end of temperance. The particular means used to attain this particular end had many consequences other than the specific end being sought, and these other unsought ends had to be given their proper weight in considering the desirability of the means.

Third, the means-end terminology tends to obscure the role of the time element in decision-making. If an end is some condition or state to be realized, then only one state may be realized at one time but many states over a period of time, and choice is influenced not only by particular ends but also by expectations of what ends may be realized at different times. Choice imposes two problems: (1) If a particular end is to be realized at a given time, what alternative ends must be relinquished for that time? (2) If a particular end is to be realized at a given time, how does this limit the ends that may be realized at other times? When Louis XV said, "Après nous le déluge," he was expressing the factual judgment that achievement of his particular short-run ends entailed some unfortunate long-run consequences; and he was also expressing a value-judgment— one of indifference for long-term consequences. Economists would say that he discounted time heavily.

The time element enters into decision-making in still another way. Some decisions are irrevocable in the sense that they create a new situation which, in turn, influences the decisions that follow them. In economic situations this is illustrated by the existence of fixed costs. If a manufacturer is deciding whether he will build a factory to make shoes, his problem is to determine whether the revenue he will get by selling the shoes will reimburse him for his expenditure. But, if he already *has* a shoe factory, the cost of this factory is a "sunk" cost that cannot be recovered; and he will continue to make shoes, even at an over-all loss, provided his revenues cover any new and additional costs that he must incur to make them. The decision to build the factory, therefore, influences his subsequent decisions. It is the existence of these long-term, irrevocable decisions that more than anything else accounts for the relative consistency of both personal and organizational behavior over periods of time. It also accounts for a certain "inertia" in the adjustment to new situations.

These objections do not mean that the language of ends and means is unusable; they simply mean that it must be employed with considerable care and sophistication. Under some circumstances another terminology may be clearer, and it is the purpose of the next section of this chapter to suggest such a terminology.

ALTERNATIVES AND CONSEQUENCES

The objections that have been raised to the means-end schema are (a) that it obscures the comparative element in decision-making, (b) that it does not achieve a successful separation of the factual elements in decision from the value elements, and (c) that it gives insufficient recognition to the time variable in purposive behavior. A theory of decisions in terms of alternative behavior possibilities and their consequences meets all these objections.

Behavior Alternatives[4]

At each moment the behaving subject, or the organization composed of numbers of such individuals, is confronted with a large number of alternative behaviors, some of which are present in consciousness and some of which are not. Decision, or choice, as the term is used here, is the process by which one of these alternatives for each moment's behavior is selected to be carried out. The series of such decisions which determines behavior over some stretch of time may be called a *strategy*.

If any one of the possible strategies is chosen and followed out, certain consequences will result. The task of rational decision is to select that one of the strategies which is followed by the preferred set of consequences. It should be emphasized that *all* the consequences that follow from the chosen strategy are relevant to the evaluation of its correctness, not simply those consequences that were anticipated.

The task of decision involves three steps: (1) the listing of all the alternative strategies; (2) the determination of all the consequences that follow upon each of these strategies; (3) the comparative evaluation of these sets of consequences. The word "all" is used advisedly. It is obviously impossible for the individual to know *all* his alternatives or *all* their consequences, and this impossibility is a very important departure of actual behavior from the model of objective rationality. As such, it will receive extended consideration in Chapter V.

Time and Behavior

There is nothing which prevents the subject, or the organization, having chosen one strategy on Monday, from selecting a different one on Tuesday. But the Monday decision, in so far as it has been partly acted out before its reconsideration, has already narrowed down the strategies available on Tuesday. This has been pointed out above in the illustration of the shoe factory. Hence, the individual or organization can be committed to a particular line of action from the fact that, having once initiated it, it appears preferable to continue with it rather than to relinquish completely the portion which has already been carried out.

This time-binding character of strategies deserves the greatest

[4]The theory presented here was worked out by the author in 1941. Its present reformulation has been greatly influenced by the remarkable work of John von Neumann and Oskar Morgenstern, *The Theory of Games and Economic Behavior* (Princeton: Princeton University Press, 1944), chap. 2. It is fair to point out that von Neumann first published that portion of his theory which is germane to the present discussion in 1928, "Zur Theorie der Gesellschaftsspiele," *Math. Annalen* 100:295–320 (1928).

emphasis, for it makes possible at least a modicum of rationality in behavior, where, without it, this would be inconceivable. For example, an individual who has spent seven years of his life preparing to be a physician and ten more practicing that profession does not ordinarily have to spend any more time deciding whether he should be a physician or not. Alternative occupations are practically closed to him by virtue of the investment he has already made in the strategy pursued thus far.

Similarly, an organization that is manufacturing shoes does not need to reconsider every day (although it may need to reconsider at intervals) whether it should be in the automobile business instead. This narrows appreciably the alternatives that must be considered by the individual at each moment, and is certainly a necessary, though not a sufficient, condition of rationality.

Knowledge and Behavior

The function of knowledge in the decision-making process is to determine which consequences follow upon which of the alternative strategies. It is the task of knowledge to select from the whole class of possible consequences a more limited subclass, or even (ideally) a single set of consequences correlated with each strategy. The behaving subject cannot, of course, know directly the consequences that will follow upon his behavior. If he could, a sort of reverse causality would be operating here—future consequences would be determinants of present behavior. What he does is to form *expectations* of future consequences, these expectations being based upon known empirical relationships, and upon information about the existing situation.

This may be illustrated in the case of a typical administrative decision process—the selection of personnel. Data are gathered about each of the candidates for a position, from examinations, service ratings, and other sources. These data are used as a basis for comparative prediction to determine which of the candidates will perform most satisfactorily on the job. If the predictions are accurate, then a correct decision can be made.

It has already been remarked that the subject, in order to perform with perfect rationality in this scheme, would have to have a complete description of the consequences following from each alternative strategy and would have to compare these consequences. He would have to know in every single respect how the world would be changed by his behaving one way instead of another, and he would have to follow the consequences of behavior through unlimited stretches of time, unlimited reaches of space, and unlimited sets of values. Under such conditions even an approach to rationality in real behavior would be inconceivable.

Fortunately, the problem of choice is usually greatly simplified by the tendency of the empirical laws that describe the regularities of nature to arrange themselves in relatively isolated subsets. Two behavior alternatives, when compared, are often found to have consequences that differ in only a few respects and for the rest are identical. That is, the differential consequences of one behavior as against an alternative behavior may occur only within a brief span of time and within a limited area of description. If it were too often true that for want of a nail the kingdom was lost, the consequence chains encountered in practical life would be of such complexity that rational behavior would become virtually impossible.

In one respect the decision problem in private organizations is much simpler than in public agencies. The private organization is expected to take into consideration only those consequences of the decision which affect *it*, while the public agency must weigh the decision in terms of some comprehensive system of public or community values. For example, when the president of a private corporation decides to give his son a position in the firm, he has to take into consideration the effect the appointment will have upon the efficiency of the enterprise; but a man in the same relative position in the public service has to be concerned equally about the effect of this step upon "equality of opportunity in the public service." This distinction between private and public management is hardly one of black and white, for an increasing number of private businesses are becoming "affected with a public interest," and an increasing number of private executives are concerning themselves with their responsibilities of trusteeship toward the community, even beyond the limits that the law imposes on them.

The fact that consequences usually form "isolated" systems provides both scientist and practitioner with a powerful aid to rationality, for the scientist can isolate these closed systems in his experimental laboratory, and study their behavior, while the practitioner may use the laws discovered by the scientist to vary certain environmental conditions without significantly disturbing the remainder of the situation.

There still remain two important distinctions between a problem of scientific discovery and a problem of decision. First of all, it is a valid scientific problem to deduce the empirical laws that would hold under certain simplified hypothetical conditions, even though these conditions do not prevail in practice—the theoretical scientist can talk about "rigid bodies," "perfect vacuums," "frictionless fluids," etc. But the practitioner must allow for the effects of elasticity, air pressure, or friction, if they are present and substantial, no matter how much this complicates his problem of selecting the correct alternative. Second, the scientist can choose to study only those consequences of the system that he wishes to be concerned with, and ignore the others. It is a valid scientific problem to ask: "What effect upon the total weight of this airplane will specified changes in design have?" The problem of practical decision, however, is to balance a possible weight-saving against an increase in cost, or a loss of maneuverability, or other qualities. The practitioner can never choose to disregard conditioning facts or consequences simply because they fall outside the scope of his theory.

Group Behavior

Further complications are introduced into the picture if more than one individual is involved, for in this case the decisions of the other individuals will be included among the conditions which each individual must consider in reaching his decisions. That is, each individual, in order to determine uniquely the consequences of his actions, must know what will be the actions of the others. This is a factor of fundamental importance for the whole process of administrative decision-making.

There is really a serious circularity involved here. Before A can rationally choose his strategy, he must know which strategy B has chosen; and before B can choose his strategy, he must know A's. This may be illustrated by the game of matching pennies. There are two participants. The first, out of the sight of his opponent, places a coin with either head or tail uppermost upon a table, and covers it with his hand; the second tries to guess whether head or tail is up. The first participant must decide which choice he thinks the second will make, and then must place the coin in the opposite fashion; the second participant must decide which estimate the first has made of the situation. Both of them cannot be right for, if the first estimates correctly the second's choice, then the second will have incorrectly estimated the choice of the first, and vice versa. The resulting behavior system will be of a highly indeterminate nature, for the instability of each of the behavior choices leads to the instability of the other.

While the illustration may appear trivial, a little reflection will convince the reader that this game is a model for any purely competitive activity involving two participants—military strategy being perhaps the most important practical example.[5]

At the opposite extreme from a purely competitive situation is one where two or more participants share a common goal, and where each has sufficient information as to what the others are going to do to enable him to make correct decisions. This is precisely what is meant by "team-

[5]Cf. Col. J. F. C. Fuller, *The Foundations of the Science of War* (London: Hutchinson, 1925), p. 183.

work." The purpose of signals in football, or bidding in bridge, is to enable each player in a team to form accurate expectations as to what his teammates are going to do, so that he can determine the proper means for cooperating with them to reach the common aim. A major purpose of the planning and organizing that precedes any administrative activity is not merely to put each participant in the job he can best fill, but to permit each to form accurate expectations as to what the others are going to do. Perhaps it would clarify discussion of administrative theory to use the term "cooperation" for activity in which the participants share a common goal, and "coordination" for the process of informing each as to the planned behaviors of the others. Hence, cooperation will usually be ineffective—will not reach its goal, whatever the intentions of the participants—in the absence of coordination.

If the activity is competitive, then, it may exhibit a certain instability, for each individual will readjust his behavior if he "finds out" the intentions of his opponent, or even as a defensive tactic to prevent the opponent from finding out his own. But this same instability may result even if the activity is cooperative, provided the participants are insufficiently informed. In an organization, for example, where responsibilities have not been allocated with sufficient definiteness, two executives may write conflicting letters to the same person on the same matter, while in another case a letter may remain unwritten because each expects the other to do it.

To state the matter formally, in a cooperative pattern both participants prefer the same set of consequences; hence, if each anticipates the other correctly, they will both act so as to secure these consequences. In a competitive pattern, the optimum outcome for the first participant is not the optimum for the second. Hence the realization by the first participant of the consequences he prefers will frustrate the other participant—e.g., the rule of the market is to buy cheap and sell dear, but if the buyer buys cheap the seller will not have sold dear. Even a cooperative pattern may be unstable if each participant is unable to predict what the other is going to do. In these cases, coordination of the behaviors of the two participants is necessary in order that they may realize the possibility that they both prefer. Here conflict of aims is not in question, but imperfect knowledge.

Administrative organizations are systems of cooperative behavior.[6] The members of the organization are expected to orient their behavior with respect to certain goals that are taken as "organization objectives." This leaves the problem of coordinating their behavior—of providing each one with knowledge of the behaviors of the others upon which he

---

[6]Why and to what extent the participants in such organizations share a common goal will be discussed in chap. vi.

can base his own decisions. In cooperative systems, even though all participants are agreed on the objectives to be attained, they cannot ordinarily be left to themselves in selecting the strategies that will lead to these objectives; for the selection of a correct strategy involves a knowledge of each as to the strategies selected by the others.[7]

VALUE AND POSSIBILITY

There remains for discussion the third element in decision-making; namely, the process of determining preferences among consequences. This process may be termed *valuation*. To each strategy corresponds a unique set of consequences. Rational behavior involves a listing of the consequences in their order of preference, and the choice of that strategy which corresponds to the alternative highest on the list.

The System of Values—Utility Surfaces

Since the values that are present in the various alternatives are both numerous and diverse, the individual in exercising his preference must weigh them and choose among them. The economists have developed a conceptual scheme for describing this process which is very similar indeed to the scheme used here.

The individual's choices among competing values may be described by a set of indifference curves. These curves indicate which sets of possible consequences are equivalent to each other or mutually "indifferent" to choice. To illustrate with the economist's favorite goods—nuts and apples—the indifference curves tell whether a combination of ten nuts and five apples is preferred by an individual to a combination of five nuts and seven apples, or whether the first combination is less desirable, or whether the individual is indifferent as between the two.

Empirical limitations upon choice are introduced into the economist's scheme by the individual's stock of goods, and by the price structure. It is assumed that the individual starts with a specified number of nuts and apples, that he may exchange one for the other at a specified rate of exchange, and that he then attempts to select that amount of exchange for which his preference is greatest.[8]

---

[7]This is the fundamental criticism that the theory of anarchism has always failed to meet. That theory appears to posit that, given common goals, participants in a social scheme will automatically select for themselves their own most effective roles.

[8]Henry Schultz, *The Theory and Measurement of Demand* (Chicago: University of Chicago Press, 1938), pp. 12–35.

Relation of Value, Experience, Behavior

The significance of the "means-end" relationship now becomes clearer. It is clear that the "means-end" distinction does not correspond to the distinction between fact and value. What then is the connection between the two sets of terms? Simply this: A means-end chain is a series of anticipations that connect a value with the situations realizing it, and these situations, in turn, with the behaviors that produce them. Any element in this chain may be either "means" or "end" depending on whether its connection with the value end of the chain, or its connection with the behavior end of the chain, is in question.

The means-character of an element in a means-end chain will predominate if the element is toward the behavior end of the chain; the end-character will predominate if the element is descriptive of the consequences of behavior. If this be so, terms that are descriptive of the consequences of a behavior may be taken as indicia of the values adhering to that behavior. While the economist talks of economic goods as the values that are the goals of economic activity, in actuality, of course, the economic goods are merely indicia of the existence of a state of affairs from which value can be obtained—the possibility of consuming the goods.[9]

The psychological act of evaluating alternatives usually consists in measuring these alternatives in terms of certain value-indices that have been found in fact to be generally associated with the realization of the values themselves—money, for example, may come to stand as an index of the values that money can purchase. These value-indices involve an important factual element, for they presuppose that an alternative characterized by a high value-index will possess a correspondingly high value. For example, if a federal loan agency spends only a small percentage of its funds in the administration of its loans, this may be an index of efficiency, for, *all other things being equal,* low administrative expenses are to be desired. But of course in this case the ratio of administrative to total expenses would *not* be a good value-index, because in the absence of definite evidence that the quality of investigation is not changed, it is highly unsafe to assume that all other factors remain the same when administrative costs are reduced.

If the means-end relationship is defined in this way, it does not permit a sharp separation of value from fact, for the same behavior may have

[9]Frank Knight considers a major weakness of classical economics to be its failure to recognize economic gain as a purely intermediate link in a means-end chain, leading to "prestige" and "comfort"; and likewise its failure to recognize as an end valued for its own sake the very economic activity which leads to gain. See his *Risk, Uncertainty, and Profit* (Boston: Houghton Mifflin, 1921), pp. xii–xx.

as consequence more than one value—it may be a member of more than one means-end chain. A relief policy, for example, in which family budgets are set at a very low level in order to provide clients with an incentive to seek and accept private employment, may also have as its consequences a high incidence of malnutrition and disease among the families of relief clients. An acceptable policy cannot be determined merely by considering one of these means-end chains and ignoring the other.

DEFINITIONS OF RATIONALITY

A principal aim of this chapter has been to build the foundations upon which a clear understanding of the concept of "rationality" could be erected. Clarity does not necessarily imply simplicity, however. Roughly speaking, rationality is concerned with the selection of preferred behavior alternatives in terms of some system of values whereby the consequences of behavior can be evaluated. Does this mean that the process of adaptation must be conscious, or are unconscious processes included as well? It has been shown that many of the steps in mathematical invention—than which there can presumably be nothing more rational—are subconscious; and this is certainly true of the simpler processes of equation-solving.[10] Moreover, if consciousness is not stipulated as an element of rationality, are only deliberate processes of adaptation admitted, or non-deliberate ones as well? The typist trains herself to strike a particular key in response to the stimulus of a particular letter. Once learned, the act is unconscious, but deliberate. On the other hand, any person instinctively withdraws a finger that has been burned. This is "rational" in the sense that it serves a useful purpose, but is certainly neither a conscious nor a deliberate adaptation.

Shall we, moreover, call a behavior "rational" when it is in error, but only because the information on which it is based is faulty? When a subjective test is applied, it is rational for an individual to take medicine for a disease if he believes the medicine will cure the disease. When an objective test is applied, the behavior is rational only if the medicine is in fact efficacious.

Finally, in terms of what objectives, whose values, shall rationality be judged? Is behavior of an individual in an organization rational when it serves his personal objectives, or when it serves the organizational objectives? Two soldiers sit in a trench opposite a machine-gun nest. One of

---

[10]See Jacques Hadamard, *Essay on the Psychology of Invention in the Mathematical Field* (Princeton: Princeton University Press, 1945).

them stays under cover. The other, at the cost of his life, destroys the machine-gun nest with a grenade. Which is rational?

Perhaps the only way to avoid, or clarify, these complexities is to use the term "rational" in conjunction with appropriate adverbs. Then a decision may be called "objectively" rational if *in fact* it is the correct behavior for maximizing given values in a given situation. It is "subjectively" rational if it maximizes attainment relative to the actual knowledge of the subject. It is "consciously" rational to the degree that the adjustment of means to ends is a conscious process. It is "deliberately" rational to the degree that the adjustment of means to ends has been deliberately brought about (by the individual or by the organization). A decision is "organizationally" rational if it is oriented to the organization's goals; it is "personally" rational if it is oriented to the individual's goals. In the ensuing discussion, the term "rational" will always be qualified by one of these adverbs unless the meaning is clear from the context.

CONCLUSION

The object of this chapter has been to explore the anatomy of decision with a view to establishing a terminology and a framework of analysis that permit a realistic investigation of administrative decision. To this end, the objective environment surrounding choice was examined. This environment was described as a set of alternative behaviors, each leading to definite anticipated consequences.

Knowledge is the means of discovering which of all the possible consequences of a behavior will actually follow it. The ultimate aim of knowledge, in so far as it is part of the process of choice, is to discover a single unique possibility which is consequent on each behavior alternative, although in practice this aim is of course only imperfectly attained.

Knowledge about the consequences of behavior was thus identified as a primary influence on choice. The second influence was found to lie in the preferences of the behaving individual for one set of consequences as compared with another. The problem of choice is one of describing consequences, evaluating them, and connecting them with behavior alternatives.

It was found that means and ends do not completely correspond to facts and values, respectively, but that there is some connection between the two sets of terms. A means-end chain was defined as a series of causally related elements ranging from behaviors to the values consequent on them. Intermediate ends in such a chain serve as value-indices; and, using them, we can evaluate alternatives without a complete exploration of the final ends, or values, inhering in them.

The notion of alternatives casts considerable light on the patterns of interpersonal behavior. The relationship of the values of interacting individuals with the consequences of their joint behavior determines whether the behavior pattern will be competitive or cooperative. It was seen that instability in the behavior pattern may result when the pattern is competitive or when each of the participants in the pattern errs in predicting the behavior of the others.

Finally some definitions have been laid down to distinguish various meanings of rationality: objective, subjective, conscious, deliberate, organizational, and personal.

This chapter has barely touched on the psychological aspects of choice. In the next chapter an attempt will be made to contrast the psychological and the logical elements in the choice process. In later chapters of this study the analytic tools developed in this and the next chapter will be used to study some of the concepts that are central to administrative decision: authority, efficiency, identification, influence, and communication.

RATIONALITY IN ADMINISTRATIVE BEHAVIOR

CHAPTERS IV AND V TREAT of rational human decision-making. It may be useful to explain briefly why they are preoccupied with *rational* behavior, and why they emphasize the *limits* of rationality.

RATIONAL BEHAVIOR AND ADMINISTRATION

The social sciences suffer from acute schizophrenia in their treatment of rationality. At one extreme, economists attribute to economic man a preposterously omniscient rationality. Economic man has a complete and consistent system of preferences that allows him always to choose among the alternatives open to him; he is always completely aware of what these alternatives are; there are no limits on the complexity of the computations he can perform in order to determine which alternatives are best; probability calculations are neither frightening nor mysterious to him. Within the past generations, in its extension to competitive game situations (e.g., game theory) and to decision-making under uncertainty (e.g., rational expectations), this body of theory has reached a state of Thomistic refinement that has a great intellectual and esthetic appeal but little discernible relation to the actual or possible behavior of flesh-and-blood human beings.

At the other extreme are those tendencies in social psychology, many traceable to Freud, that try to reduce all cognition to affect. Thus, we show that coins look larger to poor children than to rich,[11] that the pressures of a social group can persuade people they see spots that are not there,[12] that the process of group problem-solving involves accumulating and discharging tensions,[13] and so on. The past generations of behavioral

[11]J. S. Bruner and L. Postman, "On the Perception of Incongruity: A Paradigm," *Journal of Personality*, 18:206–223 (1949).

[12]S. E. Asch, "The Doctrine of Suggestion, Prestige, and Imitation in Social Psychology," *Psychological Review*, 55:250–276 (1948).

[13]R. F. Bales, *Interaction Process Analysis* (Cambridge: Addison, Wesley, 1951).

scientists have been busy, following Freud, showing that people are not nearly as rational as they thought they were. Perhaps the next generation will have to show that they are far more rational than we now describe them as being—but with a rationality less grandiose than that proclaimed by economists.

This schizophrenia is reflected in Chapters IV and V. The former chapter undertakes to clarify the concept of rationality as it has been developed in economics and formal decision theory. The latter chapter discusses the boundaries that man's limited cognitive capabilities place on the exercise of rationality. Hence it is Chapter V and not Chapter IV that describes rationality as we should expect actually to see it in real life. Readers who have just finished Chapter IV must suspend judgment, until they have read its companion chapter, about the shape that rationality takes in administrative decision-making.

To anyone who has observed organizations, it seems obvious enough that human behavior in them is, if not wholly rational, at least in good part *intendedly* so. Much behavior in organizations is, or seems to be, task-oriented—and often efficacious in attaining its goals. Hence, if we are to give a psychological account of human behavior in organizations, our theory must have room in it for rational behavior. It seems equally apparent that the rationality exhibited in organizations has none of the global omniscience that is attributed to economic man. Hence, we cannot simply chuck psychology overboard and place the theory of organization on an economic foundation. Indeed—as will become increasingly evident—it is precisely in the real world where human behavior is *intendedly* rational, but only *boundedly* so, that there is room for a genuine theory of organization and administration.

Finally, to assert that behavior in organizations is boundedly rational does not imply that the behavior is always directed toward realizing the organization's goals. Individuals also strive rationally to advance their own personal goals, which may not be wholly concordant with organizational goals, and often even run counter to them. Moreover, individuals and groups in organizations often strive for power to realize their own goals and their own views of what the organization should be. To understand organizations, we must include all of these forms and objectives of rationality in our picture. We must include human selfishness and struggles for power.

When we speak of people behaving irrationally what we generally mean is that their goals are not our goals, or that they are acting on the basis of invalid or incomplete information, or that they are ignoring future consequences of their actions, or that their emotions are clouding their judgments or focusing their attention on momentary objectives. We do not often mean that their action is so apparently random as to be inexplicable. The nature of this intended and bounded rationality will be the main topic of Chapter V and its commentary.

DELIBERATE AND HABITUAL RATIONALITY

In the final pages of Chapter IV a number of distinct types of rationality were discussed briefly. In particular, it was asked whether a choice should be regarded as rational if it *served a purpose* (e.g., withdrawing a finger from a hot stove), or only if it were made with *deliberate purpose* (a skilled typist striking a particular key), or—a still stricter criterion—only if it were both *deliberate and conscious*. All of these kinds of rationality can be seen in organizations. Many actions are undertaken consciously and deliberately; but the underlying purposes or reasons for many other actions may not be known to the actor: the clerks' tasks may simply be to file certain papers according to account numbers: their's not to reason why. Even if an actor has developed a procedure quite deliberately and consciously, it may in time become wholly habitual, but still retain the same utility and purpose.

Habits and routines may not only serve their purposes effectively, but also conserve scarce and costly decision-making time and attention. For that reason, a very large part of an organization's activities (or a person's) is likely to proceed according to established rules and routines, which may be reviewed at shorter or longer intervals for possible revision. The establishment of such rules and routines is itself a rational decision, and when we speak of rationality in organizational decision-making, we must include them and the processes for establishing them.[14]

Some recent writings on organizations have suggested that, because of the large role played by habit and routine in organizations, it is not appropriate to describe organizational behavior in decision-making terms.[15] But this is mostly a misconception. As we have just seen, the routines themselves are embodiments of "once and for all" decisions, and applying them in particular circumstances is a decision, albeit often itself a routine one. When routines take over, our analysis must turn to the processes that created them, and those that lead, from time to time, to questioning, reviewing, and periodically revising them. Since Barnard, we have been aware that determining the occasions for decision (or for not taking a decision) is itself a key element in the decision process.

[14]R. Nelson and S. Winter, *An Evolutionary Theory of Economic Change* (Cambridge: Harvard University Press, 1982).

[15]For a brief but balanced discussion of this point, see M. D. Cohen and Lee S. Sproull (eds.), *Organizational Learning* (Thousand Oaks, Calif.: Sage Publications, 1996), pp. xii–xiii.

MOTIVATION AND EMOTION IN DECISION-MAKING[16]

In everyday thinking about human behavior, we often treat reason and emotion as polar opposites, the expression of our emotions preventing our behavior from being rational (perhaps even from being boundedly rational), and our rationality preventing us from expressing our genuine emotions. To find the measure of truth that resides in this popular view, we must examine the function of emotions and the role they play in behavior.

Human beings, like most other complex organisms, can only deal consciously with one or a very few things at a time. Of course, we breathe, our hearts beat, our food digests while we are doing other things, but actions requiring thought have to be done more or less one at a time. When traffic is light, we can time-share our mind between driving and a not-too-serious conversation. But when the traffic gets heavier, we had better focus attention on the road. The bottleneck of attention means that we operate largely in serial fashion: the more demanding the task, the more we are single-minded.

However, over the course of a day, and especially over longer intervals of time, we must address many needs, and seek to attain many goals. We must share our time among these many agenda items, some requiring prompt attention, some allowing more flexibility; and we must therefore have mechanisms that allow us to allocate attention to particular tasks and to shift attention rapidly when a task presents itself with real-time urgency (a flying brick heading in our direction). Motivation and emotion are the mechanisms responsible for this allocation of attention.

A rapidly moving object, even in the periphery of vision, and a loud noise are familiar interruptive stimuli. By interrupting attention they allow it to be refocused on an urgent, real-time need. At the same time that they interrupt us, they arouse emotions that prepare us to attack or flee. The arousal is accomplished by the internal or autonomic nervous system, which, among other things, may stimulate a greatly increased flow of adrenaline. Hunger and thirst, and many other emotions, are more gradual in their onset, but have ultimately the same attention-interrupting effect.

Oversimplifying vastly, we may say that emotions are associated either directly with external stimuli, or with particular contents of our memory stored there by past experiences. When these stimuli appear, or

---

[16]I have discussed the relation of motivation and emotion with cognition more generally in two papers, "Motivational and Emotional Controls of Cognition," *Psychological Review*, 74:29–39 (1967); and "Bottleneck of Attention: Connecting Thought with Motivation," in W. D. Spaulding, ed., *Integrative Views of Motivation, Cognition, and Emotion* (Lincoln: University of Nebraska Press, 1994).

these memories are evoked by events or thoughts, we feel the associated fear, or anger, or love, or happiness, or sadness, or hunger, or sexual urge, and these emotions tend to interrupt what we have previously been attending to and to bind our attention to the situation or thoughts that evoked them.

There is no intrinsic opposition between emotion and reason: emotion is a principal source of motivation, focusing us toward particular goals; and it can direct great powers of thought on the goals it evokes. We sometimes think of emotion as inimical to thought (and thought as inimical to emotion) when an emotion is aroused in us that interferes with the task we have been engaged in—when it turns our rationality to other goals. But to think hard about a subject, in particular to be able to resist interruption of our thought, requires our attention to be fixed by powerful motivational forces.

However, when emotion is strong, the focus of attention may be narrowed to a very specific, and perhaps transient, goal, and we may ignore important matters that we would otherwise take into account before acting. (Hence the advice to "count to ten.") In producing this narrowness of focus, emotion does sometimes stand in opposition to reason. But we must be very careful in our evaluations, for it is this same intensity of thought that, under other circumstances, allows us to concentrate on solving highly complex problems and dealing with extremely difficult situations.

Perhaps the most useful way to think about emotion in relation to administration and to decision-making in organizations is to think of it as a force that helps direct actions toward particular goals by holding attention on them and the means of their realization. Emotion works with reason when it attaches to broad and permanent goals, assuring that action will not be narrowly conceived; it works against reason when it hastens decision unduly and narrows too far the range of possibilities and consequences that receive consideration in the decision process.

CHAPTER V

The Psychology of
Administrative Decisions

THE ARGUMENT OF THE PRESENT CHAPTER can be stated very simply. It is impossible for the behavior of a single, isolated individual to reach any high degree of rationality. The number of alternatives he must explore is so great, the information he would need to evaluate them so vast that even an approximation to objective rationality is hard to conceive. Individual choice takes place in an environment of "givens"— premises that are accepted by the subject as bases for his choice; and behavior is adaptive only within the limits set by these "givens."

If the psychological environment of choice, the "givens," were determined in some accidental fashion, then adult behavior would show little more pattern or integration than the behavior of children. A higher degree of integration and rationality can, however, be achieved, because the environment of choice itself can be chosen and deliberately modified. Partly this is an individual matter: the individual places himself in a situation where certain stimuli and certain items of information will impinge on him. To a very important extent, however, it is an organizational matter. One function that organization performs is to place the organization members in a psychological environment that will adapt their decisions to the organization objectives, and will provide them with the information needed to make these decisions correctly.

The material of the chapter will be presented in three parts. In the first part, the reasons will be set forth in detail why individual behavior must perforce fall far short of the standard of rationality.

The second part of the chapter will examine how the psychological environment of choice is, in fact, formed. It will be shown that this environment is the unifying element that fits a whole sequence of momentary choices into a consistent pattern.

In the final part, the role of the organization in establishing the psychological environment of choice will be studied. It will be seen how the organization selects the individual's ends, how it trains him in skills, and how it provides him with information. In the course of this discussion it will begin to appear that organization permits the individual to approach reasonably near to objective rationality.[1]

THE LIMITS OF RATIONALITY

Objective rationality, as that term was defined in the previous chapter, would imply that the behaving subject molds all his behavior into an integrated pattern by (a) viewing the behavior alternatives prior to decision in panoramic fashion, (b) considering the whole complex of consequences that would follow on each choice, and (c) with the system of values as criterion singling out one from the whole set of alternatives.

Real behavior, even that which is ordinarily thought of as "rational," possesses many elements of disconnectedness not present in this idealized picture. If behavior is viewed over a stretch of time, it exhibits a mosaic character. Each piece of the pattern is integrated with others by their orientation to a common purpose; but these purposes shift from time to time with shifts in knowledge and attention, and are held together in only slight measure by any conception of an over-all criterion of choice. It might be said that behavior reveals "segments" of rationality—that behavior shows rational organization within each segment, but the segments themselves have no very strong interconnections.

Actual behavior falls short, in at least three ways, of objective rationality as defined in the last chapter:

(1) Rationality requires a complete knowledge and anticipation of the consequences that will follow on each choice. In fact, knowledge of consequences is always fragmentary.

(2) Since these consequences lie in the future, imagination must supply the lack of experienced feeling in attaching value to them. But values can be only imperfectly anticipated.

---

[1]The entire chapter draws heavily upon psychology for its premises. A fundamental difficulty that must be faced by any social scientist who wishes to use the products of psychological research in dealing with his subject is that the psychologists themselves are divided into warring schools. Fortunately, most of the psychological topics that are relevant to the present study are not subjects of controversy among these schools. Because it is one of the few psychological theories that are oriented around the concepts of choice and purpose, Tolman's analysis of *Purposive Behavior in Animals and Men* (New York: D. Appleton-Century, 1932) has perhaps contributed more than any other treatise to the terminology and viewpoint of this chapter. For traditional psychological topics such as "habit," "attention," and the like, an analysis sufficient for the purposes of this study may be found in any of the numerous textbooks. As a matter of fact, most of the references here are to William James, *The Principles of Psychology* (New York: Henry Holt, 1925), and to John Dewey, *Human Nature and Conduct* (New York: Modern Library, 1930).

(3) Rationality requires a choice among all possible alternative behaviors. In actual behavior, only a very few of all these possible alternatives ever come to mind.

Incompleteness of Knowledge

The first limitation upon rationality in actual behavior has been mentioned in Chapter IV.[2] Rationality implies a complete, and unattainable, knowledge of the exact consequences of each choice. In actuality, the human being never has more than a fragmentary knowledge of the conditions surrounding his action, nor more than a slight insight into the regularities and laws that would permit him to induce future consequences from a knowledge of present circumstances.

For instance, to achieve a completely successful application of resources to a city's fire protection problem, the members of the fire department would need to know in comprehensive detail the probabilities of fire in each portion of the city—in fact, in each structure—and the exact effect upon fire losses of any change in administrative procedure or any redistribution of the fire-fighting forces.

Even to state the problem in this form is to recognize the extent to which complete rationality is limited by lack of knowledge. If each fire were reported to the department at the moment ignition occurred, fire losses would miraculously decline. Lacking such omniscience, the fire department must devote considerable effort to securing as promptly as possible, through special alarm systems and otherwise, information regarding situations where its action is needed.[3]

This point has been developed in some detail in order to emphasize that it poses an extremely practical problem of administration—to secure an organization of the decision-making process such that relevant knowledge will be brought to bear at the point where the decision is made. The same point might have been illustrated with respect to a business organization—the dependence of its decisions, for example, on the correct prediction of market prices.

The human being striving for rationality and restricted within the limits of his knowledge has developed some working procedures that partially overcome this difficulty. These procedures consist in assuming that he can isolate from the rest of the world a closed system containing only a limited number of variables and a limited range of consequences.

---

[2]See pp. 78–80, *supra*.

[3]With respect to similar considerations involved in military tactics, see *United States Army Field Service Regulations, 1923* (Washington: Government Printing Office, 1924), p. 4.

There is a story to the effect that a statistician once found a very high correlation between the number of old maids and the size of the clover crop in different English countries. After puzzling over this relation for some time, he was able to trace what appeared to him to be the causal chain. Old maids, it appeared, kept cats; and cats ate mice. Field mice, however, were natural enemies of bumblebees, and these latter were, in turn, the chief agents in fertilizing the flowers of the clover plants. The implication, of course, is that the British Parliament should never legislate on the subject of marriage bonuses without first evaluating the effect upon the clover crop of reducing the spinster population.

In practical decision-making, devious consequences of this sort must of necessity be ignored.[4] Only those factors that are most closely connected with the decision in cause and time can be taken into consideration. The problem of discovering what factors are, and what are not, important in any given situation is quite as essential to correct choice as a knowledge of the empirical laws governing those factors that are finally selected as relevant.

Rational choice will be feasible to the extent that the limited set of factors upon which decision is based corresponds, in nature, to a closed system of variables—that is, to the extent that significant indirect effects are absent. Only in the cases of extremely important decisions is it possible to bring to bear sufficient resources to unravel a very involved chain of effects. For instance, a very large amount spent for research to determine the indirect effects of a governmental fiscal policy upon employment in the economy would, if it achieved its aim, be well spent. On the other hand, a physician treating a patient does not take time to determine what difference the life or death of his patient will make to the community.

Difficulties of Anticipation

It is a commonplace of experience that an anticipated pleasure may be a very different sort of thing from a realized pleasure. The actual experience may be considerably more or less desirable than anticipated.

This does not result merely from failure to anticipate consequences. Even when the consequences of a choice have been rather completely described, the anticipation of them can hardly act with the same force upon the emotions as the experiencing of them. One reason for this is that the mind cannot at a single moment grasp the consequences in their

---

[4]Cf. Dewey, *The Public and Its Problems* (New York: Henry Holt, 1927), pp. 106–107.

entirety. Instead, attention shifts from one value to another with consequent shifts in preference.

Valuation, therefore, is limited in its accuracy and consistency by the power of the individual to trace the varied value elements in the imagined consequence and to give them the same weight in anticipation as they will have for him in experience.

This is probably an important influence in "risky" behavior. The more vividly the consequences of losing in a risky venture are visualized—either through past experience of such consequences or for other reasons—the less desirable does the risk assumption appear. It is not so much that the experience of loss leads to attaching a higher probability to the occurrence of loss as that the desire to avoid the consequences of loss has been strengthened.

The Scope of Behavior Possibilities

Imagination falls down also in conceiving all the possible patterns of behavior that the individual might undertake. The number of things that a man, restricted only by physical and biological limitations, could do in even so short an interval as a minute is inconceivable. He has two legs, two arms, a head, two eyes, a neck, a trunk, ten fingers, ten toes, and many sets of voluntary muscles governing each. Each of these members is capable of complex movements individually or in coordination.

Of all these possible movements, only a very few come to mind at any moment as possible behavior alternatives. Since each alternative has distinct consequences, it follows that many sets of possible consequences never reach the stage of valuation, since it is not recognized that they are possible consequents of available behavior alternatives.

Relatively speaking, of course, human beings come much closer to exploiting in purposive action their physiological capacities of movement than other animals. The relatively simple "tool behaviors" of which the great apes are capable[5] are very elementary, judged by human standards.

In some fields, considerable ingenuity has been shown in devising methods for exploiting possibilities of behavior. Elaborate devices have been constructed in phonetics for observing and correcting lip and tongue movements. Time-and-motion studies are made to observe, in great detail, hand movements in industrial processes, to improve these movements, and to facilitate them through revision of the process. In the same category could be placed the whole field of tool-invention and

[5]See Tolman, *op. cit.*, pp. 219–226, and the literature there cited.

skill-training. Both involve a close observation of behavior processes, and a consequent enlargement of the alternatives available for choice.

PURPOSIVE BEHAVIOR IN THE INDIVIDUAL

These remarks concerning the departure of actual behavior from the norm of rationality serve already to indicate some of the characteristics of the psychological process of choice. It is time now to examine these characteristics more systematically.

Docility

As was pointed out in Chapter IV, the simplest movement—taking a step, focusing the eyes on an object—is purposive in nature, and only gradually develops in the infant from its earliest random undirected movements. In achieving the integration the human being exhibits *docility;* that is, he observes the consequences of his movements and adjusts them to achieve the desired purpose.[6]

Docility is characterized, then, by a stage of exploration and inquiry followed by a stage of adaptation. It can be observed in the behavior of individuals and in the behavior of organizations. A man learning to operate an overhead crane first obtains information from someone skilled in its operation as to how it is controlled and what the functions are of the various instruments and levers. He then supplements his information by experimenting with the crane, gradually learning from practice what reaction he can expect from the equipment when he manipulates it in a particular way. When he has reached this point, he is able to use the crane to accomplish his purposes—to adapt the manipulation to his ends.

Similarly, a new publishing firm must learn, from its own experience or from that of other firms, how many copies of a particular book are likely to be sold, and what kind of advertising is effective in selling it. Having learned what results a particular advertising technique will produce, the organization can intelligently adjust its techniques to the particular objectives it is trying to reach. This last example illustrates also

[6]The term "docility" is used here in its proper dictionary sense of "teachability." Since the word has no good synonym, it is unfortunate that in general speech it has taken on the connotations of tractability, submissiveness, or pliancy. Tolman, whose treatment is closely followed in this discussion, defines docility as "that character of behavior . . . which consists in the fact that, if a given behavior-act in a given environment proves relatively unsuccessful, i.e., does not get the demanded type of goal-object at all or gets there only by a relatively long distance, it will, on subsequent occasions, tend to give way to an act or acts which will tend to get the organism to this demanded type of goal-object and will tend to get him to it by a relatively short route" (*op. cit.*, pp. 442–443).

the great part that judgment and estimate play in the adaptive process in most practical situations.

Characteristics of Human Docility

Docility is of course, quite as characteristic of the behavior of higher animals as it is of human behavior. There are, however, a number of rather striking differences between animal and human docility. The animal's learning is primarily of a trial-and-error character. That is, learning does not show itself until he has had an opportunity, by actually experiencing them, to observe the consequences of his behaviors. The human being's power to observe regularities in nature of a very general sort, and to communicate with other human beings, helps him to shorten materially this learning process.

In the first place, a previous experience with other choices (of the same sort) may enable him to infer something about the character of the particular choice with which he is faced. Likewise, he may experiment ideationally rather than in actual behavior: he may trace in his mind the consequences of each behavior alternative and select one of them without actually trying any of them out. For example, an engineer may explore in his mind or on paper several plans for a sewer, and may be able to determine quite accurately their respective performance without putting any of them to an actual trial.[7]

In the second place, communication gives the human being a tremendous advantage over the animal in learning. The engineer designing a pavement does not base his attempts entirely upon experimentation, ideational or actual, but uses reference sources, descriptions of the conclusions that other persons have reached on the basis of long experimentation and research in this field—although he may select and modify this accumulated experience on the basis of his own success and failure. Under some circumstances, moreover, learning is dependent entirely on communication, and even the subsequent test of success or failure is not available to the individual. This is true of many professional disciplines. In the field of medicine, for instance, the individual practitioner is seldom able to determine from what happens to his small group of patients the efficacy of particular modes of treatment, especially in the case of diseases he meets only infrequently. He must base his treatment on doctrine developed by medical scientists with special facilities for controlled

---

[7]As a matter of fact, the difference between men and animals in this respect is probably one of degree rather than kind. Tolman, for instance, shows that the rat has a considerable capacity for generalization (*ibid.*, pp. 187–190).

research. The function of research, and especially experimental research, is to adapt behavior to purpose when the consequences of behavior are not easily evaluated outside the controlled conditions of the laboratory.

The possibility of purposive behavior derives, then, from recognition of the consequences that follow on particular behaviors. The human being's advantage is that he does not have to determine these consequences separately for each particular decision with which he is faced. By the use of the experimental method, by communication of knowledge, by theoretical prediction of consequences, a relatively little bit of experience can be made to serve as the basis for a wide range of decisions. As a result a remarkable economy of thought and observation is achieved.

Memory

The role of memory in rational behavior hardly requires comment. When similar problems recur, it is memory that stores up the information gathered, or even the conclusions reached, in solving the first problem, and makes these available, without new inquiry, when the next problem of the same kind is encountered.

It has often been remarked that memory may be either natural or artificial—information may be stored in the mind, or it may be recorded on paper in such a way as to be accessible. The artificial kind of memory that consists of libraries, files, and records is the kind of most importance in organization.

For any kind of memory, whether natural or artificial, to be useful, there must be mechanisms that permit the memory to be drawn upon when needed. The letter that is lost in the files and the figure that has slipped the mind are equally useless items of memory unless they can be located. Hence human rationality relies heavily upon the psychological and artificial associational and indexing devices that make the store of memory accessible when it is needed for the making of decisions.

Habit

An equally important mechanism that assists in the preservation of useful behavior patterns is habit.[8] Habit permits conservation of mental effort by withdrawing from the area of conscious thought those aspects of the situation that are repetitive.

[8]Dewey (*Human Nature and Conduct*, pp. 14–131, 172–181) early emphasized the important role of habit in social behavior. James, in his *Psychology*, contributed a classic chapter to the psychological literature on habit (chap. iv).

In learning to typewrite, the student tries to pay close attention to each minute movement of his fingers, and to the relation of each mark on the copy to each key on the instrument. Only through a gradual and fumbling adjustment of his movements does he achieve the necessary coordination of eye with hand. When, by practice, a certain point in skill has been reached, it proves no longer necessary to give attention to integrations at this lowest level. The mere desire for the end of the action—the letter to be printed—brings about the act without further will. When this step has been reached, habit or skill takes over the integration which was first achieved by attention and desire to learn.

Habit performs an extremely important task in purposive behavior, for it permits similar stimuli or situations to be met with similar responses or reactions, without the need for a conscious rethinking of the decision to bring about the proper action. Habit permits attention to be devoted to the novel aspects of a situation requiring decision. A large part of the training that goes to make a championship football team, crew, army battalion, or fire company is devoted to developing habitual responses that will permit immediate reactions to rapidly changing situations.[9]

Habit, like memory, has an artificial organization counterpart, which has been termed by Stene "organization routine."[10] In so far as methods of handling recurring questions become matters of organization practice, perhaps embodied in manuals of practice and procedure, they cease to be objects of reconsideration when these questions arise. The close relation between habit and memory is evident here as it is in the case of the habits of individual persons. If a formal criterion were needed, it might be said that a matter has become part of the organization routine when it is settled by reference to accepted or approved practices rather than by consideration of the alternatives on their merits.

Habit must not be thought of as a purely passive element in behavior (either individual or organizational), for once a habit has been established the mere presence of the stimulus tends to release the habitual behavior without further conscious thought. Under such circumstances, it may actually require conscious attention to prevent the response from occurring even if changed circumstances have made it inappropriate. The automobile driver who is habituated to the application of his brakes on the approach of danger has difficulty restraining himself from this response when he skids on an icy pavement. This is a point that has far-reaching implications for organization, and must be considered at greater length.

[9]John Dewey, *The Public and Its Problems*, pp. 159–161.

[10]Edwin O. Stene, "An Approach to a Science of Administration," *American Political Science Review*, 34:1129 (Dec., 1940).

Role of Positive Stimuli

If rationality is to be achieved, a period of hesitation must precede choice, during which the behavior alternatives, knowledge bearing on environmental conditions and consequences, and the anticipated values must be brought into the focus of attention. Psychologically speaking, such a hesitation marks a relatively sophisticated level of behavior. Simpler behavior patterns may be described as those responses to stimuli that occur upon presentation of the stimulus and with little or no hesitation.

The distinction between the stimulus-response pattern of behavior and the hesitation-choice pattern gives a clue to the respective roles of nonrational and rational in the complete behavior pattern. Considering the limitations, just described, in human capacity to meet the demands of rationality, the hesitation preceding choice could conceivably lengthen into inaction. The individual, realizing his inability to take into consideration all the factors relevant to his choice, and despairing of rationality, might vacillate among the available alternatives until the time for action was past. In fact, choice and action usually take place long before attention has been given even to those elements in the situation that are within grasp. A stimulus, external or internal, directs attention to selected aspects of the situation to the exclusion of competing aspects that might turn choice in another direction. Within the central nervous system are built up channels that permit impulses to be translated into action while leaving large portions of the central system undisturbed.

Conscious attention is not a necessary element in this process. The consciousness that accompanies the "startle pattern" of behavior is not the cause of the response—it merely accompanies, or even succeeds, the response. However, since we are concerned primarily with decision points, and with responses to new situations, we may consider first the role of attention in the selective process—that is, in the channelizing of stimuli.

William James, who was not troubled by behavioristic scruples, described attention as follows:

> Every one knows what attention is. It is the taking possession by the mind, in clear and vivid form, of one out of what seem several simultaneously possible objects or trains of thought. Focalization, concentration, of consciousness are of its essence. It implies withdrawal from some things in order to deal effectively with others, and is a condition which has a real opposite in the confused, dazed, scatterbrained state which in French is called *distraction*, and *Zerstreutheit* in German.[11]

---

[11] *The Principles of Psychology*, 1:403–404.

Tolman, more cautiously, prefers to avoid the term and speaks instead of "selective responsiveness to stimuli."[12]

Attention, then, refers to the set of elements that enter into consciousness at any given time. It is clear that consciousness is not a necessary precondition to docility, and that even behaviors that are not in the focus of attention are capable of purposive adjustment. Certainly consciousness and attention are not involved in the simpler types of conditioned response—e.g., in the development of motor skills. In most cases, there seems to be a close relation, however, between the spheres of attention and of rationality. That is, docility is largely limited by (1) the span of attention, and (2) the area within which skills and other appropriate behaviors have become habitual. Hence to a considerable extent, the limits upon rationality described above are resultants of the limits of the area of attention.

Now it has already been noted that in so far as a part of behavior is governed by habit, it passes out of the area of conscious attention. For example, in a consideration of behavior alternatives, attention is not usually directed to possible movements of individual muscles. Instead, the behavior alternatives that actually come to attention are habitual integrations of such unitary movements—walking, writing, pronouncing, etc.; only under unusual circumstances is there a conscious attempt to analyze these integrations. Once the stimulus is received for the initiation of such movements, they go to completion without further consideration.

The same responsiveness in habitual manner to stimuli occurs at even higher levels of integration. A typist who receives some printed matter for copying converts it into typewritten form almost without the necessity of a single conscious or original decision. To the man on an assembly line, the presence on the belt in front of him of a partially finished product is the only stimulus necessary to initiate the whole series of skilled movements that represent his contribution to the manufacture of the product. The individual sitting down at the dinner table finds in the food before him the sufficient stimulus for the complex process of eating and can carry on this process without conscious attention—meanwhile devoting his attention to conversation.

It appears, then, that in actual behavior, as distinguished from objectively rational behavior, decision is initiated by stimuli which channel attention in definite directions, and that the response to the stimuli is partly reasoned, but in large part habitual. The habitual portion is not, of course, necessarily or even usually irrational, since it may represent a previously conditioned adjustment or adaptation of behavior to its ends.

[12]*Op. cit.*, pp. 35–36.

In executive positions characterized by great busyness on the part of their occupants, a great many stimuli for decision come from outside the individual. A difficult case is referred upward for appellate review; a caller or a member of another organization insists on discussing a problem with the "top man." Innumerable other persons, problems, and things are constantly being forced on his attention. In any such position the particular questions to be decided will depend largely on the accident of what stimuli are presented.

Not only do the stimuli determine what decisions the administrator is likely to make, but they also have a considerable influence on the conclusion he reaches. An important reason for this is that the very stimulus which initiates the decision also directs attention to selected aspects of the situation, with the exclusion of others. For example, a fire chief pictures a city in which fire losses are extremely low—which seems to him a good thing. His knowledge tells him that progress toward this desirable state of affairs could be made by purchase of a new piece of equipment. The demands of rationality would require, of course, that before deciding whether a new piece of equipment is needed he consider the other purposes for which the money could be spent: street repairs, an addition to the municipal hospital, and so on. That this description is not far from the actualities of administrative behavior will be amply demonstrated in later chapters.[13]

Almost all human beings have the feeling, at one time or another, that there are more things that they would like to do than there is time to do them. That is, there are more possible stimuli for behavior than could be acted out if they were all simultaneously present to the attention. Rationality demands that a conscious choice be made among competing "goods" instead of leaving the choice to the caprice of the attention-directing stimuli.

Determinants of the Psychological Environment

In so far, then, as choice is initiated by impingement upon the individual of accidental and arbitrary stimuli, it would seem that the integrated busyness of the adult is simply a more patterned busyness than the ran-

[13]The reader who is interested in further examples of this stimulus-response type of thinking will find fascinating materials in several fields. First, let him turn to autobiography and try to ascertain how each subject chose his particular profession. The autobiographies of Viscount Haldane and of William Alanson White both illustrate the point well: *Richard Burdon Haldane: An Autobiography* (London: Hodder & Stoughton, 1931), and *The Autobiography of a Purpose* (Garden City: Doubleday, Doran, 1938). Next, let him turn to recent literature on propaganda technique and note the generous use of attention-directing devices by the propagandist. The supporting schedules of budget documents and the testimony taken at budget hearings are also filled with examples of attention channelized toward particular values.

dom movements and shifting attentions of the child. The organized wholes of which it is composed are larger and more complex but, as wholes, no more closely related to any overall system of values than those of the child. The study of administrative behavior as a rational activity would hardly seem useful unless this difficulty can be removed by showing that the stimuli that initiate choice are not, or at least need not be, arbitrary, when viewed from the standpoint of the organization as a whole rather than from that of an individual member.[14]

The next question that must be considered, then, is how the stimuli themselves originate that are instrumental in initiating the decisional process.

A man in a room with a shelf full of books may glance over the titles and deliberately choose one of them to read for an hour. Once he has opened the book, if it is not too dull and he is not interrupted, the symbols which it places before his eyes will be the most important, perhaps the only, stimuli engaging his attention during the ensuing hour. Hence, his choice of a book determines these subsequent stimuli.

Now consider an illustration of a slightly more practical sort. A man has formed the habit of glancing at his calendar pad when he comes to the office each morning. On Thursday he receives a letter which will need to be answered the next Tuesday. He places a note on his pad, knowing that this note will provide the stimulus to act on the following Tuesday.

A third illustration involves the deliberate development of a skill. A person who uses the typewriter once in a while may fall into the "hunt and peck" system of typing because, at any given moment when he wishes to type, this is the fastest way of spelling out the words. If he anticipates, however, that he will make considerable use of the typewriter over a period of time, he may take the pains to develop the habits associated with the touch system. Then in the long run the stimuli that he wishes to translate into typewritten words will receive a more effective response than if he had not previously developed this skill.

[14]The pragmatists would seem to take the position that human beings are concerned with rationality only in the first sense—in terms of adjustive responses to arbitrary stimuli. John Dewey, in *Human Nature and Conduct* (pp. 261–262), says: "The action of deliberation, as we have seen, consists in selecting some foreseen consequence to serve as a stimulus to present action. . . . But the selected consequence is set in an indefinite context of other consequences just as real as it is. . . . The 'ends' that are foreseen and utilized mark out a little island in an infinite sea. This limitation would be fatal were the proper function of ends anything else than to liberate and guide present action out of its perplexities and confusions. But this service constitutes the sole meaning of aims and purposes. Hence their slight extent in comparison with ignored and unforeseen consequences is of no import in itself." See also *The Public and Its Problems*, p. 200. Dewey's later views set forth in *Logic. The Theory of Inquiry*, chap. ix, pp. 159–180 (New York: Henry Holt, 1938), are in closer accord with the point of view of the present study—that the behavior of the individual acquires a wider context of rationality through the environment of choice social organization provides for him.

A final illustration is provided by the lines of communication in an administrative organization. Each member of the organization requires certain information in order to make correctly those decisions for which he is responsible. To make certain that the necessary information is presented to each member, a regular system of records and reports is devised, which automatically directs these stimuli into the proper channels.

These illustrations give some notion of the mechanisms that bring about the integration of behavior in a broad pattern. Two principal sets of mechanisms may be distinguished: (1) those that cause behavior to persist in a particular direction once it has been turned in that direction, and (2) those that initiate behavior in a particular direction. The former are for the most part—though by no means entirely—internal. Their situs is the human mind, and to this extent their description and functioning is a problem for psychology, and can only be touched upon in the present study.

Behavior-initiating mechanisms, on the other hand, are largely external to the individual, although they usually imply his sensitivity to particular stimuli. Being external, they can be interpersonal—they can be invoked by someone other than the person they are intended to influence, and consequently, they play a central role in administrative organization.

The mechanisms of initiation have already been sufficiently illustrated for present purposes. The next few pages will dispose briefly of the mechanisms of behavior-persistence. That done, it will be possible to reconstruct a picture of rational behavior, giving a central place to the mechanisms of integration.

The Mechanisms of Behavior-Persistence

Attention and behavior, once initiated in a particular direction, tend to persist in that direction for a considerable interval of time. This is true even when the original choice of activity was a matter of relative indifference.

One important reason for behavior-persistence has already been discussed in Chapter IV. Activity very often results in "sunk costs" of one sort or another that make persistence in the same direction advantageous. An administrator may feel considerable doubt that a particular activity should be undertaken; but, once the responsibility has been assumed, it may be advantageous to continue rather than lose the time and effort that have already been expended. Another way of stating this is to say that activities are usually continued at least until a point of "consummation" has been reached—a point where the values produced by sunk costs have been harvested.

A second reason for persistence is that the activity itself creates stimuli that direct attention toward its continuance and completion. This has already been pointed out—a book, if it is well written, tends to hold attention to the limits of its covers until it has been read through. But the same thing can be equally well illustrated from almost any administrative situation. An engineer, arriving at his office, finds on his desk a set of plans for a street on which he was working the previous day. Immediately, his attention is directed to these plans and the problems involved in completing them, and no further external stimuli may be needed to keep him at work on the plans for the remainder of the day.

It may be seen that a large part of this stimulation is "internal," and proceeds along the associational paths that have been built up in the mind. If the pattern of associations is rich, the mind acts as a sort of closed circuit, repeatedly bringing thought back to the subject of concern whenever it strays. As is well known, any considerable degree of concentration (i.e., internal stimulation) will actually decrease the individual's sensitivity to external stimuli.[15]

A third factor making for persistence, and one closely related to "sunk costs," is one that might be labeled "make-ready" costs. In the case of many repetitive tasks, the time of preparing to perform the task, and the time required to turn from that task to another, make it advantageous to persist in the performance of the one task rather than to perform a variety.

THE INTEGRATION OF BEHAVIOR

It is time now to turn from the mechanisms that make integration possible to the pattern of behavior that results from the operation of these mechanisms. The process involves three principal steps:

(1) The individual (or organization) makes broad decisions regarding the values to which he is going to direct his activities, the general methods he is going to use to attain these values, and the knowledge, skills, and information he will need to make particular decisions within the limits of the policy laid down and to carry out the decisions. The decisional activity just described might be called *substantive planning*.

(2) He designs and establishes mechanisms that will direct his attention, channel information and knowledge, etc., in such a way as to cause the specific day-to-day decisions to conform with the substantive

---

[15]The subject cannot be pursued further at this point, but a wealth of illustrative material will be found in the psychological literature. See, for example, James' chapters in *The Principles of Psychology* on "The Stream of Thought," "Association," and "Will" (chaps. ix, xiv, and xxvi).

plan. This decisional activity might be called *procedural planning,* and corresponds to what was earlier described as "constructing the psychological environment of decision."

(3) He executes the plan through day-to-day decisions and activities that fit in the framework provided by steps (1) and (2).

In reality, the process involves not just three steps but a whole hierarchy of steps, the decisions at any given level of generality providing the environment for the more particular decisions at the next level below. The integration of behavior at the highest level is brought about by decisions that determine in very broad terms the values, knowledge, and possibilities that will receive consideration. The next lower level of integration, which gives greater specificity to these very general determinants, results from those decisions that determine what activities shall be undertaken. Other levels follow, each one determining in greater detail a subarea lying within the area of the level above.

At the higher levels of integration only the very general aspects of the situation can be given consideration. Particularization can take place only when attention is directed to the more detailed possibilities and consequences. Hence, a fundamental problem of administrative theory is to determine how this plexus of decisions should be constructed—what the proper division of labor is between the broad "planning" decisions and the narrower "executory" decisions. A second fundamental problem is that of procedural planning—to devise mechanisms that will make effective the control of the executory decisions by the planning decisions.

Types of General Decisions

It should be made clear that actual events are determined by choice among on-the-spot alternatives for immediate behavior. In a strict sense, a decision can influence the future in only two ways: (1) present behavior, determined by this decision, may limit future possibilities,[16] and (2) future decisions may be guided to a greater or lesser degree by the present decision. It is from this possibility of influencing future choice by present decisions that the idea of an interconnected plexus of decisions derives. The first type of influence has already been discussed, but the second requires further consideration.

When a problem of a particular kind has several times arisen for decision, it may lead to a generalized query of the following kind: "What

[16]See chap. iv, pp. 77–78, *supra.*

criteria can I discover which can be used as a basis for choice whenever a problem of this kind arises?" For example, the experienced fire fighter asks, "Are there any underlying principles of fire fighting which can be applied to the many fire situations with which I deal?"

When the problem has been posed and a solution reached, then a decision has been made that will guide all further decisions on this subject. This it may do by selecting (1) particular values as criteria for the later decisions, (2) particular items of empirical knowledge as relevant to the later decisions, (3) particular behavior alternatives as the only ones needing consideration for later choice.

(1) The specialization of administrative functions, each with its own "objective," directs each portion of the organization toward the realization of a particular restricted set of values. To accept "reducing fire losses" as the objective of a fire department is to establish a criterion of value that will guide the fire department administrator in all his decisions.

(2) In many fields, general decisions are reached as to the facts that should be taken into consideration in making any subsidiary decision. The engineer, for instance, has routine procedures of calculation for determining whether a given bridge design allows the required factor of safety in bearing its stresses.

(3) Similarly, in many fields, general decisions determine the behavior alternatives that are to be considered when a specific choice is faced. A football team goes on the field with a definite repertoire of "plays" which it can call into use at appropriate moments. A policeman, seeing an infraction of the law, is trained to respond in terms of "arrest," "warning," or "report."

The psychological mechanisms by which these general criteria, previously decided upon, are brought to bear upon an immediate problem for choice have already been described.[17] By creating internal and external stimuli, these prior decisions determine the framework of attention with which the mind responds to the specific choice-situation. This narrow frame of attention is in distinct contrast with the broader area of reference that is involved when the prior, controlling decision is made. That is, the set of factors taken into consideration when it is determined that "a fire department will be established with the objective of minimizing fire losses" is quite different from the set that influences a fire-fighter to decide, "I had better connect a 2½-inch line to this hydrant." This

---

[17]*Supra.*

stratification of decisions makes it possible for each choice to be guided directly or indirectly by much broader considerations of rationality than would be possible if it had to be made "on the spot" without benefit of previous consideration. Hence, we are led to a concept of "planned" behavior as the proper means for maintaining rationality at a high level.

The Planning Process

The psychological processes involved in planning consist in selecting general criteria of choice, and then particularizing them by application to specific situations.[18] A designing engineer selects as his objective a railroad to extend between cities A and B through mountainous country. After a preliminary examination of the topography, he selects two or three general routes that seem feasible. He then takes each of these routes as his new "end"—an intermediate end—and particularizes it further, using more detailed topographical maps.

His thought processes might be described as a series of hypothetical implications: "If I am to go from A to B, routes (1), (2), and (3) seem more feasible than the others; if I am to follow route (1), plan (1a) seems preferable; if route (2), plan (2c); if route (3), plan (3a)"—and so on, until the most minute details of the design have been determined for two or three alternative plans. His final choice is among these detailed alternatives.

This process of thought may be contrasted with a single choice among *all* the possible routes. The latter method is the one dictated by logic, and is the only procedure that guarantees that the decision finally arrived at is the best. On the other hand, this method requires that all the possible plans be worked out in full detail before any decision is reached. The practical impossibility of such a procedure is evident. The planning procedure is a compromise, whereby only the most "plausible" alternatives are worked out in detail.

Let us present another illustration. Suppose the problem is to select a dam site for a storage reservoir. For simplicity, it will be assumed that the desideratum is to secure a specified volume of water storage at a minimum cost, and that water storage above the specified amount will be of no value. Usually the real problem is not so simple. The cost can be estimated, for each point along the river, of building a dam with the required storage capacity. However, to make an accurate estimate, detailed studies would need to be made of the foundation conditions at each point. Then, this huge array of cost estimates could be compiled and the dam site with least cost selected.

[18]Cf. MacMahon, Millet, and Ogden, *op. cit.*, p. 17.

Actually, the engineer proceeds quite differently. By inspection of a topographic map, he immediately picks out a half-dozen "plausible" dam sites, and forgets the rest. He is sufficiently familiar with dam construction costs to know—with a fair degree of certainty—that any other site he might choose would have a higher construction cost. Next, he makes an approximate estimate of dam costs for each of the plausible sites, assuming "normal" foundation conditions. Finally, he selects the most promising sites and makes careful foundation studies as a basis for final estimates.

At each step in this process there is a chance that the dam site which really is most desirable will be eliminated without complete analysis. He must exercise great skill in determining the degree of approximation that is allowable at each point in the procedure.

The Function of Social Organization

It was mentioned several times in this chapter that the mechanisms leading to the integration of behavior might be interpersonal. If organizations and social institutions be conceived, in the broad sense, as patterns of group behavior, it is not hard to see that the individual's participation in such organizations and institutions may be the source of some of his most fundamental and far-reaching integrations. The organizational influences on the individual are of two principal kinds:

(1) Organizations and institutions permit stable expectations to be formed by each member of the group as to the behavior of the other members under specified conditions. Such stable expectations are an essential precondition to a rational consideration of the consequences of action in a social group.[19]

(2) Organizations and institutions provide the general stimuli and attention-directors that channelize the behaviors of the members of the group, and that provide those members with the intermediate objectives that stimulate action.[20]

No pattern of social behavior could survive, of course, that did not anticipate and provide in some manner for the satiation of the stimuli of hunger, sexual desire, and fatigue. Beyond this, institutional arrangements are subject to infinite variation, and can hardly be said to follow from any innate characteristics of man. Since these institutions largely

[19]Cf. Stene's discussion of "organization routine" *op. cit.*, p. 1129.

[20]Cf. Dewey, *The Public and Its Problems*, p. 54.

determine the mental sets of the participants, they set the conditions for the exercise of docility, and hence of rationality in human society.

The highest level of integration that man achieves consists in taking an existing set of institutions as one alternative and comparing it with other sets. That is, when man turns his attention to the institutional setting which, in turn, provides the framework within which his own mental processes operate, he is truly considering the consequences of behavior alternatives at the very highest level of integration. Thought at this comprehensive level has not been common to all cultures. In our Western civilization it has perhaps been confined to (1) the writings of utopian political theorists and (2) the thought and writings surrounding modern legislative processes.[21]

Human rationality, then, gets its higher goals and integrations from the institutional setting in which it operates and by which it is molded. In our democratic culture, legislation is the principal designer and arbiter of these institutions. Administrative organizations cannot perhaps claim the same importance as repositories of the fundamental human values as that possessed by older traditional institutions like the family. Nevertheless, with man's growing economic interdependence, and with his growing dependence upon the community for essential governmental services, formal organization is rapidly assuming a role of broader significance than it has ever before possessed. This is not without its advantages, for administrative organizations are usually constructed and modified with a deliberation and freedom from tradition which—though far from complete—gives them great adaptability to meet new needs with new arrangements.

The behavior patterns which we call organizations are fundamental, then, to the achievement of human rationality in any broad sense. The rational individual is, and must be, an organized and institutionalized individual. If the severe limits imposed by human psychology upon deliberation are to be relaxed, the individual must in his decisions be subject to the influence of the organized group in which he participates. His decisions must not only be the product of his own mental processes, but also reflect the broader considerations to which it is the function of the organized group to give effect.

---

[21]It has often been shown that the concept of "law-making" as distinct from "law-finding" is a relatively recent development. See, for example, C. J. Friedrich, *Constitutional Government and Politics* (New York: Harper & Bros., 1937), and Charles G. Haines, *The American Doctrine of Judicial Supremacy* (New York: Macmillan, 1914), pp. 12–13, 18–24. Hence, only in recent times has legislation involved a conscious consideration of the possibilities of alternative institutional patterns. Karl Mannheim has emphasized the importance of the deliberate fashioning of the institutional environment in his recent study, *Man and Society in an Age of Reconstruction* (London: Kegan Paul, 1940), pp. 149–155.

Mechanisms of Organization Influence

The means that the organization employs to influence the decisions of individual members have already been outlined in the introductory chapter. They will be analyzed at length in later chapters and therefore require only brief discussion at this point.

(1) The organization divides work among its members. By giving each a particular task to accomplish, it directs and limits his attention to that task. The personnel officer concerns himself with recruitment, training, classification, and other personnel operations. He need not give particular concern to the accounting, purchasing, planning, or operative functions, which are equally vital to the accomplishment of the organization's task, because he knows they have been provided for elsewhere in the organization structure.

(2) The organization establishes standard practices. By deciding once for all (or at least for a period of time) that a particular task shall be done in a particular way, it relieves the individual who actually performs the task of the necessity of determining each time how it shall be done.

(3) The organization transmits decisions downward (and laterally or even upward) through its ranks by establishing systems of authority and influence. The most familiar form this takes is the hierarchy of formal authority; but of equal importance are the assignment to particular individuals of the formal function of advising, and the growth in any actual organization of an informal system of influence based partly upon formal status, and partly upon social relationships.

(4) The organization provides channels of communication running in all directions through which information for decision-making flows. Again these channels are both formal and informal. The formal channels are partly based on, and partly separate from, the lines of formal authority, and the informal channels are closely related to the informal social organization.

(5) The organization trains and indoctrinates its members. This might be called the "internalization" of influence, because it injects into the very nervous systems of the organization members the criteria of decision that the organization wishes to employ. The organization member acquires knowledge, skill, and identifications or loyalties that enable him to make decisions, by himself, as the organization would like him to decide.

The Process of Coordination

One of the principal functions of these organizational influences has already been alluded to in this and the previous chapter: to bring about coordination in the activities of the organization members. As has been explained, the effectiveness of an individual in achieving his aims in any social situation will depend not only upon his own activity, but also on how well that activity relates to what the other individuals concerned are doing. In any large organization—the Federal government is an excellent example—the task of relating the activities of one individual or unit to those of others becomes one of the greatest importance, complexity, and difficulty. War activities have illustrated this strikingly on numerous occasions. An administrator responsible for airplane gasoline production may wish to issue orders—quite logical for the execution of his task—that would interfere with the task of another administrator responsible for rubber production. The procurement of steel for merchant shipping may conflict with the procurement of steel for warships, or for tanks. The execution of a large military operation may require the coordination, in time, of a host of preparatory activities. These illustrations could be multiplied many times.

Viewed from the position of the individual in organization, coordination involves several elements: the relation of the individual's objectives and intermediate aims to those of other segments of the organization; the individual's assessment of the alternatives available to him and to the other members of the group; and his expectations as to the courses of action that will be followed by the others.

Self-Coordination. In the simplest situations, the individual participant can bring his activities into coordination with the activities of others through simple observation of what they are doing. In a group of three or four painters working together, each one may take a part of the job, and the entire group may work as a team with each one fitting in where he thinks his efforts will be most effective and will interfere least with the others. Occasionally a command may be given; but most of the adjustments take place silently and without discussion.

Anyone who has observed an unorganized group of persons act in an emergency has seen organized behavior of this variety. Of course, if the group has been organized previously to the emergency or if one or more members of the group are recognized as "leaders," the mechanism of coordination may be much more elaborate, involving vocal commands.

In most situations, the successful performance of a task by a group of persons requires a slightly higher degree of coordination. For instance, it may be necessary for effective performance that they all apply their efforts simultaneously. Even under such circumstances, the coordination may not be deliberate nor involve explicit commands. The various members of the group may merely accept one member as the "leader" and adjust their movements to his—a group of men moving a heavy load, for example.

All these situations where self-coordination is possible require that the individual be able to observe the behaviors of the organization members and adjust his to theirs. Where this direct observation is not possible—as in most situations of any complexity—the organization itself must provide for the coordination.

Group Versus Individual Alternatives. The individual views the attainment of his objectives as dependent upon the particular course of behavior he follows. For each of the courses of action open to him there is a distinct set of consequences or results. Rational choice, as has been explained, consists in selecting and bringing about the result that is preferred to the others.

When choice takes place in a group situation, the consequences of a course of action become dependent not only upon the individual's selection of a particular alternative, but upon the selections of the other members of the group as well. Only when the behaviors of the others are taken as "constants"—that is, when expectations are formed regarding their behaviors—does the problem of choice take on a determinate form. When such expectations have been formed, the only remaining independent variable is the individual's own choice, and the problem of decision reduces to the former case.

Hence, the set of alternatives available to the *group* must be carefully distinguished from the set of alternatives available to the *individual.* The latter is only a subset of the former, a different subset for each given set of behaviors of the other members of the group. The alternative that the individual actually selects for his own behavior may be quite distinct from the alternative that he would select if he could determine the behaviors of all the other group members.

If the individual's expectations of the behaviors of his colleagues are accurate they will usually be rather different from the way he wishes his colleagues would behave. Since his own decision, to be rational, must be related to his expectations rather than his wishes, he must aim not at that alternative *among all those possible for the group* which he prefers, but at that alternative *among all those possible for him* which he prefers.

That a distinction must be made between a plan of campaign that depends on the opponent's doing the wished-for thing, and a plan that depends upon the opponent's doing the "correct" thing is a cardinal principle of military tactics, and indeed of any competitive activity. A plan of the first kind never succeeds, for its success depends upon the false assumption that the opponent will do what you want him to do. In the practical world, plans are characterized as "utopian" whose success depends on wished-for behavior on the part of many individuals, but which fail to explain how this wished-for behavior will, or can, be brought about.

Now a very special situation arises when all the members of the group exhibit a preference for the same values and for the same outcomes out of all those possible of realization by the group. All the firemen fighting a fire are agreed on the aim of their joint behavior—to extinguish the fire as quickly as possible. In such a case there is one set of behaviors for the members of the group which, on entirely objective empirical grounds, is the most expeditious for the accomplishment of this aim. The members of the group may disagree as to what this best solution is, but any such disagreement is on a factual level—a question of judgment, not of values.

The attainment of the "best" result implies that each member of the group knows his place in the scheme and is prepared to carry out his job with the others. But, unless the intentions of each member of the group can be communicated to the others, such coordination is hardly possible. Each will base his behavior on his expectations of the behaviors of the others, but he will have no reason to expect that they will fit into any preconceived plan. Lacking formal coordination, the result will be highly fortuitous.

Under most practical conditions, self-coordination is infinitely less effective than a predetermined scheme of action that relieves each member of the group of the task of anticipating the behavior of the others as a basis for his own.

Communication, then, is essential to the more complex forms of cooperative behavior. The process of coordination in these more complicated situations consists of at least three steps: (1) the development of a plan of behavior for *all* the members of the group (not a set of individual plans for each member); (2) the communication of the relevant portions of this plan to each member; and (3) a willingness on the part of the individual members to permit their behavior to be guided by the plan.

This process is not unlike that whereby the individual integrates his own behavior into a coordinated pattern. In the integration of the group, communication fills the gap—supplies the nerve tissue, so to speak—left by the absence of any organic connection among the individuals.

The Group Plan. The idea of a plan for the behavior of a group does not involve any metaphysical notions of a "group mind." It is a specification as to how a number of persons shall behave, rather than a specification as to how one person shall behave. The plan has its existence on paper, or in the respective minds of the individuals who create it. These individuals may be many, or few; they may belong to the group, or they may not. All that is required is that, before the plan is acted out, it shall be communicated to the group members who are to do the acting.

In the discussion thus far, it has been assumed that a plan will come into being only when there is perfect agreement among the group members as to which of all the possibilities available to the group they would like to see realized. As a matter of fact, this is not strictly necessary. Group coordination may be possible in many cases where different individuals have different notions of the "optimum." It is necessary only that they agree in finding one plan preferable to any alternative that would be open to them *as individuals* if there were no cooperation.[22]

Since the present discussion is concerned not so much with the reasons why individuals cooperate as with the mechanisms that make cooperation possible, the subject of the "group plan" may now be left, to be more fully discussed in the next chapter.

Communication. General organization decisions can control the behavior of the individual only through psychological mechanisms that bring values and knowledge to bear upon each individual decision at the time it is made. In group behavior, there is a similar necessity of communicating the group plan to the individuals who are to carry it out. This does not mean that the whole plan must be communicated, but that each individual must know what he is to do.

No step in the administrative process is more generally ignored, or more poorly performed, than the task of communicating decisions. All too often, plans are "ordered" into effect without any consideration of the manner in which they can be brought to influence the behavior of the individual members of the group. Procedural manuals are promulgated without follow-up to determine whether the contents of the manuals are used by the individuals to guide their decisions. Organization plans are drawn on paper, although the members of the organization are ignorant of the plan that purports to describe their relationships.

Failures in communication result whenever it is forgotten that the behavior of individuals is the tool with which organization achieves its purposes. The question to be asked of any administrative process is: How does it influence the decisions of these individuals? Without communication, the answer must always be: It does not influence them at all.

Acceptance of the Plan. The final step in coordination is acceptance by each of the organization members of his part in the group plan. The

[22]An extreme form of this proposition was used by Hobbes in his demonstration that social organization can arise even from a state of *bellum omnium contra omnes*. Other contract theorists, notably Locke, felt impelled to postulate a natural identity of interests. For a penetrating discussion of the motivational bases of cooperation see R. M. MacIver, *Community: A Sociological Study* (London: Macmillan, 3rd ed., 1924), particularly Bk. II, chaps. ii and iii.

problem of securing this acceptance will furnish the principal topic of the next two chapters.

SUMMARY

In the course of this chapter both the limits and the possibilities of human rationality have been examined. The limits of rationality have been seen to derive from the inability of the human mind to bring to bear upon a single decision all the aspects of value, knowledge, and behavior that would be relevant. The pattern of human choice is often more nearly a stimulus-response pattern than a choice among alternatives. Human rationality operates, then, within the limits of a psychological environment. This environment imposes on the individual as "givens" a selection of factors upon which he must base his decisions. However, the stimuli of decision can themselves be controlled so as to serve broader ends, and a sequence of individual decisions can be integrated into a well conceived plan.

The deliberate control of the environment of decision permits not only the integration of choice, but its socialization as well. Social institutions may be viewed as regularizations of the behavior of individuals through subjection of their behavior to stimulus-patterns socially imposed on them. It is in these patterns that an understanding of the meaning and function of organization is to be found.

THE PSYCHOLOGY OF
ADMINISTRATIVE DECISIONS

IN ONE SENTENCE, the thesis of Chapters IV and V is this: *The central concern of administrative theory is with the boundary between the rational and the nonrational aspects of human social behavior.* Administrative theory is peculiarly the theory of intended and bounded rationality—of the behavior of human beings who *satisfice* because they have not the wits to *maximize*.[23]

At the time the first edition of *Administrative Behavior* was written, the model of economic man was far more completely and formally developed than the model of the satisficing administrator. Consequently, limited rationality was defined largely as a residual category—as a departure from rationality—and the positive characterization of the process of choice was very incomplete. It is the intent of the commentaries to Chapter IV and the present chapter to remedy this deficiency.

EMPIRICAL EVIDENCE FOR BOUNDED RATIONALITY

In psychology during the past fifty years, there has been a great renaissance of interest in human thinking. As a result, it is more feasible now than when *Administrative Behavior* was first written to construct a model of rational choice that incorporates the actual properties of human behavior and at the same time matches some of the formal clarity of the economic model. Two crucial alterations are needed to transmute the economic man of Chapter IV into the administrator of Chapter V—the person of bounded rationality whom we recognize from everyday life.[24]

---

[23]As editors sometimes look askance at the word "satisfice," or even replace it by "satisfy," I note that it is defined, with the meaning given here, in the second edition of the *Oxford English Dictionary*.

[24]See my "A Behavioral Model of Rational Choice," *op. cit.*; and "Rational Choice and the Structure of the Environment," in the *Psychological Review*, April 1956, both of which are reprinted in *Models of Thought* (New Haven, Conn.: Yale University Press, 1979). For later developments in the psychology of cognition, see also chaps. 3 and 4 of *The Sciences of the Artificial*, 3rd ed. (Cambridge: MIT Press, 1996).

(1) Whereas economic man supposedly maximizes—selects the best alternative from among all those available to him—his cousin, the administrator, satisfices—looks for a course of action that is satisfactory or "good enough." Examples of satisficing criteria, familiar enough to business people, if unfamiliar to most economists, are "share of market," "reasonable profit," "fair price."[25]

(2) Economic man purports to deal with the "real world" in all its complexity. The administrator recognizes that the perceived world is a drastically simplified model of the buzzing, blooming confusion that constitutes the real world. The administrator treats situations as only loosely connected with each other—most of the facts of the real world have no great relevance to any single situation and the most significant chains of causes and consequences are short and simple. One can leave out of account those aspects of reality—and that means *most* aspects—that appear irrelevant at a given time. Administrators (and everyone else, for that matter) take into account just a few of the factors of the situation regarded as most relevant and crucial. In particular, they deal with one or a few problems at a time, because the limits on attention simply don't permit everything to be attended to at once.

Because administrators satisfice rather than maximize, they can choose without first examining all possible behavior alternatives and without ascertaining that these *are* in fact all the alternatives. Because they treat the world as rather empty and ignore the interrelatedness of all things (so stupefying to thought and action), they can make their decisions with relatively simple rules of thumb that do not make impossible demands upon their capacity for thought. Simplification may lead to error, but there is no realistic alternative in the face of the limits on human knowledge and reasoning.

But how do we know that this is a *correct* description of administrative decision-making—more accurate, for example, than the model of economic man? The first test, and perhaps not the least important, is the test of common sense. It is not difficult to imagine the decision-making mechanisms that the administrator of bounded rationality would use. Our picture of decision-making fits pretty well our introspective knowledge of our own judgmental processes.

But the theory also passes a more severe test: It fits the mass of observations of human decision processes that have been made by the psychologists and researchers on organization and management who have

[25]See, for example, R. M. Cyert and J. G. March, "Organizational Factors in the Theory of Oligopoly," *Quarterly Journal of Economics*, 70:44–64 (Feb., 1956).

studied them. The past forty years have seen enormous progress in what has come to be called "information processing psychology." Human thought processes in difficult problem-solving, concept-attainment, and decision-making tasks have been described successfully in terms of basic symbol-manipulating processes. These explanations have been carried out in sufficient detail so that computer programs have been written to simulate the human behavior, and close matches have been obtained between the outputs of the computer programs and the thinking-aloud protocols of human subjects engaged in the same tasks.[26]

This is not the place to describe these developments in detail. What is important for our purposes is that the basic postulates about human rationality supported by these simulations of behavior are essentially the postulates of the satisficing decision-maker, described above. Nor have the tests of these new theories been limited to laboratory tasks. To cite a few examples, a careful analysis has been carried out, in information-processing terms, of how students completing a graduate program in business made their first job selections; programs have been written that are capable of making medical diagnoses and one of these is marketed commercially; a program simulates the processes an expert accountant uses to identify corporate problems by examination of financial records; the screening of applicants for credit has been simulated.[27] Other examples will be supplied later in this commentary.

In view of the large body of evidence that now supports the concepts of bounded rationality and satisficing, the description of human rationality in Chapters IV and V is no longer hypothetical but has been verified in its main features.

RELATION TO CURRENT DEVELOPMENTS IN FORMAL DECISION THEORY

It is interesting and even a bit ironical that at the very time when we have learned to build rather precise and empirically verified theories of

[26]See *The Sciences of the Artificial, op. cit.*, chaps. 3 and 4. A more complete account of the research on problem solving will be found in Allen Newell and Herbert A. Simon, *Human Problem Solving* (Englewood Cliffs, N.J.: Prentice-Hall, 1972). For some recent developments, see Allen Newell, *Unified Theories of Cognition* (Cambridge: Harvard University Press, 1990).

[27]The job choice study is described briefly in Peer Soelberg, "Unprogrammed Decision Making," in J. H. Turner, A. X. Filley, and Robert J. House, eds., *Studies in Managerial Process and Organizational Behavior* (Glenview, Ill.: Scott Foresman, 1972). Several empirical studies on organizational decision-making are included in R. Cyert and J. G. March, *A Behavioral Theory of the Form* (Englewood Cliffs, N.J.: Prentice-Hall, 1963). Philip Bromiley, in *Corporate Capital Investment: A Behavioral Approach* (Cambridge, Eng.: Cambridge University Press, 1986), reports a careful empirical study in four manufacturing concerns of the decision process for making new investments.

rational human decision-making there should be a vigorous renaissance of formal theorizing about economic man. The renaissance can be dated from the remarkable progress in game theory, owing initially to von Neumann and Morgenstern, on the one hand, and, on the other hand, the equally remarkable and closely related progress in statistical decision theory, owing to Neyman and Pearson, to Wald, and to Savage.[28]

The von Neumann and Morgenstern game theory involves at least five separate and distinct concepts, all of them important.

1. Representing possible future behavior as a "tree," with branches radiating from each choice point, so that the individual must select at each such point the appropriate branch to follow.
2. Taking the minimax (selecting the branch that will give the best result in the face of a competitive opponent) as the definition of rational choice in a competitive situation.
3. Using a mixed strategy (e.g., bluffing) in a competitive situation to prevent one's move from being anticipated by the opponent.
4. Defining rational choice in competitive situations with more than two players in terms of the possibilities of forming coalitions.
5. Assuming that, in the face of uncertainty, where only the probability distribution of outcomes is known, the decision-maker has a cardinal utility function and is choosing so as to maximize its expected value.

The theory of bounded rationality in *Administrative Behavior* incorporates item (1) of this list and is compatible with items (3) and (4), but the remaining items characterize economic man rather than the administrator and are not part of the model used here. This vital distinction has sometimes been overlooked by commentators, who have mistakenly supposed that the term "rational" in this book has essentially the same meaning as it has for classical economists, game theorists, and statistical decision theorists.

Closely related to game theory is the hypothesis in modern economics of *rational expectations*. The idea underlying rational expectations is that all decision-makers have accurate knowledge of the true equilibrium level of the economic system, that each decision-maker assumes that all the others have the same knowledge and beliefs based on it, and that all actors form expectations about the future and make decisions on the basis of this knowledge and these beliefs.

---

[28]On game theory, see J. von Neumann and O. Morgenstern, *Theory of Games and Economic Behavior* (Princeton: Princeton University Press, 1947). On statistical decision theory see L. J. Savage, *The Foundations of Statistics* (New York: Wiley, 1954). Developments in game theory in recent years are well covered in *The New Palgrave Dictionary of Economics*.

Neither game theory nor rational expectations take into account the severe limits of the decision-maker's actual knowledge and computational powers in the face of the real world. They lead in almost a diametrically opposite direction to that followed by a theory of bounded rationality.

COMPONENTS MISSING FROM THE CLASSICAL THEORY

Empirical study of decision-making quickly revealed that three basic components of the process were absent from the classical theory. One omission is the process of setting the agenda that determines what decisions will be made at what particular times. The second is the process of obtaining or constructing a representation for the problem selected for attention. The third is the set of processes that generate the alternative actions among which the decision-makers choose. These processes call for more elaboration than they receive in Chapter V.

Setting an Agenda

In the classical theory, it is supposed that the same set of decisions is made at each point in time. In that theory there is no such thing as an agenda, for there is no need to choose which specific decision problems will be dealt with. In the real world, the available attention must be directed to those matters on which timely action is required instead of those about which there is no urgency; there must be processes for setting and revising the agenda.

Simple Procedures for Setting Agendas. If two or more needs express themselves at the same time, organisms and organizations must decide which to put first on the agenda. These priorities are usually settled by simple rules: attend first to the need whose inventory of satisfiers is more nearly exhausted. Agendas are set very much in the manner of the familiar two-bin inventory systems of industrial practice. For each need or want there is an "order point" and an "order quantity." At some level of deprivation, signals sent to decision centers secure attention to the want unless more urgent signals are present. If the matter is not attended to immediately, the signals become gradually more insistent until the want gains first priority.

This system for fixing the agenda requires nothing like a comprehensive utility function. The urgency of needs is compared only to set search priorities. All that is required is a simple mechanism that will signal urgency and gradually increase the intensity of its signal. Nothing needs to be maximized. This crude procedure will work satisfactorily (not optimally) as long as there is time to carry out searches to meet wants before inventories are completely exhausted. With some slack available, searches can be interrupted in the face of more urgent demands.

A mere increase in the number of issues for decision does not complicate the agenda-setting task, provided that attention to all of them is not essential for survival. Those that are not urgent enough simply never get on the active agenda. (Most of us are familiar with this phenomenon in our personal lives.) Most potential agenda items are either problems or opportunities. Problems are items that, if not attended to, will cause trouble. Opportunities are items that, if attended to, may increase profit or probability of surviving.

Nor is there a definite list of opportunities, or even problems, among which the priorities are set. Neither problems nor opportunities can be considered for the agenda unless they are noticed, and except for those that attract attention by means of an internal signaling system, they must be picked out from a complex external sensory environment. Until they are noticed, opportunities are not opportunities. In the world in which we actually live, at any given time we notice only a tiny fraction of the opportunities that are objectively present, and only a small part of the problems. A major initial step—and by no means an assured one—in technological or social invention is to extract opportunities and problems from the confusion of the environment—to attend to the right cues.

How Opportunities Are Noticed. Today, we have the beginnings of a theory of how opportunities (or problems) are noticed. The greatest progress has been made in the domain of scientific discovery.[29] One of the mechanisms that focuses human attention on important problems is surprise. Alexander Fleming noticed a Petri dish in his laboratory in which the bacteria were disintegrating. He was surprised—there was no obvious reason why the bacteria should be dying. On the edge of the dish, near where the lysis was occurring, was a mold of the genus *Penicillium*.

What are the conditions for such a surprise? We are surprised when we are knowledgeable about a situation and something unusual (contrary to our knowledge) occurs. Fleming was knowledgeable about bacteria and molds, and nothing in his knowledge led him to expect that bacteria would die in the presence of a mold. Surprise put the problem (or opportunity) of explaining why the bacteria were dying on Fleming's research agenda; it would not have been noticed by anyone who lacked his knowledge. A great many opportunities, including many of the first order of magnitude, secure their place on the agenda through informed surprise.

We can generalize from the surprise mechanism to a more general

[29]See P. Langley et al., *Scientific Discovery* (Cambridge: The MIT Press, 1987).

theory of what it is that focuses human attention on specific parts of the environment. In the contemporary world all of us are surrounded by, even drowned in, a sea of information, only an infinitesimal part of which can be attended to. Although we may wish to have certain kinds of information that are not available (e.g., reliable forecasts), the critical scarce factor in decision-making is not information but attention. What we attend to, by plan or by chance, is a major determinant of our decisions.

Given the general scarcity of attention, people and organizations can enhance the quality of their decision-making by searching systematically, but selectively, among potential information sources to find those that deserve most careful attention, and that might provide items for the agenda. This is a major function of so-called "intelligence" units in organizations, and also of research and development units, and even planning units.

For example, a company laboratory is seldom the major source of basic discoveries from which new products can be developed. More often, the laboratory serves as an intelligence link to the community of academic and other science from which ideas may be drawn. Its task is to observe and communicate with that community, and to notice and develop further the opportunities that are presented by it. Of course, the experimental laboratory also has its window on the natural world, but that is a rather narrow window unless supplemented by close interaction with the scientific community.

A common responsibility of planning units, not always explicitly recognized in the definition of their function, is early recognition of problems. One mechanism for problem recognition is to build computational models of the system of interest and use them to make predictions. Selective surveillance of information available in the environment may provide an even more reliable early warning system than prediction.

Perhaps I have said enough to demonstrate that a theory of agenda formation—which is, in turn, a theory of attention focusing—is an essential part of a theory of rational decision. We can find ideas on this topic useful for decision-making in the literature of artificial intelligence and cognitive science—for example, recent research on the processes of scientific discovery.

Representing the Problem

The commentary on Chapter II noted that an organization's structure is itself a representation of the task the organization was designed to deal with. Representation also has significance at the level of decision-making. Whenever a new occasion for decision arises, a representation must be found for the decision problem.

Perhaps even less is known today about the mechanisms of problem formulation than about agenda-setting processes. Of course, if the item placed on the agenda by the attention-directing mechanisms is of a familiar kind, standard procedures will usually be available for casting it in a solvable form. If we can formulate a problem as an equation, then we know how to solve it.

Or, to return to items placed on the agenda by surprise, scientists have a rather standard procedure for exploiting surprises. In case of surprise, they first try to characterize the scope of the surprising phenomenon. If bacteria are dying in the presence of a mold, what kinds of bacteria are affected? (Fleming found that many kinds were.) What kinds of mold? (Evidently only the mold *Penicillium*.) And when the scope of the phenomenon has been defined, try to find its mechanism. (Can we extract from *Penicillium*, by crushing, treating with alcohol, heating, crystallizing, etc., a substance that retains, or even enhances, its effect upon bacteria? If we find such a substance, can we purify it and characterize it chemically? A whole sequence of experiments, first by Fleming, then by Howard Florey and Ernst Chain, achieved just this.)

Some problems are very hard as the world presents them, but very easy when they are reformulated properly. The Mutilated Checkerboard problem is a celebrated example. Consider a checkerboard (eight-by-eight) and 32 dominoes, each of which covers exactly two squares of the board. Clearly, we can entirely cover the checkerboard with the dominoes. Now suppose that two squares are cut out of the checkerboard— the upper left corner and the lower right corner. Can we cover the remaining 62 squares with 31 dominoes?

We cannot, but the answer is not obvious. None of us would have the patience to demonstrate the impossibility by trying all possible coverings; we must find some other way. Let us abstract the problem, considering just the number of dominoes, the number of black squares, and the number of red squares. Each domino will cover exactly one black and one red square. But the two squares we removed are of the same color (they are at opposites ends of a diagonal). Hence there will now be two fewer squares of one color than of the other (let's say 30 black and 32 red). But dominoes can cover only the same number of black and red squares, hence a covering is impossible.

Problem representations, like the problems themselves, are not presented to us automatically. They are either retrieved from memory, when we recognize a situation as being of a familiar kind, or discovered through selective search. Formulating a problem is itself a problem-solving task.

For example, American and European firms have been fully aware for some years now of the challenge presented by Japanese and other Far

Eastern competition. The problem is on the agenda, but finding an appropriate problem representation is difficult, and has not yet been fully achieved. Is the problem one of quality control, of manufacturing efficiency, of managerial style, of worker motivation, of wage levels, of exchange rates, of foreign trade regulations, of investment incentives? The list is endless; and different representations of the problem will produce different proposals for solution.

It is apparent that developing a veridical theory of problem representation must stand high on the agenda of decision-making research.

Discovering and Choosing Alternatives

One of the striking features of the theory of the rational economic man is that all of the alternatives among which he chooses are given at the outset. He lives in a static (imaginary) world that presents a fixed repertory of goods, processes, and actions of every sort. This classical view of rationality provides no explanation of where alternative courses of action originate; it simply presents them as a free gift to the decision-makers.

Yet, a very large part of the managerial effort in any organization is devoted to discovering possible alternatives of action. To take some obvious examples, there is search for new products, for new marketing methods, for new manufacturing methods, even for new organization structures. All of this search activity is aimed at enabling the organization to go beyond actions that are already known and understood and to choose novel ones.

Even Chapter V, which includes some discussion of alternative-finding under the heading of "The Planning Process," gives rather short shrift to the subject of generating alternatives, and we must count this as a serious shortcoming in our treatment of decision.

House-hunting and job-hunting are market activities that normally require extensive search among an ill-bounded set of alternatives. A graduating student, searching for a first job, must not only have procedures for discovering prospective employers, but stop rules for determining when the search should end, and procedures for obtaining relevant information about each employment opportunity. In just the same way, in organizations the alternatives for choice are not usually given but are generated through selective search.

Finding alternatives is sometimes a search of the sort just described for a house or a job. Here the alternatives already exist; they must simply be located. But in many cases, including perhaps the most important, the alternatives for which an organization is seeking do not exist but have to be created and designed. The task is not to search but to synthesize: to design. Many economic products are not manufactured for the open market or to be sold from the shelf, but are designed specially on contract with a particular customer. And shelf goods, too, initially have to be conceived and designed, a task that becomes central and continual in industries, like clothing or pharmaceuticals, where new products are constantly coming onto the market.

In recent years, research in cognitive science has taught us a great deal about the processes of design.[30] In any problem-solving process, we have a goal, or a set of goals, formulated as tests to be applied to prospective solutions. (A solution is something that satisfies these tests of goal satisfaction.) Design calls for a generator that produces prospective solutions. If it cannot simply produce items, one by one, for test and acceptance or rejection, it must synthesize prospective solutions in a series of steps, applying tests of progress along the way to direct the search. The more we know about the problem space in which we are searching (the problem representation), the more information we can extract from that space to direct the search, and the more efficient the exploration will be.

Stages in Decision-Making

The division of the decision-making process into such subprocesses as setting the agenda, representing the problem, finding alternatives, and selecting alternatives has sometimes been criticized as describing decision-making falsely as a "linear" process, and thereby rigidifying it.[31] Of course there is no implication in anything that we have said that these subprocesses must follow in a set order. Agenda-setting—and resetting—is a continual process, as is the search for new decision alternatives (e.g., new products), and the selection of alternatives as new occasions for decisions arise. An alternative discovered in one decision process may find its effective application at some much later time and in connection with a quite different decision.

Moreover, each of the subprocesses in decision-making itself poses a problem that may again require agenda setting, finding alternatives, selecting them, and evaluating them. This becomes clear when we automate decisions in computer programs and observe the complex hierarchy of goals and subgoals that emerges in the course of executing them. There is nothing "linear" about the decision process described here, nor any barrier to flexibility as new situations arise and new facts are discovered. All of this is pointed out, if briefly, in Chapter V.

[30]See *The Sciences of the Artificial, op. cit.,* chaps. 5 and 6.

[31]For a recent example of this misunderstanding, see Langley, Mintzberg, et al., "Opening up Decision Making: The View from the Black Stool," *Organization Science,* 6: 260–279 (1995), at p. 262.

Well-structured and Ill-structured Problems

The problem-solving we understand best concerns well-structured problems. Problems are well structured when the goal tests are clear and easily applied, and when there is a well-defined set of generators for synthesizing potential solutions. Problems are ill structured to the extent that they lack these characteristics. Many, if not most, of the problems that confront us in the everyday world are ill structured. An architect designing a house, an engineer designing a bridge or a power-generating station, a chemist seeking a molecule with desired properties and a way of manufacturing it cheaply, a manager judging whether a new factory should be built to meet increasing demand—all of these are solving problems with many ill-defined components.

To the best of our current knowledge, the underlying processes used to solve ill-defined problems are not different from those used to solve well-defined problems. Sometimes it is argued, to the contrary, that solving ill-defined problems involves processes that are "intuitive," "judgmental," or even "creative," and that such processes are fundamentally different from the run-of-the-mill, routine, logical, or analytical processes employed in well-structured problem-solving.

We can refute this argument empirically, because we have strong evidence today about the nature of intuitive, judgmental, and creative processes that shows how they are carried out. We know that experts in any domain have stored in their memories a very large number of pieces of knowledge about that domain. Where it has been possible to measure the knowledge, at least crudely, it appears that the expert may have 50,000 or even 200,000 "chunks" (familiar units) of information—but probably not 5,000,000.

This information is held in memory in a particular way: it is associated with an "index"—a network of tests that discriminate among different stimuli. When the expert is confronted with a situation in his or her domain, various features or cues in the situation will attract attention. A chess player, for example, will notice such familiar cues as an "open file," "doubled pawns," or a "pinned knight." Each familiar feature that is noticed gives access to the chunks of information stored in memory that are relevant to that cue. An accountant who sees a low cash balance on the balance sheet will be reminded of what he or she knows about cash flow and liquidity problems.

The ability, often noticed, of the expert to respond "intuitively," and often very rapidly, with a relatively high degree of accuracy and correctness, is simply the product of this stored knowledge and the problem-solving by recognition that it permits. Intuition, judgment, creativity are basically expressions of capabilities for recognition and response based upon experience and knowledge. There is nothing more mysterious about them than about our recognizing our friend "instantly" when we meet him on the street, and gaining access to all sorts of information we have about that friend. However, as the ideas of intuition, judgment, and creativity are widely believed to be beyond scientific explanation, we will take some pains in the next section of this commentary to say more about what is known about them.

As we shall see, we do not need to postulate two problem-solving styles, the analytic and the intuitive. The power of analysis depends on expert knowledge for its speed and effectiveness. Without knowledge that becomes available by recognition, only tiny, slow, painful steps can be taken in reasoning. We may see relative differences among experts in their reliance on analysis as against recognition (intuition), but we may expect to find large components of both, closely intermingled, in virtually all expert behavior.

THE ROLE OF INTUITION[32]

Objections are frequently raised to current decision-making theory on the grounds that almost exclusive attention is given to the systematic and "logical" aspects of the process without taking sufficient account of the large role that is played in these matters by human intuition and emotion. The dispute about "logical" versus "intuitive" decision-making goes back many years, antedating the first edition of *Administrative Behavior*. One of its starting points was a well-known essay by Chester Barnard on "Mind in Everyday Affairs," which was published in 1938 as an appendix to his *Functions of the Executive*. More recently, the supposed neglect of intuition in the "logical" approach attributed to the decision-making framework has been the object of strong criticism by, among other writers, Chris Argyris and Henry Mintzberg.[33]

Barnard's Thesis of Non-logical Decision Processes

The Barnard essay will provide a good starting point for our own discussion. Its central motif was a contrast between what Barnard called "logical" and "non-logical" processes for making decisions.

[32]This section draws heavily on H. A. Simon, "Making Management Decisions: the Role of Intuition and Emotion," *Academy of Management EXECUTIVE*, February 1987, pp. 57–64.

[33]As recent examples, see *Mintzberg on Management* (New York: The Free Press, 1989), especially chap. 4; and Langley, Mintzberg, et al., *op. cit.* I will have more to say about Argyris's position later. A reader who compares these critiques with the theories they are criticizing will quickly recognize the gross inaccuracies of their caricature. But when authors are misinterpreted, I suppose they must face the charge of unclear exposition.

By "logical processes" I mean conscious thinking which could be expressed in words or by other symbols, that is, reasoning. By "non-logical processes" I mean those not capable of being expressed in words or as reasoning, which are only made known by a judgment, decision or action.

Barnard's thesis is that executives, as contrasted, say, with scientists, do not often enjoy the luxury of making their decisions on the basis of orderly rational analysis, but depend largely on intuitive or judgmental responses to decision-demanding situations. No neglect of the non-logical or intuitive here! Although Barnard did not provide a set of formal criteria for distinguishing between logical and judgmental decision-making, he did provide a characterization of the two styles that makes them easily recognizable, at least in their more extreme forms. In "logical" decision-making, goals and alternatives are made explicit, the consequences of pursuing different alternatives are calculated, and these consequences are evaluated in terms of how close they are to the goals.

In "judgmental" decision-making, the response to the need for a decision is usually too rapid to permit an orderly sequential analysis of the situation, and the decision-maker cannot usually give a valid account of either the process by which the decision was reached or the grounds for judging it correct. Nevertheless, decision-makers may have great confidence in the correctness of their intuitive decisions and are likely to attribute their ability to make them rapidly to their experience.

Most executives probably find Barnard's account of their decision processes persuasive; it captures their own feelings of how the processes work. On the other hand, some students of management, especially those whose goal is to improve management decision processes, have felt less comfortable with it. It appears to vindicate snap judgments and to cast doubt on the relevance of management science tools, which almost all involve deliberation and calculation.

Barnard did not regard the non-logical processes of decision as magical in any sense. On the contrary, he felt they were mostly grounded in knowledge and experience:

> The sources of these non-logical processes lie in physiological conditions or factors, or in the physical and social environment, mostly impressed upon us unconsciously or without conscious effort on our part. They also consist of the mass of facts, patterns, concepts, techniques, abstractions, and generally what we call formal knowledge or beliefs, which are impressed upon our minds more or less by conscious effort and study. This second source of non-logical mental processes greatly increases with directed experience, study and education. (p. 302)

At the time I wrote *Administrative Behavior* (1941–42) I was troubled by Barnard's account of intuitive judgment (see footnote 10 of Chapter III), largely because he left no clues as to what subconscious processes go on while judgments are being made. Wholly persuaded, however, that a theory of decision-making had to give an account of both conscious and subconscious processes, I finessed the issue by assuming that both these processes were essentially the same: that they draw on factual premises and value premises, and operate on them to form conclusions that become the decisions.

Because I used logic (drawing conclusions from premises) as a central metaphor to describe the decision-making process, many readers of *Administrative Behavior* have concluded that the theory advanced here applies only to "logical" decision-making, and not to decisions that involve intuition and judgment. That was certainly not my intent. But now, the ambiguity can be resolved, because we have acquired a solid understanding of what the judgmental and intuitive processes are. I have already given a brief glimpse of them in the previous section of this commentary. I will take up the new evidence in a moment; but first, a word must be said about the "two brains" hypothesis, which argues that rational and intuitive processes are so different that they are carried out in distinct parts of the brain.

Split Brains and the Forms of Thought

Physiological research on "split brains"—brains in which the corpus callosum, which connects the two hemispheres of the cerebrum, has been severed—has provided encouragement to the idea of two qualitatively different kinds of decision-making—the analytical, corresponding to Barnard's "logical," and the intuitive or creative, corresponding to his "judgmental." The primary evidence for this dichotomy is that (in right-handed people) the right hemisphere plays a special role in the recognition of visual patterns, and the left hemisphere in analytical processes and the use of language. Other evidence in addition to the split-brain research also suggests similar hemispheric specialization. EEG techniques, for example, can be used to measure relative activity in different parts of the brain. For most right-handed subjects, when the brain is engaged in a task involving recognition of visual pattern, activity is stronger in the right than in the left hemisphere; with more analytical tasks, the pattern is reversed.[34] This

[34]For some experiments and a review of the evidence as applied to managements tasks, see R. H. Doktor, "Problem Solving Styles of Executives and Management Scientists," in A. Charnes, W. W. Cooper, and R. J. Neihaus, eds., *Management Science Approaches to Manpower: Planning and Organization Design* (Amsterdam: North-Holland, 1978); and R. H. Dokter and W. F. Hamilton, "Cognitive Style and the Acceptance of Management Science Recommendations," *Management Science*, 19: 884–894 (1973).

specialization is supported also by more recent evidence derived with the addition of CAT scans and MRI techniques.

The more romantic versions of the split-brain doctrine extrapolate this evidence into the two polar forms of thought labeled above as analytical and creative. The analytical left hemisphere, so this story goes, carries on the humdrum, practical, everyday work of the brain, while the creative right hemisphere is responsible for those flights of imagination that produce great music, literature, art, science, and great management. The evidence for this romantic extrapolation cannot be derived from the physiological research, which has demonstrated only some measure of specialization between the hemispheres—in particular that the right hemisphere plays a special role in recognizing visual patterns (but another part of the brain in recording their locations in the visual field).

The physiological evidence does not in any way imply that either hemisphere is capable of problem-solving, decision-making, or discovery independently of the other. The real evidence for two different forms of thought is essentially that on which Barnard relied: the observation that, in everyday affairs, men and women often make competent judgments or reach reasonable decisions rapidly—without any overt indication that they have engaged in systematic reasoning, and without their being able to report the thought processes that took them to their conclusions. There is also some evidence for the very plausible hypothesis that some people, when confronted with a particular problem, make major use of intuitive processes in solving it, while other people make relatively more use of analytical processes.

For our purposes, it is the differences in behavior, not the differences in the hemispheres, that are important. Reference to the two hemispheres is a diversion that can only impede our understanding of intuitive, "non-logical" thought. The important questions for us are "What is intuition?" and "How is it accomplished?" not "In which cubic centimeters of the brain tissue does it take place?"

New Evidence on the Processes of Intuition

We have already seen that in recent years a great deal has been learned about the processes human beings use to solve ill-structured problems, and even to create works of art and science. This knowledge has been gained in the psychological laboratory, by observing the behavior of people who are demonstrably creative in some realm of human endeavor, and by using computers to model human thought processes at expert levels. Using these materials, we can give a rather detailed account of the processes that underlie intuitive judgment, even though most of these processes are not within the conscious awareness of the person using them.

Cognitive science and artificial intelligence have devoted a great deal of attention to the nature of expert problem-solving and decision-making in professional-level tasks, in order to gain an understanding of the differences in behavior between experts and novices and to learn more about how novices can become experts. The goal of the cognitive science research has been to model the human processes; of the artificial intelligence research, to build "expert systems." Both lines of research have greatly deepened our understanding of expertise.[35]

Intuition in Chess-Playing. Chess may seem remote from management, but it is a game requiring a high level of intellect and careful thought, and grand masters are normally full-time professionals who have devoted many years to acquiring their mastery. Much research has been done to discover the basis for expertise in chess and the nature of the intuitive judgments that appear to play such an important part in the game.

Chess might also seem an unlikely domain in which to study intuition. Chess-playing is thought to involve a highly analytical approach, with players working out systematically the consequences of moves and countermoves, so that a single move may take as much as a half hour's thought, or more. But chess professionals can play simultaneous games, sometimes against as many as 50 opponents, and exhibit only a moderately lower level of skill than when playing under tournament conditions. In simultaneous play, the professional takes much less than a minute, often only a few seconds, for each move. There is no time for careful analysis.

When we ask the grand master how good moves can be found under these circumstances, we get the same answer that we get from other professionals when they are questioned about rapid decisions: It is done by "intuition," by applying professional "judgment" to the situation. A few seconds' glance at the position suggests a good move, although the player has no awareness of how the judgment was evoked. Even under tournament conditions, good moves usually come to a player's mind after only a few seconds' consideration of the board. The remainder of the analysis time is generally spent verifying that an apparently plausible move does not have a hidden weakness.

We encounter this same kind of behavior in other professional domains where intuitive judgments are usually subjected to tests of vari-

[35]For a survey of cognitive science research on problem-solving and decision-making, see *The Sciences of the Artificial, op. cit.*

ous kinds before they are actually implemented. The main exceptions are situations where the decision has to be made before a deadline or almost instantly. Of course we know that under these circumstances (as in professional chess when the allowed time is nearly exhausted), mistakes are sometimes made.

How do we account for the judgment or intuition that allows the chess grand master usually to find good moves in a few seconds? A good deal of the answer can be derived from an experiment that is easily repeated. If a grand master and a novice are shown, for five seconds, a position from an actual but unfamiliar chess game, and asked to reproduce the position, the grand master will usually do so with about 95 per cent accuracy (23 or 24 out of 25 pieces), while the novice will average about 25 per cent (5 or 6 pieces). Does this mean that chess expertise is based on superior visual imagery? No; because if we now present boards with the same pieces placed *at random*, the novice will still replace about 6 pieces, but the grand master only about 7. The difference lies not in imagery, but in the expert's knowledge. For the grand master, a position from a well-played game is not a clutter of 25 pieces, but an arrangement of a half dozen familiar patterns, recognizable old friends. On the random board there are no such patterns, only the 25 individual pieces in an unfamiliar arrangement.

The grand master's memory holds more than a set of patterns. Associated in memory with each pattern is information about its significance— what dangers it holds, what offensive or defensive moves it suggests. Recognizing the pattern brings to the grand master's mind at once moves that may be appropriate to the situation, and it is this recognition that enables the professional to play very strong chess at a rapid rate. Previous learning that has stored a large indexed chess encyclopedia in the expert's head makes this performance possible. This, then, is the secret of the grand master's intuition or judgment.

We mentioned earlier in this commentary the estimates that have been made of the number of familiar patterns in the expert's memory— estimates in the neighborhood of 50,000. The natural language vocabularies of college graduates have been estimated to be in the range of 50,000 to 200,000 words—nearly the same range. Recognizing a word accesses our memory's store of its meanings, in the same way that recognizing a chess pattern accesses knowledge of its chess significance.

Intuition in Computerized Expert Systems. A growing number of successful expert computer systems are capable of matching professional human performance in specific domains. These systems have stored in memory tens of thousand of *productions*. Productions are computer instructions that take the form of "if-then" pairs. The "if" is a set of conditions or patterns to be recognized; the "then" is a body of information associated with the "if" and evoked from memory whenever the pattern is recognized in the current situation.

In medical diagnosis, where there has been much study of both human intuition and expert systems, diagnosis systems like CADUCEUS and MYCIN consist of a large number of such if-then pairs, combined with an inference machine of modest powers. These systems are now capable of medical diagnosis at a good clinical level within their respective limited domains. Their recognition capabilities, the if-then pairs, account for their intuitive or judgmental ability; their inferencing processes account for their analytical ability.

Medical diagnosis is just one of a number of domains for which expert systems have been built. For many years, electric motors, generators, and transformers have been designed automatically by expert systems developed by large electrical manufacturers. These computer programs have taken over from professional engineers many standard and relatively routine design tasks. They imitate rather closely the rule-of-thumb procedures that human designers have used, the result of a large stock of theoretical and practical information about electrical machinery. Recognition plays a large role in these systems. For example, examination of the customer's specifications reminds the program of a particular class of devices, which is used as the basis for the design. Parameters for the design are then selected to meet the performance requirements of the device.

In chemistry, reaction paths for synthesizing organic molecules can be designed by expert systems. These chemical synthesis programs employ the same mixture of intuition and analysis that is used in the other expert systems, and by human experts as well. Other examples of expert systems can be cited, all of them exhibiting reasoning or analytic processes combined with processes for accessing knowledge banks with the help of recognition cues. This appears to be a universal scheme for the organization of expert systems—and of expert human problem-solving as well.

Notice that there is nothing "irrational" about intuitive or judgmental reasoning based on productions. The conditions in a production constitute a set of premises. Whenever these conditions are satisfied, the production draws the appropriate conclusion—it evokes from memory information implied by these conditions, or even initiates motor responses. A person learning to drive a car may notice a red light, be aware that a red light calls for a stop, and be aware that stopping requires applying the brakes. For an experienced driver, the sight of the red light simply evokes the application of brakes. How conscious the actor is of the process—or inversely, how automatic the response is—may differ, but the one response is not more "logical" than the other.

Intuition in Management. It seems important to present this evidence, much of it from professional domains remote from management, because the notion has such wide currency that "intuitive" judgment has quite different properties (mostly thought to be wholly unknown) from "logical" judgment. The evidence indicates strongly that the intuitive skills of managers depend on the same kinds of mechanisms as the intuitive skills of chess masters or physicians. It would be surprising if it were otherwise. The experienced manager, too, has in his or her memory a large amount of knowledge gained from training and experience, and organized in terms of recognizable chunks and associated information.

Marinus J. Bouwman, for example, has constructed a computer program capable of detecting company problems from an examination of accounting statements.[36] The program was modeled on detailed thinking-aloud protocols of experienced financial analysts interpreting such statements, and it captures the knowledge that enables analysts to spot problems intuitively, usually at a very rapid rate. When a comparison was made between the responses of the program and the responses of expert human financial analysts, a close match was usually found.

In another study, R. Bhaskar gathered thinking-aloud protocols from business school students and experienced businessmen, who were all asked to analyze a business policy case.[37] The final analyses produced by the students and the businessmen were quite similar. What discriminated most sharply between the novices and the experts was the time required to identify the key features of the case. This was done very rapidly, with the usual appearances of intuition, by the experts; it was done slowly, with much conscious and explicit analysis, by the novices.

Some Conclusions. The description, in detail, of the use of judgmental and analytical processes in expert problem-solving and decision-making deserves a high priority in the agenda of management research. However, on the basis of the research that has already been done, it appears exceedingly doubtful that there are two types of managers (at least, of good managers), one of whom relies almost exclusively on recognition (alias, intuition), the other on analytic techniques. More likely, there is a

[36]*Financial Diagnosis.* Doctoral dissertation, Graduate School of Industrial Administration, Carnegie Mellon University, 1978.

[37]*Problem Solving in Semantically Rich Domains.* Doctoral dissertation, Graduate School of Industrial Administration. Carnegie Mellon University, 1978.

continuum of decision-making styles involving an intimate combination of the two kinds of skill. We will likely also find that the nature of the problem to be solved will be a principal determinant of what mix will be most efficacious.

With our growing understanding of the organization of judgmental and intuitive processes, of the specific knowledge that is required to perform particular judgmental tasks, and of the cues that evoke such knowledge in situations in which it is relevant, we have a powerful new tool for improving expert judgment. We can specify the knowledge *and* the recognition capabilities that experts in a domain need to acquire, and use these specifications for designing appropriate learning procedures.

We can also, in more and more situations, design expert systems capable of automating the expertise, or alternatively, of providing the human decision-maker with an expert computerized consultant. Increasingly, we see decision aids for managers that are highly interactive, with both knowledge and analysis shared between the human and the automated components of the system. A vast research and development task of extracting and cataloging the knowledge and cues used by experts in different kinds of managerial tasks lies ahead. We have seen that in the area of management, the analysis of company financial statements is a domain where some progress has been made in constructing expert systems. The areas of corporate policy and strategy are excellent candidates for early development of such systems.

What about the other aspects of executive work—very central aspects—that involve managing people? What help can we expect in improving this crucial component of the management task? We will take up an important aspect of this question in the next section.

KNOWLEDGE AND BEHAVIOR

What managers know they should do, whether by analysis or intuition, is very often different from what they actually do. One common failing of managers, which all of us have observed (sometimes in ourselves), is the postponement of difficult decisions. What is it that makes decisions difficult and hence tends to cause postponement? Often, the problem is that all of the alternatives have undesired consequences. When people have to choose the lesser of two evils, they do not simply behave like Bayesian statisticians, weighing the bad against the worse in the light of their respective possibilities. Instead, they postpone the decision, searching for new alternatives that do not have negative outcomes. If such alternatives are not found, they are likely to continue to postpone choice. A choice between undesirables is not a choice but a dilemma, something to be avoided or evaded. "Disutility" minimization turns out not to be an acceptable answer.

In other cases, uncertainty is the cause for postponement of choice. Each choice may have a good outcome under one set of environmental contingencies, but a bad outcome under another. When this occurs, we also do not usually observe classically rational behavior; the situation is again treated as a dilemma. An alternative is sought that will have at least tolerable outcomes under all prospective conditions.

There is a third common reason for temporizing. The bad consequences that lead a manager to postpone a decision are often bad for other people. Managers sometimes have to dismiss employees or, even more frequently, have to speak to them about unsatisfactory work. Dealing with such matters face to face is stressful to many, perhaps most, executives. The stress is magnified if the employee is a close associate or friend. If the unpleasant task cannot be delegated, it may be postponed.

Finally, the manager who has made a mistake (as all of us do at one time or another) also finds himself or herself in a stressful situation. The matter must be dealt with sooner or later, but why not later instead of sooner? Moreover, when it is addressed, it can be approached in different ways. A manager may try to avoid blame: "It wasn't my fault!" A different path is to propose a remedy to the situation. I know of no systematic data on how often the one or the other course is taken, but most of us could probably agree that blame-avoiding behavior is far more common than problem-solving behavior after a serious error has been made.

The Consequences of Stress

What all of these unpleasant decision-making situations have in common is stress, a powerful emotional force that can divert behavior from the urgings of reason. They are examples of a much broader class of situations in which managers frequently behave in clearly nonproductive ways. Nonproductive responses are especially common when actions have to be made under time pressure. The need to allay feelings of guilt, anxiety, and embarrassment may lead to behavior that produces temporary personal comfort at the expense of bad long-run consequences for the organization.

Behavior of these kinds is "intuitive" in a very different sense from the intuitive action we discussed earlier. It is "intuitive" in the sense that it represents response without careful analysis and calculation. Lying, for example, is probably more often the result of panic than of Machiavellian scheming. The intuition of the emotion-driven manager is very different from the intuition of the expert whom we discussed earlier. The latter's behavior is the product of learning and experience, and is largely adaptive; the former's behavior is a response to more primitive urges and an emotion-narrowed span of attention, and is more often than not inappropriate. We must not confuse the "nonrational" decisions of the experts—the decisions that derive from expert intuition and judgment—with the irrational decisions that stressful emotions may produce.

I will not attempt to produce a comprehensive taxonomy of the pathologies of organizational decision-making. I have simply given some examples of the ways that stress interacts with cognition to elicit counterproductive behavior. Such responses can become so habitual for individuals or even for organizations that they represent a recognizable managerial "style." A bit more will be said about these matters in the commentary to the next chapter.

In conclusion, it is a fallacy to contrast "analytic" and "intuitive" styles of management. Intuition and judgment—at least good judgment—are simply analyses frozen into habit and into the capacity for rapid response through recognition of familiar kinds of situations. Every manager needs to be able to analyze problems systematically (and with the aid of the modern arsenal of analytical tools provided by management science and artificial intelligence). Every manager needs also to be able to respond to situations rapidly, a skill that requires the cultivation of intuition and judgment over many years of experience and training. The effective manager does not have the luxury of choosing between "analytic" and "intuitive" approaches to problems. Behaving like a manager means having command of the whole range of management skills and applying them whenever they become appropriate.

CHAPTER VI

The Equilibrium of the Organization

IN CHAPTER V SOME MECHANISMS WERE DESCRIBED that permit the behavior of the individual to be integrated with that of the rest of the organization of which he is a part. These mechanisms do not explain, however, why the individual is willing to participate in the organized group at all, and to submit his personal aims to the established organization objectives. An organization is, after all, a collection of people, and what the organization does is done by people. The activities of a group of people become organized only to the extent that they permit their decisions and their behavior to be influenced by their participation in the organization.

INDUCEMENTS

The clue to the participation of individuals in organization lies in the remarks made in Chapter I regarding the organized group as a system in equilibrium. Individuals are willing to accept organization membership when their activity in the organization contributes, directly or indirectly, to their own personal goals. The contribution is direct if the goals set for the organization have direct personal value for the individual—church membership is a typical example of this. The contribution is indirect if the organization offers personal rewards—monetary or other—to the individual in return for his willingness to contribute his activity to the organization. Employment in a business concern is a typical example of this. Sometimes these personal rewards are directly related to the size and growth of the organization—as in the case of the stockholders of a business; sometimes, not very directly—as in the case of most wage earners. The characteristics of these three bases for participation are sufficiently distinct to make it worth while to consider them separately: personal rewards deriving directly from the accomplishment of the organization objective; personal inducements offered by the organization and closely related to its size and growth; and personal rewards derived from inducements offered by the organization but unrelated to the organization size and growth. Organizations are ordinarily made up of three groups of individuals, in each of which one of these types of motivation prevails; and it is the presence of these three groups that gives administration its specific character.

The phrase "personal goals" which is used here should be understood in a broad sense. It is by no means restricted to egoistic goals, much less to economic goals. "World peace" or "aid to the starving Chinese" may be just as much a personal goal for a particular individual as another dollar in his pay envelope. The fact that economic incentives frequently predominate in business and governmental organizations should not obscure the importance of other types of inducements. Nor should intangible egoistic values, such as status, prestige, or enjoyment of organization associations, be forgotten.

In Chapter I it was explained that in business organizations the "customers" are a group that has, predominantly, the first type of motivation—direct interest in organization objectives; employees, the third type; and the entrepreneur the second type. This is true, of course, only to a very rough approximation, and the necessary qualifications will be set forth later in the chapter.

The members of an organization, then, contribute to the organization in return for inducements that the organization offers them. The contributions of one group are the source of the inducements that the organization offers others. If the sum of the contributions is sufficient, in quantity and kind, to supply the necessary quantity and kinds of inducements, the organization survives and grows; otherwise it shrinks and ultimately disappears unless an equilibrium is reached.[1]

TYPES OF ORGANIZATION PARTICIPANTS

Organization members may be classified in other ways than in terms of the inducements they receive for their participation. They may be classified in terms of the types of contributions they make to the organization: specific services (a supplier of material); money or other neutral services that may be employed as incentives (customers); and time and effort (employees).

Still a third method of classification would distinguish those who control the organization—that is, have a right to fix the terms on which the others will be permitted to participate in it—from the remaining participants. The various possible combinations of inducements, contributions, and control arrangements make for a considerable variety of organizational forms, and this variety must be taken into consideration in the succeeding discussion.

[1]This idea of an equilibrium is due to C. I. Barnard. See his *The Functions of the Executive* (Cambridge: Harvard University Press, 1938), pp. 56–59 and chaps. xi and xvi.

ORGANIZATION GOALS AS INDUCEMENTS

Most organizations are oriented around some goal or objective which provides the purpose toward which the organization decisions and activities are directed. If the goal is relatively tangible—e.g., making shoes—it is usually not too difficult to assess the contribution of specific activities toward it, and hence to evaluate their usefulness. If the goal is less tangible—like that of a religious organization—it becomes more debatable whether a particular activity contributes to the goal; and hence there may be considerable controversy, even among those who wish to work for the goal, as to how it is to be attained. Even where the goal is tangible there may be some activities whose relation to it is so indirect, though not necessarily any less substantial for that indirectness, that the problem of evaluation is difficult. It is much easier to budget, for example, for the production line than for the advertising department or for supervision.

It has been fashionable in the literature of business administration to debate whether "the" purpose of a business organization is service or profit. There really is no problem to debate about. Certain individuals, primarily the customers, contribute to the organization because of the service it provides; others, the entrepreneurs, because of the profits they may derive. When the system of organization behavior itself is examined, it is found that both service and profit aims influence decisions. It is for terminological convenience that the label of "organization objective" is here applied to the service aim.

Application to Specific Organization Types

In the case of the business organization the organization goal—the output of product—is a personal goal for individuals who are ordinarily not considered members of the organization, that is, the customers.[2] In return for this product the customers are willing to offer money, which provides a principal inducement for the employees and entrepreneurs to participate in the group. The relation of customers to the organization is distinguished not only by the type of inducement they receive, but also by the fact that it is based on a contract or bargain for a specific product without, ordinarily, any assumption of permanence or continuity in the relationship.

In the case of a government agency the organization goal is a personal

---

[2]Barnard, in *The Functions of the Executive,* was perhaps the first writer to insist that the customers must be considered as a part of the system of organization activity in any theory of administration. His views on this point have still apparently not gained wide acceptance among writers on administration. As pointed out earlier, the important question here is not how "organization membership" is to be defined but whether or not the behavior of customers is to be included in the analysis of the organization.

goal for the ultimate controlling body of the organization—the legislature—and for the citizen. The relationship here is in part the same as in a business organization, in that the legislators, viewed as "customers," furnish the agency with its funds. It is decidedly different in that, first, they retain final legal control over the organization, and second, their "personal" motivation is based, in turn, on their peculiar status as elected representatives. To examine the way in which legislators make value judgments in determining the policy of governmental agencies would lead away from the present study into a study of the whole legislative process.

In volunteer organizations the organization objective is ordinarily the direct inducement that secures the services of the organization members. The peculiar problems of administration in volunteer organizations derive from the facts that the contributions are often on a part-time basis, that the various participants may have conflicting interpretations of the organization objective, and that the organization objective may play such a modest role in the participant's system of values that it offers only a mild inducement for cooperation. In this respect, the volunteer shares many of the characteristics of the customer of a business organization, although the former contributes services to the organization instead of money.

Adaptation of the Organization Objective

The organization objective is by no means a static thing. In order to survive, the organization must have an objective that appeals to its customers,[3] so that they will make the contributions necessary to sustain it. Hence, organization objectives are constantly adapted to conform to the changing values of customers, or to secure new groups of customers in place of customers who have dropped away. The organization may also undertake special activities to induce acceptance of its objectives by customers—advertising, missionary work, and propaganda of all sorts.

Hence, although it is correct to say that organization behavior is oriented toward the organization objective, this is not the whole story; for the organization objective itself changes in response to the influence of those for whom the accomplishment of that objective secures personal values.

The modification of the organization objective usually represents a compromise of the interests of several groups of potential participants, in order to secure their joint cooperation where each group individually is unable to attain its own objectives unaided. Hence the organization objective will seldom coincide exactly with the personal objectives of

[3]The word "customer" is used in a generic sense here to refer to any individual—customer, legislator, or volunteer—for whom the organization objective has personal value.

even those participants whose interest in the organization lies in its attainment of its goal. The crucial issue for any such individual is whether the organization objective is sufficiently close to his personal goal to make him choose to participate in the group rather than try to attain his goal by himself or in some other group. As will be seen, this process of compromise takes place, whether the controlling group of the organization is itself directly interested in the organization objective, or whether the inducement it receives from the organization is of some other type.

Loyalty of Employees to Organization Objective

Although the organization objective is of greatest importance in relation to the behavior of those participants who have been called "customers," almost all the members of an organization become imbued, to a greater or lesser degree, with the organization aim, and are influenced by it in their behavior. This has already been pointed out in the case of volunteer organizations; it is also true, although to a lesser extent, of governmental agencies and commercial organizations. It is one component, and a very important one, of organizational loyalty. If the objective has any appearance of usefulness, the organization members, whose attention is continually directed to it by their everyday work, will acquire an appreciation of its importance and value (often an exaggerated appreciation), and the attainment of the value will come, to that extent, to have personal value for them. It will be seen later that, in addition to this loyalty to the organization objective, there may also develop in employees a very different loyalty—a loyalty to the organization itself and an interest in its survival and growth.

INCENTIVES FOR EMPLOYEE PARTICIPATION

To an employee of a non-volunteer organization the most obvious personal incentive that the organization offers is a salary or wage. It is a peculiar and important characteristic of his relation with the organization that, in return for this inducement, he offers the organization not a specific service but his undifferentiated time and effort. He places this time and effort at the disposal of those directing the organization, to be used as they see fit. Thus, both the customer relation (in the commercial organization) and the employee relation originate in contract, but in contracts of very different sorts. The employment contract results in the creation of a continuing authority relation between the organization and the employee.

How can this be? Why does the employee sign a blank check, so to speak, in entering upon his employment? First, from the viewpoint of the organization, nothing would be gained by offering an inducement to the employee unless the latter's behavior could be brought into the system of organization behavior through his acceptance of its authority. Second, from the viewpoint of the employee, the precise activities with which his time of employment is occupied may, within certain limits, be a matter of relative indifference to him. If the orders transmitted to him by the organization remain within these limits of acceptance, he will permit his behavior to be guided by them.

What determines the breadth of the area of acceptance within which the employee will accept the authority of the organization? It certainly depends on the nature and magnitude of the incentives the organization offers. In addition to the salary he receives, he may value the status and prestige that his position in the organization gives him, and he may value his relations with the working group of which he is part. In setting his task, the organization must take into consideration the effect that its orders may have upon the employee's realization of these values. If the employee values white-collar status, for example, he may be completely unwilling to accept assignments that deprive him of that status even when the work he is asked to perform is not inherently unpleasant or difficult.

There is great variation among individuals in the extent to which opportunities for promotion act as incentives for participation. Promotion is, of course, both an economic and a prestige incentive. Burleigh Gardner has pointed out the importance for administrative theory of the presence in organizations of certain highly "mobile" individuals, i.e. individuals who have a strong desire for advancement. It would be a mistake (which Gardner carefully avoids) to assume that these desires provide a strong incentive in all individuals.[4]

We find, then, that those participants in organization who are called its employees are offered a variety of material and nonmaterial incentives, generally not directly related to the attainment of the organization objective nor to the size and growth of the organization, in return for their willingness to accept organization decisions as the basis for their behavior during the time of their employment. The area within which organization authority will be accepted is not unlimited, and the boundaries will depend on the incentives that the organization is able to provide. In so far as these incentives are not directly dependent upon the organization objective, modification of that objective will not affect the willingness of employees to participate, and hence the latter group will exert little influence in the determination of the objectives.

---

[4]On this and other aspects of the problem of incentives see Burleigh B. Gardner, *Human Relations in Industry* (Chicago: Richard D. Irwin, 1945), particularly chaps. i and viii.

VALUES DERIVED FROM ORGANIZATION
SIZE AND GROWTH

The third type of incentive that induces individual participation in organization derives from the size and growth of the organization. These might be referred to as "conservation" values. Most prominent in the group for whom these values are important is the entrepreneur. It is true that the entrepreneur, to the extent that he is an "economic man," is interested in profits, and not in size and growth. In practice this objection is not serious: first because profits usually are, or are thought to be, closely related to size and growth; and secondly because most entrepreneurs are interested in nonmaterial values, such as prestige and power, as well as profit. This attachment to conservation objectives is even more characteristic of the professional managerial group who exercise the active control of most large business enterprises.

Conservation objectives may provide important values, also, for the other employees of the organization as well, particularly those who are mobile. An organization that is growing and prospering offers greater opportunities for prestige and advancement than one that is static or declining. Conservation values are not, therefore, completely independent in practice from values of the second type, though for purposes of analysis there is some advantage in considering them separately.

Interest in conservation of the organization provides the basis for an organizational loyalty distinct from that previously mentioned. The individual who is loyal to the *objectives* of the organization will resist modification of those objectives, and may even refuse to continue his participation if they are changed too radically. The individual who is loyal to the *organization* will support opportunistic changes in its objectives that are calculated to promote its survival and growth.

Loyalty to the organization itself is perhaps the type of loyalty most characteristic of commercial organizations, but both species prevail widely in both public and private administration, commercial and noncommercial. Some of the most striking manifestations of conflict between these two types of loyalty are to be found in religious and reform organizations, where there is often controversy as to the extent to which organization objectives shall be modified to insure survival. This was certainly one basis for the Stalinist-Trotskyist rivalry. As previously indicated, the motives of the opportunists in such a controversy may, of course, be tactical rather than egoistic. The opportunist, assessing unfavorably the chances of survival without adaptation, may prefer half a loaf to no bread, while the "idealist" may assess the chances of survival more optimistically, or may consider that the concession in objectives more than outweighs the improvement in survival chances. Both types of loyalty will be discussed more fully in a later chapter.

ORGANIZATION EQUILIBRIUM AND EFFICIENCY

The basic value criteria that will be employed in making decisions and choices among alternatives in an organization will be selected for the organization primarily by the controlling group—the group that has the power to set the terms of membership for all the participants. If the group that holds the legal control fails to exercise this power, then, of course, it will devolve on individuals further down the administrative hierarchy.

Whatever group exercises the power of determining the basic value criteria will attempt to secure through the organization its own personal values—whether these be identified with the organization objective, with the conservation objectives, with profits or what not. But their power of control does not in any sense imply that the control group exercises an unlimited option to direct the organization in any path it desires, for the power will continue to exist only so long as the controlling group is able to offer sufficient incentives to retain the contributions of the other participants to the organization. No matter what the personal objectives of the control group, their decisions will be heavily influenced by the fact that they can attain their objectives through the organization only if they can maintain a positive balance of contributions over inducements, or at least an equilibrium between the two.

For this reason the controlling group, regardless of its personal values, will be opportunistic—will appear to be motivated in large part at least by conservation objectives. It may be worth while to illustrate this more fully in the case of widely different organization types.

Equilibrium in Commercial Organizations

In business organizations, the control groups can ordinarily be expected to be oriented primarily toward profits and conservation.[5] They will attempt to maintain a favorable balance of incoming contributions over outgoing incentives in two ways: first by modifying the organization objective in response to customer demand; and second, by employing the resources, monetary contributions, and employees' time and effort in such a manner

---

[5]This may be less true in recent years than formerly, and less true in businesses "affected with a public interest" than in others. In some areas of enterprise, particularly the public utility field, a "trusteeship" concept has grown up that leads the active control group to identify itself—to what degree the writer is not prepared to estimate—with the organization objective.

as to attain a maximum of inducement to employees, and a maximum of attainment of organization objectives with these resources. A detailed examination of the way in which this is accomplished leads to the theory of what the economist calls "the economics of the firm." Such an examination cannot be undertaken here. One point does require notice, however: the second type of adjustment—that of using the given resources as effectively as possible in the light of the organization objective—makes efficiency a basic value criterion of administrative decision in such organizations.

It might be asked why most commercial organizations, if their basic adjustment is opportunistic, do tend usually to maintain fairly stable objectives. The answer to this is threefold. First, there are "sunk costs" which make immediate and rapid adjustment unprofitable even from the standpoint of conservation. Second, the organization acquires know-how in a particular field—really an intangible sunk cost, or more properly, "sunk asset." Third, the organization acquires goodwill, which is also a sunk asset that may not be readily transferable to another area of activity. Stated differently, a change in organization objectives ordinarily entails decreased efficiency in use of resources (sunk costs and know-how) and a loss of incentives otherwise available to maintain a favorable balance (goodwill).

Equilibrium in Governmental Agencies

In the governmental agency the "customer," i.e., the legislative body, is the ultimate controlling group. Since this group can contribute to the organization whatever funds are necessary to attain the organization objective, it is less obvious on casual examination that such an organization is a system in equilibrium. It may be expected, also, that opportunistic modification of the organization objective is less prominent in such organizations than in commercial organizations.

Closer examination tends to reduce the importance of these differences. First, the legislature and the electorate to which it is responsive have changing tastes and objectives. Second, the control of the legislative body over the public agency is usually of a relatively passive and general nature, and the real initiative for the formulation of objectives often—perhaps almost always—lies in the top administrative group. This group may be strongly imbued with the organization objectives, with conservation aims, or both, and, within the limits of its discretion, may play very much the same role as the management group in commercial organizations.

In any event, efficiency comes forth again as a basic criterion of decision in the public organization, since the controlling group will attempt to attain a maximum of organization objectives, however these be determined, with the resources at its disposal.

Equilibrium in Non-Profit Private Organizations

The non-profit organization (a professional association, or a private school, for example) is likely to differ from the ordinary business organization in several respects. For one thing, there is not a conflict—always possible in business organizations—between profit aims and the other types of objectives discussed. Moreover, the control group is likely to be identified closely with the organization objective, and hence opportunism, though an important element in the equilibrium of such orgnizations, is likely to be of the type previously described as "tactical." On the other hand, the criterion of efficiency will play the same role in these organizations as in the others that have been described.

Elements in Common

These illustrations will perhaps serve to suggest the wide variety of possible organization forms. The reader undoubtedly can suggest other forms from his own experience and is aware of the numerous modifications these forms can undergo, particularly with respect to the motivation of the control group.

The same analysis can be applied to *segments* of organizations, the departments, divisions, and sections of which they are built. The administrators directing these segments, within the limits of discretion permitted them, behave in a fashion quite comparable to the groups that control autonomous organizations.

These illustrations indicate that there are at least two elements common to all organizational forms. They all have some equilibrating mechanism or mechanisms; and in all of them efficiency is a basic criterion of administrative choice.

The Criterion of Efficiency

The criterion of efficiency is such an important element in organization decision-making that an entire chapter will be devoted to it. Before leaving the present discussion, however, it may be well to give the term a more precise definition. The criterion of efficiency demands that, of two alternatives having the same cost, that one be chosen which will lead to the greater attainment of the organization objectives; and that, of two alternatives leading to the same degree of attainment, that one be chosen which entails the lesser cost.

Where resources, objectives, and costs are all variable, organization decisions cannot be reached purely on the basis of considerations of efficiency. Where the amount of resources and the organization objectives are givens, outside the control of the administrator, efficiency becomes the controlling determinant of administrative choice.

CONCLUSION

The organization has been described in this chapter as a system in equilibrium, which receives contributions in the form of money or effort, and offers inducements in return for these contributions. These inducements include the organization goal itself, conservation and growth of the organization, and incentives unrelated to these two.

The organization equilibrium is maintained by the control group, whose personal values may be of various kinds, but who assume the responsibility of maintaining the life of the organization in order that they may attain these values.

The remaining chapters of this volume will contain a development of the topics introduced thus far. The authority relationship will be examined more closely, the concept of efficiency will be analyzed, a study will be made of organizational loyalties, and the mechanisms of organization influence over the individual will be discussed in some detail. With this material at hand, it will be possible to draw a comprehensive picture of the anatomy of organization and the processes of decision in administration.

THE EQUILIBRIUM OF THE ORGANIZATION

TWO MAIN TOPICS ARE DISCUSSED in this commentary: first, the distinctions among "motives," "goals," and "constraints," and their respective roles in the decision process; and second, the kinds of work environments organizations typically offer to their employees, and how work in an organization interacts with employees' personal motives and lives.

ON THE CONCEPT OF ORGANIZATION GOAL[6]

In Chapter VI, the survival and success of organizations was discussed in terms of *organizational* goals and two kinds of *personal* goals (obtaining rewards associated with organizational growth and success, and earning wages and other rewards not so associated). Viewed as forces motivating individuals to participate in the organization's activities, organizational goals (i.e., the production of goods and services) are of most direct interest to customers, the first category of personal goals to stockholders and top executives, and the second category to the other employees. Although this is a great simplification, it indicates roughly how organizations form a collaborative endeavor by drawing upon a great diversity of individual interests.

There is some ambiguity in this terminology, however. We call one set of goals (those of most direct interest to customers) "organizational," and the other two sets "personal." For clarity, we need, instead, to distinguish between (1) the motives for individuals' participation in an organization and (2) the goals and constraints that enter directly as premises into organizational decisions.[7] Chapter VI is addressed to the former, and says little about the latter. In this commentary, we will use the term

---

[6]These comments represent a substantial revision of my paper of this title, published in the *Administrative Science Quarterly*, 9: 1–22 (1964), and used with permission. I am grateful to Herbert Kaufman for helpful comments on the manuscript.

[7]The present discussion is generally compatible with, but not identical to, that of my colleagues, R. M. Cyert and J. G. March, who discuss organizational goals in chap. 3 of *A Behavioral Theory of the Firm* (Englewood Cliffs, N.J.: Prentice-Hall, 1963).

"motives" to refer to the aims of individuals (customers, employees, and owners) and the terms "goals" and "constraints" to refer to premises used in organizational decision processes.

On the basis of legal powers, we might suppose that the motives of owners and top managers would be the major determinants of the goals that enter into an organization's decisions. But we often observe that the goals that actually underlie the decisions do not coincide fully with these motives but have been modified by managers and employees at all echelons. Must we conclude, then, that it is the motives of the latter—of subordinate managers and employees—that govern organizational behavior? Presumably not, because the kinds of behavior taking place are not those we would expect if the managers and employees were consulting only their personal motives.

Multiple Criteria for Decisions

The first step toward clarification is to enforce the distinction just made between goals, on the one hand, and motives, on the other. By goals we mean value premises that can serve as inputs to decisions. By motives we mean the causes, whatever they are, that lead individuals to select some goals rather than others as premises for their decisions. As a starting point, we will examine how goals enter into a complex decision, ignoring for the moment the organizational setting.

An Example. In recent years we have learned to build formal operations research models for reaching "optimal" decisions. Our example employs a linear programming model to describe the decision situation. English translations are provided for the equations, so the example can be followed with or without attention to the algebra.[8]

The optimal diet problem is a typical linear programming problem. We are given a list of foods, and for each, its price, its calorie content, and its mineral and vitamin contents. Then we are given a set of nutritional requirements, which may include minimum daily intake of minerals, vitamins, and calories, and may also limit maximum intake of some or all of these. The diet problem is to find the sublist of foods and their quantities that will meet the nutritional requirements at the least cost. The problem can be formalized as follows:

Let the various foods be numbered from 1 through N, and the vari-

[8]There are a substantial number of elementary discussions of linear programming in the management science literature. For a treatment that develops the point of view proposed here, see A. Charnes and W. W. Cooper, *Management Models and Industrial Applications of Linear Programming* (New York: Wiley, 1961), chap. 1. See also Charnes and Cooper, "Deterministic Equivalents for Optimizing and Satisfying Under Chance Constraints," *Operations Research*, 11:18–39 (1963).

ous nutritional components from 1 through M. Let x_i be the quantity of the ith food in the diet, y_j be the total quantity of the jth nutritional component in the diet, and p_i the price of the ith food. Let a_{ij} be the amount of the jth nutritional component in a unit quantity of the ith food; let b_j be the minimum requirement of the jth nutritional component, and c_j the maximum allowance. (Some of the b_j's may be zero, and some of the c_j's infinite.) Then:

$$\sum_i a_{ij} x_i = y_j, \text{ for } j = 1, \ldots, M; \tag{1}$$

that is, the total consumption of the jth nutritional element is the sum of the quantities of that element for each of the foods consumed. The nutritional requirements can be stated:

$$c_j \geq y_j \geq b_j, \text{ for } j = 1, \ldots, M; \tag{2}$$

that is, the total quantity of the jth element must lie between b_j and c_j. The quantity of each food consumed must be non-negative, although it may be zero:

$$x_i \geq 0, i = 1, \ldots, N. \tag{3}$$

Finally, the total cost of the diet is to be minimized; we are to find:

$$\operatorname*{Min}_x \sum_i x_i p_i. \tag{4}$$

A diet (the solution is not necessarily unique) that satisfies all the relations (2), (3), (4) is called an optimal diet. A diet that satisfies the inequalities (2) and (3) (called constraints), but that is not necessarily a minimum cost diet, is called a feasible diet.

What is the goal of the diet decision? We might say that the goal is to minimize the cost of an adequate diet, for we are minimizing the condition (4). This criterion puts the emphasis on economy as the goal. Alternatively, directing our attention primarily to the nutritional requirements (2), we might say that the goal is to find a nutritionally satisfactory diet that is economical. Although we still mention costs, the primary goal has now become good nutrition.

The relation between the criterion function (4) and the constraints (2) can be made even more symmetrical. Let us replace (4) with a new constraint:

$$\sum_i x_i p_i \leq k. \tag{5}$$

That is to say, the total cost of the diet must not exceed some constant, k. Now the set of feasible diets has been restricted to those that satisfy (5) as well as (2) and (3). But since the minimization condition has been removed, there is apparently no basis for choosing one of these diets over another.

Under some circumstances, we can, however, restrict the set of acceptable diets to a subset of the feasible set. Suppose that all the nutritional constraints (2) are minimal constraints, and that we would always prefer, *ceteris paribus*, a greater amount of any nutritional factor to a smaller amount. We will say that diet A is dominated by diet B if diet B costs no more than diet A, and if diet B contains at least as much of each nutrient as does diet A, and more of at least one. Economists call the set of diets in the feasible set that is undominated by other diets in that set the Pareto optimal set.

Our preference for one or the other of the diets in the Pareto optimal set will depend on the relative importance we assign to cost in comparison with nutrients, and to the relative amounts of these nutrients. If cost is the most important factor, then we will again choose the diet that is selected by criterion (4). On the other hand, if we attach great importance to nutrient j, we will generally choose a quite different feasible diet—one in which the quantity of j is as great as possible. Within the limits set by the constraints, it would be quite reasonable to regard as our goal whatever criterion led us to select a particular member of the Pareto optimal set.

But if the constraints are strong enough, so that the feasible set and, *a fortiori*, the Pareto optimal set is very small, then the constraints will have as much or more influence on what diet we finally select than will the cost minimization goal. For example, if we set one or more of the nutritional requirements very high, so that only a narrow range of diets also satisfy the budget constraint (5), then introducing cost minimization as the final selection rule will have relatively little effect on what diet we choose.

Under such circumstances it might be well to give up the idea that the decision situation can be described in terms of a single goal. Instead, it would be more reasonable to speak of a whole set of goals: the whole set of nutritional and budgetary constraints that the decision-maker is trying to attain. To paraphrase a familiar epigram: "If you let me determine the constraints, I don't care who selects the optimization criterion."

Multiple Criteria in Organizations. To see the organizational relevance of our example, suppose that the occasion for decision has arisen within a business firm that manufactures commercial stock feeds, that the nutrients are requirements for hogs and the prices those of available feed ingredients, and that the finished feed prices facing the firm are fixed. Then minimizing the cost of feed meeting certain nutritional standards is identical with maximizing the profit from selling feed meeting those standards. Cost minimization represents the profit-maximizing goal of the company.

We can equally well say that the goal of the feed company is to provide its customers with the best feed possible, in terms of nutrition, at a given price. Presumably this is what industry spokesmen mean when they say that the goal of business is not profit but efficient production of goods and services. If we had enlarged our model to convert some of the prices to constraints, instead of fixing them as constants, we could have introduced other goals, for example, the goal of suppliers' profits, or, if there were a labor input, the goal of high wages.[9]

Summarizing the discussion to this point: In the decision-making situations of real life, a course of action, to be acceptable, must satisfy a whole set of requirements, or constraints. Sometimes one of these requirements is singled out and referred to as the goal of the action. But the choice of one constraint from many is to a large extent arbitrary. For many purposes it is more meaningful to refer to the whole set of requirements as the (complex) goal of the action. This conclusion applies both to individual and organizational decision-making.

Search for a Course of Action

In Chapter V, we saw that in most real-life situations, possible courses of action must be discovered, designed, or synthesized. In searching for a satisfactory solution, the goals—that is, the constraints—may play a guiding role in two ways. First, they may be used to synthesize proposed solutions (*alternative generation*). Second, they may be used to test the satisfactoriness of a proposed solution (*alternative testing*). The former set of constraints will generally appear to us the more goal-like.[10]

A bank officer who is investing trust funds in stocks and bonds may, because of the terms of the trust document, take as the goal increasing the capital value of the fund, and thereby consider buying common stock in firms in growth industries (alternative generation). But the trust officer will check each possible purchase against other requirements: that the firm's financial structure be sound, its past earnings record satisfactory, and so on (alternative testing). All these considerations can be

[9]See "A Comparison of Organization Theories," in my *Models of Man* (New York: Wiley, 1957), pp. 170–182.

[10]For further discussion of the role of generators and tests in decision-making and problem-solving, see A. Newell and H. A. Simon, "The Processes of Creative Thinking," in H. E. Gruber, G. Terrell, and M. Wertheimer, eds., *Contemporary Approaches to Creative Thinking* (New York: Atherton, 1962), particularly pp. 77–91.

counted among the goals in constructing the portfolio, but some of the goals serve as generators of possible portfolios, others as checks.[11]

Designing courses of action introduces an important asymmetry between the "goal-like" constraints that guide synthesis and the constraints that test potential solutions. In general, the search will continue until one decision in the feasible set is found, or, at most, a very few alternatives. Which member of the set is discovered and selected may depend critically on the order of search, that is, on which requirements serve as generators and which as tests.

In a multiperson situation, one person's goals may be another's constraints. The feed manufacturer may seek to produce feed as cheaply as possible, searching, for example, for possible new ingredients. The feed, however, has to meet certain nutritional specifications. The hog farmer may seek the best quality of feed, searching, for example, for new manufacturers. The feed, however, cannot cost more than available funds allow; if it is too expensive, quality or quantity must be cut. A sale will be made when a lot of feed meets the requirements of both manufacturer and farmer.

Do manufacturer and farmer have the same goals? In one sense, clearly not. The farmer wishes to buy cheap, the manufacturer to sell dear. But if a bargain can be struck that meets the requirements of both, then, in another sense they do have a common goal. In the limiting case of perfect competition, the constraints narrow down the feasible set to a single point, determining uniquely the quantity of goods they will exchange and the price.

The neatness and definiteness of the limiting case of perfect competition should not blind us to the fact that most real-life situations do not fit this case at all closely. Typically, generating alternatives (e.g., inventing, developing, and designing products) is a laborious, costly process. Typically, also, there is a practically unlimited sea of potential alternatives. A river valley development plan that aims at the generation of electric power, subject to appropriate provision for irrigation, flood control, and recreation, will look quite different from a plan that aims at flood control, subject to appropriate provision for the other goals mentioned. Even though the plans generated in both cases will be examined for their suitability along all the dimensions, quite different plans will almost certainly be devised and proposed for consideration in the two cases, and the plans finally selected will represent quite distinct points in the feasible set.

Later, we will state why the total sets of constraints considered by decision-makers in different parts of an organization are likely to be similar, although different decision-makers are likely to divide the constraints between generators and tests in quite different ways. Under these circum-

---

[11]G. P. E. Clarkson, "A Model of Trust Investment Behavior," in Cyert and March, *op. cit.*

stances, if we use "organization goals" broadly to denote the constraint sets, we will conclude that organizations do, indeed, have goals (widely shared constraint sets). If we use the phrase narrowly to denote the generators, we will conclude that there is little communality of goals among the several parts of large organizations and that subgoal formation and goal conflict are prominent and significant features of organizational life. It is important always to make explicit which sense of goal is intended.

Motivation for Achieving Goals

As motivation means whatever it is that causes someone to follow a particular course of action, every action is motivated. But the relation between motives and action is not usually simple; it is mediated by a whole chain of events and surrounding conditions. If asked about goals, the investment trust officer whose behavior we considered earlier could answer: "I am trying to select a stock for this investment portfolio." "I am assembling a portfolio that will provide retirement income for my client." "I am employed as an investment trust officer." Now it is the step of indirectness between the second and third answers that has special interest for organization theory. The investment trust officer presumably has no "personal" interest in the retirement income of the client, only a "professional" interest in his or her role as trust officer and bank employee. The trust officer does have, on the other hand, a personal interest in maintaining that role and employment status.

Role Behavior. In real life the line of demarcation between personal and professional interests is not sharp, for personal satisfactions may arise from performing a professional role competently, and both satisfactions and dissatisfactions may result from innumerable conditions that surround the employment. Nevertheless, it is important to distinguish between the answers to two questions of motive: "Why do you keep (or take) this job?" and "Why do you make this particular investment decision?" The first question addresses the personal motives of the occupant of the role, the second question, the goals that define behavior appropriate to the role.

Corresponding to this separation of personal motives from goals defined by a role, organization theory is sometimes divided into two subparts: (1) a theory explaining the decisions of people to participate in and remain in organizations; and (2) a theory of decision-making within organizations comprised of such people.[12] Chapter VI deals with the first

[12]For further discussion and references, see J. G. March and H. A. Simon, *Organizations* (Cambridge: Blackwell, 2nd ed., 1993), chap. 4.

subpart: the inducements and contributions of organization members, and their effects on organizational equilibrium.

In separating organizational role-enacting behavior from personal motivation, we are abstracting from the complexities of real life. A good deal of the significant research on human relations and informal organization, which has contributed heavily to our understanding of organizational behavior, has been concerned specifically with the phenomena that this abstraction excludes. Desire for power and concern for personal advancement mingle personal goals with organizational role, as do the social and craft satisfactions and dissatisfactions associated with work.

However, this abstraction is often useful. First, many organizational decisions hardly affect personal motives at all. As a trivial example, the secretary's inducement-contribution balance is generally unaffected by the choice between typing a letter to A or a letter to B or by the content of the letter. Second, personal motives may enter the decision process as fixed constraints (only courses of action that satisfy the constraints are considered, but the constraints have no influence on the choice of action within the set). Thus, the terms of the employment contract may limit work to a forty-hour week but may have little to say about what goes on during the forty hours.[13]

The (partial) separation of organizational role from personal goals is consonant with human bounded rationality. Of all the knowledge, attitudes, and values stored in a human memory, only a very small fraction are evoked in any given situation. Thus, an individual can assume a variety of roles when these are evoked by appropriate circumstances, each of which may interact only weakly with the others. At one time a person may be a father, at another a machinist, at another a bridge player. The day-to-day organizational environment evokes from memory quite different associations from those evoked when one is considering a change of jobs. To the extent this is so, one's "personal" system of inducements and contributions will not affect one's "organizational" decisions.

The ability of an individual to shift from one role to another as a function of the environment thus helps to explain the extent to which organizational goals become internalized, that is, are automatically evoked and applied during performance of the role. No matter how one was originally motivated to adopt the role, the goals and constraints appropriate to it become a part of the decision-making program, stored in memory, that defines one's role behavior.

Interpersonal Differences. Differences among individuals can, however, affect substantially their behavior in roles that are identical from an orga-

---

[13] See "A Formal Theory of the Employment Relation," in *Models of Man, op. cit.*

nizational standpoint. A role is not a specific, stereotyped set of behaviors but a process for determining courses of action. While we may conceive of an ideal type of role having only organizational goals among its premises, actual roles in organizations invariably incorporate both organizational and personal goals.

Interpersonal differences in role behavior go far beyond differences in personal goals; they arise also from differences in knowledge. Thus, particular professional training provides an individual with specific techniques and knowledge for solving problems (accounting techniques, legal techniques, and so on), which are then drawn upon as part of the program evoked by the role. A chief executive with an accounting background may find different problem solutions from a chief executive, in the same position, with a legal background. An individual may incorporate in the role not only a professional style but also a personal style, bringing to the role habits and beliefs that provide crucial premises for handling interpersonal relations. An authoritarian personality will behave quite differently from a more permissive person when both are in the same organizational role and pursuing the same organizational goals.

The leeway for expressing individual differences is commonly narrowest in handling matters that come to the role occupant at the initiative of others and broadest in exercising initiative and in selecting the agenda of discretionary matters. Premises supplied by the organization generally control alternative selection more closely than alternative generation.

The Organizational Decision-Making System

What are the implications of factoring behavior into its personal and organizational components? It permits us to assemble the decision-making programs of all the participants, together with the connecting flow of communication, into a composite description of the organizational decision-making system. In the simplest case, of a small, relatively unspecialized organization, we are back to something like the optimal diet problem. The language of "goals," "requirements," "constraints" that we applied there is equally applicable to simple organizational situations. In more complicated cases, abstracting out personal motives does not remove inter-role differences from the decision-making process. For when many persons in specialized roles participate in making an organization's decisions, individuals will differ in the communications they receive and the parts of the environment from which they receive them. They will differ in their search programs. Hence, even if we neglect personal motives, we find many causes for differential perception and subgoal formation. (See Chapter X and its commentary, below.)

Consider, for example, a system for controlling factory inventory and production. Decisions have to be made about (1) the aggregate rate of production (the work force and the hours employees will work), (2) the allocation of aggregate production among products, and (3) scheduling the sequence in which the individual products will be processed by the machines: the aggregate production decision, item allocation decision, and scheduling decision, respectively. The three sets of decisions may be made by different roles in the organization; in general, we would expect the aggregate decision to be handled at more central levels than the others. The real-world situation will always include additional complications, for it will involve decisions about shipments to warehouses, about warehouse inventories, and many others.

Now we could conceive of an omniscient Planner (the entrepreneur of classical economic theory) who, by solving a set of simultaneous equations, would make each and all of these interrelated decisions. But we now know a great deal about the mathematical structure of the problem, and we know in particular that discovering the optimal solution of a complete problem of this kind is well beyond the powers of existing or prospective computational equipment. In actual practice, no one tries to find an optimal solution for the whole problem. Instead, various particular decisions are made by particular units of the organization. In making their decisions, the specialized units find a "satisfactory" solution for one or more subproblems, where some of the effects of the solution on other parts of the system are incorporated, as constraints, in the definition of "satisfactory."

For example, standard costs may be set as constraints for a manufacturing executive. Finding that operations are not meeting those constraints, the executive will search for ways of lowering costs. Longer production runs may be proposed, but these can be achieved only if the variety of products is reduced, so product standardization may be proposed as a solution to the cost problem. Presumably, before implementing the solution it will be tested against constraints introduced by the sales department— objections that refusal to meet special requirements of customers will lose sales.

Anyone familiar with organizational life can multiply examples of this sort, where different problems come to attention in different parts of the organization, or where different solutions are generated for a problem, depending on where it arises in the organization. We do not have to postulate conflict in personal goals or motivations in order to explain organizational conflicts or discrepancies. They could and would equally well arise if each of the organizational decision-making roles were being enacted by computers, in a total absence of the usual sorts of personal limits on acceptance. The discrepancies arise out of the cognitive inability of the decision-making to deal with the entire problem as a set of simultaneous relations.[14]

In virtually all organizations, the kinds of aggregative decisions that are made at high levels of the organization are separated from the kinds of specific, item-by-item decisions that are made at low levels. When executives at high levels make decisions about total inventory, this factorization already involves radical simplification and approximation. For example, there is no single, well-defined total cost associated with a given aggregate of inventories. Different costs will be associated with each kind of item (for example, different items may have different spoilage rates or obsolescence rates), and different probabilities and costs will be associated with stock-outs of each kind of item. Thus, an aggregate inventory will have different costs depending on its composition.

Designing a system for making decisions about the aggregate work force, production rate, and inventories requires an assumption that the total inventory will never depart very far from a typical product mix. The assumption required for aggregation is like that made for measuring the temperature of a tank of water with a single thermometer: it works if you stir well.

If decisions are made on this approximate basis about aggregate work force, production rate, and inventories, then these decisions can serve as constraints on detailed decisions made elsewhere about the inventory or production of particular items. If the decision has been reached to make one million gallons of paint next month, then other decisions can determine how much paint of each kind to make, subject to the constraint that the individual items should add up to one million gallons.[15]

This simple example suggests how the whole mass of decisions that are continually being made in a complex organization can be viewed as an organized system. Particular decision-making processes aim at finding courses of action that are feasible or satisfactory in the light of multiple goals and constraints; and decisions reached in any one part of the organization enter as goals or constraints for the decisions being made in other parts. In this loosely coupled system, there is no guarantee that the decisions will be optimal with respect to any specific goal. Nevertheless,

---

[14]For some empirical evidence, see the section on "Evidence for Cognitive Mechanisms in Identification" in the commentary to chap. x, below.

[15]A system of this kind is developed in detail in "Determining Production Quantities under Aggregate Constraints," in C. Holt, F. Modigliani, J. Muth, and H. A. Simon, *Planning Production, Inventories, and Work Force* (Englewood Cliffs, N.J.: Prentice-Hall, 1960). Compare the discussion of composite decision in chap. xi, below.

the results of the overall system can be measured against organizational goals, and changes can be made in the decision-making structure when these results are adjudged unsatisfactory.

The decision-making structure in an actual organization is usually put together in such a way that the decisions made by specialized units will take cognizance of the more general goals. Individual units are linked to the total system by production schedules, systems of rewards and penalties based on cost and profit goals, inventory limits, and so on. The loose coupling among the parts permits specific constraints in great variety to be imposed on subsystems without rendering their decision-making mechanisms complex beyond practicality.

Inducements and Contributions, and Organizational Behavior

We have seen that the system of personal inducements and contributions imposes constraints that the organization must satisfy if it is to retain its members and survive; while the constraints incorporated in the organizational decision-making system are imposed in the course of conceiving and adopting actions. There is no necessary logical connection between these two sets of constraints. After all, organizations sometimes fail to survive, and their demise can often be attributed to failure to incorporate all the important motivational concerns of participants among the constraints in the organizational decision-making system.

For example, a major cause of small business failure is working capital shortage, a result of failure to constrain actions to those that are consistent with creditors' demands for prompt payment. Similarly, new products often fail because incorrect assumptions about the inducements important to consumers shaped the constraints that guided product design. (Some of the major troubles of the Chrysler Corporation in the post–World War II period stemmed from the design premise that car purchasers were primarily interested in buying a good piece of machinery.)

In general, however, there is a strong empirical connection between the two sets of constraints, for the organizations we usually observe— those that have survived for some time—are precisely those that have developed organizational decision-making systems whose constraints guarantee that their actions maintain a favorable balance of inducements to contributions for their participants.[16] Thus, the functional requisites for survival can usually give us good clues for predicting organizational

---

[16]The relation between the functional requisites for survival and the actual constraints of the operating system is a central concept in W. R. Ashby's notion of a multi-stable system. See his *Design for a Brain* (New York: Wiley, 2nd ed., 1960).

goals; however, concordance is empirical, not definitional. The goals must be inferred from observation of the organization's decision-making processes, whether these processes be directed toward survival or suicide.

Conclusions

We can now summarize what is meant by "organizational goal." First, decisions are seldom directed toward a single goal; rather, decisions are concerned with discovering courses of action that satisfy a whole set of constraints. It is this set, and not any one of its members, that is most accurately viewed as the goal of the action. Sometimes we select a constraint for special attention because of its relation to the motivations of the decision-maker, or because of its relation to the search process that is generating or designing particular courses of action.

When we come to organizational decisions, many of the constraints that define a satisfactory course of action are associated with an organizational role and hence only indirectly with the personal motives of the individual who assumes that role. We may use the phrase "organization goal" for sets of constraints imposed by the organizational role, which has only this indirect relation to personal motives. As an organizational decision-making system generally contains constraints that reflect virtually all the inducements and contributions important to various classes of participants, courses of action that are inimical to survival tend to be removed from consideration.

In view of the hierarchical structure of most formal organizations, we usually employ "organizational goal" to refer particularly to the constraints and criteria of search that define roles at the upper levels. Thus we speak of conservation of forest resources as a principal goal of the U.S. Forest Service, or reducing fire losses as a principal goal of a city fire department. For high-level executives in these organizations will seek out and support actions that advance these goals, and subordinate employees will tailor their choices to constraints established by the higher echelons with these ends in view.

Finally, as there are large elements of decentralization in the decision-making in any large organization, different constraints may define the decision problems of different positions or specialized units. For example, "profit" may not enter directly into the decision-making of most members of a business organization. This does not mean that it is meaningless to regard profit as a principal goal of the business. It simply means that the decision-making mechanism is loosely coupled, so that the profit constraint enters into most subsystems only in indirect ways. Most business firms are directed toward profit making, subject to side constraints that introduce many gross approximations into the search for profitable courses of action. Furthermore, the goal ascription does not imply that any employee is motivated by the firm's profit goal, although some may be.

This view of the nature of organization goals leaves us with a picture of decision-making that is not simple. But it provides us with an operational way of showing, by describing the structure of the organizational decision-making mechanism, how and to what extent overall goals, like "profit" or "conserving forest resources," help to determine the actual courses of action that are chosen.

THE ORGANIZATION AS WORKPLACE: SATISFACTION[17]

The central thesis of Chapter VI is that the survival and success of organizations depend on their providing sufficient incentives to their members to secure the contributions that are needed to carry out the organizations' tasks. Monetary rewards are, of course, important; but willingness to do the work and the enthusiasm with which work is done may depend very much on how pleasant or unpleasant workers find the job and its physical and social environments.

Many cultures, including our own, cherish a myth of an earlier Golden Age, in which life was delightful and men and women were happy. During the eighteenth century, the Age of Reason, such myths flourished. "Man," said Jean Jacques Rousseau, "was born free, but everywhere he is in chains." The ideal of a Golden Age has not died. In our own day, we cast nostalgic eyes on the past, imagining that we see there simpler and happier times that have been taken from us by the complexities and confusions of our present industrial society.

This section of the commentary will examine some of our present discontents that center on the workplace, to assess their severity and to ask how far they differ from the discontents of the past. Are our modern factory, office, and shop fit places for human beings to work in and live out their days? In particular, are the changes taking place in the workplace—changes resulting from the continuing advance of technology, or from rising levels of education in our society, or from our responses to resource scarcities and environmental pollution—are these changes improving the quality of life in the workplace, or causing it to deteriorate?

Of course the conditions of some people may have improved, of others deteriorated. We may have something different to say about the life of

[17]This section draws upon *On the Alienation of Workers and Management*, The Zucker Lectures, Hamilton, Ontario: McMaster University, 1981.

the executive and the life of the blue-collar or clerical worker. Moreover, the quality of life has many dimensions. We may observe progress along some of them, regress along others. I will focus on levels of work satisfaction: people's attachment to or alienation from their work. I will begin with executive work.

The Work of the Executive

Forty years ago we learned from William H. Whyte a new phrase, "the Organization Man."[18] The Organization Man was an executive who had sold his soul to the Corporation. He dressed as it wanted him to, married as it wanted him to, and thought as it wanted him to. But most important, the Organization Man was a member of a group. He was loyal to the group, conformed to the group norms, and made his decisions and did his work through group processes. It was no part of his role to express his individuality, to innovate in solitude, or to dissent from the group consensus.

Whyte's argument has been widely interpreted as an attack on modern business institutions and industrial society. It was no such thing. It was an expression of nostalgia for an individualistic ethic—the Protestant ethic, as it is often called—which Whyte thought was rapidly being displaced by a social ethic.[19]

We may share Whyte's sympathy for the rugged individualists of the past—the Henry Fords and the Andrew Carnegies, but we must remember that there was generally room for only one of those individualists in any single company. Henry Ford could be an individualist because he could hire many organization men to work for him.

Second, we must not imagine that there is no place for individualists in the business and industrial world today. Their main opportunities arise, as they have always done, in the spawning of new industries and companies. I can think, offhand, of a dozen examples in the electronics industry alone—men like William Hewlett of Hewlett-Packard, Pat Haggerty of Texas Instruments, or Bill Gates of Microsoft. Moreover, these contemporary individualists seem often to have acquired a managerial style that allows them to work effectively with others. They seem to have

---

[18]New York: Simon & Schuster, 1956.

[19]*Ibid.*, p. 17. "By social ethic I mean that contemporary body of thought which makes morally legitimate the pressures of society against the individual. Its major propositions are three: a belief in the group as the source of creativity; a belief in 'belongingness' as the ultimate need of the individual; and a belief in the application of science to achieve the belongingness." By "science," Whyte meant specifically social psychology as applied to human relations.

absorbed at least some elements of the social ethic. But we find that that was also true of men of the past, like Carnegie, when we examine their careers carefully.

So we are left with the question of whether the portrait of the Organization Man revealed a genuine trend or just rediscovered that most people, most of the time, need a supportive social environment—need to "belong"—and are capable, at most, of only modest bursts of creativity, whether in isolation or in groups. Whyte himself spoke quite cautiously of a needed balance between the individualist ethic and the social ethic, and argued only that the balance had moved too far toward the latter.

Let us accept the premise that the social ethic describes—if with a bit of exaggeration—the ways of thought and action of most business managers today. What does this say of their satisfactions, of the quality of life in the executive workplace, of their attachment to it, or alienation from it?

One can doubt that there has been any massive shift during the past few generations in the nature of the manager's work or social environment. Conformity to social pressure is not an invention of our generation. Nor should we go to the other extreme and assume that ours is peculiarly an age of nonconformity. The solid ranks of blue jeans I see in my classes disabuse me of that idea. What kind of nonconformity produces this coincidental convergence on blue jeans, and informal living arrangements? We are not solitary savages but social animals. Most of us are not productive, or even comfortable, when placed in isolation and asked to solve vague, complex, unstructured problems. We cannot conclude that the office, which provides us with social support and social interaction, is a hostile environment for us.

How then are we to account for the boredom and lack of satisfaction that many executives experience in their jobs? If the workplace is humane, why do many persons express their alienation from it, and why do they seek their satisfaction outside it? Daniel Berlyne, in his research on what makes things boring or interesting, showed that activities can hold people's interest and attention only if they are sufficiently complex to continue to present elements of novelty, but sufficiently simple to be understandable, so that pattern can be discerned in them. The level of complexity of a task does not, of course, remain constant. Experience with it gradually reduces its complexity, so that in time almost any task can become routine, uninteresting, boring. Nor is the complexity of a task the same for all persons. What is incomprehensible to some may be banal to others.

Of course, maintaining the average complexity of executive tasks at the level that would maximize job interest and job satisfaction cannot be our main aim. The goals of successful company operation have to take some priority over the goals of immediate work satisfaction for managers. Put in simplest terms—which apply to all kinds of work and not just to managerial jobs—lots of dull tasks have to be done in the world each day, and to each of us falls a larger or a smaller share of them. Some of these dull tasks, particularly those requiring mechanical effort, we have passed off to machines, but more than enough remain for the human beings in almost all occupations.

People whose jobs are unrewarding look for their main satisfactions in other parts of their lives, and we say that they are alienated. Again, this is not a peculiarity of contemporary life. The novels and letters of Stendhal complain constantly of the tedium of executive life in the French army and government a century and a half ago.[20] Samuel Pepys, writing his diary in England three centuries ago, gives us only glimpses of the work of his office at the Admiralty, because, apart from periodic political crises that endanger his position, he finds his life outside the office much more interesting.[21] The testimony of these witnesses is especially valuable, in that both were reputedly effective executives, and both were intensely interested in and curious about life, even though their curiosity was more often satisfied outside the workplace than in it.

How has the introduction of computers into business changed this picture? To date, the computer has had very modest impact on executive work, particularly at higher executive levels. In some middle management areas (e.g., scheduling and inventory control) the computer has assumed responsibility for routine, repetitive decisions that managers had previously made. Here, the consequence, in addition to downsizing, has been to transfer the manager's attention to somewhat longer-run concerns, and to the management of people.

At higher executive levels, even these kinds of effects have not been visible. To a limited extent, the computer has changed and improved the flow of information to top executives—the information that is available to them, for example, when they are engaged in collective bargaining, about the cost of particular provisions in the labor contract. Changes of this sort, however, have little significance for the human quality of the executive's job. They do not change the nature of interactions with associates or subordinates. Of course, we cannot be sure that this will continue to be the case—that later developments in the computer revolution, like the current proliferation of data bases and communication networks, will not impinge on the manager's job in more fundamental

[20]To the Happy Few: Selected Letters of Stendhal (New York: Grove Press, 1952).

[21]Diary and Correspondence of Samuel Pepys, F.R.S (London: George Bell and Sons, 1875), 4 vols.

ways. Nothing we have seen up to the present time allows us to predict with any confidence what the shape of such developments might be, or their consequences for alienation or for the balance between the social ethic and individualism.

What I have said should not be taken as an argument against making the executive workplace a more challenging and humane environment. Using the computer to automate routine work is one possible direction of improvement, although we should remember that the human jobs left behind after the automation may sometimes be simpler instead of more complex than those they replaced. Other possibilities for work enrichment may be found in more frequent lateral transfer of executives from one responsibility to another.

Thus far, I have presented no systematic evidence, but have relied on anecdotes and appeals to your own personal experiences for support of my position. Turning now to a domain where at least a modicum of objective evidence is available to discipline our personal viewpoints, I should like to examine work satisfactions and alienation of blue-collar and clerical workers, and particularly the impacts on work satisfaction of factory and office automation.

Work Before Industrialization

Golden Age myths do not all describe a happy savage. There is also a Golden Age of preindustrialized society, supposedly inhabited by happy craftsmen and even happy peasants. The contrast of this Golden Age with the bleak realities of life in factory and mine during the early Industrial Revolution provides a central topic for nineteenth-century social criticism. The theme of alienation finds a clear voice in the writings of Karl Marx; the *Communist Manifesto*[22] contains a succinct statement:

> Owing to the extensive use of machinery and to the division of labor, the work of the proletarians has lost all individual character, and consequently, all charm for the workman. He becomes an appendage of the machine, and it is only the most simple, most monotonous, and most easily acquired knack that is required of him.

One hundred years after the publication of the Communist Manifesto the same fears were expressed about the introduction of the computer to automate factory and office work. Two charges, then, have been

---

[22]Chicago: Charles H. Kerr & Company, n.d.

leveled: that the Industrial Revolution dehumanized work, and that the appearance of the electronic computer has dehumanized it further.

Again, few statistics are forthcoming that would settle these questions in any definitive way. We know that, prior to the Industrial Revolution, almost all people were poorer in material goods than they are in the industrialized nations today. Perhaps, however, they were poor but happy. Perhaps they have given up their pleasant and challenging occupations for the potage of a goods-filled unsatisfying leisure.

An English writer, Alasdair Clayre,[23] searched out what the preindustrial workers in England themselves said about work. Of course, much more was written *about* workers and peasants, than *by* workers and peasants. Nevertheless, Clayre was able to find a little diary material, some reasonably concrete reports by observers, and, most important, the evidence of poems and work songs that were current among the people. Here is a typical example of what he found, part of a poem written about 1730 by one Stephen Duck:[24]

> Week after Week we this dull Task pursue, / Unless when winnowing Days produce a new; / A new indeed, but frequently a worse, / The Threshall yields but to the Master's Curse: / He counts the Bushels, counts how much a Day, / Then swears we've idled half our Time away.

The evidence is wholly consistent. Work—whether on farm or at sea—is hard and wearisome. After work is done there may be time for pleasure. As Clayre sums it up:[25]

> It is not often, in the whole body of traditional songs, that we find a reference to work as an activity valued in itself, independent of love, of the chances of interruption by girls, of play, or of rewards.

Although the evidence is less full then we might wish, the weight of it is clearly opposed to the reality of a Golden Age of work that was destroyed by the machine and the factory. We should not go to the other extreme of supposing that the Industrial Revolution was itself a Golden Age. We know too much about the brutalities of the first century of the factory system to fall into that error. But our concern is with alienation in the twentieth century, not in the nineteenth.

[23]See his book, *Work and Play* (New York: Harper & Row, 1974).

[24]*Ibid.*, p. 93.

[25]*Ibid.*, p. 134.

Automation and Alienation

We are now only about four decades into the computer revolution. There is no doubt that it is a revolution of the most profound kind, which has only begun to run its course. Because the computer is such a recent innovation, we do have some reasonably reliable and comparable data on levels of work satisfaction before its introduction and today. We also have evidence from a few careful studies of the changes experienced by workers at the time computers were introduced into their factories and offices.

Polling data from at least fifteen job satisfaction surveys of national samples of workers provide no evidence of decline in the average levels of job satisfaction reported by respondents. Thirty-five or forty years ago, most workers (80 to 90 per cent) said they were "satisfied" or "reasonably satisfied" with their jobs. About the same percentage say the same things today.[26]

Of course we must be careful how we interpret these findings. Workers who say they are reasonably satisfied with their jobs may not be especially happy in them. They might have a long list of things they would like to see changed. They might not even be particularly pleased with their choices of occupations, and might wish that they had entered others. We do not have good measuring sticks for absolute levels of satisfaction. But we can conclude from the findings of the polls that, however high or low the absolute levels of satisfaction, there has been no discernible trend in those levels since computers began to be used by business and industry on a large scale. Automation, as far as it has gone to date, has not produced new alienation.

A person whose conception of automation was formed by viewing Charlie Chaplin's *Modern Times* might understandably be puzzled at these poll results. The dehumanizing effects of machines appear so blatant that it would seem that workers could not fail to notice them, unless they were numbed by their work experiences. But of course *Modern Times* is a caricature, and it is a caricature of a form of mechanization that is becoming increasingly outmoded. To get a more factual picture of the meaning of automation for workers, we must examine the automated workplace itself and study its characteristics.

A substantial number of published studies, especially from the decades of the 1960s and '70s, describe factories and offices operating at one or another level of mechanization and automation, including before-and-after studies of the installation of new computing systems. First there are studies of the short-term, transient effects of introducing computers,

---

[26]Robert P. Quinn and Linda J. Shepard, *The 1972–73 Quality of Employment Survey* (Ann Arbor: Survey Research Center, Institute for Social Research, University of Michigan).

like the observations reported by Ida Hoos.[27] In these studies, we see considerable evidence of psychological trauma produced by the changes. Workers are often fearful of the new technology, and express feelings that their work has been dehumanized. They worry about the prospects of their being displaced by the computer, and about their abilities to cope with their altered jobs.

That such reactions to computerization have occurred cannot be doubted, but their interpretation is more problematic. Are they reactions to computers and a computerized workplace; or may they be, instead, reactions to change? And even more particularly, may they be reactions to the particular ways in which change was introduced and implemented? Writers on human relations have been pointing out for years that the way in which an innovation will be received by workers depends critically upon the way in which it is presented to them. Change may be feared and resisted, or it may be accepted as a welcome challenge.

Human nature is not inherently hostile to change, for human beings seek out novelty as often as they flee it. Whether their reactions will be positive or negative depends in large part on the nature and extent of their participation in the change process. In simplest terms, people usually react positively to actions that they perceive as being done by them, and negatively to those they perceive as being done to them without their consent. It is not change, but feelings of anxiety and helplessness in being subjected to change over which they have no control or influence that causes malaise and opposition.

We cannot be sure, therefore, whether studies that show negative attitudes toward a newly computerized workplace reflect characteristics of the technology or are simply the consequences of a poorly managed change process. We know that managements in the past have frequently been guilty of failing to consult workers and secure their participation in all sorts of changes, most of them unconnected with mechanization. We know that these failures in communication quite consistently produced exactly the sorts of reactions that have been observed in the before-and-after computer studies. Hence, we are left with two different possible causes for these reactions, and no basis for disconfounding them. For further enlightenment, we must turn to other sorts of studies.

Thirty years ago, Robert Blauner carried out an important series of case studies which he reported in his book *Alienation and Freedom: The Factory Worker and his Industry*.[28] Blauner's idea was that there are many forms of manufacturing technology—the assembly line is only one of

---

[27]*Automation in the Office* (Washington, D.C.: Public Affairs Press, 1961).

[28]Chicago: University of Chicago Press, 1964.

them—and different forms might have quite different psychological significance. Some of them might be severely dehumanizing and alienating, and others less so or not at all.

Blauner looked at companies using four different technologies: a printing concern, a textile manufacturer, an automobile assembly plant, and a continuous process chemical manufacturing plant. He found substantial differences in the levels of satisfaction or dissatisfaction of workers in these four situations. Some of the diversity could be attributed to differences in the ethnic and social origins of the workers, but even when allowance was made for this factor, large differences remained. Worker satisfactions were relatively high in the printing concern and the chemical plant, relatively low in the textile mill and the auto assembly plant.

We can conjecture some of the reasons for these findings. Printing was, at the time of Blauner's study, a relatively traditional technology employing skilled craftsmen. The textile mill and the assembly line fit more closely to the *Modern Times* stereotype. Most of the jobs in these factories were highly routine and repetitive, and the human work was paced by the rhythm of the machines.

The finding that job satisfaction at the chemical plant was relatively high requires a little more consideration. It was a modern, highly automated plant, in which humans served primarily in a backup role—not operating the process but monitoring it, and intervening only when it malfunctioned. The human staff also had, of course, the responsibilities for maintenance and repair. Some parts of the engineering staff were continually engaged in the longer-term concerns of improving and expanding the plant, and introducing new operations. A relatively large fraction of the jobs associated with the plant called for a high level of skill, and few were paced by the tempo of the manufacturing processes. The worker supervised the machine, maintained the machine, designed and modified the machine, but was not driven by the machine. The worker's pace did not have to be matched, from moment to moment, to the machine's pace.

It is the chemical plant, and not the textile mill or the auto assembly line, that most nearly typifies the direction in which highly automated and computerized factory and office work are moving. The newer technology appears to be substantially more congenial to its human operators than the technology that was typical of an earlier phase of the Industrial Revolution. The current and continuing trend toward high levels of automation is eliminating some of the routine and boredom of semi-automated technologies.

Another series of studies that deserves attention was carried out by

Thomas L. Whisler in a score of insurance offices.[29] Like Hoos, Whisler compared attitudes toward work prior to and subsequent to the computerization of large-scale clerical operations. The difference between Whisler's studies and those of Hoos is that Whisler examined the offices, not immediately after the change had been introduced, but some years later. He did not observe strongly negative attitudes of the sort that Hoos had reported. On average, the clerical workers reported that their jobs were now more demanding—a higher level of accuracy and reliability was expected of them. At the same time, they reported that their jobs were no less pleasant or more boring than they had been before. Evidently the higher demands of the jobs produced as much challenge as tension. Whisler also found that all of the changes in attitude were very small in magnitude, and often in opposite directions in different firms. A rather radical alteration of the data processing technology had produced only small, almost insignificant, changes in the perceived human quality of the work environment.

We need many more studies like those of Blauner and Whisler before we can be satisfied that their results may safely be extrapolated to the whole spectrum of manufacturing and clerical operations that are now being automated. However, the findings should be surprising only to persons who have not examined in detail the new technology—who still view it as if it were in a direct line of descent from the traditional mechanized factory, instead of representing a quite distinct and different line of evolution.

Alienation and Authority Relations

A good deal of the discussion of alienation in the workplace has been focused on the role of authority in organizations, and the alienating effects of authoritarian environments. Because the next chapter, Chapter VII, takes up the topic of authority, we will postpone our discussion of the relation between authority and alienation to the commentary to that chapter.

Systems Effects of Automation

To understand the effects of automation upon job satisfaction, it is not enough to observe the direct impact of automation upon the factory or office where it takes place. The purpose and economic justification of automation is to save human labor. After automation, fewer persons will be employed for a given level of output than before. This increase in pro-

[29]*The Impact of Computers on Organizations* (New York: Praeger, 1970); and *Information Technology and Organizational Change* (Belmont, Calif.: Wadsworth, 1970).

ductivity produces shifts in the distribution of the labor force among occupations and industries. Under present conditions, and those of the foreseeable future, these shifts are bringing about a relative decline in the fraction of the labor force that is engaged in manufacturing and routine clerical occupations, and an increase in the fraction engaged in service occupations, a change that has already been going on for a generation and is likely to continue into the indefinite future.

The shifts raise the important question of whether service jobs tend, on average, to be more or less satisfying than jobs in manufacturing industries or large clerical offices. The data from opinion polls do not show large differences in satisfaction among these categories, but the categories are too gross to allow us to reach conclusions with any great assurance. In particular, "service occupations" is a most heterogeneous category that includes school teachers, cosmetics salesmen, medical technicians, and innumerable other groups. Unless we know which of these occupations are going to be most expanded, we cannot easily decide whether work is going to become, on average, more pleasant or less pleasant.

Probably, on average, service occupations are not less routine than occupations in factories and offices. On the other hand, most service occupations appear to afford more-than-average human contact in their performance. This is generally considered a positive and humanizing aspect of a job, and a majority of people probably regard it as so.

We arrive at the conclusion that automation, by producing a net shift in the employment spectrum toward the service occupations, may make a small contribution toward increasing job satisfactions and the humaneness of the workplace, and very probably is not deleterious in its net effects. In all of this discussion, the assumption has been made implicitly that the levels of employment and unemployment are independent of how much automation has been introduced into the economy. Most economists would accept that assumption, and I have given the arguments for it in Chapter 5 of my *New Science of Management Decision*.[30]

Organizations of the Future

At the very end of the commentary on Chapter I, some observations were made about ongoing and potential changes in the nature of organizations with the spread of computing and networking technology and the broadening ranges of their application. Some work, it was argued, was being transferred from the factory or office to the home; networking and

[30]Revised edition, Englewood Cliffs, N.J.: Prentice-Hall, 1977.

"groupware" were encouraging and facilitating collaborative work; with the networking of organizations, hierarchy was becoming a less important component in the total system of communications channels.

These developments are sufficiently new that it is not possible to predict with great assurance either the rate at which they are likely to spread or their effects on work satisfaction.[31] Each of these developments raises its own issues. One issue about home work is the extent to which employees will prefer working in a remote environment, tied to their co-workers by electronic links, as compared with a social environment permitting face-to-face interaction in the office. A central issue with respect to networking, which will be explored more fully in the commentary to Chapter VIII, on communications, is how the load that is placed on human attention by each-to-all communication nets is to be kept within acceptable bounds. An obvious issue with respect to hierarchy is how top management is to retain its ability to steer the general course of the organization and maintain adherence to its goals.

Until we have more experience with these developments, the prudent course is to render a Scottish verdict, "Not proven." Meanwhile, events are proceeding sufficiently slowly that we will have many opportunities to study the consequences of these changes in specific work situations when they are first attempted.

Conclusion

In this survey of the evidence for and against a trend toward the alienation of executives and workers from their jobs, I have considered the possibility both of a long-term trend, having its beginnings with the Industrial Revolution, and a short-term trend over the past forty years, resulting from the widespread introduction of the computer into factory and office.

The evidence for either trend is almost wholly absent. There was no Golden Age of work prior to the Industrial Revolution—or at least, the workers themselves seemed unaware that they lived in one. Similarly, it appears that workers are about as satisfied or dissatisfied with their jobs today as they were forty years ago (but less certain about the durability of these jobs).

[31]Informative studies of the social effects of networking in university and business settings will be found in Kiesler and Sproull, eds., *Computing and Change on Campus* (New York: Cambridge University Press, 1987). Much of the evidence that they report comes from the experience of Carnegie Mellon University, a pioneer in campus networking, during the initial years of its Andrew system. On the new employment relations that may arise out of the computer technology, see also, Denise M. Rousseau, "Organizational Behavior in the New Organizational Era," *Annual Review of Psychology*, vol. 48 (Palo Alto, Cal.: Annual Reviews Inc., 1997).

A similar conclusion can be reached about the satisfaction of executives. The Organization Man and his discontents are not a phenomenon that is peculiar to our generation. Our attention has simply been called to a "social ethic" that has probably been the rule of executive behavior rather than the exception as long as we have had organizations.

Denial of trends in alienation does not mean that alienation is not extensive in all of the industrialized nations—Eastern European as well as Western. The main cause for it is not that work has been industrialized, but that people must work to live, and that, on average, jobs are not as complex as they would have to be to enlist the deep interest of those who fill them.

There is no reason for great optimism that the problem of alienation from work will ever be solved—that we will be freed entirely from the curse of Adam. Some degree of alienation is probably an integral part of the human condition. But there is no reason why we should not search as diligently and intelligently as we can for ways to reduce the level of alienation in our society—ways that will make the workplace a more frequent locus for important life satisfactions to a larger fraction of the people who spend so many of their waking hours there. Although modern trends toward automation have not, so far, had a visible impact on worker alienation, still the highly automated workplace appears to be a somewhat more humane environment than the typical workplace of earlier forms of manufacturing. We may therefore legitimately hope that automation will in time make a modest contribution to increasing work satisfaction.

Lacking a crystal ball, it is very hard to foresee the extent to which the workplace will be altered or de-localized by networking and "groupware," or what the consequences of such changes will be for employee satisfaction.

The Role of Authority

HAVING DISCUSSED THE PROCESSES whereby the individual becomes a member of an organization, we come to the next problem, which is how the organization fits the individual's behavior into an overall pattern—how it influences his decisions. Two aspects of influence may be distinguished: the stimuli with which the organization seeks to influence the individual; and the psychological "set" of the individual, which determines his response to the stimuli. These may be termed the "external" and "internal" aspects of influence, respectively.

For purposes of exposition, it is not convenient to separate completely the external and internal aspects of influence. Each plays a greater or lesser role in all the principal modes of influence: authority, communication, training, efficiency, and identification (organizational loyalty). Each of these topics will be considered, in turn, in the following chapters.

In this and the following chapters it is necessary to keep constantly in mind the idea of a decision as a conclusion drawn from a set of premises—value premises, and factual premises. Organizational influence upon the individual may then be interpreted not as determination by the organization of the decisions of the individual, but as determination for him of *some* of the premises upon which his decisions are based. Hence the several modes of influence by no means exclude one another. When the individual decides upon a particular course of action, some of the premises upon which this decision is based may have been imposed upon him by the exercise of the organization's authority over him, some may have been the result of his training, others of his desire for efficiency, still others of his organizational loyalty, and so forth.

Of all the modes of influence, authority is the one that chiefly distinguishes the behavior of individuals as participants of organizations from their behavior outside such organizations. It is authority that gives an organization its formal structure, and the other modes of influence may best be discussed after this structure has been specified.

In the behavior of organized human groups we often find a unity and coordination of behavior so striking that it has led many social thinkers to draw an analogy between the group and the individual, and even to postulate a "group mind."[1] The mechanism whereby this coordination is achieved is not easily perceived. In the case of the individual, there is a perfectly tangible structure of nerve fibers, capable of transmitting impulses from any part of the body to any other part, and capable of storing and transforming those impulses in a central nucleus. In the case of the social group, no physiological structure is present whose anatomy can be explored in the search for clues to the underlying mechanism.

The way in which such coordination is accomplished has already been partly described, in the last part of Chapter V. A plan of action is developed for the group, and this plan is then communicated to the members of the group. The final step in the process is the *acceptance* of this plan by the members. Authority plays a central role in this acceptance.

Coordination then results when the behavior of the individual is guided by his expectations of the behavior of the other members of the group. In the simplest cases, as we have seen, this adaptation may be self-induced. But for the coordination to reach any degree of complexity, it is necessary for the individual to make his specific decisions conform to some sort of group plan. Psychologically speaking, his realization that a particular behavior is a part of his role under the plan must be a sufficient stimulus to bring about the behavior in question.

The mental processes involved are seldom entirely deliberate or conscious. Most of the behaviors resulting in coordination are in large part habitual or reflexive. A soldier obeying a command does not reflect on the philosophy of obedience, but he *does* set himself a rule of behavior which makes his choices responsive to the command. Instead of being guided at each moment by a decision, "I will attack now," the soldier comprehends all such decisions under the general rule, "I will attack when ordered to do so."

An analysis of organized behavior of all sorts will demonstrate that such behavior results when each of the coordinated individuals sets for himself a criterion of choice that makes his own behavior dependent upon the behavior of others. In the simplest cases he makes his own decision at each point as to what those adjustments should be. In slightly more complex forms of organization, *he sets himself a general rule which permits the communicated decision of another to guide his own choices* (i.e. to

---

[1]For two decisive refutations of "group mind" theories see Floyd H. Allport, *Institutional Behavior* (Chapel Hill: University of North Carolina Press, 1933), chaps. i–iii, and R. M. MacIver, *Community*, Bk. II, chap. ii, and App. A.

serve as a premise of those choices) *without deliberation on his own part on the expediency of those premises.*

AUTHORITY

Even the very simple illustrations that have been presented of organized behavior exhibit, in embryo at least, the phenomenon of authority. "Authority" may be defined as the power to make decisions which guide the actions of another. It is a relationship between two individuals, one "superior," the other "subordinate." The superior frames and transmits decisions with the expectation that they will be accepted by the subordinate. The subordinate expects such decisions, and his conduct is determined by them.[2]

The relationship of authority can be defined, therefore, in purely objective and behavioristic terms. It involves behaviors on the part of both superior and subordinate. When, and only when, these behaviors occur does a relation of authority exist between the two persons involved. When the behaviors do not occur there is no authority, whatever may be the "paper" theory of organization.

The behavior pattern of the superior involves a command—an imperative statement concerning the choice of a behavior alternative by the other—and an expectation that the command will be accepted by the other as a criterion of choice.[3]

The behavior pattern of the subordinate is governed by a single indeterminate decision, or criterion for decision, to "follow that behavior alternative which is selected for me by the superior." That is, he holds in abeyance his own critical faculties for choosing between alternatives and uses the formal criterion of the receipt of a command or signal as his basis for choice.[4]

Now since the relation of authority involves a particular criterion of choice as the basis for the subordinate's behavior, it is clear that two persons may stand in a relation of authority at one moment and not at the next. For the subordinate's behavior may be governed at the first moment by a command, and not at the next. Nor does it follow that when two persons recognize each other as "superior" and "subordinate"

---

[2]For other descriptions of authority see L. D. White, *Introduction to the Study of Public Administration* (New York: Macmillan, 1939), pp. 44–46, and C. I. Barnard, *The Functions of the Executive*, p. 163.

[3]This idea was central to the utilitarian concept of the state. See, for example, Jeremy Bentham, *A Fragment on Government* (Oxford: Clarendon Press).

[4]Cf. Ordway Tead, *Human Nature and Management* (New York: McGraw-Hill, 1929), p. 149, and Stene, *op. cit.*, p. 1131.

respectively, all the verbalizations of the first which affect the behaviors of the second are "commands." The willingness of the subordinate to accept a command, *if given*, does not imply that all, or even most, of his behavior choices are governed by commands.

It is necessary to distinguish, therefore, between specific behaviors which are momentary instances of the exercise of authority, and the roles played by two persons over a period of time which involve an *expectation of obedience* by the one and a *willingness to obey* by the other.

Distinction Between Influence and Authority

The relation of authority by no means comprehends all situations where the verbalizations of one person influence the behavior of another. The verbs "persuade," "suggest," etc., describe several kinds of influence which do not necessarily involve any relationship of authority. The characteristic which distinguishes authority from other kinds of influence is one already mentioned above, namely, that a subordinate holds in abeyance his own critical faculties for choosing between alternatives and uses the formal criterion of the receipt of a command or signal as his basis for choice. On the other hand, a person who receives a suggestion accepts it as only one of the evidential bases for making his choice—but the choice he will make depends upon conviction. Persuasion, too, centers around the reasons for or against a course of action. Persuasion and suggestion result in a change in the evidential environment of choice which may, but need not, lead to conviction. Obedience, on the other hand, is an abdication of choice.

Confusion among these terms results from the fact that all three phenomena—persuasion, suggestion, and command—are frequently present in a single situation. Even where a behavior can be secured by the exercise of authority, a superior often and perhaps usually prefers to employ suggestion or persuasion. Some reasons for this will be discussed presently. But confusion will be avoided if it is remembered—as has been pointed out already—that the mere fact that two persons accept the roles of superior and subordinate does not imply that all, or even most, of their behaviors will be instances of the exercise of authority.

The line of demarcation between suggestion and command is perhaps not so clear as would be suggested by this discussion, however. Certain subtleties are concealed in the term "conviction," which was used as the distinguishing criterion.

A conviction, as used in this connection, is a belief in a factual or value premise which is relevant to a particular decision. Belief in a factual proposition may be induced in a number of ways, one of which is *proof*.

But we are convinced of a great number of things which never have been proved to us logically or empirically. Most persons in this country would agree that the atom bomb has been invented, though they would be hard put to demonstrate this either by pure logic or by the evidence of the senses. Likewise, few persons before taking prescribed medicines ask their physicians for a demonstration of the curative properties of the prescription.

In other words, conviction often results from the social transmission of factual statements, even in the absence of proof. So, a secretary who has been instructed by her employer to investigate a particular question of office procedure may report: "I have looked into the problem, and suggest that you act in this manner." This suggestion may be accepted without any review of its evidential basis by the employer, merely on the strength of his confidence in the secretary. Here is evident the same relaxation of critical faculties that we have said was characteristic of the relation of authority.

Statements, then, may convince without proving by virtue of the status or position of the person making the statement. An individual who does not have a recognized status, or who is not recognized by his associates as expert with respect to a certain kind of knowledge, will have a more difficult time convincing his listeners that a recommendation is sound than one who possesses the credentials of "expertness." Recommendations are judged partly on their merits, but partly on the merits of the persons making the recommendations. This is true both because the individuals acting upon the recommendations often do not have the expertise needed to judge them, and because pressure of time requires them to accept the recommendations of those whom they trust. This is an important reason for the resistance that is usually experienced in any organization to suggestions that are made outside the line of duty, or that are volunteered through other than the usual lines of communication.

It should not be implied that this resistance to "irregular" suggestions is entirely a weakness of organization. The specialization of decision-making functions, and the fixing of responsibility for particular kinds of expertness upon particular individuals is an important source of organizational efficiency that must be balanced against the potential loss of independent ideas which results.

At the expense of a possible abuse of the term, we shall use "authority" broadly, and comprehend under it all situations where suggestions are accepted without any critical review or consideration. If this definition is accepted, it follows that when A is superior to B at one moment, B may act as superior to A at the next moment. What is meant, then, when A is described as *the* superior of B?

Authority and the "Last Word"

In the situations that have been discussed, a subordinate accepts commands in the absence of a determinate choice of his own. But a subordinate may also accept commands in opposition to a determinate choice of his own. In such a case, the element of authority in the behavior pattern is unequivocal. When there is a disagreement between two persons, and when the disagreement is not resolved by discussion, persuasion, or other means of conviction, then it must be decided by the authority of one or the other participant. It is this "right to the last word" which is usually meant in speaking of "lines of authority" in an administrative organization. Too often, however, the element of disagreement in obedience is overemphasized at the expense of the other elements of the situation. The term "authority" would be too narrowly employed if it were restricted to such instances of disagreement.

A final complication must be added to the notion of authority. If authority were evidenced entirely in the acceptance of explicit commands, or in the resolution of disagreements, its presence or absence in any relationship could be sought in the presence or absence of these tangible concomitants. But it is equally possible for obedience to anticipate commands. The subordinate may, and is expected to, ask himself "How would my superior wish me to behave under these circumstances?" Under such circumstances, authority is implemented by a subsequent review of completed actions, rather than a prior command. Further, the more obedient the subordinate, the less tangible will be the evidences of authority. For authority will need to be exercised only to reverse an incorrect decision.

This phenomenon has been pointed out by Friedrich,[5] who calls it a "rule of anticipated reactions." It affords a striking example of the manner in which expectations and anticipations govern human behavior, and the difficulties which result from this for the analysis of human institutions. The difficulty in determining authority relations because of the operation of the rule of anticipated reactions is common to all "power" situations. Any study, for instance, of a governor's veto power must take into consideration what bills failed of passage in the legislature because of the anticipation of veto, and what bills were passed for the very same reason.[6]

Any study of power relations which confines itself to instances where the sanctions of power were invoked misses the essential fact of the situa-

[5]C. J. Friedrich, *op. cit.*, p. 16. Cf. Bentham's very interesting definition: "A tacit *expression of will* is that which is conveyed by any other signs than words whatsoever; among which none are so efficacious as acts of punishment annexed in times past, to the non-performance of acts of the same sort with those that are the objects of the will that is in question" (*A Fragment on Government*, p. 138).

[6]Leslie Lipson, *The American Governor: From Figurehead to Executive* (Chicago: University of Chicago Press, 1939), pp. 210–212.

tion. To avoid this fallacy, authority has been defined in this study not in terms of the sanctions of the superior, but in terms of the behaviors of the subordinate.

The Sanctions of Authority

Having decided, tentatively at least, what authority is, we must examine the circumstances surrounding its exercise. Why and to what extent will a subordinate accept the decisions of another as governing his own conduct?

The superior-subordinate relationship is one of many possible examples of the role-taking which characterizes broad areas of human conduct. Perhaps the most important basis for such role-taking is custom. That is, a great deal of conduct requires no further explanation than that, under the circumstances, it is the socially "expected" conduct. For the reasons why particular conduct is dictated by custom it would be necessary to study the social history of the society in question.[7]

The "institutions" of a society may be regarded as rules specifying the roles that particular persons will assume in relation to one another under certain circumstances. The range of possible roles and possible behaviors is as broad as the ingenuity of man for dramatic invention.[8]

One of the socially determined roles in many societies is that of "employee." The particular content of the role—the degree of obedience expected—will vary with the social situation. The American working man today, for example, probably has a somewhat narrower zone of acceptance, so far as the employer's instructions are concerned, than his father had. In part this may be due to his stronger bargaining position, or conversely, the weaker sanctions of the employer; but there is probably also present here a more fundamental change in social attitudes as to what it is "proper" for an employer to ask an employee to do. This changed attitude is reflected also in social legislation limiting the terms of the employment contract.

There are wide differences, too, among different types of employees in their expectations of the authority relations in their positions. Professional men and skilled workmen are apt to have relatively narrow zones of acceptance, particularly in the areas of their own professional competences or skills.

No attempt will be made here to explain the genesis of these social attitudes that establish an expectation of obedience in certain situations, nor their dependence upon and relation to other attitude clusters in the

---

[7]This is, of course, a central problem of sociology and social psychology.

[8]For a further discussion of this problem, see Charner M. Perry, "The Relation Between Ethics and Political Science," *International Journal of Ethics*, 47:169–170, 172–174 (Jan., 1937).

society. There has been much speculation that the central attitudes of a society must be reflected in administrative organization, so that administration in a democracy will be in some sense "democratic" while administration in a totalitarian system will be "authoritarian." Thus far, the thesis has been expounded, but by no means demonstrated.

There are a number of other, more specific, factors which induce acceptance of authority in organization. In a broad sense they might be called "sanctions," although that word is usually confined to the stimuli which act through punishment, while some of the factors listed below are more properly classified as rewards.

(1) The social sanctions are the first to be noted, and perhaps the most important. Not only does society set up in the individual expectations of obedience in certain social situations, but the individual who fails to accept his role will feel, in one way or another, the social disapprobation of his fellows. Insubordination can be as embarrassing, under these circumstances, as failure to wear a necktie to church.

On the other hand, in so far as fellow employees may receive vicarious satisfaction when an individual "tells off" the boss, social sanctions may operate to decrease the effectiveness of authority. The extent to which group attitudes of acceptance or resistance will condition the individual's reactions to authority has been much emphasized in the Hawthorne studies.[9]

(2) Psychological differences between individuals may play an important part in enforcing such relations. Though the study of leadership is in a very primitive stage, there are some indications that there may be certain personality types that lead, and others that follow.[10]

(3) Purpose has been stressed by students of administration as a sanction of prime importance. As already pointed out in Chapter VI, in voluntary organizations efforts are contributed largely because the contributor is sympathetic to the purpose of the organization. He is willing to obey commands because he realizes that the coordination secured thereby is useful to the attainment of the joint purpose.[11]

Several conditions must be satisfied if purpose is to be an effective sanction of authority. The subordinate must have confidence that the

[9]See, for example, F. J. Roethlisberger and W. J. Dickson, *Management and the Worker* (Cambridge: Harvard University Press, 1939).

[10]Charles E. Merriam, *Political Power* (New York: McGraw-Hill, 1934), pp. 24–46, and Harold D. Lasswell, *Psychopathology and Politics*, pp. 38–64, 78–152.

[11]C. I. Barnard, *op. cit.*, pp. 165–166, and Luther Gulick, "Notes on the Theory of Organization," in Gulick and Urwick, eds., *op. cit.*, pp. 37–38.

command is issued in furtherance of a purpose with which he is in sympathy. Second, he must have confidence that the command will be effective in achieving this purpose. This confidence may be based less on his own knowledge of the correctness of the command (as a matter of fact, such acceptance would fall outside our definition of authority) than on his faith in the ability of those who issued the command, his recognition that they have information he does not have, and his realization that his efforts and those of fellow workers will be ineffective in reaching the desired objective without some coordination from above. Within limits, he will even accept commands he knows to be incorrect because he does not wish to challenge or unsettle a system of authority that he believes to be beneficial to his aims in the long run.

(4) More formal sanctions in our society are based on the relation between the "job" and economic security and status. Thus, obedience may be the price of retaining the position, securing a higher salary, or other advantages. The facts that most organizations will tolerate large quantities of insubordination—particularly if it is not verbalized—without dismissal, and that many organization members are not desirous of promotion, diminish the importance of these sanctions as means for securing acceptance of authority in the day-by-day work of an organization.

(5) Particularly in the case of individuals not much affected by influences in the third and fourth categories, simple unwillingness or disinclination to accept responsibility may be a major reason for the acceptance of decisions made by others. If the assigned task is not unduly unpleasant, many individuals would prefer being told what to do to being forced to make the decisions themselves. As a matter of fact, this is probably characteristic of most individuals when the decision in question lies outside the area of their experience and competence. The psychological roots of this lie deeper than a mere fear of the consequences which may be forthcoming in case of an incorrect decision, and there is great variability among individuals in this characteristic.

The Limits of Authority

The most striking characteristic of the "subordinate" role is that it establishes an area of acceptance[12] in behavior within which the subordinate is willing to accept the decisions made for him by his superior. His choice is then determined, always within the area of acceptance, by his superior,

---

[12]This concept is adopted from Barnard (*op. cit.*, pp. 168–169), who, however, does not develop to any great extent the positive significance of what he calls the "zone of indifference."

and the relation of superior-subordinate holds only within this area. Acceptance may be due to any of the influences discussed in the previous section, and may take place when the subordinate does not care which alternative is selected, or when the sanctions are sufficiently strong to induce him to carry out an undesired alternative.

The magnitude of the area is influenced by a large number of circumstances. A voluntary organization with poorly defined objectives has perhaps the narrowest range of acceptance.[13] An army, where the sanctions as well as the customs are of extreme severity, has the broadest area of acceptance.[14]

Restraint of the superior is as important as obedience of the subordinate in maintaining the relationship. Modern writers on administration have emphasized the need for restraint by recommending the use when possible of other means of influence, leading to conviction, rather than authority, leading often to nothing more than acquiescence.

The corresponding limitations of political authority have been discussed by Professor Charles E. Merriam.[15] Theoreticians of history have often questioned the extent to which "leaders" really lead. How broad is the area of indifference within which a group will continue to follow its leadership? In a very real sense, the leader, or the superior, is merely a bus driver whose passengers will leave him unless he takes them in the direction they wish to go. They leave him only minor discretion as to the road to be followed.

THE USES OF AUTHORITY

Authority has been described as a relation that secures coordinated behavior in a group by subordinating the decisions of the individual to the communicated decisions of others. Thus, the exercise of authority in a group makes possible a large degree of separation of the decision-making processes from actual performance, or what might be called vertical "specialization" in decision-making.

Just as a steersman may permit his moment-to-moment decisions to be controlled by a course laid out beforehand on the map, so a member of an organization submits his behavior to the control of the decision-making portion of the organization. In the first case, the coordination takes place in the behavior of a single individual over a period of time. In the

---

[13]*Ibid.*, p. 155.

[14]Military literature shows a clear recognition of the importance of the area of acceptance as a fundamental element in tactics. Cf. Col. J. F. C. Fuller's graphic description of the psychology of battle (*op. cit.*, pp. 140–141).

[15]See the chapter "The Poverty of Power" in his *Political Power* (pp. 156–183).

second case, the coordination takes place in the behavior of a number of individuals, over a short or long period of time. The principle involved in both cases is the same: the subordination of specific to general decisions.

Vertical specialization, or specialization in decision-making, is possible, of course, without the use of authority. A unit may be given a purely advisory or "staff" status in an organization, and yet, through its recommendations, actually make decisions that are accepted elsewhere in the organization. However, in so far as the recommendations of a staff agency are accepted without reexamination on their merits, the agency is really exercising authority, as we have defined that term; and it would be difficult to cite examples from organization where an effective specialization of the decision-making process exists without the exercise of at least some authority to maintain it.

The wide employment of authority as a tool for coordination of group activity reflects the important uses to which this tool may be put. Three functions of authority deserve special notice:

1. It enforces responsibility of the individual to those who wield the authority;
2. It secures expertise in the making of decisions;
3. It permits coordination of activity.

Responsibility

Writers on the political and legal aspects of authority have emphasized that its function is to enforce the conformity of the individual to norms laid down by the group, or by its authority-wielding members.[16] The enactments of a legislature, for instance, are accepted as authoritative not only by the administrative hierarchy employed by the state, but by all the persons subject to its jurisdiction. When disobedience occurs, an elaborate set of sanctions may be invoked and applied against the recalcitrant member. The central core of many of the most important social institutions consists of a system of authority, and a set of sanctions for enforcing it. The state itself is the primary example, but the law of property, the church, and even the family also fall in this category.[17]

---

[16]Charles E. Merriam, *Political Power*, p. 16, and *History of the Theory of Sovereignty Since Rousseau* (New York: Columbia University Press, 1900); C. J. Friedrich, *Responsible Bureaucracy* (Cambridge: Harvard University Press, 1932), pp. 20–24.

[17]For an interpretation of "property" in terms of power and decision, see John R. Commons, *Institutional Economics* (New York: Macmillan, 1934), pp. 397–401; Morris R. Cohen, *Law and the Social Order* (New York: Harcourt, Brace, 1933), pp. 44–45; and Albert Kocourek, *Jural Relations* (Indianapolis: Bobbs-Merrill, 1927), pp. 305–334.

This aspect of authority is of considerable importance for our own discussion. The notion of an administrative hierarchy in a democratic state would be unthinkable without the corresponding notion of a mechanism whereby that hierarchy is held to account.[18] The question of responsibility must be a central issue in any discussion of the relation between administrative and legislative bodies, or in any analysis of administrative law.

When authority is employed to enforce responsibility, sanctions will probably play an important part in the process; and this accounts for the attention which is usually given to the subject of sanctions in discussions of authority. Even in this connection, the importance of sanctions should not be overemphasized, however. The person who accepts the authority of a legislature, a property holder, or a father within a particular institutional setting, is probably motivated much more by socially indoctrinated ethical notions than by the fear of sanctions. That is, the individual in a particular society believes that he *ought* to obey the laws adopted by the constituted authorities and that he *ought* to recognize property rights. To explain away the whole system of authority and responsibility in terms of sanctions is to oversimplify the situation.

Expertise

An extremely important function of authority is to secure decisions of a high quality of rationality and effectiveness. It has long been recognized that specialization is of fundamental importance to administrative efficiency, and it is hardly necessary to repeat here the stock examples which show how specialization may increase productivity.[19] These advantages of specialization are quite as important when the specialization concerns the process of "deciding" as when it concerns the processes of "doing."

The city manager of a small community is a jack-of-all-trades: he must have the skills of an engineer, accountant, executive, foreman, bill collector, and mechanic. He is also an intellectual jack-of-all-trades: he must, by himself, make almost all the decisions that guide his activities and those of his few subordinates during the working day; he must decide when to repair a street, or build a sewer; he must anticipate his equip-

---

[18]For variant notions as to the form this responsibility should take, see John M. Gaus, "The Responsibility of Public Administration," in *The Frontiers of Public Administration*, ed. Gaus, White, and Dimock (Chicago: University of Chicago Press, 1936), pp. 26–44; C. J. Friedrich, *Responsible Bureaucracy*; C. J. Friedrich, "Public Policy and the Nature of Administrative Responsibility," in *Public Policy, 1940* (Cambridge: Harvard University Press, 1940), pp. 3–24: Herman Finer, "Administrative Responsibility in Democratic Government," *Public Administration Review*, I:335–350 (Summer, 1941).

[19]L. Gulick, "Notes on the Theory of Organization," in Gulick and Urwick, *op. cit.*, pp. 3–4.

ment and personnel needs, purchase the equipment, and hire employees; he must decide what policing is needed, and what health services.

The administrator of a large city's governmental organization is in a very different situation. If his staff is large enough, he may hire an engineer to direct public-works activities, and to make the technical decisions in that area. He may have one or more personnel specialists and a purchasing agent. Foremen will exercise actual supervision over working crews. Every decision for the city's operation will receive relatively specialized and expert consideration.

To gain the advantages of specialized skill in a large organization, the work of the organization is subdivided, so far as possible, in such a way that all processes requiring a particular skill can be performed by persons possessing that skill. Likewise, to gain the advantages of expertise in decision-making, the responsibility for decisions is allocated, so far as possible, in such a way that decisions requiring particular knowledge or skill will rest with individuals possessing that knowledge or skill. This involves a subdivision of the decisions governing the organization into numerous component decisions, and a restriction of the activities of each member of the organization to a very few of these components.

A fundamental device for securing expertise in organization decisions is to locate the expert in a strategic position in the formal hierarchy of authority—that is, in a position where his decisions will be accepted as decisional premises by the other organizational members. This is a major advantage of organization by "process." When all activities to which engineering decisions are relevant are organized in a single department, then it is easy to allocate the function of decision in such a way as to secure the necessary technical competence.[20]

So long as the communication of decisions is restricted to the formal hierarchy of authority, however, it is not possible to secure the several kinds of technical assistance that are often needed for a single decision. A small school department, for instance, may lack the technical medical facilities for making decisions with regard to its school health services, or the engineering advice needed in the maintenance of the school plant.

To secure all the advantages, therefore, of expertise in decision-making, it is necessary to go beyond the formal structure of authority. The "authority of ideas" must gain an importance in the organization coordinate with the "authority of sanctions."

The emphasis in this discussion has thus far been on the *technical* knowledge needed for decisions. Expertise may apply to other types of

[20]Cf. Frederick W. Taylor, *The Principles of Scientific Management* (New York: Harper & Bros., 1911), pp. 99–113.

information as well. Modern police departments in large cities have central dispatching rooms which receive information, by telephone or otherwise, of incidents requiring police attention, and which assign policemen by radio, to investigate these incidents. The importance which the dispatching rooms have for the process of decision (in this case the assignment of policemen) lies in their strategic location with respect to relevant incoming information. Again, the formal structure of authority may play only a small part in this process, and may actually, except in cases of disagreement, be disregarded by the lines of communication.

In the organizational hierarchy, the superior ordinarily enjoys, by virtue of his position, the same advantage of information over his subordinate. The extent to which this advantage is real, and the extent to which it is mythical, may depend in large part upon the design of the lines of communication in the organization. The superior who possesses such advantages of information will have much less occasion to invoke the formal sanctions of authority than the superior whose subordinates are in a better situation than he, from the standpoint of information, to make the decision.

Coordination

The third function of authority, to secure coordination, was discussed at some length in the earlier sections of this chapter. Coordination should be clearly distinguished from expertise. Expertise involves the adoption of a *good* decision. Coordination is aimed at the adoption by all the members of the group of the *same* decision, or more precisely of mutually consistent decisions in combination attaining the established goal.

Suppose ten persons decide to cooperate in building a boat. If each has his own plan, and they don't bother to communicate their plans, it is doubtful that the resulting craft will be very seaworthy. They would probably have better success if they adopted even a very mediocre design, and then all followed this same design.

In the first portion of the Waterloo campaign, Napoleon's army was divided in two parts. The right wing, commanded by the Emperor himself, faced Blücher at Ligny; the left wing, under Marshal Ney, faced Wellington at Quatre Bras. Both Ney and the Emperor prepared to attack, and both had prepared excellent plans for their respective operations. Unfortunately, both plans contemplated the use of Erlon's corps to deliver the final blow on the flank of the enemy. Because they failed to communicate these plans, and because orders were unclear on the day of the battle, Erlon's corps spent the day marching back and forth between the two fields without engaging in the action on either. Somewhat less brilliant tactical plans, coordinated, would have had greater success.

By the exercise of authority, it is possible to centralize the function of deciding, so that a general plan of operations will govern the activities of all members of the organization. Again, this procedure is analogous to the process whereby an individual plans his own activities over an extended period of time.

Coordination may be exercised in both a procedural and a substantive sense. By procedural coordination is meant the specification of the organization itself—that is, the generalized description of the behaviors and relationships of the members of the organization. Procedural coordination establishes the lines of authority, and outlines the sphere of activity and authority of each member of the organization.

Substantive coordination is concerned with the *content* of the organization's activities. In an automobile factory, an organization chart is an aspect of procedural coordination, while blueprints for the engine block of the car being manufactured are an aspect of substantive coordination.

UNITY OF COMMAND

In Chapter II some remarks were made on the inadequacy of the doctrine of unity of command, as that doctrine is usually stated. It was pointed out there that, in a trivial sense, unity of command is always achieved, for if a subordinate is instructed to base a decision on two conflicting premises he will obviously be able to accept only one of them, and has to disregard the other. Hence, when unity of command is urged, this cannot be all that is meant.

As was also explained in Chapter II, unity of command is usually taken to mean that any one individual in an administrative organization will accept the authority of only one other person in the organization. The validity of this principle as a part of sound organization procedure was criticized on the ground that it does not give any reason why an individual cannot accept certain decisional premises from one superior and other non-conflicting premises from another. He may, for example, accept the authority of a "line" superior in determining the program of his unit, while he accepts the authority of the accounting department as to what financial records he shall keep. Or, to use the example of Taylor's "functional foremanship," he may accept the instructions of one foreman as to the speed of his lathe, and those of another foreman as to its proper maintenance.

Perhaps the purpose that is to be served by establishing unity of command will be better understood if the results which such unity is supposed to bring about are examined. It is certainly undesirable for the organization that the subordinate who receives conflicting commands relating to the *same* decisional premise should be either punished for not carrying out both commands, or placed in a position where he may carry out either command that he prefers. In the first case the subordinate will be demoralized by the impossible situation in which he is placed; in the second case he will retain his original discretion, hence will not be subject to any real authority. Moreover the superior, unless he can hold the subordinate responsible for carrying out instructions, cannot himself be held responsible for results. There is no question that these difficulties are real and fundamental; the only issue is whether unity of command is the sole or best solution.

On the contrary, there would seem to be at least four methods in common use for preventing or resolving conflicts in authority:

(1) Unity of command in the traditional sense—each individual receives orders from one and only one superior.

(2) Unity of command in the narrower sense defined in Chapter II—an individual may receive orders from several superiors, but in case of a conflict there is one and only one whom he is supposed to obey.

(3) Division of authority—each unit in the organization is assigned some specific area over which it has exclusive authority, and the decisional premises of any individual that fall within this area are subject to that authority.

(4) A system of rank—an individual is subject to the authority of all other individuals of a certain rank. If he receives conflicting orders, he follows the last one received, but is bound to bring the conflict to the attention of the person issuing the order. Authority relations between commissioned officers and men in the Army and Navy follow this general procedure.

These procedures, particularly the second, third, and fourth, are not necessarily mutually exclusive, and may be used in combination in a single organization.

The Hierarchy of Authority

The arrangement of the organization members in a hierarchy or pyramid of command affords the basis for either the first or the second method of avoiding conflicts in authority. Consistent adherence to such an arrangement either prevents the issuance of conflicting commands to a subordinate by different supervisors, or, if two individuals on the same level of the pyramid happen to work at cross purposes, automatically terminates the conflict between them by submitting it to the decision of a common superior in the hierarchy. The administrative hierarchy, therefore, provides a determinate procedure that decides who is to decide.

In actual practice, the hierarchy of authority usually represents a compromise between the two theories of unity of command listed above; that is, the lines of authority in the hierarchy provide the normal (but almost never the exclusive) channels for the transmission of commands and orders, and when overlapping of orders does occur the hierarchy is referred to in resolving the conflict.

Division of Authority

The hierarchy of authority might be described as a division of authority according to persons—each individual is assigned authority (exclusive authority, if the first theory is followed) over a specified group of subordinates. It is equally possible to divide authority according to subject matter—each individual is assigned authority over some specified aspect of the organization's work. In the literature this is often termed a "functional" allocation of authority.

Authority over subject matter is allocated by the issuance of authoritative communications—instructions, duties manuals, and the like—delineating the area within which each member of the group is to confine his activities, and within which the decisions of each member are to have an authoritative character in the group. Instead of deciding, in each particular case of conflict, what decisions are to be obeyed and what decisions are not, a general rule is laid down beforehand, granting each member of the group a certain sphere of decision within which he is to have authority.

If the work of members of the group were carried on in mutual isolation, there would be no need of a division of authority, beyond the establishment of the hierarchy. Normally, however, the manner in which each member of the group performs his work closely affects the work of each other member. The slowdown of one man on the assembly line may disrupt the entire line. The delay of a purchasing agent may affect a construction gang. A backlog on a reviewing officer's desk may hold up correspondence.

Even where there is a hierarchy of authority, then, it is usually necessary to divide the organization also along functional, or subject-matter, lines. There are two criteria for measuring the success of an allocation of authority: (1) the extent to which it aids or hinders the work of the group, and (2) the extent to which it minimizes jurisdictional disputes. The two criteria do not necessarily coincide. For instance, a division of authority in an automobile plant on the basis of the place of residence of the buyer of each car would probably be univocal, but would hardly facilitate the process of manufacture. To be successful, the division of authority must be adapted to the division of work—that is, to the technology of the work process.

Even under the best conditions, cases will occur where jurisdiction is doubtful. This is especially probable where two portions of the organization are organized on diverse principles: line and auxiliary, functional and geographical. In such cases, the need reappears for an appellate process to settle the dispute. The hierarchy of authority may be used for this purpose, or special appellate agencies may be used.

Where a formal division of authority on a subject-matter basis exists, however, a dispute is settled on a somewhat different basis from that in a simple hierarchy, where it is referred to a common superior—even though the process may be the same. When there is no division of authority, each separate dispute is submitted to the superior and is decided by him on its merits. Where there is a division of authority, the issue to be decided is not the specific question in dispute so much as the question of jurisdiction.

In the latter process, which we may call "adjudication," the superior must concern himself not so much with the content of the decision or its expediency, as with its "legality"—that is, the competence of the decider, in terms of the formal organizational structure. Without this division of authority, the superior would be concerned principally with the merits of the specific case.

For example, there may be a disagreement between a purchasing agent and a line officer as to the specifications for stationery. The line officer may wish one brand and quality, the purchasing agent may insist on delivering another to him. If this were merely a question of a hierarchy of authority, the common superior to these two men would be faced with the question of which type of paper was more desirable for the contemplated use.

In an organization with formal allocations of authority, the question would not be submitted to the superior in this form. Instead, each subordinate would claim that decisions specifying the quality of paper lay within *his* sphere of authority. Instead of deciding which paper was best, the superior would be forced to decide *which officer should decide which paper was best*. Instead of a question of technology, he would be faced with a *question of administration*.

In practice, of course, the issue is seldom decided on such a clearcut basis. The administrative superior will generally inquire both into questions of authority and into the merits of the case. Considerations of expediency influence him more when jurisdictional lines are vague than when the allocation of authority is clear. On the other hand, in order to maintain the lines of authority and the division of work in his organization, he must often support a particular decision because it lay within the sphere of authority of the decider rather than because it was the correct decision.

Even with these qualifications the illustration just given is a grave oversimplification of the actual problem, for it gives consideration only to the maintenance of the authority relation. In practice, when a conflict of authority is appealed to an administrator he must take into consideration (1) the effect his decision will have on the lines of authority, (2) the effect it will have upon organization policy, and (3) the information the conflict gives him with respect to the soundness and competence of his subordinates. The first point has already been discussed.

With respect to the second point, it is probably true that the administrator will be inclined to look into the merits of the dispute rather than to decide it on jurisdictional grounds, if it is an important question of organizational policy. As a matter of fact, jurisdictional disputes are an important means of bringing to the top administrator significant issues of policy, and of preventing these from being decided at lower levels without his knowledge. Similarly (this bears on the third point), they are a means of informing him about the characteristics and viewpoints of his subordinates. Particularly when policy in the organization is in its formative stages, there may be important advantages, therefore, to the top administrator in a somewhat indefinite allocation of authority that would permit such disputes to arise. Certainly the technique of "playing one against the other" is used by top administrators so often that it cannot be casually dismissed as poor administration.

If the administrator uses this technique of maintaining control over the decisions of his subordinates, he is faced with the very delicate tasks of preventing organizational and jurisdictional lines from dissolving completely, and of preventing the differences among subordinates which he adjudicates from degenerating into personal quarrels or feuds among subunits of the organization for power and influence. Regardless of these dangers, to avoid the use of such methods may lead to virtual abdication.

Rank

Rank, as a basis for authority relations, is always employed in connection with a hierarchy of authority. In military organizations, and some others, it is absolutely necessary to provide a continuity of authority, and a certainty in authority relations at all times. This is accomplished by the system of rank. When emergency, death, or absence of an officer temporarily disrupts the normal organizational pattern, rank is used to reestablish a system of authority.

This device, too, creates administrative complexities. An enlisted man, on a mission for one office, may be given conflicting instructions by another officer. The only safeguard here is the restraint of each officer, and his knowledge that he will be held to an accounting for a disruption of the administrative organization through the abuse of his authority.

The Application of Sanctions

It may be well to repeat at this point that authority, as the term is used in this volume, refers to the *acceptance* by the subordinate of the decisions of the superior and not the power of the superior to apply sanctions in case of noncompliance. In most present-day organizations an employee's immediate superior does not possess the unregulated power of hiring and firing, although, regardless of whether there is a formal service rating scheme, that superior's estimate of him will probably be a major factor in determining his chances of promotions, pay increases, and the like.

As the power of the immediate superior to impose sanctions is circumscribed, he must rely more and more on other more positive incentives to enforce his authority. On the other hand those who have the power to apply sanctions will, by their use of this power, either reinforce or weaken the lines of authority that have been established. Inability to discipline, either directly or by appeal to his superiors, a subordinate who is disloyal will rapidly destroy the authority of any individual in the administrative hierarchy.

Hence, when the power to discipline rests with the immediate superior, the system of authority in the organization will generally take on and retain rather definite hierarchical structure. Each individual will know who the "boss" is. It may be conjectured that under these conditions those individuals who, according to the plan of organization, exercise zoned "functional" authority without disciplinary powers will take on more nearly an advisory than an authoritative role.

It will be noticed that, regardless of whether the power to apply sanctions is distributed throughout the administrative hierarchy or is concentrated in the higher levels of that hierarchy, "unity of command" will generally be observed to the extent that a given individual will not be subjected to sanctions from two independent sources. This is a distinct, and narrower, concept of unity of command than the two stated previously, for it refers not to the right to issue orders, but to the power to impose sanctions for noncompliance with orders.

Concluding Comments

This volume is primarily a work of description rather than prescription. No attempt will be made to state definite principles as to the proper use of these several devices for the allocation of authority, but some tentative comments may be offered. Virtually no organization attempts to get along without some sort of hierarchy of authority. Some organizations operate on the theory that this hierarchy defines the sole channels of authority, others on the theory that the hierarchy is to be reverted to only in case of conflicts of authority. Whatever the theory, the practice almost always represents some compromise between these two.

In almost all organizations, authority is also zoned by subject matter; and the subject-matter allocation will sometimes conflict with the hierarchical allocation. In these cases the hierarchy is used as a mechanism for resolving jurisdictional disputes. These disputes afford the top administrator an important source of information as to what is going on at lower levels, and he will not be inclined to try to eliminate them entirely, even if he could, by a watertight allocation of authority. The distribution of the power to apply sanctions, and the use of this power, will have a considerable influence on the sharpness of the lines of authority and on the relative importance of hierarchical and subject-matter authority.

In some organizations the hierarchy and the zoning of authority will need to be supplemented by a system of rank to prevent breaks in the continuity of command.

FORMAL AND INFORMAL ORGANIZATION

The manner in which authority is used to maintain coordination in organization has already been discussed. Procedural coordination—the specification of the lines of authority, and the spheres of activity and authority of each organization member—creates a *formal organization,* a set of abstract, more or less permanent relations that govern the behavior of each participant. It will be noticed that authority enters into the formal organization in two ways: first, the authority of those individuals who exercise control over the group is employed to establish and enforce the scheme of formal organization; second, the scheme of formal organization itself prescribes the lines of authority and division of work that shall be followed in carrying out the work of the organization.

To illustrate, Acts of Congress may set up a Department of Agriculture, specify the general departmental organization, and the responsibilities of the agency. The Secretary of Agriculture, deriving authority from this formal organization plan, may then himself create a formal structure *within* the department, dividing work, and further delegating his authority.

In addition to allocating zones of activity and establishing authority relationships, the scheme of formal organization may also establish procedures and lines of communication. The body of regulations will establish who may employ or fire whom; who will give orders to whom; who is responsible for particular jobs; whose signature a particular type of decision must have; and so forth. For the most part, these relationships can be described rather abstractly, without reference to the particular content of the organization's work.

This formal scheme of organization will always differ from the organization as it actually operates in several important respects. First, there will be many omissions in it—the actual organization will exhibit many interpersonal relationships that are nowhere specified in the formal scheme. The vice president in charge of sales frequently plays golf with the comptroller, and on these occasions they discuss business problems. Second, the interpersonal relations in the organization as it operates may be in actual contradiction to the specifications. The operator of a lathe may refuse to accept his foreman's instructions as to the speed at which he should operate his machine on a particular job. The organization scheme may provide that Department A will be informed of certain decisions made in Department B, but this is not done.

The term "informal organization" refers to interpersonal relations in the organization that affect decisions within it but either are omitted from the formal scheme or are not consistent with that scheme. It would probably be fair to say that no formal organization will operate effectively without an accompanying informal organization. Every new organization must have its initial "shakedown cruise" before it will run smoothly; and each new organization member must establish informal relations with his colleagues before he becomes a significant part of the working organization.

Even if it were desirable, the formal structure could not be specified in such detail as to obviate the need for an informal supplement. On the other hand, the formal structure performs no function unless it actually sets limits to the informal relations that are permitted to develop within it. In particular, it is an important function of the formal organization to prevent the development of organization politics—struggle for influence and authority—to a point that would be deleterious to the functioning of the organization; and a further function to detect and eliminate unnecessary duplication and overlapping in the work of the parts of the organization. Perhaps a more positive function of the formal, in relation to the informal, structure is to encourage the development of the latter along constructive lines. That is, a proper allocation of duties and the maintenance of adequate channels of communication may both relieve the need for the growth of informal channels, and encourage cross-fertilization and attitudes of cooperation within the informal structure.

PSYCHOLOGY AND THE THEORY OF AUTHORITY

It is important to note that propositions about human behavior, *in so far as it is rational*, do not ordinarily involve propositions about the psychology of the person who is behaving. Let us explain this rather paradoxical statement. In a given situation, and with a given system of values, there is only one course of action which an individual can rationally pursue. It is that course which under the given circumstances maximizes the attainment of value. Hence, psychological propositions, other than descriptions of an individual's value system, are needed only to explain why his behavior, in any given instance, *departs* from the norm of rationality.

Likewise, propositions about the behavior of members of an organization, *in so far as that behavior is governed by the system of authority in the organization*, do not ordinarily involve propositions about the psychology of the person who is behaving. That is, in so far as a person is obedient to the decisions of another, his psychology has nothing to do with his behavior. Hence, psychological propositions are important for determining the area within which authority will be respected, but have no significance for determining what behavior will be *within this area*.

It should be added, of course, that in many cases it is very difficult for the superior to control the interpretation and application that is given his orders by the subordinate, and in so far as this is true the attitudes of the latter are of very considerable importance. Apart from actual insubordination, an order may be carried out intelligently or unintelligently, promptly or slowly, enthusiastically or grudgingly. The statement of the previous paragraph might be more cautiously restated: Psychological propositions are important for determining the area within which authority will be respected, and the degree to which the intent of the order-giver will actually be carried out; but in so far as the authority is actually accepted they have no significance for determining what the subordinate's behaviors will be.

For illustration let us consider the literature on military psychology. This literature is concerned with one central problem—how to enlarge the area within which the soldier, when faced with the dangers of battle and the hardships of campaign life, will obey his superiors.[21]

---

[21]Col. J. F. C. Fuller, *op. cit.*, pp. 140–141; Ardant du Picq, *Etudes sur le combat* (Paris: Hachette et Cie., 1880), pp. 7–8, and *passim*.

If the obedience of soldiers were perfect, then military operations would be limited only by the soldiers' physiological endurance—their marching endurance, and their vulnerability to the effects of bullets. A unit could fail in an attack only through the physical extermination of its members by the enemy, and the only data needed in planning operations would be statistical information on the effects of fire under different conditions.[22]

Actually, however, before a unit is exterminated, it will usually reach a point where its members will refuse obedience. They will refuse to advance when ordered to do so, or they will surrender to the enemy. The real limiting factors, then, in an attack, are the psychological factors which determine when the soldiers will refuse further obedience to commands. To be sure, behind disobedience or surrender will lie the fear of extermination, but the actual amount of destruction necessary before morale fails varies within wide limits under different circumstances.[23]

Psychology, then, enters into administration as a *condition*, just as physiological, physical, or other environmental factors may enter in. It is part of the technology of administration, rather than a part of the administrative theory itself.

SUMMARY

In this chapter the behavior of the organized group was explored with a view to isolating some of its salient characteristics. An individual acts as a member of a group when he applies the same general scale of values to his choices as do other members of the group, and when his expectations of the behavior of other members influence his own decisions.

In all but the simplest varieties of group behavior, definite procedures are adopted for securing coordination. A procedure is coordinative when it adapts the behavior of each individual to a plan for the group. In all cases, coordination requires communication of at least certain critical elements in the group situation to the members of the group.

When coordination goes farther than mere communication, when it deliberately influences the behavior of group members in desired directions, it ordinarily involves some measure of authority. Authority is exercised over an individual whenever that individual, relaxing his own critical faculties, permits the communicated decision of another person to guide his own choice.

[22]In the recent war this was evidently nearly true of Japanese soldiers. If so, the limits of authority here were physiological rather than psychological.

[23]Col. Gen. von Balck, *Tactics*, trans. Walter Krueger (Fort Leavenworth, Kans.: U.S. Cavalry Association, 1911), pp. 185–200.

Authority is only one of a number of forms of influence. Its distinguishing characteristic is that it does not seek to convince the subordinate, but only to obtain his acquiescence. In actual exercise, of course, authority is usually liberally admixed with suggestion and persuasion. An important function of authority is to permit a decision to be made and carried out, even when agreement cannot be reached. Perhaps this arbitrary aspect of authority has been overemphasized, however, in discussions of the concept. In any case, the arbitrary element in authority is limited to the "area of acceptance" of the subordinate.

The magnitude of the area of acceptance depends upon the sanctions which authority has available to enforce its commands. At least as important as the negative sanctions—physical and economic force—are community of purpose, social acceptance, and personality.

In administration the avoidance of contradictory authority-relations is sometimes an important problem. The problem is met by establishing a determinate hierarchy of authority, and by zoning authority along functional or other lines. It is seldom possible, however, to eliminate twilight zones within which conflicts of authority may occur. It is an important administrative task to maintain the organization structure by adjudicating "boundary disputes" with respect to authority.

Coordination is only one of the three functions which authority performs in administrative organization. Authority is also an important factor in the enforcement of responsibility, and in the specialization of decision-making.

The problem of responsibility, which has already been discussed at length in Chapter III, arises whenever it is desirable or necessary to enforce the adherence of the individual to the group plan. Sanctions play a more important part in the responsibility-enforcing function of authority than in its other uses.

The advantages which are obtained from the division and specialization of work may also be claimed for the division and specialization of the decision-making function. Authority, by permitting the decision reached by one member in an organization to influence the behavior of other members, makes possible the specialization of decision-making.

A formal organization is a plan for the division of work and the allocation of authority. The organization plan gives to each member of the group his status and role in relation to the other members, but it specifies the *content* of his work and his decisional function only in very general terms. It is to the substantive aspects of decision—the criteria of choice rather than the procedure of choice—that we must turn next.

THE ROLE OF AUTHORITY

THE USES OF AUTHORITY IN ORGANIZATIONS have been the topic of much discussion and social criticism in the last generation or two, and even the need for a traditional hierarchy of authority has sometimes been questioned.[24] This commentary will address three issues: the extent to which formal authority causes alienation from the organization and inhibits self-actualization, the potential of employee participation in decision-making for increasing worker satisfaction and productivity, and the effects of an appetite for power on the functioning of organizations.

AUTHORITY AND ALIENATION[25]

Chapter VII describes how authority is used in organizations, and especially its role in the decision-making process. It will be informative to link that discussion of authority with the discussion of work satisfaction in the commentary to Chapter VI.

Sometimes it is said that the main problem with organizations is that they require people to exercise and to accept authority—as they certainly do—and that authority is inimical to the mature development of the human personality.[26] Acceptance of authority, it is said by these critics, induces attitudes of dependency and passivity and inhibits self-actualization.

Accepting authority in an organization, we have seen, means accepting premises provided by other organization members as part of the basis for one's own behavior. There are many reasons why people might accept a greater or lesser exercise of authority over their behavior. If the premises employees are asked to accept and the things they are asked to

[24]D. P. McCaffrey, S. R. Faerman, and D. W. Hart, "The Appeal and Difficulties of Participative Systems," *Organization Science*, 6:603–627 (1995), provides valuable recent discussion of these issues and numerous references to the literature.

[25]This section draws upon "Are We Alienated from Our Organizations?" *SUPALUM* (School of Urban and Public Affairs Alumni Magazine, Carnegie Mellon University), vol. 6, no. 1, pp. 6–7 (1979).

[26]A prominent exponent of this point of view is Chris Argyris. See his *Personality and Organization* (New York: Harper & Bros., 1957).

do are not antithetical to their own beliefs and values, they may regard a wage or some other kind of extrinsic reward as a sufficient reason for acceptance. A belief that the organization's product was socially valuable, or valuable to the employee, would provide additional reasons for acceptance. That is to say, authority might be obeyed in an organization because it was believed that the authority structure was instrumental in getting the organization's job done, and because the utility of getting that job done was accepted by reason of either intrinsic or extrinsic motives.

When authority is exercised in this way and accepted with these motives, there is no reason to suppose that most people regard it as demeaning, or that it creates attitudes of dependency and passivity in them. It is a myth—widely believed but not less mythical for that—that people are most creative when they are most free. All of the psychological evidence suggests instead that people are most creative, and most capable of self-actualization, when their environment provides them with an appropriate amount of structure, not too much and not too little. When the environment is too strictly structured, creativity suffers from lack of opportunities for exploration and problem-solving. When the environment demands too little, creativity suffers for lack of structure that can be discovered and exploited. The Gothic cathedrals are a great example of the flowering of creativity operating within a framework of strict physical and social constraints, imposed by the law of gravity and the tenets of religion, respectively. There is no reason to believe that more freedom would have made the cathedral builders more creative.

Human beings seek to satisfy in organizations a wide variety of needs—including needs for achievement, for affiliation with others, and for power. Organizations can be cogent instruments for satisfying needs for achievement and affiliation, and to the extent to which these needs predominate among their members, the exercise of authority creates no special problems. With needs for power, matters are different, for if these needs are satisfied for those who exercise power, they are thwarted for those who submit to it.

The contemporary challenge to authority in organizations may well be a symptom of a more general shift in our society from concerns with achievement and affiliation to concerns with power. Certainly the same challenge to authority has affected institutions like the family, including parent-child relations. There is narrower and more reluctant acceptance of authority than in the past in all our social institutions, and not just in formal organizations. Most of us would, I think, regard the muting of authority that has taken place in our lifetimes as desirable. It does not follow that an indefinite continuation of the same trend would be equally desirable, particularly if it is motivated by a preoccupation with the distribution of power rather than the effectiveness of organizations as instruments toward personal and social goals.

Those who criticize modern organizations as authoritarian and creativity-suppressing seem to proceed from two premises:

1. That the exercise of authority in organizations is directly inimical to self-actualization.
2. That the workplace is the principal arena for self-actualization and for realizing central life satisfactions.

As we have seen, this second premise may represent a misconception of the role that organizations play in most people's lives, and that people want them to play. Some people—some managers, some professional people, some craftsmen—may find their major satisfactions in their work and during their working hours. They must be careful not to ascribe the same value system to all the other members of their society, or to assume it would be better if all who did not have these values would acquire them.

Most people appear to see organizations primarily or even exclusively as instrumental systems—systems that produce society's goods and services, and that provide their employees with the wherewithal to lead pleasant and satisfying lives, primarily during the leisure time that is left them. From the accounts we reviewed in the commentary to Chapter VI, this is probably the role that organizations and work have always played in the lives of people, pre-industrial as well as industrial.

These remarks should not be interpreted as a claim that contemporary organizations represent the best of all possible worlds. There are many ways they can be improved, and a continued application of automation in order to reduce the need for those occupations that seem most routine and "alienating" is just one of those ways. But while we are improving our organizations, it is important that we enhance their abilities to do their main job, which is to serve as social instruments: to get work done, and thereby to increase the goods, services, and leisure that they make available to their members and to all members of society. The employment relation and the authority associated with it have been essential means for using organizations to perform these tasks.

EMPLOYEE PARTICIPATION IN DECISION-MAKING

For nearly a half century, a central theme in social psychological and sociological research on organizations and in the work of consultants on organizational behavior has been the idea of broadening employee participation in the decision-making process. The claim usually made is that participation increases both employee satisfaction and productivity. The evidence from the numerous empirical studies that have been carried out is mixed. In general, participation does increase employee satisfaction, but it does not appear to have a consistent effect upon productivity.[27]

Interest in the subject has been reawakened by the use of quality circles in Japan, and their presumptive role as one of the elements in the rapid growth of Japanese productivity. To work our way around the sometimes conflicting empirical evidence, let us start at the other end and ask what theory would predict. The issues are both motivational and cognitive. On the motivational side, we might postulate that participation increases satisfaction; which increases employee identification with the organization's goals, including productivity goals; which leads to increased effort, care in work, and desire to solve problems; which increases production. On the cognitive side, we might postulate that workers have certain kinds of information about the work that is not as directly available to their supervisors or to management, and that employees' participation in decision-making leads them to contribute this information to diagnosing and solving quality problems (and other kinds of problems as well).[28]

If these are the important underlying mechanisms then at least two crucial conditions must be satisfied in order for participation to increase production: (1) the basic attitude of the employees to the organization must be sufficiently positive that the opportunity to participate is welcomed and leads to an increase in identification with organization goals; (2) the employees must, through observation or otherwise, have access to information about the manufacturing process that is important to maintaining product quality. It is easy to see that these conditions might be satisfied in some factory situations and not in others. It can also be seen that success with participative activities will depend on how they are conducted, and requires focusing on what employees are in a position to contribute. There is no reason to suppose that employees will be willing or able to increase productivity unless these conditions are met.

The theory just outlined is quite different from the proposition that employees who have the opportunity to participate in decision-making will "work harder." The idea of the quality circles was not to induce employees to work harder, but to enable them to apply knowledge and intelligence toward improving the manufacturing process, including their

---

[27]See V. Vroom, *The New Leadership: Managing Participation in Organization* (Englewood Cliffs, N.J.: Prentice-Hall, 1988); K. E. Weick, *The Social Psychology of Organizing*, 2nd ed. (Reading, Mass.: Addison-Wesley, 1979).

[28]McCaffrey, Faerman, and Hart, *op. cit.*

part in it. Application of the principles of quality control, which empha-sizes preventing defective work by tightening the manufacturing process rather than screening out defective products, can, in situations where standards are at all hard to meet, lead to very great increases in produc-tivity. If 80 per cent of the products are defective (not unusual, for exam-ple, in the early days of computer chip manufacture), then reducing defects to 20 per cent increases productivity by a factor of four.

Returning to the general topic of participation, we see that it is something quite different from "democratization" of the workplace or the general withering away of the hierarchy of formal organizational author-ity. There is little evidence that many employees wish to participate in decisions that are not directly related to their own work experience and knowledge, except for decisions that bear directly on wages and other employment issues and thereby affect achievement of their personal goals. These latter issues, of course, raise questions of union representa-tion of workers and of employee representation on company boards of directors. These are important questions, but they fall outside the scope of this book.

ATTRACTION TO POWER

We do need to discuss briefly, however, the attraction that the prospect of holding power exerts on some people, both employees and their employers. Power, and formal authority as a form of power, is a frequently useful tool for attaining one's objectives. But it is not uncommon for power to become a goal in its own right, sought for its own sake. There are large interpersonal differences among people in the needs they feel for power, relative to their needs for affiliation with others or for achieve-ment.[29] A balanced account of human motivation in organizations has to provide a significant role for all of these needs, and others, in shaping the feelings, thoughts, and actions of participants.

The need for power can be felt and expressed both by those who exercise it and by those over whom it is exercised. We call a manager authoritarian if he or she has a paramount need for power and little need for achievement or affiliation. But the alienated worker may be the very same person in the reciprocal role: this time urged by a need for power to rebel against attempts to control or influence his or her behavior.

In a world oriented toward power, "who controls" becomes the cen-tral issue that overshadows "what is accomplished." It is in precisely such

[29]See J. W. Atkinson, An Introduction to Motivation (Princeton, N.J.: Van Nostrand, 1964); and D. C. McClelland et al., The Achievement Motive (New York: Appleton, 1953).

a power-focused world that it becomes most difficult to establish openness and trust among participants and self-actualization becomes synonymous with anarchy. Among the most unpleasant consequences of the expression of power needs is a dramatic upsurge of mistrust, anger, and fear between the contending groups.

Notice that this witch's brew of dysfunctional consequences cannot be concocted from power alone. It arises out of interaction between a system of interdependencies on the one hand, and a high *need* for power among the participants (managers and managed alike) on the other. A classical issue in the design of organizations and societies is to determine how these dysfunctional consequences can be avoided or mitigated while permitting the accomplishment of the organization's tasks (i.e., meeting needs for achievement and affiliation). The so-called "human relations school" of research on organizations has tended to choose de-emphasis of authority relations as the way out, but sometimes at the price of downplaying the consequences for organizational effectiveness.

Another way out, of course, is to find means for shifting human attention from needs for power to needs for achievement and affiliation. Lord Acton observed that "power corrupts and absolute power corrupts absolutely." A new Lord Acton might say: "What corrupts is not power, but the need for power; and it corrupts both the powerful and the powerless." Readers who can recall the student unrest of the 1960s and '70s will remember the students' remarkable preoccupation with student power and with freedom from adult power, and their incoherence about the goals that the newly won power was to serve.

These phenomena are quite familiar to theorists of revolution. Destabilization of a social system, for whatever reason, creates needs for power within each of the self-identified social groups that now find the relations between "we" and "they" full of uncertainty and threat. It is in this context, too, that we must interpret the self-destructive behavior of both employees and employers that often emerges during industrial strikes.

It is an essential managerial task to create an environment in the organization in which authority can be used effectively as a tool for accomplishing the organization's objectives rather than as an end in itself, without stimulating the latent urges of either managers or employees to use power for power's sake.

CHAPTER VIII

Communication

THE ROLE OF COMMUNICATION in the influencing of decisions has been mentioned many times in the preceding pages and particularly in the last chapter. It is time now to examine more systematically this important aspect of the decisional process.

The first topic to be taken up will be the nature and functions of communication systems. This will be followed by a discussion of formal and informal channels of communication. A third section of the chapter will be devoted to those elements in an administrative organization which are specialized for the function of communication; while the final section will discuss the role of training in communication.

NATURE AND FUNCTIONS OF COMMUNICATION

Communication may be formally defined as any process whereby decisional premises are transmitted from one member of an organization to another. It is obvious that without communication there can be no organization, for there is no possibility then of the group influencing the behavior of the individual. Not only is communication absolutely essential to organization, but the availability of particular techniques of communication will in large part determine the way in which decision-making functions can and should be distributed throughout the organization. The possibility of permitting a particular individual to make a particular decision will often hinge on whether there can be transmitted to him the information he will need to make a wise decision, and whether he, in turn, will be able to transmit his decision to other members of the organization whose behavior it is supposed to influence.

Communication in organizations is a two-way process: it comprehends both the transmittal *to* a decisional center (i.e. an individual vested with the responsibility for making particular decisions) of orders, information, and advice; and the transmittal of the decisions reached *from* this center to other parts of the organization. Moreover, it is a process that takes place upward, downward, and laterally throughout the organization. The information and orders that flow downward through the formal channels of authority and the information that flows upward through these same channels are only a small part of the total network of communications in any actual organization.[1]

The information and knowledge that have a bearing on decisions arise at various points in the organization. Sometimes the organization has its own "sensory organs"—the intelligence unit of a military organization, or the market analysis section of a business firm. Sometimes individuals are recruited and installed in positions for the knowledge they are presumed already to possess—a legal division. Sometimes the knowledge develops on the job itself—the lathe operator is the first one to know when his machine breaks down. Sometimes the knowledge is knowledge of other decisions that have been made—the executive turns down one request for expenditure of funds because he knows that he has already committed these funds to another use.

In all these cases particular individuals in the organization are possessed of information that is relevant to particular decisions that have to be made. An apparently simple way to allocate the function of decision-making would be to assign to each member of the organization those decisions for which he possesses the relevant information. The basic difficulty in this is that not all the information relevant to a particular decision is possessed by a single individual. If the decision is then dismembered into its component premises and these allocated to separate individuals, a communication process must be set up for transmitting these components from the separate centers to some point where they can be combined and transmitted, in turn, to those members in the organization who will have to carry them out.

Only in the case where the man who is to carry out a decision is also the man best fitted to make that decision is there no problem of communication—and in this exceptional case there is of course no reason for organization. In all other cases means must be devised for transmitting information from its organizational sources to decisional centers, from centers where component decisions are made to centers where these are combined, and from the latter to the points in the organization where the decisions are to be carried out.

Military organization has developed especially elaborate procedures for accomplishing the gathering and transmittal of information. An important reason for this is that the information on which military deci-

---

[1] Barnard's discussion of communications (*op. cit.* pp. 175–181) suffers somewhat from his identification of communication channels with channels of authority.

sions—particularly tactical decisions—depend is of a rapidly changing nature, ascertainable only at the moment of decision.

> Military information is essential to the efficient preparation and execu-
> tion of strategical and tactical plans. It constitutes a vital element in
> the commander's estimate of the situation and decision. Continuous
> research of information by all available means throughout the course of
> operations is necessary to the successful operations of all units . . .
> Information collected by combat units in the field relates chiefly to
> the enemy forces with which they are in contact . . .
> The necessary orientation is given to the research of information by
> the issuance of instructions to subordinate units indicating the points
> of greatest importance to the execution of the commander's plan of
> operations and to the security of the command. . . .
> Each unit commander, in his own zone of operation, directs the
> research of information in accordance with instructions received, and
> in addition independently carries out such researches as are dictated by
> his special situation or required for the execution of the operation in
> which he is engaged.
> The evaluation, collation, and analysis of military information is the
> duty of the intelligence division of the general staff of large units and of
> the intelligence agencies of brigades, regiments, and battalions . . .
> Analysis of the information received leads to a more or less com-
> plete reconstruction of the enemy's situation and activities and fre-
> quently furnishes the best indication of his intentions.[2]

The difficulties of transmission from sources of information to decision centers tend to draw the latter toward the former, while the difficulties of transmission from decision centers to points of action create a pull
in the opposite direction. The task of properly locating decision centers
is one of balancing these opposing pulls.

The pulls that tend to bring about a centralization of the decision-
making functions and a consequent separation of decision from action
have already been discussed from a slightly different viewpoint in the
previous chapter. These pulls are the need for responsibility, expertise,
and coordination. The two principal pulls in the opposite direction—
that of decentralization—are, first, the fact that a very large portion of
the information that is relevant to decisions originates at the operating
level, and second, that the separation of decision from action increases
the time and man-power costs of making and transmitting decisions.

[2]U.S. Army Field Service Regulations, 1923, pp. 25–26.

FORMAL AND INFORMAL COMMUNICATION

The formal system of communications in any organization—those channels and media of communication which have been consciously and deliberately established—is soon supplemented by an equally important informal network of communications based on social relations within the organization. The relationship between the formal and the informal system is best understood through an examination of the media of communication.

Media of Formal Communication

The most obvious media of communication are the spoken word and memoranda and letters addressed from one member of an organization to another. A number of specialized written media need to be distinguished from the ordinary memorandum or letter. First, there is "paper flow"—the movement of a document from one point to another of an organization where it is successively processed. Next there are records and formal reports. Finally, there are manuals of organization practice and procedure.

Oral Communications. Only to a limited extent is any formal system of oral communications ordinarily established in the scheme of organization. To a certain degree the system of formal authority creates a presumption that oral communication will take place primarily between individuals and their immediate superiors or subordinates; but these are certainly never the exclusive channels of communications.

To a certain degree, also, the formal organization may place limits upon the ease with which upward communication takes place. Individuals at higher levels of the organization may be relatively inaccessible to all except their immediate subordinates. In military organizations, formal rules are developed to govern this matter of "accessibility"—the private speaks to the captain by permission of the sergeant—but in other organizations, even when the executive maintains an official "open door" policy, accessibility is regulated by informal social controls plus the device of a private secretary. In this case accessibility is really governed by the informal rather than the formal organization.

Physical propinquity may be a very real factor in determining the frequency of oral communication, and hence, the layout of offices is one of the important formal determinants of the communication system. Even the advent of the telephone has not very much diminished the importance of this factor, since a telephone conversation is by no means equivalent to a face-to-face contact.

Memoranda and Letters. The flow of memoranda and letters is more often subjected to formal control, particularly in large organizations, than is oral communication. In some organizations it is actually required that all written communications follow the lines of authority; but this is not common. Slightly more common is the requirement that communications skip not more than one link in the chain of authority. That is, if two individuals in different divisions of the same department wish to communicate, the communication must go to the first division head, from him to the second division head, and thence to the second individual, by-passing the head of the department.

In most organizations, however, no such strict requirements are imposed, except in the transmission of orders—a topic that has been covered in the previous chapter. "Clearance" rules are quite frequently established, however, that require copies of communications to be sent up the regular channels when the communication itself has cut across lines.

Paper-Flow. In certain cases—this is typical of organizations handling financial matters, like insurance companies, accounting departments, and Federal lending agencies—the organization's work, or some part of it, centers around the processing of a piece of paper. In a life insurance company, for example, applications are received, examined, accepted or rejected, policies issued, policy-holders billed for premiums, premiums processed, and benefits paid. The file representing the individual policy is the focal center of the organization's work. This file is moved from one point in the organization to another for various types of action—reviewing the application, recording a change of beneficiary, approving payment of benefits, and so on. As it moves it carries with it all the information regarding that policy which is needed in taking the required administrative action. The individual at that point *to which* it is moved for a particular action presumably possesses the knowledge of company regulations that must be applied to the policy information in order to reach a decision as to its disposition. The file permits the combining of the information relating to the individual policy-holder, which originates in the field, with the information relating to the company's practices and obligations, which originates in the central office. In this case the combining is accomplished by moving the information obtained in the field into the central office for decision through the flow of paper. In other situations this might be done by transmitting the central office information to the field through instructions, manuals, and the like.

Records and Reports. A vital part of the formal communications system of almost every organization is the system of records and reports. In the case of letters and memoranda, the individual initiating the communication must reach the decision that there is a need for transmission of certain information, and will decide what is to be transmitted. The distinguishing characteristic of records and reports is that they specify for the person who makes them out on what occasions he is expected to make reports (periodically or on the occurrence of a particular event or circumstance), and what information he is to include in them. This is highly important, for it largely relieves each organization member of the important but difficult task of continually deciding what part of the information he possesses should be passed on to other organization members, and in what form.

Manuals. The function of manuals is to communicate those organization practices which are intended to have relatively permanent application. In their absence, permanent policies will reside only in the minds of permanent organization members, and will soon cease to have any great influence upon practice. The preparation and revision of manuals serves to determine whether the organization members have a common understanding of the organization structure and policies. An important use of manuals, either in connection with or apart from a period of vestibule training, is to acquaint new organization members with these policies.

An almost inevitable consequence of the preparation and use of manuals is to increase the degree of centralization in decision-making. In the interest of "completeness" and "uniformity" the individuals preparing a manual almost always include in it matters that have previously been left to individuals to decide, and embody these matters in organization policy. This is by no means all sheer gain, for "completeness" and "uniformity," unless required in the interest of coordination, do not have any particular value for an organization.

Informal Communications

No matter how elaborate a system of formal communications is set up in the organization, this system will always be supplemented by informal channels. Through these informal channels will flow information, advice, and even orders (the reader will recall that, in terms of our definitions, an authority relation can exist even though the superior is not vested with any sanctions). In time, the actual system of relationships may come to differ widely from those specified in the formal organization scheme.

The informal communications system is built around the social relationships of the members of the organization. Friendship between two individuals creates frequent occasions for contact and "shop talk." It may also create an authority relationship if one of the individuals comes to accept the leadership of the other. In this way "natural leaders" secure a role in the organization that is not always reflected in the organization chart.

The informal communication system takes on additional importance when it is remembered that the behavior of individuals in organizations is oriented not only toward the organization's goals but also to a certain extent toward their personal goals, and that these two sets of goals are not always mutually consistent. Hence, when organization members deal with one another, each must attempt to assess the extent to which the other's attitudes and actions are conditioned by personal rather than organizational motives. When a primary relationship has been estab- lished between them, it becomes easier for each to make this assessment, and easier for them to be frank in regard to their motives. Requests for cooperation will less often meet with the reaction: "You run your depart- ment, and I will run mine." (This problem of identification with, or loy- alty to, a particular segment of the organization will be discussed more fully in Chapter X below.)

Primary relationships can be unfriendly, of course, just as easily as they can be friendly, although there is what might be called a "presump- tion of friendliness" in most social relationships in our society. It becomes a major task of the executives, then, to maintain attitudes of friendliness and cooperation in these direct personal relationships so that the infor- mal communication system will contribute to the efficient operation of the organization rather than hinder it.

The informal communications system is sometimes used by organiza- tion members to advance their personal aims. From this arises the phe- nomenon of cliques—groups that build up an informal network of commu- nications and use this as a means of securing power in the organization. Rivalry among cliques, in turn, may lead to general unfriendliness in social relationships and defeat the purpose of the informal communica- tions system.

There has been little systematic analysis of the way in which the for- mal organization structure encourages or hinders the formation of cliques, or of the techniques that can be used by executives to deal with cliques and minimize their harmfulness. On the first score, it may be con- jectured that weakness of the formal system of communications and fail- ure to secure an adequate measure of coordination through that system probably encourage the development of cliques. The coordinating func- tion that cliques perform under such circumstances is closely analogous to the coordinating function performed by political machines in a highly decentralized governmental structure like the American system.

A great deal of the informal communication in any organization is far less deliberate than the activities of cliques or even the conversations of executives who lunch together. In addition to these there is the great mass of communication that goes under the head of "gossip." In most organizations the "grapevine" probably plays, on the whole, a constructive role. Its chief disadvantages are, first, that it discourages frankness, since confidential remarks may be spread about, and, second, that the information transmitted by the grapevine is very often inaccurate. On the other hand, in addition to transmitting information that no one has thought to transmit formally, the grapevine is valuable as a barometer of "public opinion" in the organization. If the administrator listens to it, it apprises him of the topics that are subjects of interest to organization members, and their attitudes toward these topics. Even for this latter purpose, of course, the grapevine needs to be supplemented by other channels of information.

Personal Motivation and Communication

We have just seen that personal motivation may have considerable influence upon the growth of the informal communication system. In particular, individuals may develop this system as a means of increasing their own power and influence in the organization. There is another way in which personal motivation affects communication—both formal and informal. Information does not *automatically* transmit itself from its point of origin to the rest of the organization; the individual who first obtains it must transmit it. In transmitting it, he will naturally be aware of the consequences its transmission will have for him. When he knows that the boss is going to be "burned up" by the news, the news is very likely to be suppressed.[3]

Hence, information tends to be transmitted upward in the organization only if (1) its transmission will not have unpleasant consequences for the transmitter, or (2) the superior will hear of it anyway from other channels, and it is better to tell him first, or (3) it is information that the superior needs in his dealings with his own superiors, and he will be displeased if he is caught without it. In addition, there is often failure to transmit information upward simply because the subordinate cannot visualize accurately what information his superior needs in order to make his decisions.

A major communications problem, then, of the higher levels of the administrative hierarchy is that much of the information relevant to the decisions at this level originates at lower levels, and may not ever reach

---

[3]This point has been very well discussed by Burleigh Gardner in *Human Relations in Industry*, chap. ii, and the present exposition follows closely Gardner's analysis.

the higher levels unless the executive is extraordinarily alert. As has already been pointed out, an important function of a system of formal records and reports is to transfer from the subordinate to the superior the responsibility for deciding what information will be transmitted upward.

There is a converse problem that arises when a superior withholds information from a subordinate. This, again, may be accidental—the superior does not realize that his subordinate needs the information. On the other hand, the superior may use his exclusive possession of information as a means of maintaining his authority over the subordinate. It is hard to see that the latter, which is usually a symptom of an incompetent and insecure executive, has any constructive function in organization. The former, equally unfortunate, is of frequent occurrence in most organizations, largely because of lack of sufficient consideration to the needs of downward transmission of information other than orders.

Receptivity to Communications

Consideration has been given thus far principally to the source of communications. Attention must be given also to their destination. It has been pointed out that the attention that will be given a communication by its recipient is not simply a matter of logic. The source of the communication, and the way in which it is presented, will determine for its recipient how much consideration he will give it. If formal channels are maintained, communications flowing through these channels will have their effect enhanced by the authority which their "official" character gives them. Unsolicited information or advice, on the other hand, may be given little or no attention.

This dependence of the weight of a communication upon its source applies in upward as well as downward transmittal—suggestions transmitted upward may receive scanty consideration unless the person offering the suggestion is in a formal advisory position and transmits it "through channels." Much frustration results therefrom, particularly in the lower levels of the organization, but it is hard to see how this can be completely eliminated without destroying the organization structure.

The attention a communication will receive will also depend upon its form. In the discussion of the authority relation in the previous chapter, emphasis was placed on the acceptance of authority by the subordinate. The crucial point is whether the recipient of an order, or of any other kind of communication, is influenced by the communication in his actions or decisions, or whether he is not. The problem of securing employees' compliance with a safety rule is not very different from the problem of securing a customer's acceptance of a particular brand of soap.

In some cases formal authority may be a sufficient inducement for the subordinate to comply; but usually the communication must reason, plead, and persuade, as well as order, if it is to be effective.

In the same connection, consideration must be given to whether the communication should be oral or written; and whether it should be in formal or informal language. In every case the state of mind of the recipient, his attitudes and motivations, must be the basic factors in determining the design of the communication. The function of the communication, after all, is not to get something off the mind of the person transmitting it, but to get something into the mind and actions of the person receiving it.

SPECIALIZED ORGANS OF COMMUNICATION

Because of the great importance of communication to their functioning, most organizations, even of moderate size, develop certain specialized communications tasks. Decision-centers themselves—that is, executive positions—must often be staffed with persons who can assist the executive in his communications functions. The organization develops specialized repositories of its official "memory"—files, records, libraries, follow-up systems. Organization units may be established to handle specific information-gathering functions: accounting, inspection, administrative analysis, intelligence, and the like. The larger the organization, the farther it becomes possible to carry this specialization.

Organization of Decision-Centers

A number of the communications tasks of the administrator need not be performed personally, but may be delegated to staff assistants in his office. Included among these are the drafting of outgoing communications, the screening of incoming communications, and liaison.

The drafting of outgoing communications hardly requires comment. It is one of the common functions of secretaries, and important executives often have assistants with such functions. Perhaps the most elaborate specialization of this sort is the Bureau of the Budget in the Executive Office of the President, which has, as one of its important functions, the drafting of presidential orders, as well as the drafting of bills for submission to Congress.

The possibility of this type of division of work does have one important consequence. It means that, by the attachment of specialists to the executive's office, outgoing communications can receive a review from the standpoint of their respective specialties without complicating the scheme of authority. This system is perhaps best developed in military organization, where an artillery officer, for example, on the divisional commander's staff will work out the artillery phases of an operational plan, and so forth. The executive himself—and in the military example, his chief of staff—exercises the function of coordinating and balancing these specialties.

The review of incoming communications to determine which should receive the personal attention of the executive is also a delegable function that is specialized for important executive positions. In some cases this extends to the preparation of analyses and recommendations for the executive which are transmitted to him with the communication. In other cases, the executive's staff may be able to take action on the communication, by-passing him completely.

The delegation by the executive to his staff of the function of liaison with subordinates or with other organization units creates somewhat more delicate problems than the other two types of delegation. Unless the relationships are carefully defined, the subordinates of the executive may fail to recognize that the liaison officer is exercising authority not on his own initiative, but as representative of his chief. As a result of this ambiguity, considerable resentment may develop against the liaison officer and he may lose his usefulness. In many civilian organizations the distinction between an assistant department head and an assistant to the department head is not clearly understood, and such organizations would do well to observe the care with which this distinction is made in military organization.

Repositories of Organization "Memory"

Since an organization is not an organism the only memory it possesses, in the proper sense of the term, is the collective memory of its participants. This is insufficient for organization purposes, first, because what is in one man's mind is not necessarily available to other members of the organization, and, second, because when an individual leaves an organization the organization loses that part of its "memory."

Hence organizations, to a far greater extent than individuals, need artificial "memories." Practices which would become simply habitual in the case of the individual must be recorded in manuals for the instruction of new organization members. Among the repositories which organizations may use for their information are records systems, correspondence and other files, libraries, and follow-up systems.

All these devices are familiar. They in themselves create difficult problems of organization—what types of information are to be recorded, in what manner they are to be classified and filed, the physical location of the files, and so forth; but it is hardly profitable to discuss these problems in the abstract.

Investigatory Facilities

Most organizations, or particular decision-centers in organization, require information in addition to that which comes to them normally in the course of their work. This necessary information is of two kinds: external— that which is to be obtained from sources outside the organization; and internal—that which is to be obtained within the organization. In any large organization units can be identified whose function it is to secure one or the other of these types of information. The patent department in industrial concerns is such a unit, one of whose primary functions is to keep continual watch on patent and product development in the company's field by checking the *Patent Office Gazette*, manufacturers' catalogues, periodicals, and trade literature. The accounting department is the outstanding example of a unit whose function it is to obtain internal information.

The external investigatory unit does not require much discussion. The chief problem in fitting it into the organization is to locate it in such a manner that the information it receives will be transmitted promptly and in usable form to the appropriate points in the organization. This inevitably leads to questions, like those asked of any service unit, as to how far the function should be specialized and how far it should be decentralized among the operating units. Other such units are the intelligence units in military organization, market research units in business concerns, a fire alarm bureau, and a police communications system.

There are several varieties of internal investigatory units in addition to accounting. Perhaps the most significant are independent inspectional units (like the Inspector General's Office of the Army) and analysis units (the Department of Investigation of New York City, or the Division of Administrative Management of the United States Bureau of the Budget).

In the case of accounting for money, the need for a flow of information independent of the regular channels of authority is universally accepted as almost self-evident. The functions of the typical accounting unit have been very much broadened, however, beyond the simple audit for honesty. It is quite frequently used nowadays as a source of information for determining whether expenditures are conforming to the plan laid down in the budget. Accounts are used also as a basis for cost analysis which, in turn, contributes to future executive decisions. In these capacities, accounting information has become one of the most important tools in the executive review of operations.

Accounting controls have probably never been carried further than they have by the Comptroller General of the United States. That office has for a number of years maintained a continual pre-audit of Federal expenditures and has disallowed those which it considered to be not in conformity with Congressional authorizations. This has created a system of dual authority over expenditures in the Federal government that has generally received adverse comment from persons who have studied it. It should be recognized, however, that this is merely an extreme form of the problem that arises whenever control functions of *any* sort are vested in an accounting unit. To the extent that the accountant has authority to set limits to the actions of executives in the line organization, his authority cuts across the regular lines of authority, and unity of command in the broad sense of that term is violated.

Independent inspectional organizations create problems of dual command similar to those created by accounting controls. Even where, as is usually the case, the inspectional unit has no power but that of reporting its findings to the top executive, the line organization will become responsive to its viewpoints. The seriousness of this problem is mitigated somewhat—with a weakening in the effectiveness of the inspectional unit—by the fact that its intervention is usually intermittent rather than continuous. At any rate, whatever the problems it creates, the top administrator often finds the inspectional unit an invaluable aid because it gives him information that simply would not be transmitted up through the line organization.

Another way in which the top levels of the hierarchy gain knowledge about the operation of the organization is by undertaking, at intervals, a comprehensive analysis and survey of the organization or some part of it. In this they may be assisted by an administrative analysis unit which specializes in such work. Such a survey may be confined to questions of organization structure, or it may include an analysis of the program of activity. In most cases these two are so inextricably interwoven that both are involved.

TRAINING AND COMMUNICATION

The whole subject of training involves other questions than those of communication. Nevertheless the role of training in administration is perhaps best understood by viewing it as one of several alternative means for communicating decisional premises to organization members. If, for example, a particular job in an organization requires certain legal knowledge, (a) a lawyer may be appointed to the position; (b) instructions and manuals may be provided to the person selected, with careful supervision of his work; or (c) he may be trained after selection. All these are, in a sense, training procedures, but in (a) the organization depends upon pre-service training, in (b) upon day-to-day supervision as a training device, in (c) upon formal training.

Military organizations have long provided striking demonstrations of the use that can be made of formal training in indoctrinating large numbers of new members in highly complicated and unfamiliar tasks in a short time. In civilian organizations, where new members are seldom employed in such large numbers, and where the new employees are usually at least partly trained at the time of their recruitment, the possibilities of formal training have been much less fully realized. In military organizations instruction in "how to do it" is carried on almost entirely through the formal training process, while operational orders are generally restricted to "what to do." In many civilian organizations instruction in "how to do it" is left pretty much to the supervisory staff. Undoubtedly the poorest method of communicating operational procedures is to rely solely on written instructions and manuals.

Perhaps the greatest difficulty in the use of formal training methods is to secure in the group being trained an attitude of receptivity. Every teacher recognizes—often with a great feeling of helplessness—that motivation is the key to the learning process. The trainee must have an interest in learning, and, moreover, he must be convinced that he does not already know the things in which he is to be trained. The problem of motivation is at a minimum in the vestibule training of new employees. It may be very serious indeed in the training of employees who have already been performing their jobs for a considerable period of time.

Training requires of the trainee a certain attitude of deference toward the teacher, and an admission of incomplete knowledge that many individuals who have reached a mature age and a responsible position find quite galling. When in-service training deals with such individuals—skilled workmen, supervisors, executives—considerable attention must be given to the prestige and acceptability of the instructor and the practicality of the training materials. One of the reasons for the success of the conference method in training such groups is that it minimizes the "teaching" role of the instructor, and creates the illusion that the new ideas are originating in the group itself. Of course this is not entirely an illusion; but it is more of an illusion than the theorists of conference-method training like to admit.

Training is applicable to the process of decision wherever the same elements are involved in a large number of decisions. Training may supply the trainee with the facts necessary in dealing with these decisions; it may provide him a frame of reference for his thinking; it may teach him "approved" solutions, or it may indoctrinate him with the values in terms of which his decisions are to be made.

Training, as a mode of influence upon decisions, has its greatest value in those situations where the exercise of formal authority through commands proves difficult. The difficulty may lie in the need for prompt action, in spatial dispersion of the organization, or in the complexity of the subject matter of decision which defies summarization in rules and regulations. Training permits a higher degree of decentralization of the decision-making process by bringing the necessary competence into the very lowest levels of the organizational hierarchy.

CONCLUSION

This chapter has been concerned with the organization communications system—particularly those aspects of it which supplement the system of authority. It has been shown that the specialization of decision-making functions is largely dependent upon the possibility of developing adequate channels of communication to and from decision-centers. Generally the organization structure will include the specification of a formal system of communication—including channels for oral and written communications, paper-flow, records and reports, and manuals—but this will be supplemented by a rich network of informal communications based upon the social relationships that develop in the organization.

Personal motives may lead organization members to try to divert the communications system to their own uses, and may lead them also to withhold information from superiors and colleagues. Personal motives and attitudes also influence the reception given to those communications that are transmitted, and the ability of an individual to influence others by his communications will depend upon his formal and informal position of authority, and upon the intelligibility and persuasiveness of the communication itself.

Organizations usually develop units that are specialized for particular communications functions. These include staff aids, repositories of organization "memory," and investigatory units, both internal and external.

Training is one of several alternative methods of communication that proves particularly useful in transmitting job "know-how." Its successful use, however, hinges on the possibility of obtaining favorable attitudes in the trainees toward the training program.

COMMUNICATION

IN 1947 IT WAS POSSIBLE to write a chapter on communications in organizations without mentioning electronic computers. Today such a chapter might be regarded as downright quaint. However, rereading Chapter VIII in the light of the events of the past fifty years does not reveal anything in it that is clearly wrong. As it errs by omission rather than commission, I shall try to make good some of the omissions in this commentary. Another section of the commentary will discuss learning in organizations, a topic that has attracted a good deal of research attention in recent years, and which, especially in a world in rapid transition, is of central importance for understanding how organizations adjust to change (or resist it).

In discussing communications, we should not be too hasty to conclude that "the medium is the message." It might be better to focus the discussion on the contents of the messages instead of the medium. Nevertheless, computers are here in force today and there will be many more of them tomorrow. If, contrary to McLuhan, the medium is not the message, still the medium does exert a strong influence on the flow and contents of messages in organizations, and it is important to assess its significance for organizational decision-making and organization structure.

IS THERE AN INFORMATION REVOLUTION?[4]

Is there in fact, as is so often claimed, an "information explosion"? Why do we think so? What does it signify? Certainly the press has had no doubts for some years that information is exploding. A single issue of the Sunday *New York Times* a decade or more ago yielded the following two items:

> Will a full week of shorter trading hours bring happiness to brokerage firms whose back offices are jammed with paperwork?

[4]This section draws upon "The Future of Information Processing," which appeared in *Management Science*, 14:619–624 (1968).

George A. Miller, a professor of psychology at Harvard, warned that by 2000, the limit of man's mind to absorb information may be reached. "We may already be nearing some kind of limit for many of the less gifted among us, and those still able to handle the present level of complexity are in ever increasing demand."

This is simply a tiny sample from a very much larger number of items—the first two that came to hand. The first conjures up a fascinating picture of the Stock Exchange slowly submerging under a tide of paper; the second promises prosperity to "those still able to handle the present level of complexity"—and I assume that means all of my readers. How valid are the predictions of the impending Flood? To answer those questions, we must sort out the elements of stability and the elements of change in human affairs.

Change—extremely rapid change—there certainly is along technological and economic dimensions. We know that technology is advancing with great speed. We know that it is beginning to make technically possible for the first time in human history the elimination of acute poverty (provided that we give adequate attention to problems of distribution as well as total production). We know that it is even providing means, if not yet the will, for combating the over-rapid growth of population—the most serious threat to the prospect of banishing poverty.

But (there is always a "but" at this point in the argument), if we measure the world by the values and goals of our species, we have good reason to doubt whether it is changing very much at all. We must not suppose that with the progress of technology, or even with the progress of our economies, mankind will become deliriously happy. For human aspirations have a way of adjusting to opportunities. We must not expect that technological progress will produce Utopia; it is reasonable to hope that it can bring relief to acute hardship and acute pain.

Evidences for the Revolution

With these cautions and reservations, let us examine the changes that are taking place in information production and processing. Forty years ago, at a meeting of the Operations Research Society of America, Allen Newell and I made some very specific ten-year predictions. I wish I could tell you that each one had been exactly fulfilled. The last of them (a computer as world chess champion) is still not quite there—but very close. But rather than either defend or explain away these past predictions, I will simply make a few general comments about them.

All the predictions were wrong in detail, but they were correct in the trend they foresaw and the overall rate of change. We did not guess correctly how research efforts would be allocated to particular areas or the relative difficulties of specific problems. Hence, although chess-playing by computer has made enormous progress, it is, in forty years, just reaching our ten-year target. On the other side of the account, fundamental understanding of natural language, including speech recognition and understanding, the construction of high-level computer languages, automatic design by computers, visual pattern recognition, and robotics, among others, have advanced more rapidly than we would have dared to predict in 1957.

Hence, in the light of the actual progress, there is no reason to revise our basic thesis: that electronic computers are general-purpose information-processing devices; that we will continue to learn step by step to do with them any kind of thinking that people can do; that, with the help of computer simulation techniques, we are learning how human beings learn and think and how to help them to learn and think better.

My discussion in this chapter of the consequences for organizations of the computer and communication network culture has been strongly influenced by my having lived in that culture for many years, with e-mail since 1972, and with a campus-wide network since 1985.[5]

Attending to the Information That Is There

Given the rate at which the technology of information processing is progressing, why won't there be an information explosion? The mountain climber, Mallory, when asked why he wanted to climb Everest, gave his famous reply: "Because it is there." Not all of us accept that reply for ourselves. Not all of us aspire to climb Everest or would look forward to the prospect with any relish or sense of purpose.

Now it is possible to be just as skeptical about processing information as about climbing mountains. Specifically, information doesn't have to be processed just because it is there. The telephone doesn't have to be answered just because it is ringing; or the newspaper read just because it was tossed on our doorstep. Information is sometimes ignored at our own peril, but we are more often guilty of the opposite error—of supposing that all would be well "if we just had more information," a pathetically naïve belief in the technological fix. The following is an old example, but one that remains quite relevant today:

The U.S. State Department, drowning in a river of words estimated

---

[5]A series of research studies of the initial impact of the installation of the network on the Carnegie Mellon campus will be found in S. B. Kiesler and L. S. Sproull (eds.), *Computing and Change on Campus* (New York: Cambridge University Press, 1987).

at 15 million a month to and from 278 diplomatic outposts around the world, contracted, a number of years ago, for a $3.5 million combination of computers, high-speed printers, and other electronic devices. These were aimed at eliminating transmission bottlenecks in the system, especially during crises that bring in torrents of cabled messages from world trouble spots. With the new system, computers could absorb cable messages at 1,200 lines a minute. The old teletypes could receive messages at only 100 words a minute.

Leave aside the fact that the technology mentioned in this example is already, thirty years later, buried with the dinosaurs, and that the flow of cable messages has undoubtedly increased by several orders of magnitude. What is most instructive about the example is that the new system was designed without anyone asking about the capacity of the human users to process the greatly accelerated flow of information. The sorcerer's apprentice is at large. Who will read the flood of words that the new enlarged communications channels will deliver? The bottleneck is no longer the capacity of the electronic channels but the capacity of the human users.

Attending Selectively

We cannot save ourselves from drowning in information by installing faster printing devices. Lack of information is not the typical problem in our decision processes (although lack of the *right* information sometimes is). The world is constantly drenching us with information through eyes and ears—millions of bits per second. According to the best evidence, we can handle only about fifty. The limit is not information but our capacity to attend to it.

Saturation with information is no new thing. The movements of the stars, visible to us throughout the tens of thousands of years of our history, contain all the information that is needed for Newton's laws of motion or the law of gravitation. The information was there all along. What was lacking, until a few hundred years ago, was the basis for selecting the tiny fraction of it that could be used to establish powerful generalizations.

If we cannot avoid living in a world that drenches us with information—whether made by ourselves or nature—still, we can and must select for our processing the information that is likely to be useful to us and ignore the rest. Our scientific and technological knowledge, our decision-making and information-processing systems should permit us to absorb information very selectively, extracting from it just the parts we want.

In the same vein, most of the contemporary concern about the information explosion in science is misconceived, because it is based on an invalid model of the nature of scientific progress. Science does not advance by piling up information—it organizes information and compresses it. A generation or two ago, for example, organic chemistry was a mass of particulars only weakly organized by known theoretical generalizations. Today, although knowledge of organic chemistry has grown vastly, the principles of quantum mechanics provide powerful organizing means for that knowledge. As a result, it is undoubtedly easier today to gain a mastery of organic chemistry adequate for doing significant original work than it was in an earlier era when very much less was known.

The example I have chosen is not an isolated one. In the scientific endeavor, "knowing" has always meant "knowing parsimoniously." The information that nature presents to us is unimaginably redundant. When we find the right way to summarize and characterize that information—when we find the pattern hidden in it—its vast bulk compresses into succinct laws, each one enormously informative. Herein lies the real significance of today's information revolution. Information and the processing of information are themselves for the first time becoming the objects of systematic scientific investigation. We are laying the foundations for a science of information processing that we can expect will greatly increase our effectiveness in handling the information around us.

Thus, at a time when we are acquiring devices that will transmit, store, and process symbols at unprecedented rates and volumes, the most important change is not the growth of these devices but the growth of a science that helps us understand how information can be transmitted, how it can be organized for storage and retrieval, how it can be used (and how it is used) in thinking, in problem-solving, in decision-making. This growing understanding of information processing returns to us the decision of whether information must overflow and we must drown in it.

A major task ahead is to design effective information-processing systems for making decisions in business and in government. It is important that we talk about designing information-processing systems and not just designing computers and electronic networks. The design must encompass far more than the computer hardware and software; it must handle with equal care the information-processing characteristics and capabilities of the human members of organizations who constitute the other half of the systems.

For generations to come, although organizations will have many mechanized components, their most numerous and crucial elements will continue to be people. Their effectiveness in handling problems will depend as heavily on the effectiveness of the thinking, problem-solving, and decision-making that people do as upon the operation of the computers and their programs. Hence, in the period ahead, as important as advances in hardware and software design will be advances in our understanding of human information processing—of thinking, problem-solving, and decision-making.

ORGANIZATIONAL LEARNING[6]

One of the important uses of communication, in organizations and else-where, is for teaching and learning. An organization's knowledge com-prises the (relevant) knowledge stored in the memories of its members together with the knowledge stored in its files and records, including, nowadays, the data banks in its computers. Organizational learning is the set of processes that lead to the acquisition of this knowledge. Both employees and computers can participate in instructional processes either as teachers or learners. (A venerable example of a non-human teacher is a book; a more contemporary example is an intelligent com-puter tutor.)

The boundary between one biological organism and others is defined by identity of the shared DNA of all the organism's cells. In a similar way, one might say that shared information determines the boundary of an organization—although the sharing is not nearly as complete as it is among an organism's cells. Understanding the processes of organizational learning is critical to understanding the respective roles of organizations and markets in the economy. Shared knowledge makes it possible for organizations to behave in effectively coordinated ways that are not as easily available to coteries of independent firms.

Organizations acquire knowledge in the forms both of facts and pro-cedures. Much of the knowledge contained in human memories and machines resides in programs that govern the day-to-day activities of organization members and information processors. These procedures affect not only the behavior of individual employees, but also their rela-tions with each other.

The Individual and Organizational Levels

The first question one must raise is whether organizational learning is different from learning by individuals. A recruiter who is interviewing a job prospect is learning about the candidate, and on the basis of that learning, together with other information, will or won't make a job offer. As this learning by an individual has consequences for an organizational decision, providing new facts about the qualifications of the candidate, it must count as organizational learning.

If we adopt too strict a definition of organizational learning, we will define the topic out of existence. All human learning takes place inside

[6]See M. D. Cohen and L. S. Sproull, eds., *Organizational Learning* (Thousand Oaks, Calif.: Sage, 1996). In this section I have drawn particularly from my chapter in that book: "Bounded Rationality and Organizational Learning."

individual human heads; an organization learns in only three ways: (a) by
the learning of its members, (b) by ingesting new members who have
knowledge the organization didn't previously have, (c) by introducing
new knowledge into its files and computing systems. For the moment, I
will limit the discussion to human learning; learning by computers will
be considered later.

What is stored in any one head in an organization may not be unrelated to what is stored in other heads; and the relation between those
two (and other) stores will have a great bearing on how the organization
operates. What an individual learns in an organization is very much
dependent on what is already known to (or believed by) other members
and what kinds of information are present in the organizational environment. As we shall see, an important component of organizational learning is internal learning—that is, transmission of information from one
organizational member or group of members to another. Individual learning in organizations is very much a social, not a solitary, phenomenon.

However, we must also be careful about reifying the organization
when talking about it as "knowing" something or "learning" something.
It is usually important to specify where in the organization particular
knowledge is stored, or who has learned it. Depending on its actual locus,
knowledge may or may not be available at the decision points where it
would be relevant. Since what has been learned is stored in individual
heads (or in files or data banks), its transience or permanence depends
on what people leave behind them when they depart from an organization or move from one position to another. It also depends on what
records remain readable when computer software is changed. Has the
knowledge been transmitted to others or stored in ways that will permit
it to be recovered when relevant? Human learning in the context of an
organization is very much influenced by the organization, has consequences for the organization, and produces phenomena at the organizational level that go beyond anything we could infer simply by observing
learning processes in isolated individuals.

Let me perseverate for a moment on that term "organizational level."
Readers of March and Simon's *Organizations*[7] have sometimes complained that it was not a book on organizations at all but on the social
psychology of people living in an organizational environment. The complaint was usually registered by sociologists, and was not without merit.
We need an organization theory because some phenomena are more conveniently described in terms of organizations and parts of organizations
than in terms of the individual human beings who inhabit those parts.

[7]2nd ed., Cambridge, Mass.: Blackwell, 1993.

There is nothing more surprising in the existence of those phenomena than in the existence of phenomena that make it convenient for chemists to speak about molecules rather than quarks. Employing a more aggregate level of discourse is not a declaration of philosophical anti-reductionism, but simply a recognition that most natural systems do have hierarchical structure, and that it is often possible to say a great deal about aggregate components without specifying the details of activity within these components.

Hence, the remarks that follow have little or nothing to say about the detailed mechanisms that enable an individual human being to learn, but focus on how information is acquired by organizations, is stored in them, and is transmitted from one part of an organization to another. They are concerned with what are usually called emergent phenomena at the organizational level.

The Structure of Roles

For purposes of discussing organization learning, organizations are best viewed as systems of interrelated roles. As has been explained in the commentary on Chapter VI, a role is not a system of prescribed behaviors but a system of prescribed decision premises. Roles tell organization members how to reason about the problems and decisions that face them: where to look for appropriate and legitimate informational premises and goal (evaluative) premises, and what techniques to use in processing these premises. The fact that behavior is structured in roles says nothing, one way or the other, about how flexible or inflexible it is.

Each of the roles in an organization presumes the appropriate enactment of the other roles that surround it and interact with it. Thus, the organization is a role system.

Organizational Learning and Innovation

Since the organizations I know best are universities, I will draw upon my university experiences for most of my examples of organizational learning phenomena. Consider a university that wants to innovate along some dimension of educational practice—perhaps by building its instruction around the Great Books, or by focusing on something it calls liberal-professional education. I'll use the latter example, which is closer to home.

The graduate schools from which a university draws its new teachers are organized in disciplines, some of which are saturated with the values of liberal education (and transmit them to their students), others of which are devoted to professional education. There are no disciplines, to the best of my knowledge, that fly the banner of "liberal-professional" education. Clearly, a university that wishes to implement this view of instruction is faced with a major learning problem for its new (and probably its old) faculty members. It has no chance of accomplishing its goal without substantial education, and re-education, of its inductees. Moreover, the re-education is not a one-time task but a continuing one, unless the educational climate of the environing society changes so that it begins to produce graduates already indoctrinated with the desired goals and information.

Effects of Turnover. Turnover in organizations is sometimes considered a process that facilitates organizational innovation—getting out of the current rut. But in the case before us, where the organization is trying to distance itself from general social norms, turnover becomes a barrier to this kind of innovation, because it increases training (socialization) costs. To preserve its distinct culture, an organization of this kind may try to train its own personnel from the ground up, instead of relying on outside institutions to provide that training. Such inbreeding will have other organizational consequences.

Contrast this with the organization that finds in its environment training organizations that share a common culture with it. The Forest Service, in Herbert Kaufman's classical account of it, is such an organization, counting on schools of forestry to provide it with new employees who are already indoctrinated with its values and even its standard operating procedures.[8] The same thing occurs, less specifically but on a larger scale, in such professions as engineering, where there are close links between the engineering colleges and the industries, with a feedback of influence from industry to the engineering curricula.

An Experiment on Stability. If turnover is sufficiently low, organizational values and practices can be stabilized by the fact that each new inductee finds himself or herself confronted with a social system that is already well established and prepared to mold newcomers to its procedures. This phenomenon can be produced in the laboratory (and I believe actually has been produced, but I cannot put my hands on the appropriate reference).

In a certain experimental paradigm in social psychology (often called the Bavelas communication network) different patterns of communication are imposed on five-person groups. In one pattern (the wheel) one member of the group serves as leader or coordinator and all the other

[8]H. Kaufman, *The Forest Ranger* (Baltimore: Johns Hopkins Press, 1960).

members communicate with him or her, and not directly with each other. In another pattern (the circle) the members are arranged in a symmetric circular network, each member communicating only with the two who are immediately adjacent. The groups are performing a task that requires them to share information that is given to the members individually.[9]

Now consider two groups whose members are A1, A2, A3, A4, A5, and B1, B2, B3, B4, B5, respectively, where the A's are in the wheel pattern and the B's in the circle pattern. After they are thoroughly trained in the task, we open all the communication channels so that each member can communicate directly with all the others in that group. If they are under sufficient pressure to perform rapidly, the first group will likely continue to use the wheel pattern of communication and the second group the circle pattern.

After a number of additional trials, interchange A1 and B1. One would predict that the groups would continue to use their respective patterns. After a few more trials, interchange A2 with B2, then A3 with B3, and so on until the original wheel group is populated by B1 through B5, and the original circle group by A1 through A5. We would predict that the A's would now be communicating in a circle pattern and the B's in a wheel pattern. If the experiment works as predicted, it demonstrates an emergent property of an organization—a persistence of pattern that survives a complete replacement of the individuals who enact the pattern.

The Problem of Sustaining Distinctiveness. The example of the deviant university can be extended to virtually all organizational innovation. Among the costs of being first—whether in products, in methods of marketing, in organizational procedures, or what not—are the costs of instilling in members of the organization the knowledge, beliefs, and values that are necessary for implementing the new goals. And these costs can be exceedingly large (as they are in the case of a university). The tasks of management are quite different in organizations that can recruit employees who are prefashioned, so to speak, than they are in organizations that wish to create and maintain, along some dimensions, idiosyncratic subcultures.

The mechanisms that can enable an organization to deviate from the culture in which it is embedded are, therefore, a major topic in organizational learning. As my university example suggests, this topic can be examined in the field, and particularly in a historical vein, by following the course of events in organizations that seek to distance themselves along one or more dimensions from the surrounding culture.

---

[9]A. Bavelas, "Communication Patterns in Task-Oriented Groups," *Journal of Acoustical Society of America*, 22: 725–730 (1950).

Organizational Memory

Retaining the unique traits of an organization is a part of the more general phenomena of organizational memory. Because much of the memory of organizations is stored in human heads, and only a little of it in procedures put down on paper (or held in computer memories), turnover of personnel is a great enemy of long-term organizational memory. This natural erosion of memory with time has, of course, both its advantages and disadvantages. In the previous section I emphasized one of its disadvantages. Its advantage is that it automatically removes outdated irrelevancies (but without discriminating between the relevant and the irrelevant).

Turning from the erosion problem, how are we to characterize an organization's memories? Research in cognitive psychology in recent years has made great progress in understanding human expertise, and what has been learned was summarized in the commentary on Chapter V. The knowledge of experts is stored in the form of an indexed encyclopedia, which is technically referred to as a production system, so that whenever appropriate cues are evoked by a stimulus, access is provided to the corresponding chunk in semantic memory. Armed with knowledge stored in his or her production system, the expert is prepared (but only in the domain of expertise) to respond to many situations "intuitively"—that is, by recognizing the situation and evoking an appropriate response—and also to draw on the stored productions for more protracted and systematic analysis of difficult problems.

Against the background of this picture of expertise, the memories of an organization can be represented as a vast collection of production systems. This representation becomes much more than a metaphor as we see more and more examples of human expertise captured in automated expert systems. One motive for such automation, but certainly not the only one, is that it makes organizational memory less vulnerable to personnel turnover.

Ingesting Innovations from Without

My previous example had to do with organizations trying to retain their identities in a world of alien ideas, fighting the threat of increasing entropy that comes with the absorption of new personnel. The other side of the coin is the problem of assimilating innovations that originate outside the organization, or that have to be transmitted from a point of origin in the organization to points of implementation. Here, let me take the research and design process as my example, but again in the context of universities. The translation to corporate situations will follow.

Research as a Learning Mechanism. So-called research universities have a dual mission: to create new knowledge and to transmit that knowledge to their students. Research accomplishes the former, and instruction the latter. Of course the real pattern is much more complicated than this. In the first place, the new knowledge produced by research is usually not initially transmitted only to students at the same university, but to researchers throughout the world, mainly by publication. In the second place, most of the knowledge transmitted to students in a university is not produced at that university. Is there really any reason why the research (which is one process of learning) and the instruction (another learning process) should go on in the same institution?

When we examine the research process more closely, we see that it differs rather fundamentally from the usual description. In any given research laboratory, only a tiny fraction of the new knowledge acquired by the research staff is knowledge created by that laboratory; most of it is knowledge created by research elsewhere. We can think of a research scientist as a person who keeps one eye on Nature and the other on the literature of his or her field. And in most laboratories, probably all laboratories, much more information comes in through the eye that is scanning the journals than the eye that is looking through the microscope.

It is probably true, and certainly widely suspected, that in any field of research a large fraction of the less distinguished laboratories could vanish without seriously reducing the rate at which new knowledge is created. Does that mean that these dispensable laboratories (dispensable in terms of the creation of knowledge) do not pay their way? The conclusion does not follow if the main function of a laboratory is not the creation of knowledge but the acquisition of knowledge. In military parlance, we would label such laboratories intelligence units rather than research units. They are units of the organization that are specialized for the function of learning from the outside world (and perhaps sometimes creating new knowledge themselves).

As a matter of fact, in universities we sometimes recognize the intelligence function of "research." When we are asked why we require faculty members who are primarily teachers to publish in order to gain promotion or tenure, we answer that if they do not do research, they will not remain intellectually alive. Their teaching will not keep up with the progress of their disciplines. It is not their research products that we value, but their engagement in research which guarantees their attention to the new knowledge being produced elsewhere.

It can be highly dysfunctional for a laboratory to live with the belief that its main product is the new knowledge produced by its in-house research. Such a belief produces the NIH (not invented here) phenomenon, with a consequent reinvention of many wheels.

R&D and Manufacturing. The problem of developing new products from (local or imported) research ideas and of carrying them to the stage of successful manufacture and marketing is a classical organizational problem of creating and transferring information. It has already been discussed briefly in the commentary on Chapter II and will receive further attention in the commentary on Chapter XI.

In whichever direction the ideas flow through the organization, it is clear that nothing will happen unless they do flow. Normally, the learning associated with a new product must be highly diffused through the organization—many people have to learn many things—and such lateral diffusion and transfer is far from automatic or easy. It must overcome motivation obstacles (I have already mentioned the NIH syndrome), and it must cross cognitive boundaries.

Manufacturing Constraints. A common complaint about contemporary American practice in new product design is that the design process is carried quite far before manufacturing expertise is brought to bear on it. But ease and cheapness of manufacture can be a key to the prospects of a product in competitive markets, and failure to consider manufacturability at an early stage usually causes extensive redesign with a corresponding increase in the time interval from initial idea to a manufactured product. These time delays are thought to be a major factor in the poor showing of many American industries in competing with the Japanese.

We know some, if not all, of the conditions for making communications between designers and manufacturing engineers effective. Each group must respect the expertise of the other, and must acknowledge the relevance of that expertise to their own problems. Moreover, each must have a sufficient knowledge and understanding of the others' problems to be able to communicate effectively about them. Experience shows that these conditions are unlikely to be satisfied unless members of each group (or a sufficient number of members of each group) have had actual experience with the activities and responsibilities of the other group. In typical Japanese manufacturing practice, this shared understanding and ability to communicate is brought about by extensive lateral transfer of engineers in the course of their careers.

These examples will illustrate some of the kinds of learning involved, some of the problems of bringing it about, and some of the mechanisms for solving those problems when an organization brings in innovations from outside or tries to transport them from one organizational unit to another.

Acquiring New Problem Representations

In my earlier discussion of a culturally deviant organization, I contrasted the way in which roles (decision premises) are acquired in such an organization with the way in which they are acquired in an organization that builds upon the culture of the society that provides it with new members. Learning may bring new knowledge to bear within an existing culture and learning may change the culture itself in fundamental ways. I would like to turn now to that distinction.

In the past thirty years, a great deal has been learned about how people solve problems by searching selectively through a problem space defined by a particular problem representation. Much less has been learned about how people acquire a representation for dealing with a new problem—one they haven't previously encountered.[10]

Two cases must be distinguished: (1) The learner is presented with an appropriate problem representation, and has to learn how to use it effectively. That is essentially what is involved when organizations, already formed, ingest new members from an alien culture. (2) The organization is faced with a totally new situation, and must create a problem representation to deal with it, then enable its members to acquire skill in using that representation. In the extreme case, a new organization is created to deal with a new task. A new problem representation and a role system are created.

Creating an Organization. Some years ago I was fortunate enough to have a grandstand seat at the creation of the Economic Cooperation Administration, the U.S. governmental organization that administered the Marshall Plan of aid to Western European countries. In that process, which extended through most of the year 1948, competing problem representations emerged from the very first days, each implying a quite different organization structure and set of organizational roles from the others. These problem representations were not made out of whole cloth, but arose from analogies between the presumed task of the ECA and other tasks that were familiar to the inventors of the representations from their previous training and experience.

For example, some participants in the planning drew an analogy between the ECA and wartime organizations that had supplied essential goods to the allies. Others thought of it as an exercise in investment banking. Others were reminded of the theory of international trade balances. From each of these views, a set of organizational roles could be

[10]But see A. H. Van de Ven, "Central Problems in the Management of Innovation," *Management Science*, 32:590–607 (1986), and J. G. March, L. S. Sproull, and M. Tamuz, "Learning from Samples of One or Fewer," in M. D. Cohen and L. S. Sproull, eds., *op. cit.*

inferred, and each such structure of roles was quite different from the others. Which representations took root in which parts of the burgeoning organization depended heavily on the cultures from which these parts recruited their new members. The commentary to Chapter XI will recount how this competition was resolved.

Why Representation Matters. Attention to the limits of human rationality helps us to understand why representation is important, and how policy may imply a representation. About two decades ago, the U.S. Steel Corporation began to contract its steel operations and to invest a major part of its capital in the oil industry, becoming USX in the process. The motivation of these moves was a particular representation of the corporation's purposes.

If, a few years ago, you had asked executives of U.S. Steel what the corporation's goals were, they might have answered: "To manufacture and market steel efficiently and profitably." If you had persisted further, they might even have agreed that profit was the "bottom line." But it would have been hard or impossible for them to describe the company without strong emphasis on its focus on steel. Their views might have been paraphrased: "We are out to make profits, but the way for us to make profits is to be an efficient steel manufacturer. That is a domain in which we have knowledge and expertise, and in which we can make good decisions."

For the conglomerate that it became, an entirely different representation was required. The corporation has product divisions that can still be described in ways that resemble the earlier corporation—the word "steel" applying to some divisions, and "oil" to others. But in the new representation, these divisions are only components operating within a larger framework in which the fundamental policy is to invest available funds in the directions that will yield the greatest returns. Within that framework, new expertise is required: essentially the expertise of an investment banker.

Change in representation implies fundamental change in organizational knowledge and skills. It should not be surprising that under these conditions we often see massive turnover of personnel at all levels. It is often cheaper and quicker to import the new expertise and dismiss the old than to engage in massive re-education.

Conclusion

This section has been aimed at showing how concepts that have arisen in contemporary cognitive psychology for describing human learning processes can be applied to the analysis of organizational learning. I have made no attempt to be complete or comprehensive in my account, but have been satisfied to present some examples of how specific organizational situations can be understood in terms of these concepts.

Among the contents of organizational memories perhaps the most important is the representation of the organization itself and its goals, for it is this representation (or representations, if it is not uniform throughout the organization) that provides the basis for defining the roles of organization members.

APPLYING INFORMATION TECHNOLOGY
TO ORGANIZATION DESIGN[11]

In the past, organization theory has been mainly concerned with what might be called "organization for production." The theory traditionally paid special attention to two problems: how to divide up the work for its efficient performance and in such a way as to keep the needs for coordination of the parts within manageable bounds; and how to construct and maintain mechanisms for coordinating the several organizational parts.

Research on human relations in organizations, beginning on a substantial scale in the 1930s, turned attention in organizational design to the linkage between the individual as organization member and the total pattern of organizational activity. The principal normative concern here was to create organizational environments in which employees would be motivated to join the organization, to remain in it, and to contribute vigorously and effectively to its goals.

With the introduction of highly automated machinery, and particularly with the introduction of mechanized information-processing equipment, the assembly line becomes a rather rare form of organization of production, as does the repetitive unautomated clerical process. The human operative or clerk is more and more an observer, moderator, maintenance and repair person for a nearly autonomous process that can carry on for significant intervals of time without direct human intervention. More and more of the human work becomes work of thought and communication, and as a consequence, the design of organizations becomes a central topic in the study and application of information technology, and vice versa.

The Post-Industrial Society

Peter Drucker used the phrase "post-industrial society" to describe the emerging world in which manufacturing and the activities associated

---

[11]This section had its origins in a paper with this title that appeared in *Public Administration Review*, 33:268–78 (1973). The present version is much revised from the original.

with it play a much less central role than they did in the world of the past century. Providing services tends to pose different organizational problems from producing tangible goods. It is usually more difficult to define appropriate output measures for service organizations than for organizations that produce commodities. Whatever problems are present in measuring the quality of goods are magnified greatly in measuring the quality of services. The point can be illustrated by comparing two versions of the same economic activity, first viewed as a goods-producing activity, then as a service-producing activity: that is, producing houses and housing respectively.

A house is a tangible commodity that can be manufactured and distributed through the usual market mechanisms; housing is a bundle of services provided by a dwelling in the context of a neighborhood, with schools, streets, shopping facilities, and a pattern of social interaction among the inhabitants. However complex it may be to define the qualities of a house, narrowly conceived as a structure, it is far more complex to define the qualities of housing, conceived as a situation that creates and supports a pattern of social activity, the life of a family, say.

Related to the tendency of organizations in our society to broaden the definition of their goals from the production of tangible commodities to the production of bundles of services that may or may not be associated with tangible commodities, is a tendency to broaden their concern for the externalities associated with their activities. Externalities are those consequences of action that are not charged, through the existing market mechanisms, to the actors. The classical example is the factory smoke whose social costs have not generally been paid by the consumers of the factory's product.

It may be that organizations producing services usually have more and larger externalities associated with their activities than organizations producing goods; or it may be that we are simply becoming more sensitive in our society to the indirect consequences of organizational activity directed toward specialized goals; or it may be that, with the growth of population and technology, the actual interdependencies of organizations, and hence the externalities they cause, are becoming more extensive and significant. Whatever the reasons—and all three of those mentioned probably contribute to the trend—organizational decision-making in the organizations of the post-industrial world shows every sign of becoming a great deal more complex than the decision-making of the past. As a consequence, the decision-making processes—rather than the processes contributing immediately and directly to the production of the organization's final output—bulk larger and larger as the central activity in which the organization is engaged.

Organizing the Information-Processing Structure

In the post-industrial society, then, the key problem is how to organize to make decisions—that is, to process information. Until recent years, decision-making was exclusively a human activity; it involved processes going on inside the human head and symbolic communication among humans. In our present world, decision-making is shared between the human and mechanized components of man-machine systems. The division of labor between the human and computer components in these systems has changed steadily over the past forty years, and it will continue to change as the sophistication of computer technology—and particularly computer programming or software technology—grows.

The anatomy of an organization viewed as a decision-making and information-processing system may look very different from the anatomy of the same organization viewed as a collection of people. The latter viewpoint, which is the traditional one, focuses attention on the groupings of human beings—that is, departmentalization. The former viewpoint, on the other hand, focuses on the decision-making process itself—that is, upon the flows and transformations of symbols. If we carve an organization, conceptually, into subsystems on the basis of the principal components into which the decision-making process divides, we may, and probably will, arrive at a very different dissection than if we carve it into its departmental and subdepartmental components. Moreover, the greater the interdependencies among departmental components, the greater will be the difference in these two ways of conceptualizing the organization.

Both of these viewpoints are useful and even essential in arriving at sound designs for organizations. In this analysis, I shall emphasize the less conventional point of view and discuss the decision-making process disembodied, so to speak, from the flesh and blood (or glass and metal, as the case may be) decision-makers who actually carry out this process. Instead of watching a person or computer as information arrives and is processed, and new information transmitted in its turn, we will follow information as it flows from one person or computer to another and is transformed in the course of flow. This approach, apart from any other advantages, will give us a fresh look at the design of organizations.

Factorization of Decisions and Allocation of Attention

From the information processing point of view, division of labor means factoring the total system of decisions that need to be made into relatively independent subsystems, each of which can be designed with only minimal concern for its interactions with the others. As in subdividing other kinds of work, the division is necessary because of the bounded rationality of both humans and computers. The number of alternatives that can be considered, the intricacy of the chains of consequences that can be traced—all these are severely restricted by the limited capacities of the available processors.

Any division of labor among decisional subsystems must take account of the interdependencies that are ignored. What is wanted is a factorization that minimizes these interdependencies and consequently permits a maximum degree of decentralization of final decision to the subsystems, and a maximum use of relatively simple and cheap coordinating devices to relate each of the decisional subsystems with the others.

Not only must the size of decision problems handled by organizations be reduced to manageable proportions by factorization, but the number of decisions to be processed must be limited by applying good principles of attention management. Attention management for an organization means exactly what it means for an individual human being: Processing capacity must be allocated to specific decision tasks, and if the total capacity is not adequate to the totality of tasks, then priorities must be set so that the most important or critical tasks are attended to.

The bottleneck of attention becomes narrower and narrower as we move to the tops of organizations, where parallel processing capacity becomes less easy to provide without damaging the coordinating function that is a prime responsibility of these levels. Only a few items can simultaneously be on the active agenda at the top.

The difficulty of coping with an information-rich environment is compounded by the fact that most information relevant to top-level and long-run organizational decisions typically originates outside the organization, and hence in forms and quantities that are beyond its control. This means that the organization must have an "interface" for identifying, obtaining, and ingesting such information selectively and for translating it into formats that are compatible with its internal information flows and systems.

Second, if attention is the scarce resource, then it becomes particularly important to distinguish between problems for decision that come with deadlines attached (real-time decisions) and problems that have relatively flexible deadlines. Rather different system designs are called for to handle these different kinds of decisions.

In summary, the inherent capacity limits of information-processing systems impose two requirements on organizational design: that the totality of decision problems be factored in such a way as to minimize the interdependence of the components; and that the entire system be so structured as to conserve the scarce resource, attention. The organizational design must provide for interfaces to handle information that originates outside the organization, and special provision must be made for real-time decisions that have deadlines.

Applying these basic design requirements makes it easy to see the fallacy lurking in some standard but more or less abortive approaches to the improvement of information systems: for example, municipal data banks and management information systems. There was a great enthusiasm, when computers first became available to municipal organizations, for developing comprehensive data banks for metropolitan areas—these data banks to incorporate in a single system all the myriad pieces of information about land and its uses, and about people and their activities, that are generated by the operations of urban government.

As the result of several attempts to construct such systems, the enthusiasm has been much moderated, and several incipient undertakings of this kind have been abandoned. There were several reasons for the disenchantment that followed the initial attempts at construction. First, the data processing and data storage tasks proved much larger and more complex than had been imagined. Perhaps more crucial, it became less and less clear just how the data were to enter into the decision-making process, or indeed to just what decisions they were relevant.

There is no magic in comprehensiveness. The mere existence of a mass of data is not a sufficient reason for collecting it into a single, comprehensive information system. Indeed, the problem is quite the opposite: of finding a way of factoring decision problems in order to relate the several components to their respective relevant data sources. Analysis of the decision-making system and its data requirements must come first; only then can a reasonable approach be made to defining the data systems that will support the decision-making process.

The history of management information systems has been nearly the same as the history of municipal data banks. In the enthusiasm to make use of the enormous power of computers, there was a tendency, in designing such systems, to take the existing finance and production records as a starting point and to try to give top management access to all this information. The question was not asked, or not asked with sufficient seriousness, whether top or middle management either wanted or needed such information, nor whether the information that management at various levels needed and should want could in fact be derived from these particular source records. The systems were not designed to conserve the critical scarce resource—the attention of managers—and they tended to ignore the fact that the information most important to top managers comes mainly from external sources and not from the internal records that were immediately accessible for mechanized processing.

Thus many of the efforts to design information systems for municipalities and corporations fell prey to the fallacy of thinking that "more information is better." They took over, implicitly, the assumptions of a past society where information rather than attention was the scarce resource.

Components of the New Information Technology

In designing decision-making organizations, we must understand not only the structure of the decisions to be made, but also the decision-making tools at our disposal, both human and mechanical—men and computers.

The Human Components. In our fascination with the new capabilities that computers offer us, we must not forget that our human decision-makers have some pretty remarkable qualities too. Each person is provided with a sizable memory that is stocked cumulatively over a long period of years with various kinds of relevant and irrelevant information and skills. Each can recover relevant portions of that memory by recognition of audible or visible cues in the current situation. Each is able to communicate in natural language with others, either in direct face-to-face settings or by remote devices like the telephone or fax or e-mail.

Suppose, for example, that we were interested in designing an organization that would lead us to the most expert source of information in the United States about any particular question that happened to arise. Our first impulse, today, might be to turn to the World Wide Web. Should that impulse be encouraged?

The information we are seeking is stored both in human heads and in books and data banks. Moreover, the information in books is also indexed in human heads, so that usually the most expeditious way to find the right book is to ask a human who is an expert on the subject of interest. Not only is information available from books indexed in human heads, but information about people is also. Taking these resources into account, the most powerful information-processing system for carrying out a search for the best expert in the United States is still the aggregate of memory that is distributed among 250 million human heads, together with the telephone system that links these distributed memories.

On receipt of an inquiry, I pick up the phone and call the person, among my acquaintances, whose field of expertness is as close as possible to the target (it need not be very close at all). I ask my respondent, not for the answer to the question, but for the name of the person in his or her circle of acquaintance who is closest to being an expert on the topic. I repeat the process until I have the information I want. It will be a rare occasion when more than three or four calls are required.

Suppose that the question is whether whales have spleens. (I can't imagine why we would want to know, but this example is as good as any other.) I call a biologist, who refers me to an ichthyologist, who refers me to a specialist on whales, who either knows the answer or can refer me to the source where I will find it.

I do not mean to propose that we junk all our other information systems and place sole reliance on the telephone and the vast distributed memory with which it connects us. However, this is a useful thought experiment on how we must regard information-processing systems— including both electronic and human systems—their components and interconnections. We must learn to characterize them in terms of the sizes of their memories, the ways in which those memories are indexed, their processing rates, and the rapidity with which they can respond. The human components of information systems are just as describable as the machine components, and today we know a great deal through psychological research about the parameters of the human system.

Our new and growing understanding of information processing enables us to look at familiar processing systems—man and telephone—in new ways. It also introduces us to new kinds of systems, under the general rubric of "computers," that have capabilities of the most varied kinds.

The Computer as Memory. The computer is, first of all, a memory. I have already expressed my qualms about confusing the design of an information-collecting system with the design of an information-processing system. The fault, of course, is not in collecting information (although that may be costly in itself); it is in demanding the scarce attention of decision-makers to process the information that has been collected. Memories, as components of information-processing systems, need to be viewed as stores of *potential* information, which, if indexed effectively, can become available at a reasonable cost whenever it is needed as input to a decision-making process.

Even reading one book a day—a pretty good clip—a person who has collected a library of 30,000 books will take 100 years to read through all of them. We may even consider it a bit ostentatious of people to collect more books than they can possibly read—as though they were trying to impress us with their learning. However, we must not be too hasty in judging them. If their libraries are properly indexed, then each of our collectors has potential access to any of the information in the 30,000 volumes. They are quite justified in collecting more volumes than they can read if they cannot predict in advance what particular information they will need in the future, and if they have a good indexing system for finding, on demand, what they want to see.

Except for the Web, and a few specialized data banks, the computer memories that are employed today are not, in general, large compared with the paper-and-ink memories we call libraries. They are, in general, slightly better indexed for rapid retrieval of information, and one of the important directions of technological progress since the computer has appeared on the scene has been our understanding of the indexing and information-retrieval processes, and our ability to carry these out mechanically.

The Computer as Processor. In addition to being a memory, the computer is also a processor that has quite general capabilities for handling symbols of all kinds, numerical and non-numerical. This is its most novel feature. Non-human memories have been familiar to mankind since the invention of writing. Non-human symbol manipulation is something quite new, and even after forty years, we are just beginning to glimpse its potential.[12]

Up to the present time, perhaps the most important use of the computer in decision-making (though not the use that accounts for the bulk of computer time in organizations) is to model complex situations and to infer the consequences of alternative decisions. Some of this modeling makes use of mathematical techniques, like linear programming, that permit the calculation of optimal courses of action, hence serving as direct decision-making tools. In other forms of modeling, the computer serves as a simulator, calculating the alternative paths a system would follow in response to different decision strategies.

The term "management information system" has generally been construed narrowly and has been applied to large information storage and retrieval systems, like those mentioned earlier, in which the computer does only very simple processing of the information. The term would be better applied to the optimizing and simulation models that are increasingly used to illuminate various areas of management decision—models that are usually referred to as "operations research" and "strategic planning," or sometimes, "management decision aids." Such models, however they are labeled, probably give us a better preview of the future uses of computers in organizational decision systems than do the explicitly named management information systems.

Let me cite one example of an area of application for a strategic planning model. In the next decades, our society faces some important and difficult policy decisions with respect to the production and use of energy. In the past, the national energy problem was perceived mostly as a resource problem, and it was left in considerable part to private management through market mechanisms. Today, we see that the use of energy has important indirect consequences for the environment, and we see also that

---

[12]One evidence of the degree of novelty of the computer's capabilities is the resistance it evokes from those who refuse to see in it anything more than an enlarged desk calculator. Not since the Darwinian controversy of the past century have we seen such a passionate defense of the uniqueness of man against claims of kinship by systems that do not belong to his species.

the adequacy of fuel resources for producing energy will depend on such broader trends as the rates of development of industrializing countries and the decisions we make with respect to R&D for energy technology.

The number of important variables involved in the energy picture is so large, and the interconnections among variables so intricate, that common sense and everyday reasoning no longer provide adequate guides to energy policies—if, indeed, they ever did. Nor is there a simple organizational solution of a traditional kind: establishing a federal agency with comprehensive jurisdiction over energy problems, or, alternatively, tinkering with the market mechanism.

Agency reorganization is no solution for at least two reasons. First, energy problems cannot be separated neatly from other problems. What would be the relation of a comprehensive energy agency to environmental problems? The fragmentation of responsibility for energy policy in the federal government today ignores the intertwining of those problems with others. Second, even if there were such an agency, it too would need a systematic framework within which to take up its decision problems. Tinkering with market mechanisms raises the same difficulty— without a decision framework, we do not know how to tinker.

Hence, the most important organizational requirement for handling energy policy in an intelligent way is the creation of one or more models—either of an optimizing or simulation type—to provide coherence to the decision-making process. No doubt, it is of some importance to locate the responsibility for developing and exploiting such models in appropriate places in the governmental and industrial structure. But the mere existence of the models, wherever located, cannot but have a major impact on energy policy decisions. Surprisingly, comprehensive models of the energy system are still not common, although the need for them has been fairly obvious for some years. The tardiness of response to the need is evidence both of the novelty of the modeling technology and the novelty of looking at organization as a collection of decision systems rather than a collection of agencies and departments.[13]

---

[13]We have now had two generations' experience with decision models for economic policy. The construction and testing of such models in the United States has been carried out in considerable part by non-governmental agencies—the Cowles Foundation for Research in Economics and the Brookings Institution, for example. Since the day when President Nixon declared himself to be a Keynesian, the impact of decision models on government decisions could no longer be in doubt, although the impact certainly preceded that declaration by a decade or more. The econometric models have generally used classical analytic mathematical techniques, but the computer has been essential to carrying out the calculations. A somewhat different example is provided by several linear programming models that have been constructed, mainly under university auspices, to guide water policy decisions. In both these cases we see decision-making systems being designed in relative independence from reorganizations of a traditional kind. It is interesting to speculate whether all of the agency-shuffling reorganizations of federal agencies since 1937 have had as great an effect on public policy as these new decision-making systems.

Computer Access to External Information.[14] A third point must be made about the characteristics of the computer as a component of the organization's information-processing system. I have mentioned as one limitation of management information systems up to the present time their great reliance on information that is generated within the organization itself—for example, production and accounting information. A major reason for the emphasis on internal information was that, as the organization controls the production of this information, it was not hard to produce it in machine-readable form. No costly step was involved in getting it inside the computer.

If we examine the kinds of external information that executives use, we find that a large proportion of it is simply natural language text—the pages of newspapers, trade magazines, technical journals, and so on. Natural language text can, of course, be stored in computer memory after it is translated into some machine-readable form—punched cards, magnetic tape, or the like. Once stored in memory, computer programs can be written to index it automatically and to retrieve information from it in response to inquiries of a variety of kinds.

The only barrier, therefore, to making available to the mechanized components of organizational information systems the same kind of external information that executives now rely upon is the cost of putting the information into machine-readable form. Technologically, and even economically, there is no longer an obstacle; we have low-cost devices (scanners combined with optical character recognizers) that translate printed text into computer files, cheaply and accurately.

But for new materials, we do not even have to incur a cost to obtain them in machine-readable form. Every word that is now printed in a newspaper, journal, or book passes through a machine at some time during its prior history (as these words are doing while I write them)—a typewriter or typesetting machine—that can produce a machine-readable version of the text at the same time that it produces the human-readable version. Hence, the written word is becoming almost universally available in both machine-readable and human-readable editions. Personal computers and electronic networks created the market for the machine-readable versions, and the conversion process is now going very rapidly. It is a little like the telephone—the more people who have them, the more worthwhile it is to get one.

This development has opened up a whole new range of applications of computers to organizations' information systems. It enables computers to

---

[14]Because of the developments that have occurred since the publication of the 3rd edition of this book, I have had to convert the whole of this section of my discussion from the future into the present tense.

serve as initial filters for most of the information that enters the organization from outside, and thereby can reduce the attentional demands on executives. A recent example is the information system installed by the TIAA, the principal manager of university professors' retirement funds. Letters and other communications from owners of policies are typically typed or handwritten. When received, they are immediately passed through a scanner and an optical character reader so that they can be stored in computer-readable form in the TIAA computer system. An employee determines where the communication should be routed, and if it needs attention at more than one point in the organization, the system automatically prepares and distributes copies. The ability to work on the task in parallel at several places reduces turnaround time considerably. As the communication is inside the company's information system, it can be used to call up automatically records in the files that are needed for handling it.

Matching Techniques to Requirements. These comments will serve to indicate what is involved in fitting together the requirements of organization information systems with the characteristics of the information technology that is already available, and that which is emerging. The key to the successful design of information systems lies in matching the technology to the limits of the attentional resources. From this general principle, we can derive several rules of thumb to guide us when we are considering adding a component to an existing information-processing system.

In general, an additional component (man or machine) for an information-processing system will improve the system's performance only if:

1. Its output is small in comparison with its input, so that it conserves attention instead of making additional demands on attention;
2. It incorporates effective indexes of both passive and active kinds (active indexes are processes that automatically select and filter information for subsequent transmission);
3. It incorporates analytic and synthetic models that are capable not merely of storing and retrieving information, but of solving problems, evaluating solutions, and making decisions.

Conclusion

The major problems of organization today are not problems of departmentalization and coordination of operating units. Instead, they are problems of organizing information storage and information processing— not division of labor, but factorization of decision-making. These organizational problems are best attacked, at least to a first approximation, by examining the information system and the system of decisions it supports in abstraction from agency and department structure.

With the rapid development of information-processing technology, the corporate and public decision-making processes are becoming significantly more sophisticated and rational than they were in past eras. If we require any proof for this, we need only compare the Star Wars debate (regardless of whether we like its outcome) with any debate on the Acropolis reported by Thucydides—or, for that matter, with any debate in the U.S. Congress in the first half of this century. With the development of information-processing technology, we have a growing capacity to consider interactions and tradeoffs among alternatives and consequences; to cumulate our understanding of fragments of the whole problem by embedding these fragments in comprehensive models.

Barbara Ward and others have pointed out to us that the largest crises in our world today are crises of aspirations. The population problem is as old as our species. What is new about it today is that many peoples are resolved not to accept a gloomy outcome but to deal with it. For centuries, human actions have been creating all kinds of unintended and unexpected consequences. We could live in good conscience with these actions to the extent that we were unaware of their consequences. Today, we can trace minute and indirect effects of our behavior: the relation of smoking to cancer, the relation of the brittleness of eagles' eggs to the presence of DDT in the environment. With this new ability to trace effects, we feel responsible for them in a way we previously did not. The intellectual awakening is also a moral awakening.

The new problems created (or made visible) by our new scientific knowledge are symptoms of progress, not omens of doom. They demonstrate that we now possess the analytic tools that are basic to understanding our problems—basic to understanding the human condition. Of course, to understand problems is not necessarily to solve them. But it is the essential first step. The new information technology that we are creating enables us to take that step.

CHAPTER IX

The Criterion of Efficiency

IN THE PRECEDING TWO CHAPTERS attention has been concentrated on the way in which the organization brings its influence to bear on its individual members. Through the system of authority and the other types of communication that have been discussed, the organization provides the individual with some of his principal premises of decision: it specifies his fundamental value-premises—the organization objectives—and it supplies him with relevant information of all sorts that is necessary if he is to implement these values. It is time now to turn to the "internal" aspects of decision, and to see how the organizationally supplied premises are synthesized by the individual into a completed decision. Crucial to the synthesis are the decisional premises that the individual himself supplies, and the most important of these, aside from the information that originates with him, are the criterion of efficiency[1] and the individual's organizational identifications or loyalties. These will provide the subject matter of this and the following chapter, respectively.

Because the criterion of efficiency is rather more complicated in its application to noncommercial than to commercial organizations, a large part of this chapter will be taken up with the problem of extending the concept of efficiency so that it becomes applicable to the former as well as to the latter.

THE NATURE OF EFFICIENCY

The criterion of efficiency is most easily understood in its application to commercial organizations that are largely guided by the profit objective. In such organizations the criterion of efficiency dictates the selection of that alternative, of all those available to the individual, which will yield the greatest net (money) return to the organization. This "balance sheet" efficiency involves, on the one hand, the maximization of income, if costs are

[1]The theory of efficiency, along the lines developed here, has been proposed in C. E. Ridley and H. A. Simon, *Measuring Municipal Activities* (Chicago: International City Managers' Association, 1938).

considered as fixed; and on the other hand, the minimization of cost, if income is considered as fixed. In practice, of course, the maximization of income and the minimization of cost must be considered simultaneously—that is, what is really to be maximized is the difference between these two.

It will be seen that the criterion of efficiency is closely related to both organization and conservation objectives, as those terms have been defined in Chapter VI. It is related to the organization objective in so far as it is concerned with the maximization of "output." It is related to conservation objectives in so far as it is concerned with the maintenance of a positive balance of output over input.

The simplicity of the efficiency criterion in commercial organizations is due in large part to the fact that money provides a common denominator for the measurement of both output and income, and permits them to be directly compared. The concept must be broadened, therefore, if it is to be applicable to the process of decision where factors are involved that are not directly measurable in monetary terms. Such factors will certainly be present in noncommercial organizations where monetary measurement of output is usually meaningless or impossible. They will also be present in commercial organizations to the extent that those controlling the organization are not solely directed toward the profit motive—i.e. where they are concerned with questions of the public interest or employee welfare even when those factors are not directly related to the profit and loss statement. Moreover, nonmonetary factors will also be involved in the internal operation even of purely commercial organizations where specific activities are concerned whose relation to the profit-and-loss statement cannot be assessed directly. For example, decisions in a personnel department cannot always be evaluated in monetary terms, because the monetary effect of a particular personnel policy cannot be directly determined.

The Cost Element in Decision

In both commercial and noncommercial organizations (except for volunteer organizations) the "input" factor can be largely measured in money terms. This is true even when the organization objectives are broader than either profit or conservation of the organization. That is, even if the organization is concerned with the cost *for the community*, this cost can be fairly valued in terms of the goods and services that the organization buys.[2]

This point may not be entirely evident in the case of the evaluation

---

[2]For an elaboration of this point, and statements of the qualifications that must be appended to it to make it strictly accurate, the reader is referred to the literature on welfare economics. See, for example, A. C. Pigou, *The Economics of Welfare* (London: Macmillan, 1924).

of the services of employees. The tasks to which employees are assigned are not all equal with respect to agreeableness, hazard, and the like; and, to the extent that they are not, the money wage (unless this accurately reflects these elements—which it usually does not) is not an accurate measure of input in an organization where employee welfare takes its place among the organization objectives. In such cases, organization decisions must balance not only money input against output, but money input against output *and* employee welfare.

There are other cases, too, where input is not accurately measured by money cost to the organization. An industrial concern, for example, which is not penalized for the smoke and soot it distributes over the community has a cost factor, provided the organization objectives include concern for community welfare, that does not appear in the accounts.

When the decision is being made for a public agency that embraces among its objectives the general stability and prosperity of the economy—the Federal government, for example—still other considerations must enter in. In the case of a private business, interest on invested capital, at the market rate, must be included in calculations as a cost. In the case of government, if the effect of spending is to employ investment capital that would otherwise be idle, the interest on this capital is not really a cost from the standpoint of the economy as a whole. Moreover, the "output" of government investment may include effects of this investment on the level of income and employment in the economy, and these effects must be included in the measurement of product.

Likewise, when a private business employs an unemployed person his wage is an ordinary cost; while when the government employs such a person it makes use of a resource that would otherwise not be utilized, and hence the wages of those employed do not involve any real cost from the standpoint of the community.

These comments are not intended to defend any particular concept of the role of government spending in a modern economy—a subject that evokes sufficient controversy among the various competing schools of modern economists—but merely to point out that the criterion of efficiency cannot be applied to decisions in governmental agencies without consideration of the economic effects that the activities of these agencies may have. In the language of the economist, the problem of efficiency in the public agency must be approached from the standpoint of the general, rather than the partial, equilibrium.

Positive Values in Decision

While the negative values involved in decision can usually be summarized in terms of time or money costs, the positive values present a somewhat more complex picture. As we have seen, in a commercial enterprise, money value of output plays somewhat the same role as cost of production (input) in summarizing the value element involved. From a positive standpoint the kind of product manufactured is a valuationally neutral element. Not so in the case of public services. Hence, some substitute must be found in public administration for money value of output as a measure of value.

This substitute is provided by a statement of the objectives of the activity, and by the construction of indices that measure the degree of attainment of these objectives. Any measurement that indicates the effect of an administrative activity in accomplishing its final objective is termed a measurement of the *result* of that activity.[3]

Definition of Objectives. The definition of objectives for public services is far from a simple task. In the first place, it is desirable to state the objectives so far as possible in terms of values. That is, only if they are expressions of relatively final ends are they suitable value-indices. When objectives are stated in terms of intermediate goals, there is a serious danger that decisions governed by the intermediate end will continue to persist even when that end is no longer appropriate to the realization of value. The proliferation of forms and records in an administrative agency, for instance, frequently evidences a failure to reconsider activities which are aimed at some concrete end in terms of the broader values which that end is supposed to further.

On the other hand, however, the values which public services seek to realize are seldom expressible in concrete terms. Aims, such as those of a recreation department—to "improve health," "provide recreation," "develop good citizens"—must be stated in tangible and objective terms before results can be observed and measured. A serious dilemma is posed here. The values toward which these services should be directed do not provide sufficiently concrete criteria to be applied to specific decisional problems. However, if value-indices are employed as criteria in lieu of the values themselves, the "ends" are likely to be sacrificed for the more tangible means—the substance for the form.

Further difficulty arises in the lack of a common denominator of value. An activity may realize two or more values, as in the case of the recreation department mentioned above. What is the relative importance of the various values in guiding the department's activities? The health department provides an illustration of the same problem. Shall the department next year redistribute its funds to decrease infant mortality or to increase the facilities of the venereal disease clinic? Observations of results, measured in terms of value-indices, can merely tell the extent to which the several objectives are realized if one or the other course of action is taken. Unless both activities are directed toward exactly the same value, measurement of results cannot tell which course of action is preferable. Rationality can be applied in administrative decisions only after the relative weights of conflicting values have been fixed.

The question of who should construct the system of values or preferences which underlie the administrator's decisions has already been discussed in Chapter III. We wish here only to emphasize that somewhere, sometime in the administrative process weights actually are assigned to values. If this is not done consciously and deliberately, then it is achieved by implication in the decisions which are actually reached. It is not possible to avoid the problem by hiding it among the unexpressed premises of choice.

Accomplishment a Matter of Degree. Defining objectives does not exhaust the value element in an administrative decision. It is necessary to determine, in addition, the degree to which the objective is to be attained. A city charter or ordinance may define the function of the fire department as "protecting the city from damage due to fire"; but this does not imply that the city will wish to expand the fire-fighting facilities to the point where fire damage is entirely eliminated—an obviously impossible task. Moreover, it begs the question to say that the fire department should reduce losses "as far as possible," for how far it is possible to reduce losses depends on the amount of money available for fire protection and fire prevention services.

Value questions are not eliminated from the fire protection problem of that city until it has been determined that (1) the fire department should aim to limit fire losses to x dollars per capita, and (2) the city council will appropriate y dollars which, it is anticipated on the basis of available information, will permit (1) to be carried out. Values are involved, then, not only in the definition of objectives, but in the determination as well of the level of adequacy of services which is to be aimed at. Attainment of objectives is *always* a matter of degree.

The processes of "policy determination," as they take place in our governmental institutions, seldom cope with these questions of degree in determining the objectives of governmental services. It will be urged in later sections of this chapter that extension of policy determination to such questions is of fundamental importance for the maintenance of democratic control over the value elements in decision. It will be shown that a large measure of this procedural reform can be attained by a modification and extension of budgetary techniques.

Distributive Values. Thus far, the discussion has centered on values which are "aggregates." That is, the community measures its fire loss in terms of total dollars of destruction during the year. It does not distinguish the loss of $1,000 in Smith's store from a loss of $1,000 in Jones' store. The police department, in attempting to reduce the number of robberies, does not give a robbery on Third Street a different weight from a similar robbery on Fourth Street.

Nevertheless, questions of "distributive" value enter into almost every administrative decision—if in no other way than in an assumption of "equal weight" like those cited above. A playground built on the West Side will not serve children on the East Side. If chess classes are offered at the social center, there may be no facilities available for persons interested in social dancing.

Many distributive questions are geographical, but they may involve social, economic, or innumerable other "class" distinctions. The importance of such considerations in administration can be appreciated when it is recognized that agencies for assessment administration, administrative tribunals, and even welfare agencies are concerned primarily with questions of distributive rather than aggregate value.

As will be shown later, distributive questions are also of great importance when the work of an organization is specialized by "area" or by "clientele." In these cases, the objective of the organizational unit is immediately restricted to a particular set of persons, and interjurisdictional problems of the greatest consequence may arise.

A Common Denominator for Value—the Criterion of Efficiency

A fundamental problem involved in reaching a decision is the discovery of a common denominator between the two values which have been mentioned: low cost and large results. How is the choice made when the two conflict? Four relations are conceivable between choices A and B. If I_A is the input for A, and I_B for B, and O_A and O_B are the respective outputs, then these four possible relations may be expressed as follows:

1. I_A is less than I_B, and O_A is greater than O_B.
2. I_B is less than I_A, and O_B is greater than O_A.
3. I_A is less than I_B, and O_A is less than O_B.
4. I_B is less than I_A, and O_B is less than O_A.

In cases 1 and 2 the choice is unequivocal; but not so in cases 3 and 4. That is, when possibility A involves a larger cost than possibility B, but produces a smaller result, B obviously is preferable. But when possibility A involves a lower cost as well as a smaller result than B, cost must be weighed against result before a choice can be made.

The path to the solution of this difficulty has already been indicated. Underlying all administrative decisions is a limitation—a "scarcity"—of available resources. This is the fundamental reason why time and money are costs. Because they are limited in quantity, their application to one administrative purpose prevents the realization of alternative possibilities. Hence, the administrative choice among possibilities can always be framed as a choice among alternatives involving the same cost, but different positive values.

An administrative choice is incorrectly posed, then, when it is posed as a choice between possibility A, with low costs and small results, and possibility B, with high costs and large results. For A should be substituted a third possibility C, which would include A *plus* the alternative activities made possible by the cost difference between A and B. If this is done, the choice resolves itself into a comparison of the results obtainable by the application of fixed resources to the alternative activities B and C. The efficiency of a behavior is the ratio of the results obtainable from that behavior to the maximum of results obtainable from the behaviors which are alternative to the given behavior.

The criterion of efficiency dictates that choice of alternatives which produces the largest result for the given application of resources.

It should be noted that this criterion, while it supplies a common denominator for the comparison of administrative alternatives, does not supply a common numerator. Even though all decisions be made in terms of alternative applications of the same resources, the problem still remains of comparing the values which are attained by the different courses of action. The efficiency criterion neither solves nor avoids this problem of comparability.

Note on the Term "Efficiency"

The term "efficiency" has acquired during the past generation a number of unfortunate connotations which associate it with a mechanistic, profit-directed, stop-watch theory of administration. This is the result of the somewhat careless use of the term by overenthusiastic proponents of the "scientific management" movement. Nevertheless, no other term in the language comes so close as "efficiency" to representing the concept described in this chapter. The term has therefore been employed, with the hope that the reader will understand the criterion in the sense in which it has just been defined, and will be able to dissociate from it any unfortunate connotations it may have had in his mind.

Until practically the end of the nineteenth century, the terms "efficiency" and "effectiveness" were considered almost as synonymous. The Oxford Dictionary defines "efficiency": "Fitness or power to accomplish, or success in accomplishing, the purpose intended; adequate power, effectiveness, efficacy."

In recent years, however, "efficiency" has acquired a second meaning: the ratio between input and output.[4] In the words of the *Encyclopaedia of the Social Sciences:*

> Efficiency in the sense of a ratio between input and output, effort and results, expenditure and income, cost and the resulting pleasure, is a relatively recent term. In this specific sense it became current in engineering only during the latter half of the nineteenth century and in business and in economics only since the beginning of the twentieth.[5]

The use of the term by leaders of the scientific management movement added still a third meaning. Again quoting from the *Encyclopaedia of the Social Sciences:*

> The foundation of modern scientific management may be dated from F. W. Taylor's paper, *A Piece Rate System*, in which he described his pioneer method of establishing standards of job performance at the Midvale steel plant. When such standards were set, it became customary to refer to the ratio of actual performance to the standard performance as the efficiency of labor, a use somewhat different from that of the mechanical engineers, who apply the term to the ratio of actual output to an actual input.[6]

Harrington Emerson, another pioneer in the scientific management movement, and one who preferred the term "efficiency engineering," is reported to have defined efficiency as "the relation between what is accomplished and what might be accomplished." In this connection, he speaks of the "efficiency percent of the employee."[7]

It must be noted that there is a difference in computing an output-

---

[4]An early application of the engineering concept to the social field is that of F. Y. Edgeworth, who on p. 2 of his *Mathematical Psychics* (London: Kegan Paul, 1881) defined efficiency essentially as it is defined in this study: ". . . efficiency being thus defined: one engine is more efficient than another if, whenever the total quantity of fuel consumed by the former is equal to that consumed by the latter, the total quantity of energy yielded by the former is greater than that yielded by the latter."

[5]"Efficiency," *Encyclopaedia of the Social Sciences*, 5:437.

[6]*Loc. cit.*

[7]Horace Bookwalter Drury, *Scientific Management* (New York: Columbia University Press, 1915), pp. 114, 115.

input ratio in the physical and in the social sciences. For the engineer, both output and input are measured in terms of energy. The law of conservation of energy tells him that the output of useful energy cannot exceed the energy input. Hence arises the concept of "perfect" efficiency—that is, a situation in which output equals input. In the social sciences, output and input are seldom measured in comparable units; and even when they are, as in a comparison of cost of fire protection with dollar losses from fire, there is no "law of conservation of energy" which prevents the output from exceeding the input. Hence, the concept of perfect efficiency, if it is used at all, must be redefined. As a matter of fact, the concept of perfect efficiency will not be required in the present study. Actual problems, as they present themselves to the administrator, are always concerned with *relative* efficiencies, and no measure of *absolute* efficiency is ever needed. Moreover, the theory does not require a numerical measure of efficiency, but merely a comparison of *greater* or *less* between the efficiencies of two alternative possibilities. Under these circumstances, the definitions of efficiency as ratio of output to input and as ratio of the actual to the maximum possible amount to the same thing.

An Economic Analogy

It can be seen that the criterion of efficiency as applied to administrative decisions is strictly analogous to the concept of maximization of utility in economic theory. It is not asserted here that the criterion of efficiency always does dominate administrators' decisions, but rather that if they were rational it would. There is no assertion that such rationality is a common characteristic of actual behavior. On the other hand, the doctrine of maximization of utility has been commonly set forth in the economic literature as an explanatory doctrine as well, that is, as descriptive of actual behavior in the market. This difference between the two propositions should be kept carefully in mind.

The analogy between the two propositions extends also to the assumptions which underlie them. The first of these is that there is a scarcity of applicable resources. A second assumption is that the activities concerned are "instrumental" activities—that is, activities that are carried on for the positive values they produce, in the form of some kind of "result." Third, both propositions involve the comparability, at least subjectively, of the values in terms of which results are measured. (This assumption has already been discussed in the previous section.)

The broad scope of the analogy will become increasingly clear as the discussion proceeds. It will be seen that the problem of administrative decisions can be translated into a problem in the theory of production, and that concepts and theorems developed in economic theory have wide applicability to administrative decisions.

CRITICISMS OF THE EFFICIENCY CRITERION

Criticisms of "efficiency" as a guide to administration have been frequent and vociferous.[8] One group of criticisms need not concern us here, for they refer to definitions of the term different from the one proposed here. In this category must be placed attacks on efficiency which equate the term with "economy" or "expenditure reduction." As we have used "efficiency," there is no implication whatsoever that a small expenditure—or, for that matter, a large expenditure—is *per se* desirable. It has been asserted only that if two results can be obtained with the same expenditure the greater result is to be preferred. Two expenditures of different magnitude can, in general, be compared only if they are translated into opportunity costs, that is, if they are expressed in terms of alternative results.

"Mechanical" Efficiency

Others have objected to "efficiency" on the ground that it leads to a "mechanical" conception of administration. This objection, too, must result from the use of the term in quite a different sense from that proposed here. For a mere criterion of preference among possibilities does not in any manner limit the administrative techniques which may be employed in attaining the possibilities, nor, as we shall see in the next section, does it in any way reduce the role of the administrator's judgment in reaching decisions. Furthermore, the efficiency criterion is in the most complete accord with a viewpoint that places the social consequences of administration in the forefront of its determining influences.

"The Ends Justify the Means"

Two other lines of criticism assert that the criterion of efficiency leads to an incorrect relationship between "means" and "ends." On the one hand it is alleged that, in the interests of efficiency, ends are taken to justify any appropriate means. As we have noted in Chapter IV, the terms "means" and "ends" must be employed carefully in order to avoid contradictions; and for this reason we have preferred to talk of the value and

---

[8]See instances cited by Marshall E. Dimock, "The Criteria and Objectives of Public Administration," in *The Frontiers of Public Administration*, ed. Gaus, White, and Dimock, pp. 116–133.

factual aspects of alternatives. Suffice it to say that if the evaluation of the results of administrative activity takes into account *all* the significant value elements of the administrative alternatives, no undue subordination of "means" to "ends" can result.

"Ruthless" Efficiency

On the other hand, it is charged that efficiency directs all attention to the means, and neglects the ends. This charge has already been answered in pointing out the integral role which valuation plays in the employment of a criterion of efficiency. It may be freely admitted that efficiency, as a scientific problem, is concerned chiefly with "means," and that "efficient" service may be efficient with respect to any of a wide variety of ends. But merely to recognize that the process of valuation lies outside the scope of science, and that the adaptation of means to ends is the only element of the decisional problem that has a factual solution, is not to admit any indifference to the ends which efficiency serves. Efficiency, whether it be in the democratic state or in the totalitarian, is the proper criterion to be applied to the factual element in the decisional problem. Other, ethical, criteria must be applied to the problem of valuation.

Common to all these criticisms is an implication that an "efficiency" approach involves a complete separation of "means" and "ends." We have already seen that, strictly speaking, this is not the case—that the only valid distinction is one between ethical and factual elements in decision. Yet, in the actual application of the efficiency criterion to administrative situations, there is often a tendency to substitute the former distinction for the latter, and such a substitution inevitably results in the narrower, "mechanical" efficiency which has been the subject of criticism.

How this substitution comes about may be briefly explained. The ethical element in decision consists in a recognition and appraisal of all the value elements inhering in the alternative possibilities. The principal values involved are usually expressed as "results" of the administrative activity, and, as we have seen, the activity itself is usually considered as valuationally neutral. This leads to the isolation of two values: (1) the positive values expressed as "results," and (2) the negative values, or opportunity costs, expressed in terms of time or money cost.

In fact, to consider the administrative activity itself as valuationally neutral is an abstraction from reality which is permissible within broad limits but which, if carried to extremes, ignores very important human values. These values may comprehend the remuneration and working conditions (using these terms broadly) of the members of the group which carries out the activity.

We may enumerate some of these value elements more explicitly:

1. If cost is measured in money terms, then the wages of employees cannot be considered as a valuationally neutral element, but must be included among the values to be appraised in the decision.
2. The work pace of workers cannot be considered as a valuationally neutral element—else we would be led to the conclusion that a "speed-up" would always be eminently desirable.
3. The social aspects of the work situation cannot be considered as a valuationally neutral element. The decision must weigh the social and psychological consequences of substituting one type of work-situation for another.
4. Wage policies, promotional policies, and the like need to be considered not only from the viewpoint of incentives and result-efficiency, but also from that of distributive justice to the members of the group.

It must be emphasized, then, that when a choice between alternatives involves any valuationally significant difference in the work activity this difference must be included among the values to be weighed in reaching a decision.

Valuational Bias

A closely related fallacy in the application of the efficiency criterion is to include in the evaluation of alternatives only those values which have been previously selected as the *objective* of the particular administrative activity under consideration. The effects of some administrative activities are confined to a rather limited area, and indirect results do not then cause much difficulty. The activities of the fire department usually have an effect on fire losses, but very little relation to the recreation problem in the community (unless ardent fire fans form a large part of the community). Hence the fire chief does not have to take recreation values into consideration in reaching his decisions. It is very fortunate that the consequences of human activities are so strictly segregated; if they were not, the problem of reaching rational decisions would be impossible.[9] But the mere fact that activities do not *usually* have valuationally significant indirect effects does not justify us in ignoring such effects if they are, *in fact*, present. That is, the fire chief cannot, merely because he is a fire chief, ignore the possibility of accidents in determining the speed at which his equipment should respond to alarms.

[9]See pp. 94–95, *supra*.

This all seems commonplace, yet we shall devote a large portion of the next chapter to showing that, in actuality, administrators in reaching decisions commonly disclaim responsibility for the indirect results of administrative activities.[10] To this point of view we oppose the contrary opinion that the administrator, serving a public agency in a democratic state, must give a proper weight to *all* community values that are relevant to his activity, and that are reasonably ascertainable in relation thereto, and cannot restrict himself to values that happen to be his particular responsibility. Only under these conditions can a criterion of efficiency be validly postulated as a determinant of action.[11]

Of course, the extent to which administrators can, in practice, give consideration to "indirect" effects is severely limited by the psychological considerations analyzed at length in Chapter V. Many effects not directly related to the objective of the organization will perforce be ignored because the administrator's span of attention is limited, and because there are often severe limits on the time available for making decisions.

FACTUAL ELEMENTS IN DECISION[12]

We have seen that the criterion which the administrator applies to factual problems is one of efficiency. The resources, the input, at the disposal of the administrator are strictly limited. It is not his function to establish a utopia. It is his function to maximize the attainment of the governmental objectives (assuming they have been agreed upon), by the efficient employment of the limited resources that are available to him. A "good" public library, from the administrative standpoint, is not one that owns all the books that have ever been published, but one that has used the limited funds which are allowed it to build up as good a collection as possible under the circumstances.

When a decision is made in terms of the criterion of efficiency, it is necessary to have empirical knowledge of the results that will be associated with each alternative possibility. Let us consider a specific municipal

---

[10]For a superlative illustration of the difficulty of securing administrative responsibility for indirect effects see Karl E. Stromsen, "The Usefulness of Central Review of Bureau Communications," *Case Reports in Public Administration*, No. 16, compiled by a Special Committee on Research Materials, Committee on Public Administration, Social Science Research Council (Chicago: Public Administration Service, 1940). The entire analysis assumes that organizational relevance is the ruling criterion of whether an indirect effect should be given administrative consideration.

[11]Dewey finds in these indirect effects the basic characteristic which distinguishes a "public" from a "private" transaction. See *The Public and Its Problems*, pp. 12–13.

[12]This section is based on Herbert A. Simon, "Comparative Statistics and the Measurement of Efficiency," *National Municipal Review*, 26:524–527 (Nov., 1937).

function, the fire department. Its objective is the reduction of the total fire loss, and results will be measured in terms of this loss.

The extent of the fire loss will be determined by a large number of factors. Among these are natural factors (frequency of high winds, heavy snowfall, severe cold weather, hot dry weather, tornadoes, hurricanes and cyclones, earthquakes, and floods), structural and occupancy factors (exposure hazards, physical barriers, density of structures, type of building construction, roof construction, contents, and risk of occupancy), the moral hazard (carelessness and incendiarism), and finally the effectiveness of the fire department itself. The loss, then, will be a function of all these variables, including the performance of the fire department itself. The fire chief must know how the activities of his department affect the loss if he is to make intelligent decisions.

How does the fire department perform its task? It inspects buildings to eliminate fire hazards, it carries on campaigns of education against carelessness, it fights fires, it trains firemen, it investigates and prosecutes incendiaries.

But we can carry the analysis a step farther. Of what does fire-fighting consist? A piece of apparatus must be brought to the scene of action, hose laid, water pumped and directed upon the flames, ladders raised, and covers spread over goods to reduce water damage. Again, each of these activities can be analyzed into its component parts. What does laying a hose involve? The hose must be acquired and maintained. Equipment for carrying it must be acquired and maintained. Firemen must be recruited and trained. The firemen must spend a certain amount of time and energy in laying the hose.

A final level of analysis is reached by determining the cost of each of these elements of the task. Thus, the whole process of fire-fighting can be translated into a set of entries in the city's books of accounts.

The problem of efficiency is to determine, at any one of these levels of analysis, the cost of any particular element of performance, and the contribution which that element of performance makes to the accomplishment of the department's objectives. When these costs and contributions are known, the elements of performance can be combined in such a way as to achieve a maximum reduction in fire loss.

There are at least four rather distinct levels at which the analysis of the administrative situation may be carried out. At the highest level is the measurement of results, of the accomplishment of agency objectives. Contributing to these results are the elements of administrative performance. Subordinate to these, in turn, is input measured in terms of effort. Effort, finally, may be analyzed in terms of money cost.

The mathematically minded will see in this structure a set of equations—strictly identical with the economist's "production functions." The first equation expresses the results of government as a function of the performance of certain activities. Further equations express these performance units as functions of less immediate performance units, the latter in terms of units of effort; and finally effort is expressed as a function of expenditures. The problem of efficiency is to find the maximum of a production function, with the constraint that total expenditure is fixed.

The Determination of Social Production Functions

It follows from the considerations which have been advanced that that portion of the decision-making process which is factual, which is amenable to scientific treatment, resolves itself into the determination of the production functions of administrative activities. This is a research task of the first magnitude, and one which as yet has hardly been touched.

Progress toward an understanding of these functions involves a series of well defined steps:

1. The values, or objectives, affected by each activity must be defined in terms that permit their observation and measurement.
2. The variables, extra-administrative as well as administrative, that determine the degree of attainment of these functions must be enumerated.
3. Concrete, empirical investigations must be made of the way in which results change when the extra-administrative and administrative variables are altered.

The necessary scope and difficulty of a research program which would make a substantial contribution to our knowledge of these functions can hardly be exaggerated. The principal progress to date has been in the first step,[13] and, as yet, empirical studies involving steps 2 and 3 are almost nonexistent.[14]

But if such research is difficult it is also indispensable. It is hard to see how rationality can play any significant role in the formulation of administrative decisions unless these production functions are at least approximately known. Nor can the problem be avoided by falling back on the "common sense" of administrators—their "intuition" and "practical insight" in dealing with situations for which "long experience" has

[13]For a bibliography of writings on this subject see Ridley and Simon, *op. cit.*, pp. 68–74.

[14]Herbert A. Simon et al., *Determining Work Loads for Professional Staff in a Public Welfare Agency* (Berkeley: Bureau of Public Administration, University of California, 1941).

qualified them. Anyone who has had close contact with administrative situations can testify that there is no correlation between the ability of administrators and their confidence in the decisions they make—if anything the correlation is an inverse one. The ablest administrators are the first to admit that their decisions are, in general, the sheerest guesswork; that any confidence they evidence is the protective shield with which the practical man armors himself and his subordinates from his doubts.

The fact of the matter is that momentous decisions are made every day as to the allocation of resources to one or another competing purpose, and that, particularly in noncommercial organizations, the decisions are made in an almost complete absence of the evidence which would be necessary to validate them. The principal reason for this, of course, is the difficulty, except in enterprises that have a relatively tangible product, of determining the actual production functions.

To recognize how far actual decisions fall short of rationality is no criticism of the administrator, who must act whether or not he possesses the information that would be necessary for the complete rationality of his decisions. It is, however, a criticism of apologies that would make his ignorance a virtue, and would question the need for extensive programs of research in this direction.[15]

FUNCTIONALIZATION IN RELATION TO EFFICIENCY

A few words need to be said now about the bearing of this efficiency criterion upon organizational problems. In an earlier chapter it was noted that specialization in organization often follows functional lines. This functionalization involves the analysis of the organization objective into subsidiary objectives. One or more of the subsidiary objectives may be assigned to each of the organizational units.

Thus, a fire department may be divided into a fire prevention bureau, and a number of fire-fighting divisions. The function, or objective, of the former will be defined in terms of prevention, that of the latter in terms of extinguishment. A health department may include a communicable diseases division, a division for prenatal care, a vital statistics division, and so forth. Similar illustrations can be found in every field of governmental service.

Under these circumstances, there will be a hierarchy of functions and objectives corresponding to the hierarchy of divisions and bureaus in the agency. In general, the hierarchical arrangement of functions will

---

[15]Even Barnard, whose critical insight usually saves him from the "practical man" fallacy, credits the intuitional faculties with considerably more validity than seems to be due them. See his "Mind in Everyday Affairs," reprinted as an appendix in *The Functions of the Executive*, pp. 301–322.

correspond to a means-end relationship. Fire losses, for instance, can be conceived as a product of number of fires by average loss per fire. Hence, a fire department might take reduction in number of fires and reduction in average loss per fire as subsidiary objectives, and assign these objectives to subsidiary units in the organization.

There are several prerequisites to effective functionalization. First, as indicated above, the general objective must be analyzed into subsidiary objectives, standing in a means-end relation with it. But further, the technology of the activity must be such that the work of the agency can be broken into distinct portions, each contributing primarily toward one, and only one, of the subsidiary objectives. Thus, it would be useless to divide a recreation department into "good citizenship," "health," "enjoyment," and "education" divisions. Although these might be defended as subsidiary objectives of recreation work, it would be impossible to devise a scheme of organization which would break activities into component parts, each contributing to only one of these objectives.

Value and Limits of Functionalization

The so-called "functional principle" of organization is thus seen to be of a rather complex nature. It assumes the possibility of a parallel functionalization of objectives and of activities. Where such parallelism is absent, the mere analysis of an objective into its components does not afford any basis for organization.

If the limitations of functionalization are apparent, so also are some of its values. For, if the activities of an organizational unit are directed toward a particular well defined objective, then the problem of decision-making in that unit is correspondingly simplified. The value elements to be considered in weighing alternatives can all be related to the organizational objective. A fire prevention division need consider only the impact of its activities upon the number of fires that will occur.

On the other hand, if the functionalization is unrealistic—if it does not fit the technological picture—then functionalization may lead to deterioration in the quality of decisions. For in this case the values which are affected by the unit's activities, but which are not comprehended in the statement of the organizational objective, will be neglected in the decision-making process.

Specialization by "Area" and "Clientele"

It has not generally been recognized in the literature of administration that specialization by "area" and "clientele" are, in fact, merely a particular kind of functionalization. This follows from the fact, already noted, that the complete definition of an objective involves the specification of the group of persons to whom the value in question refers.

The fire department of Podunk, for instance, has as its objective not "minimization of fire losses," but "minimization of fire losses *in Podunk*."

If specialization by area and specialization by clientele are merely forms of functionalization, then, to be successful they must satisfy the conditions of effective functionalization: (1) it must be technologically feasible to split the work activity, as well as the objective, along functional lines; (2) these segregated work activities must not affect, to a substantial degree, values extraneous to the specified functions.

The first point may again be illustrated by a health department. It would not be technologically feasible to divide a contagious disease program into two portions, one aiming to reduce contagious diseases among men, the other among women.

The second point will be developed at length in Chapter X. By way of illustration we need only to recall the frequent newspaper accounts of buildings which burn to the ground when a fire department refuses, or is unable, to cross a jurisdictional line.

EFFICIENCY AND THE BUDGET[16]

As a practical application of the approach set forth in this chapter, we may consider the public budget-making process, and the form which this process will have to take if it is to conform to the requirements of rationality.

It has been asserted that the concept of efficiency involves an analysis of the administrative situation into a positive value element (the results to be attained) and a negative value element (the cost). For the practical execution of this analysis, a technique is needed that will enable the administrator to compare various expenditure alternatives in terms of results and costs. The budget document will provide the basis for such a comparison.

The essence of the public budget process is that it requires a comprehensive plan to be adopted for *all* the expenditures that are to be made in a limited period. But if the budget is to be used as an instrument for the control of efficiency, substantial improvements must be made in present techniques.

---

[16]This section is adapted from Herbert A. Simon, "Measurement Techniques in Administrative Research," *Civic Affairs,* 8:1 ff. (May, 1941).

Inadequacy of Customary Budget Methods

What does the typical governmental budget include? It tells how much each department will be allowed to spend during the subsequent year, and how it may spend it. How are the particular figures to be found in budgets arrived at? How is it determined that 14 per cent of the budget shall be devoted to fire protection and 11.6 per cent to highways?

A different answer to this question would be given in every community in which it was asked. Some budgets are made by copying off the figures of the previous year's expenditures. Some are constructed by increasing or decreasing appropriations by a fixed percentage. Some are determined by allotting to each department a certain percentage of its request—he who shouts loudest gets most. Some have even less systematic plans.

If this seems exaggerated, the following justifications for increased appropriations in the supporting schedules of one city budget should serve to convince even the most skeptical:

"Salaries should be commensurate with duties and responsibilities of office."

"Naturally with increased work more supplies will be necessary and the cost will be greater. My postage bills alone amount to $2,500 a year."

"Time and skill required for this work before and after election."

"A larger increase was asked last year and refused."[17]

There are, of course, a few exceptional cities and other agencies which attempt to substitute a more rational budget review for this hit-or-miss process. A number of federal departments, including the Department of Agriculture, may be cited in this connection.[18]

The Long-Term Budget

If budgeting is to serve as a basis for the rational allocation of expenditures, two comprehensive budgets must be substituted for the present inadequate documents: an annual budget and a long-term budget. However, since the annual budget is merely a segment of the long-term budget, only the latter need be discussed.

The long-term budget will be made up of several parts: (1) long-term estimates of trends in problem-magnitude for the various departments—distribution and concentration of burnable values which must be protected against fire, mileage of streets which must be kept clean, popula-

[17]I will permit the city from whose budget these examples are drawn to remain anonymous.

[18]Verne B. Lewis, "Budgetary Administration in the Department of Agriculture," in John M. Gaus and Leon O. Wolcott, *Public Administration and the U.S. Department of Agriculture* (Chicago: Public Administration Service, 1941), pp. 403–462; MacMahon, Millett, and Ogden, *op. cit.*, pp. 171–185.

tion which must be served by libraries, etc.; (2) long-term estimates of service adequacy—that is, the level of services which the city intends to provide its citizens—so many acres of park per 1,000 population, a specified fire loss, etc.; (3) a long-term work program, showing in work units the services which will have to be provided and facilities to be constructed to achieve the program outlined in items (1) and (2); and (4) a financial program which will relate the work program to the fiscal resources of the community.

Item (1) involves primarily factual considerations. The determination of item (2) is primarily a matter of value judgments. Items (3) and (4), after the first two items have been determined, become largely factual questions. Hence, it would seem to be a legislative task to weigh (2) against (4), and to determine the budget program. On the other hand, the legislature would need assistance in developing the factual information for (1), (2), and (3).

Under present budgetary procedure, items (1) and (2) are seldom even a part of the budget document, and the entire discussion is carried on in terms of items (3) and (4). Furthermore, usually a single budget plan is presented to the legislature, for its approval or amendment. It would seem much preferable, if the necessary information were available, to present directly to the legislature the policy issues involved in (2), and to present the legislature with alternative budget plans, indicating the implications for policy of increases and curtailments of expenditure. Modifications along these lines would seem to be absolutely essential if the legislature is to be returned to a place of influence in the determination of public policy.

Too often, under current practice, the basic decisions of policy are reached by technicians in the agency entrusted with budget review, without any opportunity for review of that policy by the legislature. That this condition is tolerated results partly from general failure to recognize the relative element in governmental objectives.[19] Since most legislative declarations of policy state objectives of governmental activity without stating the level of adequacy which the service is to reach, it is impossible for an "expert" to reach on factual grounds a conclusion as to the adequacy of a departmental appropriation. Hence, present procedures would not seem to safeguard sufficiently democratic control over the determination of policy.[20]

[19]See pp. 57–64, 254, *supra*. Cf. Gaston Jeze, *Théorie Générale du Budget* (Paris: M. Girard, 1922), pp. i–iii.

[20]John Dewey has done much to develop a democratic philosophy of the relation of expert to public. In *The Public and Its Problems* (p. 208) he states the essential thesis of the present study.

Progress Toward a Long-Term Budget

Public agencies have made considerable progress within the past few years toward long-term plans that include a work program and a financial plan. Little progress has as yet been made toward a program that will tell the legislator and the citizen what this program means to him in terms of specific governmental services. Furthermore, little progress has as yet been made toward estimating the cost of maintaining governmental services at a particular level of adequacy, or determining when expenditures should, in the interests of efficiency, be turned from present channels into other, more useful directions.

Illustration of a Rational Budget

As an illustration of the line of development which needs to be pursued, the budget procedure of the California State Relief Administration will be described briefly. The agency for several years employed a well designed procedure of budget estimating. One reason for its successful performance of this difficult task was the nature of its objectives.

The major task of an unemployment relief agency is to provide a minimum level of economic security to needy families. The family budget which the agency employs to effect its policies provides an immediate translation of "cost" into "result." That is, it is immediately possible to visualize what a specific expenditure means in terms of the level of economic assistance which the agency provides. The policy-forming body can decide how large a family budget it is willing to authorize, and this decision can be immediately translated into cost terms. In this way "service adequacy" is determined.

Similarly, the State Relief Administration had worked out a detailed procedure for estimating over a period of time how many cases would be eligible for assistance; that is, what the problem-magnitude would be. With these two steps completed—the level of service determined and the problem magnitude estimated—it was a simple matter to develop the work budget and estimate financial needs.

This illustration has been oversimplified to emphasize its salient features. An unemployment relief agency must provide certain types of service as well as cash relief. The operating expenses of the agency have been left out of consideration also.[21] But, except for this oversimplification and these omissions, the budget procedure which has been described closely approximates the ideal of a rational budget process.

[21]Simon et al., *op. cit.*

SUMMARY

In this chapter we have seen that, in the factual aspects of decision-making, the administrator must be guided by the criterion of efficiency. This criterion requires that results be maximized with limited resources.

On the other hand, criteria of "correctness" have no meaning in relation to the purely valuational elements in decision. A democratic state is committed to popular control over these value elements, and the distinction of value from fact is of basic importance in securing a proper relation between policy-making and administration.

Improvement in the quality of decision awaits empirical research into the production functions that relate activities to results. Our knowledge of these functions is fragmentary at present, yet they are indispensable as a tool of reason, without which it operates in a factual vacuum.

The value of organization along functional lines lies in its facilitation of decisional processes. Functionalization is possible, however, only when the technology permits activities to be segregated along parallel lines.

A potent device for the improvement in governmental decision-making processes, both legislative and administrative, is the budget document. The improvement of budgetary methods will (1) permit a more effective division of labor between the policy-forming and administrative agencies, and (2) focus attention upon the social production functions and their critical role in decision-making.

THE CRITERION OF EFFICIENCY

MEASURING RESULTS IN BUSINESS FIRMS

CHAPTER IX PLACES CONSIDERABLE EMPHASIS upon the difficulty of measuring results in public organizations, and argues that it is easier to do so in business organizations. The latter have profits as the "bottom line," and accountants know how to measure those—at least to a first approximation. But in spite of this, the measurement of results in business firms faces difficulties not unlike (although perhaps less severe than) those that public and non-profit organizations encounter.

First, there are difficulties with respect to tradeoffs between short-run and long-run profits (reflected, for example, in the interest rates assumed in estimating the present value of future income), and there are large ambiguities in such accounting items as "goodwill" and in the value of fixed assets that have been purchased (e.g., through mergers).

Second, even more severe problems are encountered when companies divisionalize with the aim of providing each division with a profit-and-loss statement and requiring it to make a profit. Then the pricing of transactions between divisions becomes a serious problem unless (and this is rarely the case) divisions are expected to deal with each other at arm's length and to exhibit no preference for dealing with other divisions of the company rather than using outside vendors. Unless there are genuine competitive markets constraining the transactions among divisions, some administrative pricing procedure must be imposed in order to determine division incomes, expenses, and profits.

Third, there are many departments in any company (accounting, personnel, law, planning, research and development, advertising, etc.) whose contribution to profits is indirect, deriving from the services they provide to the "line" departments. In many if not most cases, it is not feasible to create internal markets for these services, and in any event, such markets would not be competitive and would be inadequate mechanisms for setting prices.

For all of these reasons, profits cannot be the only yardsticks used to measure results in business organizations and their component units.

Long Run and Short Run

There has been a good deal of public discussion in recent years of reasons why company CEOs are tempted to emphasize short-term profits at the expense of the company's future prospects. Given the relatively brief average tenure of executives at top corporate levels, when a large part of executive compensation takes the form of bonuses based upon annual profits, horizons of five years or even two years may have more weight in decisions than longer-run horizons. This is equivalent to using a very high interest rate to evaluate investment opportunities. (The same temptation is present for the occupants of positions in public organizations. Survival in any position may be facilitated, for a time, by postponing present problems to the future.)

All might be well if it were easy, or even possible, for stockholders to estimate the tradeoffs between present and future that are governing company decisions, but the major uncertainties that always control the future (and which are more easily assessed by those in management than by owners who are outsiders) make it exceedingly difficult to arrive at such estimates. Moreover, uncertainties about the future have a tendency to convert themselves into rather spurious "certainties" on the company's books, where a definite value must be assigned to such items as "good-will," the value of factories and machinery and other tangible assets. For these reasons, stockholders' equity on a balance sheet is seldom an even approximate estimate of discounted future earnings.

As no one, to the best of my knowledge, has proposed an adequate solution to this problem, I simply record it here as one of the obstacles to the effective use of the efficiency criterion in decision-making in private corporations as well as public agencies.

Divisional Profit-and-Loss Statements

How well outcomes can be evaluated in profit-and-loss terms (or in any other terms, for that matter) for subdivisions of an organization depends on the degree of mutual independence of the components. If the company is, in fact, a holding company, performing little more than an investment banking function for its subsidiary divisions, then the divisional P&L statements can be as informative, or uninformative, as the statements for whole corporations.

A major consideration is whether the divisions are allowed to, and expected to, deal with each other at arm's length. One aspect of this, as suggested above, is the right to choose between outside and inside suppliers on a basis of price and quality, without any special preference for inside purchases. If some professional services (e.g., advertising, R&D, accounting, legal) are available from company-wide departments, then the same principle applies to such services as to parts supply.

For transactions where the arms-length rule does not apply, the internal supplier and user will constitute a single buyer facing a single seller, and some procedure other than simple buying and selling in a competitive market will have to be provided to fix the "fair" price of transactions. Of course, if there are competitive external markets, the prices in these markets can be used as guidelines for the negotiated internal prices even if outside procurement is not permitted. But this is quite different from leaving transactions to the free play of markets.

There is a great deal to be said, of course, for letting each tub rest on its own bottom. The divisional P&L statement is an attractive device for enforcing efficiency, but only when the circumstances permit interdivisional transactions to be priced at reasonable approximations to prices in competitive markets. In using this device, however, one must remember that there is no magic in it that creates independence among units when technology, common marketing organizations, or other circumstances actually enforce a high level of interdependence among them.

Evaluating Intermediate Outputs

Perhaps the greatest difficulty in applying the efficiency criterion lies in evaluating those outputs of activity that are not final products. The problem is serious enough in constructing cost accounting systems for factories in such a way as to assign costs correctly to their causes. The problem becomes many times enlarged in assigning values to work that contributes mainly to the organization's decision-making process. This includes, of course, all managerial activities, and especially those that feed only indirectly into production: research and development, legal services, advertising, and accounting being prime examples. In this domain, the difficulties that companies face in measuring the value of output are no less severe than those faced by government organizations.

The problem is illustrated by the rash of "downsizings," and especially reductions in white-collar and middle-management personnel, that have been occurring in American corporations since the early 1990s. In some cases downsizing was a reaction to losses in sales volume, but in other cases, companies apparently decided that they could continue to operate at current levels with substantially fewer employees. If they were correct in those judgments, then their judgments about the required workforce prior to downsizing must have been wrong.

Again, the uncertainties have a great deal to do with the balance between present and future. The kind of downsizing we are now considering focuses primarily on those positions that are not immediately involved in the products that are being manufactured and shipped today. To take the simplest example, it is obvious that one can always eliminate research activities without any effect whatsoever upon this week's or this month's—or perhaps this year's—sales.

Whenever a job is eliminated whose product has no immediate effect upon output or sales effort, short-run profits, as recorded in financial statements, can be expected to increase. What the effect will be on long-run profits is more problematic, and the answer will not be known for some time, if it is ever known. The arguments about staffing policies that take place in companies are no different from the arguments that take place in government agencies; they center upon the reality or unreality of the contributions that indirect activities make to the achievement of organizational goals over the more or less long run.

Evaluating "Quality"

We can divide into two (or sometimes more) parts the task of evaluating activities whose outcomes contribute only indirectly to the final product. First, we can usually find ways of evaluating the quality of the activity itself. Then we undertake the more difficult task of evaluating whether the activity, even if carried on at a high level of quality, is worthwhile in terms of final goals. As what may be a rather extreme example, consider the problem of evaluating a research professor at a research university—leaving aside for the moment his or her teaching contribution. The case would not be significantly different if we were evaluating a researcher in an industrial R&D lab.

Research in a university is a public activity. That is, the work is not complete until it has been evaluated and placed in the public record (published in a refereed journal). Then, it is evaluated again by those who do or don't find it useful for their own subsequent research. It is evaluated also during the interactions that the researcher has with colleagues in the laboratory, in seminars, and at professional meetings. The evaluators are themselves knowledgeable, some to a very high degree, about the substance of the work. As a result, there is usually considerable consensus in any given research domain as to the quality of the output of any particular researcher, and it is not usually too difficult to arrive at a rough rank order of researchers in such a domain.

In scientific circles some cynicism is often expressed about weighing and counting pages of research output, and readers will be familiar with the phrase "publish or perish." I do not want to make the evaluation process sound more valid than it is; but it is clearly far more veridical than weighing and counting. Its validity stems directly from the opportunities that professional peers have to observe both the process of research and its outcomes.

The work of managers and professionals in business—those who are part of the decision-making process—shares to some degree this public character. To be sure, most of the work is not literally "published," but its outcomes usually take the form of oral or written communications to other members of the organization (and to persons outside the firm). To the extent that the work is visible to, and thereby can be judged by peers, it affords the same opportunity for evaluation as occurs in research. People in organizations make judgments, therefore, about who is an effective or an ineffective manager, and about the level of effectiveness. Like judgments about research, these organizational judgments are fallible, but they are not random.

But both in the case of research and in the case of management what is being assessed is largely the short-run rather than the long-run value of the work. If we ask of a researcher's output what long-run impact it will have upon the science or its application, that question will be harder to answer. If we ask of the manager not merely whether he goes about his work in an effective way but whether his important decisions are generally correct, then we are back to the task of tracing out chains of causal relations, many of them still hidden in the future. What is distinctive about downsizing, as contrasted with other dismissals of employees, is that it is based, not on a judgment that the work is being done badly, but on a judgment that, even if it is done well, it is not making an adequate contribution to the organization's goals. As we have just seen, this is an exceedingly difficult judgment to make on an objective basis.

Competing Criteria of Evaluation

A very instructive example of the subtleties of evaluation, when it tries to go beyond direct measurement of the quality of activities, arose in the malaria control activities of the U.S. government just before, during, and after World War II.[22] Malaria had long been a serious public health problem in many parts of the South, but its incidence decreased very rapidly (for reasons that were largely unknown) in the immediate prewar years. During the war, many American soldiers were exposed to malaria abroad, and many contracted it, leading to the fear that new epidemics might break out when they returned to this country. Public health agencies used a variety of programs to deal with the disease, one of the most extensive being large-scale insecticide (principally DDT) attacks on the mosquitoes that transmit it.

There were, therefore, two kinds of measures of the effectiveness of malaria control: numbers of reported cases (and of deaths), and sizes of mosquito populations. Unfortunately, diagnosis and reporting of cases and deaths was very unreliable, for definitive blood smear tests were not widely used during much of this period. Nevertheless, the evidence was

---

[22]See M. Humphreys, "Kicking a Dying Dog: DDT and the Demise of Malaria in the American South, 1942–1950," *Isis*, 87: 1–17 (1996). The discussion here relates especially to evaluation of the Malaria Control in War Areas (MCWA) agency, a branch of the U.S. Public Health Service created in 1942.

strong, although not always accepted by the scientists, that by 1942 the agency was combating a disease that was nearly extinct in the United States. However, buoyed by the uncertainties of the morbidity and mortality statistics and by the prospects of reinfection of mosquitoes by returning veterans, the agency turned from morbidity and mortality statistics to the statistics on mosquito populations as the basis for effort evaluation. They could then show that the populations were (potentially) dangerously large, and that DDT spraying led to major reductions in them. During a period during which the agency spent approximately $50 million, the question of the relation of the activities of the agency to the continuing absence of malaria remained essentially unanswered.

It is not clear whether better statistics in this case would have made it easier to arrive at correct policy decisions. The most important information that was missing was information about the causes for the apparently unmotivated but nearly complete disappearance of the disease at the beginning of the 1940s, and information about the probabilities that a new epidemic could be started by the return of infected veterans.

Is comparable uncertainty common in business decision-making? Consider a multinational company (Sea Containers, Inc.) with one division in the container ship business, another in passenger ferries on several European ferry crossings, a third in luxury hotels on several continents, and a fourth operating railroad trains (e.g., the Orient Express). Decisions have to be made frequently about the purchase and disposal of ships and containers and the acquisition and termination of ferry routes. How should the long-term effects of the English Channel tunnel upon the Channel ferry business be estimated? What fluctuations can be anticipated in the container ship business, and what are the likely near-term strategies of competitors with respect to the purchase of new container capacity? What measures can be used to evaluate the effectiveness of the company's managers? The fact that the company has a "bottom line," and that its short-run return on investment can be measured, does not in fact make its problems of evaluation very different from those of a government agency.

Conclusion

Chapter IX argues that efficiency, the ratio of results achieved to resources consumed, is an appropriate and fundamental criterion for all of the decisions that are taken in an organization. It points out, however, that the assessment of efficiency can be exceedingly difficult, especially for the activities of public agencies. In this commentary, I have shown why that difficulty extends also to the assessment of the efficiency of actions taken inside private business firms.

CHAPTER X

Loyalties and Organizational Identification

THE VALUES and objectives that guide individual decisions in organizations are largely the organizational objectives—the service and conservation goals of the organization itself. Initially, these are usually imposed on the individual by the exercise of authority over him; but to a large extent the values gradually become "internalized" and are incorporated into the psychology and attitudes of the individual participant. He acquires an attachment or loyalty to the organization that automatically—i.e. without the necessity for external stimuli—guarantees that his decisions will be consistent with the organization objectives. This loyalty may itself have two aspects: it may involve an attachment to the service goals of the organization (what was called in Chapter VI the "organization objective"), and it may involve also an attachment to the conservation and growth of the organization itself.

In this way, through his subjection to organizationally determined goals, and through the gradual absorption of these goals into his own attitudes, the participant in organization acquires an "organization personality" rather distinct from his personality as an individual. The organization assigns to him a role: it specifies the particular values, facts, and alternatives upon which his decisions in the organization are to be based. For a park foreman the alternatives take the form of grass-cuttings, planting, road maintenance work, clean-up work, and so forth; the values are legislatively and socially determined standards of appearance, cleanliness, recreation use-value; the facts are budgets, work methods, unit costs. The foreman is not ordinarily expected to give serious thought to the alternative possibility of eliminating the park entirely, and making a subdivision of it. Yet this possibility may merit quite as serious attention as the proper location of a flower-bed. It is not considered because it is not his "business."[1]

The broader decisions in the organization determine what each

[1]Cf. Dewey, *The Public and Its Problems*, p. 22.

man's "business" is—what his frame of reference in decision-making is to be. It has already been explained, in Chapter V, why the creation of this organizational role and personality is essential to rationality in administrative decision. By limiting the range within which an individual's decisions and activities are to lie, the organization reduces his decisional problems to manageable proportions.

SOCIAL VERSUS ORGANIZATIONAL VALUES

When it is recognized that actual decisions must take place in some such institutional setting, it can be seen that the "correctness" of any particular decision may be judged from two different standpoints. In the broader sense it is "correct" if it is consistent with the general social value scale[2]—if its consequences are socially desirable. In the narrower sense, it is "correct" if it is consistent with the frame of reference that has been organizationally assigned to the decider.

This distinction is well illustrated in the literature of what is called "welfare economics."[3] In a private economy, the institution of private property permits a considerable degree of decentralization in decision-making. It is assumed that each individual will make his decisions in terms of the maximization of his "profit" or "utility." A decision is "correct" if it achieves this maximization. But the welfare economist evaluates decisions from another standpoint. He wants to know the extent to which the maximization of personal utility is compatible with the maximization of social value. When choice is viewed from within the individual's environment, advertising is explainable as a technique for increasing profit. Viewing choice from the social viewpoint, the welfare economist questions the social value of energies expended on advertising.[4]

This distinction between general social value and organizational value leads, in turn, to a third notion of correctness—the "correctness" of the organizational environment itself. That is, the social value of the organizational structure may be determined by noting the degree of coincidence between the organizationally correct and the socially correct decisions.

---

[2]The phrase "social value" is not entirely a happy one, particularly in view of the insistence upon ethical relativism in chap. iii. It is used here for lack of a more descriptive and accurate term, and an attempt will be made below to explain exactly what is meant.

[3]A. C. Pigou, *The Economics of Welfare* (London: Macmillan, 1924).

[4]See, for example, Elizabeth Ellis Hoyt, *Consumption in Our Society* (New York: McGraw-Hill, 1938), pp. 104–105. There is no intent to assert here that advertising is always socially valueless, but merely to point out that the value of advertising to the firm does not necessarily measure its value to society.

A private economy, for instance, is commonly justified on the ground that a high degree of coincidence exists between the two kinds of correctness. When it is recognized that under certain circumstances—conditions of monopoly, for instance—a considerable discrepancy arises, changes are demanded in the environment of decision (trust-busting, rate regulation, or the like) that will eliminate or reduce the discrepancies.

Meaning of the Phrase "Social Value"

The term "social value," as used here, is best understood in terms of a hierarchy of organizations, or social institutions. A society establishes certain very general values through its basic institutional structure, and attempts to bring about some conformity between these general values and the organizational values of the various groups that exist within it. This has already been illustrated in the previous paragraph. In the same way, any large organization—a business firm or a government—seeks to bring the organizational goals of its parts—departments, bureaus, and so forth—into conformity with the objectives of the organization as a whole.

What is meant by "social value" here is the objectives of some larger organization or social structure in relation to the "organizational values" of its components. Viewed from the standpoint of the legislative body or the citizenry, in so far as these have any formulated objectives, the objectives of the Department of the Interior or the United States Steel Corporation are organizational objectives. Viewed from the standpoint of the Secretary of the Interior or the president of the steel company, the objectives of his agency are the "social objectives" to which the organizational objectives of the component divisions and bureaus must conform.

Since it is difficult to establish subsidiary objectives that will always be consistent with the general objective, the individual who is a member of the subsidiary organization will sometimes make decisions that are consistent with the partial objective of his particular organizational component, but inconsistent with the broader goal of the organization as a whole. It is this problem—of reconciling the "role-taking" that the organization imposes on individuals with the achievement of goals transcending these particular roles—that provides the principal subject-matter of this chapter.

An Example of the Conflict

By way of illustration, let us consider the decision-making process in a specific organizational setting. In California, prior to July 1941, responsibility for the care of unemployed persons was divided between two agencies: the State Relief Administration cared for *employable* unemployed persons and their families; the county welfare departments cared for *unemployable* unemployed persons. The division of function was largely historical in origin and was not supported by any very cogent reasons; but that is beside the point.

From the standpoint of the state as a whole, the objective of welfare administration was to care for the unemployed and to guarantee them a certain minimum standard of living. It was desirable, moreover, to accomplish this objective as efficiently as possible. That is, once the rules of eligibility had been established and standards for the size of family budgets determined, the administrative task was to see that eligible persons, and only eligible persons, qualified for relief; that their budgets conformed to the standards authorized; and that these ends were attained with the least possible expenditure of funds. The State Relief Administration was presumably trying to accomplish this objective with its area of activity limited to employable persons, while the county welfare departments were aiming at the same objective with their areas of activity limited to unemployable persons.

But if these objectives are viewed organizationally, a competitive element immediately enters into the decisions of the state and county administrative officials, respectively. One way in which the state agency could increase its efficiency (measured in terms of its own limited objective, and not in terms of the objective of the state as a whole) was to make certain that any unemployable persons on its rolls were discovered and transferred to the county. One way in which the county agency could increase its efficiency (measured, again, in terms of the limited organizational objective) was to make certain that any employable persons on its rolls were discovered and transferred to the state.

As a result, each organization sought the relative maximization of its own objective, and a great deal of time, effort, and money was spent by these agencies in attempting to shift clients from one to the other in borderline cases. This competitive activity is entirely understandable from the point of view of the organizational objectives of each organization, but it contributed nothing toward the maximization of the broader social value.

It should be noted, however, that there is nothing inevitable about this development. Decisions are not made by "organizations" but by human beings behaving as members of organizations. There is no logical necessity that a member of an organization shall make his decisions in terms of values which are organizationally limited. Nevertheless, in example after example, we can find individuals behaving as though the institutions to which they belong were "economic men," always calculating the "institutional utility," in terms both of service and conservation goals, in each decision. How can this phenomenon be explained? To understand it, we must make clear first the distinction between men's personal and organizational decisions.

Impersonality of Organization Decisions

Barnard has very clearly pointed out that the decisions which a person makes as a member of an organization are quite distinct from his personal decisions:

> The system, then, to which we give the name "organization" is a system composed of the activities of human beings. What makes these activities a system is that the efforts of different persons are here coordinated. For this reason their significant aspects are not personal. They are determined by the system either as to manner, or degree, or time. Most of the efforts in cooperative systems are easily seen to be impersonal. For example, a clerk writing on a report form for a corporation is obviously doing something at a place, on a form, and about a subject that clearly never could engage his strictly personal interest. Hence, when we say that we are concerned with a system of coordinated human efforts, we mean that although persons are agents of the action, the action is not personal in the aspect important for the study of cooperative systems.[5]

At a later point, Barnard shows clearly why this is so. Personal considerations determine whether a person will participate in an organization; but, if he decides to participate, they will not determine the content of his organizational behavior:

> Every effort that is a constituent of organization, that is, every coordinated cooperative effort, may involve two acts of decision. The first is the decision of the person affected as to whether or not he will contribute this effort as a matter of personal choice. It is a detail of the process of repeated personal decisions that determine whether or not the individual will be or will continue to be a contributor to the organization. . . . This act of decision is *outside* the system of efforts constituting the organization . . . although it is, as we have seen, a subject for organized attention.
>
> The second type of decision has no direct or specific relation to personal results, but views the effort concerning which decision is to be made non-personally from the viewpoint of its organization effect and of its relation to organization purpose. This second act of decision is often made in a direct sense by individuals, but it is impersonal and organizational in its intent and effect. Very often it is also organizational in its

---

[5]C. I. Barnard, *op. cit.*, p. 77.

process, as for example in legislatures, or when boards or committees determine action. The act of decision is a part of the organization itself.

This distinction between the two types of decision is frequently recognized in ordinary affairs. We very often say or hear sentences similar to this: "If this were my business, I think I would decide the question this way—but it is not my personal affair"; or, "I think the *situation* requires such and such an answer—but I am not in a position to determine what ought to be done"; or "The decision should be made by someone else." This is in effect a restatement, with a different emphasis, of the suggestions in Chapter VII that a sort of dual personality is required of individuals contributing to organization action—the private personality, and the organization personality.[6]

Once the system of values which is to govern an administrative choice has been specified, there is one and only one "best" decision, and this decision is determined by the organizational values and situation, and not by the personal motives of the member of the organization who makes the decision. Within the area of discretion, once an individual has decided, on the basis of his personal motives, to recognize the organizational objectives, his further behavior is determined not by personal motives, but by the demands of efficiency.

There is a limit, however, to this proposition. There is an area of acceptance within which the individual will behave "organizationally." When the organizational demands fall outside this area, personal motives reassert themselves, and the organization, to that extent, ceases to exist.

When a person is behaving impersonally, then, an organizational value scale is substituted for his personal value scale as the criterion of "correctness" in his decisions. Hence, his decision may be considered as a variable, depending for its specific character upon the particular organizational value scale which governs it.

We still do not have an answer to the question of why an individual employs one particular organizational value scale as his criterion of choice, rather than one or more of all the innumerable other scales he might use. We can now turn our attention to this question.

ORGANIZATIONAL IDENTIFICATION

To designate the phenomenon we are discussing, we may introduce the term "identification" which has already had some currency in political theory. "Identification" is used in psychoanalytic literature to denote a particular kind of emotional tie. Freud describes the nature of the tie thus:

---

[6]*Ibid.*, pp. 187–188.

It is easy to state in a formula the distinction between an identification with the father and the choice of the father as an object. In the first case one's father is what one would like to *be*, and in the second he is what one would like to *have*. The distinction, that is, depends upon whether the tie attaches to the subject or to the object of the ego.[7]

Freud hypothesized, further, that identification is a fundamental mechanism in group cohesion:

We already begin to divine that the mutual tie between members of a group is in the nature of an identification of this kind, based upon an important emotional common quality; and we may suspect that this common quality lies in the nature of the tie with the leader.[8]

Lasswell, presumably adopting the term from Freud, devotes an entire chapter[9] to "Nations and Classes: The Symbols of Identification." Nowhere, however, does he define the term, other than to speak of "identifying symbols like 'nation,' 'state,' 'class,' 'race,' 'church,'" and to define a "sentiment area" as "the locus of those who are mutually identified." Further, he nowhere asserts that the underlying psychological mechanism is identical with the Freudian concept of identification.

Meaning of Identification

To make explicit the definition of the concept which Lasswell names, we will say that *a person identifies himself with a group when, in making a decision, he evaluates the several alternatives of choice in terms of their consequences for the specified group*. We shall not assume that the mechanism underlying this phenomenon is the Freudian one. In fact, in this case as in many others, the Freudian hypothesis appears to be a greatly oversimplified one.

When a person prefers a particular course of action because it is "good for America," he identifies himself with Americans; when he prefers it because it will "boost business in Berkeley," he identifies himself with Berkeleyans. A person is said to act from "personal" motives when his evaluation is based upon an identification with himself or with his family.

The group with which a person identifies himself can be characterized by the geographical area which it inhabits, its economic or social status in the society, and any number of other criteria. The "nation" is an example of geographical identification; the "proletariat" and "women"

---

[7]Sigmund Freud, *Group Psychology and the Analysis of the Ego* (New York: Boni and Liveright, 1922), p. 62.

[8]*Ibid.*, p. 66.

[9]H. D. Lasswell, *World Politics and Personal Insecurity* (New York: Whittlesey House, 1935), pp. 29–51. The quotations are from p. 7.

are examples of economic and social identification symbols. Examples of identifications which are important to our political institutions may be found in the literature on legislative processes and pressure groups.[10]

The identification of the individual may be either with the organization objective or with the conservation of the organization. For example, a person making a decision can identify himself with the function or objective of education—he can evaluate all alternatives in terms of their effect upon education. On the other hand, he may identify himself with a particular educational organization—he may resist the transfer of certain recreational functions from a school department to a park department—and seek the conservation and growth of that organization. As pointed out in Chapter VI, two types of organizational loyalty must be distinguished, corresponding to these two kinds of identification.

These identifications with group or with function are such an all-pervasive phenomenon that one cannot participate for fifteen minutes in political or administrative affairs, or read five pages in an administrative report, without meeting examples of them.

Newspapers carry frequent illustrations of such identifications. Following is a brief news item about the California highway system:

> California can hardly think of spending $150,000,000 to bring its highways up to military standards when the network of rural roads is seriously in need of reconstruction, State Highway Engineer Charles H. Purcell said today.
>
> Purcell told a legislative interim committee the chief concern of the State Division of Highways was how to obtain the $442,500,000 required to make the rural roads adequate to carry normal civilian traffic in the next ten years.
>
> If the War Department wants some 5,887 miles of California's strategic highways improved to its standards, the State engineer declared, it was the "primary responsibility" of the Federal Government to advance the money. The same highways system, he added, is considered adequate for civil use.[11]

The Highway Engineer apparently conceives it to be his function to choose between competing possibilities for highway construction in terms of the value of "civilian need" rather than the value of "military need" or some composite of both values. He further implies in his statement that, when funds are spent through a *state* agency, values to the

---

[10]Cf. E. Pendleton Herring, *Group Representation Before Congress* (Baltimore: Johns Hopkins Press, 1929), pp. 1–12, and *passim*, and H. D. Lasswell, *Politics: Who Gets What, When, How* (New York: McGraw-Hill, 1936), pp. 1–28, 29–51, 129–232.

[11]Oakland (Calif.) *Tribune*, Oct. 13, 1941.

state are to be given a weight in the decisions for allocating these funds, while values which may diffuse across state boundaries are not to be considered. Neither criticism of, nor agreement with, this position is intended here. The points to be noted are that the Engineer's judgments are consequences of his organizational identifications, and that his conclusions can be reached only if these identifications be assumed.

The hearings before the House Committee on Appropriations of the United States Congress are a fertile source of illustrations of the phenomenon of identification. The following example will suffice:

MR. OLIVER: That, of course, is all worth-while service, but how do you feel you are accomplishing practical, concrete results from the studies and surveys you are making in the different directions referred to?

MISS ANDERSON: Well, that is very difficult to say, because it is intangible in a way.

MR. OLIVER: In other words, it is information which, of course, either the States or some organizations in the States should take up, and acting on the suggestions you make, provide some remedy or relief?

MISS ANDERSON: Yes. For instance, take the State of Connecticut. There has been a great deal of information given to the State of Connecticut, and I have no doubt that the information that we gave them on these conditions, and what they have followed up themselves since, will manifest itself in certain legislation in the next session of their legislature.

MR. OLIVER: Now, why should not the States undertake to collect that information? Why should they be expected to send to Washington, many, many miles away, and call on the Federal Government to collect information which is much more readily available to them and to their own officials?

MISS ANDERSON: The Labor Department in only one or two States in the country are able to collect that material themselves. They have not set up that kind of investigational organization.

MR. OLIVER: Is not this true: So long as the Federal Government willingly responds to requests of that character—and it appears from your statement that each year you are being called on to become active in a new field—just so long as ready response is made to requests, the States will decline to do that which primarily should devolve upon them?

A little later in the dialogue the Congressman adds:

MR. OLIVER: How long, in times like these, should we continue to render a service of that character for the States which all seem to concede is primarily a duty devolving on the State?[12]

---

[12]U.S. Congress, Subcommittee of House Committee on Appropriations, *Hearing on Department of Labor Appropriation Bill for 1934* (Washington: Government Printing Office, 1933), pp. 74–76.

It is clear that although the Congressman states his first argument in terms of efficiency, the real issue in his mind is an organizational one. An activity which might be of legitimate value if pursued by a State is to be valued less highly if pursued by a Federal agency because it "is primarily a duty devolving on the State." We will forgive the Congressman the supreme illogic of his qualifying phrase "in times like these." It is significant, however, that his illogic, quite as much as his logic, stems from an organizational identification.

The Psychology of Identification

No single or simple mechanism is likely to explain realistically the phenomenon of identification. Some of the contributory factors may be enumerated:

1. *Personal Interest in Organizational Success.* The decision which is made in terms of organizational values is, to that extent, impersonal; but attachment to the organization derives from personal motives. The individual is willing to make impersonal organizational decisions because a variety of factors, or incentives, tie him to the organization—his salary, prestige, friendship, and many others.

Many of these personal values are dependent not only on his connection with the organization, but also on the growth, the prestige, or the success of the organization itself. His salary and his power are both related to the size of the unit that he administers. Growth of the organization offers to him and to his employees salary increases, advancement, and opportunity to exercise responsibility. A large budget will enable him to undertake activities and services which will excite the interest and admiration of his professional peers in other organizations. Consequently, these motives lead to an identification with conservation goals.

Conversely, failure of the organization, or curtailment of its budget, may mean salary reduction, loss of power, or even unemployment to the administrator. At the very least it forces on him the unpleasant duty of dismissing personnel and seriously impairs the incentive of possible advancement for his subordinates.

2. *Transfer of Private-Management Psychology.* The private segment of our economy operates on the assumption that management will make its decisions in terms of profit to the individual business establishment. This institutional psychology of choice may easily be carried over to the public segment of the economy through lack of recognition of the fundamental differences in the assumptions that underlie these two segments. The executive who is accustomed to thinking in terms of "my" business, is apt

to think in terms of "my" county, or "my" department. Again, this motive would lead primarily to identification with conservation rather than with particular organization objectives. These same attitudes may be present in persons who, while they never have had administrative responsibility in the private segment of the economy, have absorbed these notions from a predominantly private-economy cultural environment.[13]

It would be an interesting subject of research to determine the extent to which private-management attitudes persist in a communistic economy like that of Soviet Russia. It would be extremely difficult, however, to separate this factor from the elements of personal motivation which would continue to bind the individual to the organization even in a nationalized economy.

The illustration drawn from the administration of public welfare in the state of California[14] is a good example of the consequences which flow from a "private" conception of organizational efficiency. So zealous were the state and county agencies, respectively, in rejecting clients who were the "responsibility" of the other that it proved politically impossible in most counties of the state to set up an impartial medical board to pass on the employability of doubtful cases.

3. *Focus of Attention.* A third element in the process of identification is the focusing of the administrator's attention upon those values and those groups which are most immediately affected by the administrative program. When an administrator is entrusted with the task of *educating* Berkeley's children, he is likely to be more clearly aware of the effect of any particular proposal upon their learning, than of its possible indirect effects upon their health— and vice versa. He identifies himself, then, with the organization objective.

It is clear that attention may narrow the range of vision by selecting particular values, particular items of empirical knowledge, and particular behavior alternatives for consideration, to the exclusion of other values, other knowledge, and other possibilities. Identification, then, has a firm basis in the limitations of human psychology in coping with the problem of rational choice.

From this point of view, identification is an important mechanism for constructing the environment of decision. When identification is faulty, the resulting discrepancies between social and organizational values result

---

[13]Several individuals who read an earlier draft of this study questioned the existence of this transfer of private-management psychology. The writer knows of no available empirical evidence that would definitely prove or disprove the existence of such a transfer. He can only say that the hypothesis that such exists seems plausible to him, and that both the existence of the transfer and its importance if it does exist would be very fruitful objects of empirical investigation.

[14]See pp. 280–282, *supra.*

in a loss of social efficiency. When the organizational structure is well conceived, on the other hand, the process of identification permits the broad organizational arrangements to govern the decisions of the persons who participate in the structure. Thereby, it permits human rationality to transcend the limitations imposed upon it by the narrow span of attention.[15]

An example of the manner in which the focus of attention of participants in an administrative structure is determined by their position in the structure came to the author's attention while he was making a study of the administration of recreation activities in Milwaukee. The playgrounds in that city had been constructed by the Playground Division of the Department of Public Works, but activities on the grounds were supervised by the Extension Department of the School Board. Maintenance of the grounds had also been turned over to the latter agency, and there was some belief that maintenance was inadequate.

> It is understandable that the Extension Department, suddenly confronted with vast new financial obligations by the expansion of physical facilities, should attempt to minimize cost of maintenance so as not to divert funds from supervisory activities. The fact that the early construction work was highly experimental has resulted in maintenance costs beyond original expectations. It is likewise understandable that the Playground Division, whose work has been the construction of physical facilities, should consider it a false economy to inadequately provide for the maintenance of those facilities.
>
> There has been a difference in emphasis, for example, as to the place of landscaping in the playground design. The Playground Division has stressed the importance of proper landscaping in affecting public attitudes toward playgrounds. It has insisted that the playground should be an asset to the appearance of the neighborhood.
>
> The Extension Department spent the first ten years of its existence working with the meagerest physical facilities. The playgrounds were for the most part hot and dusty with no thought of landscaping. From those ten years of experience the Department learned that the success of a playground depends primarily upon leadership rather than upon physical plant.
>
> Each department understands fully that both objectives are desirable, and to a certain extent necessary, in the administration of a successful program. The question is not "which" but "how much," and since it is the Extension Department which has charge of the funds maintenance activities have suffered to a certain degree.[16]

[15]See chap. v, pp. 110–111. Karl Mannheim (*op. cit.*, pp. 52–57, 290) has emphasized this same point.

[16]Herbert A. Simon, "Administration of Public Recreational Facilities in Milwaukee," unpublished manuscript, 1935, p. 38.

Identification and Adequacy

One of the most common consequences of functional identification is a failure to balance costs against values in making administrative decisions. The accomplishment by an administrative program of its organizational goals can be measured in terms of *adequacy* (the degree to which its goals have been reached) or of *efficiency* (the degree to which the goals have been reached relative to the available resources). To use a very crude example, the adequacy of the recent war production program would be measured in terms of the size and equipment of the armed force put into the field; its efficiency in terms of a comparison of the production actually attained with what could have been attained with a best use of national resources. American war production turned out to be of a high degree of adequacy; whether it was efficient is quite another question.

The tendency of an administrator who identifies himself with a particular goal is to measure his organization in terms of adequacy rather than efficiency.[17] It is not always recognized by these specialists that there is absolutely no scientific basis for the construction of so-called "standards of desirable service" or "standards of minimum adequate service" for a particular function, until it is known what this service will cost, what resources are available for financing it, and what curtailment in other services or in private expenditures would be required by an increase in that particular service.

What annual report is ever published which does not include some such recommendation as the following:

> The chief and very urgent recommendation at the close of this fiscal year is for an increase in staff. This is especially necessary in the Minimum Wage Division, the work of which has increased enormously since the Supreme Court decision validated minimum-wage legislation. Many States still in the early stages of wage-law administration are looking to the Women's Bureau for help in organization, in securing the necessary wage and hour data, and in the all-important work of bringing uniformity into the setting of rates and the practice of enforcement. Frequent visits to the States, and meetings in Washington of State officials, are necessary. The staff of this Division must be increased, as it is not able to meet all the demands upon it.[18]

[17]Since, as pointed out in chap. vi, such identifications are more frequent in public administration than in the administration of commercial enterprises, the problem discussed in this section is primarily (but not entirely) a problem of public administration.

[18]U.S. Department of Labor, *25th Annual Report of the Secretary, Fiscal Year Ended June 30, 1937* (Washington: Government Printing Office, 1937), p. 136.

That is the universal administrative plaint. "The budget is *inadequate*." Now, between the white of adequacy and the black of inadequacy lie all the shades of gray which represent degrees of adequacy. Further, human wants are insatiable in relation to human resources. From these two facts we may conclude that the fundamental criterion of administrative decision must be a criterion of *efficiency* rather than a criterion of *adequacy*. The task of the administrator is to maximize social values *relative* to limited resources.[19]

If, then, the process of identification leads the administrator to give undue weight to the particular social values with which he is concerned, he is in no position, psychologically speaking, to make a satisfactory decision as to the amount of money which should be allocated to his function, or as to the relative merits of his claims upon public funds, as compared with the claims of competing units.[20]

Budgetary procedures are the most important means of translating questions of adequacy into questions of efficiency. The budget, first of all, forces a simultaneous consideration of all the competing claims for support. Second, the budget transports upward in the administrative hierarchy the decisions as to fund allocation to a point where competing values

---

[19]We must not commit the opposite error of making budget decisions in terms of *economy*—that is, reduction of expenditures without regard to service. This seems to be the fundamental objection to entrusting undue influence in budget matters to a controllership or treasury agency as recommended, for instance, by the British Machinery of Government Committee: "On the whole, experience seems to show that the interests of the taxpayer cannot be left to the spending Departments; that those interests require the careful consideration of each item of public expenditure in its relation to other items and to the available resources of the State, as well as the vigilant supervision of some authority not directly concerned in the expenditure itself; and that such supervision can be most naturally and effectively exercised by the Department which is responsible for raising the revenue required." (Great Britain, Ministry of Reconstruction, *Report of the Machinery of Government Committee*, Cd. 9230 [London: H.M. Stationery Office, 1918, reprinted 1925], pp. 18–19.)

[20]The importance of "location" to the psychology of the administrator is accepted, even in lay circles, as a natural attribute of institutional thought. This is humorously, but convincingly, illustrated by an incident reported in the gossip column of the *San Francisco News*, Feb. 12, 1942. The item refers to the San Francisco Utilities Department, which controls the city's Water Department and the Hetch Hetchy Power development as well as other local utilities:

"While Utilities Manager Cahill was in Washington for 10 days that lasted a month, Nelson Eckart, head of the Water Department, filled his own job, the top Hetch Hetchy post of the late A. T. McAfee, and Cahill's overall job, too. Forrest Gibbon, executive secretary, had to tell who he was by the hat he was wearing.

"On Cahill's return, Eckart's first words were, 'Here's the key to the powder house, here's the aspirin bottle, I quit.' But it was some days before Cahill discovered all the triple-personality kinks which had brought Eckart to the brink of madness. He discovered, in fact, a letter Waterman Eckart had written asking money for more water-works, another letter Hetch Hetchy Eckart had written asking for more HH dough, and a final letter Acting Utilities Manager Eckart had written denying both of his own requests. Naturally, Cahill asked what the devil.

"'From up here,' Eckart explained, 'things don't look the same as they do from down there.'"

Thomas Becket seems to have been a highly institutionalized personality—his loyalties shifting with his office. See his biography in the *Encyclopaedia Britannica*, 11th Ed. (Vol. III, p. 609), where his relations to Henry II are explained in institutional terms.

must be weighed, and where functional identifications will not lead to a faulty weighting of values.

MODIFYING IDENTIFICATIONS
THROUGH ORGANIZATION

It would seem that a major problem in effective organization is to specialize and subdivide activities in such a manner that the psychological forces of identification will contribute to, rather than hinder, correct decision-making.

Modes of Specialization

The way in which activities are subdivided in the organization will have a major influence on identification. The administrative segregation of a function will be satisfactory to the extent that (1) the activities involved in the performance of the function are independent of the other activities in the organization, (2) indirect effects of the activity, not measurable in terms of the functional objective, are absent, and (3) it is possible to set up lines of communication which will bring to the unit responsible for the performance of the function the knowledge necessary for its successful execution.

All three of these are technical and factual questions. This means that any attempt to devise an administrative organization for carrying on a service by means of an armchair analysis of the agency's function into its component parts is inherently sterile. Yet a large part of the administrative research, so called, which has been carried on in the last generation is exactly of this nature.

Allocation of the Decision-Making Function

To the extent that identifications modify decisions, the effective allocation of decision-making functions must take these identifications into consideration.

If any basic principle governs this allocation, it is that each decision should be located at a point where it will be of necessity approached as a question of efficiency rather than a question of adequacy. That is, it is unsound to entrust to the administrator responsible for a function the responsibility for weighing the importance of that function against the importance of other functions. The only person who can approach competently the task of weighing their relative importance is one who is responsible for both or neither.

This presupposes, however, that persons *will* identify themselves with their organizational units. While we have indicated that there are a number of factors making for such identification, it should not be supposed that it is ever complete or consistent. The administrator who is faced with a choice between social and organizational values usually feels a twinge of conscience, stronger or weaker, when he puts organizational objectives before broader social ones. There is no inevitability in any particular identification.

It might be hoped, then, that it would be feasible to broaden, to some degree, the area of identification which governs the administrator's decisions. Steps might be taken to transfer allegiance from the smaller to the larger organizational units, and from the narrower to the broader objectives. To the extent that this is achieved, the precise location of decision-making functions is of less importance.

> Lord Haldane's Committee deplored what they called the traditional attitude of antagonism between the Treasury and the other departments. I do not know myself that I have been particularly conscious of it, but there is no doubt that in many departments there are individuals who seem to believe in the Russian proverb, "Whose bread I eat his songs I sing," and who think it is incumbent upon them as members of a particular department to show what they conceive to be their loyalty to that department by supporting it, right or wrong. Such a view I believe to be a thoroughly mistaken one. The loyalty of every citizen in the State is to the country at large. It is the country's bread that he eats, not the bread of the Ministry of Health or the Department of Agriculture, or the Exchequer and Audit Department. If he finds something which he thinks it is in the interest of the country to point out, he ought not to be deterred from doing his plain duty by the feeling that he might be disliked in his own department or might prejudice his personal advancement. That, of course, is still more true when you take departments collectively, and when you get one department very jealous of another department, very angry if there is any poaching on its preserves, upon which follow barren interminable interdepartmental correspondence.[21]

Here, clearly, is the end to be aimed at; but it will take more than hope and preaching to reach it. If personal motives, private-business atti-

---

[21]Henry Higgs, "Treasury Control," *Journal of Public Administration*, 2:129 (Apr., 1924).

tudes, and limitations of the span of attention are the factors making for narrow organizational identifications, then any attempt to weaken such identifications, or to transfer them, must modify these same factors. Loyalty to the larger group will result when loyalty to that group is rewarded even in conflict with loyalty to the smaller group. Loyalty to the larger group will result when the distinction is clearly understood between the private-economy and public-economy modes of thought. Loyalty to the larger group will result when administrative situations are understood in terms of efficiency rather than adequacy.

Psychological Types in Decision

These considerations suggest that a very fundamental classification of administrative types might be developed in terms of the variant thought-processes underlying decision. The development of this theme would carry us too far afield from our main topic, but a few remarks may serve by way of illustration.

Observation indicates that, as the higher levels are approached in administrative organizations, the administrator's "internal" task (his relations with the organization subordinate to him) decreases in importance relative to his "external" task (his relations with persons outside the organization). An ever larger part of his work may be subsumed under the heads of "public relations" and "promotion." The habits of mind characteristic of the administrative roles at the lower and higher levels of an organization undoubtedly show differences corresponding to these differences in function.

At the lower levels of the hierarchy, the frame of reference within which decision is to take place is largely given. The factors to be evaluated have already been enumerated, and all that remains is to determine their values under the given circumstances. At the higher levels of the hierarchy, the task is an artistic and an inventive one. New values must be sought out and weighed; the possibilities of new administrative structures evaluated. The very framework of reference within which decision is to take place must be constructed.

It is at these higher levels that organizational identifications may have their most serious consequences. At the lower level, the identification is instrumental in bringing broad considerations to bear on individual situations. It assures that decisions will be made responsibly and impersonally. At the higher levels, identifications serve to predetermine the decision, and to introduce among its assumptions unrecognized and unverified valuations.

SUMMARY

In this chapter we have examined a specialized but fundamentally important element in the psychological environment of decision—namely, the element of identification. Identification is the process whereby the individual substitutes organizational objectives (service objectives or conservation objectives) for his own aims as the value-indices which determine his organizational decisions.

Through identification, organized society imposes upon the individual the scheme of social values in place of his personal motives. An organizational structure is socially useful to the extent that the pattern of identifications which it creates brings about a correspondence between social value and organizational value.

The psychological bases of identification are obscure, but seem to involve at least three elements: personal interest in institutional success, a transfer to public agencies of a private-management philosophy, and limitations upon the area of attention which prevent more than a restricted sphere of values from coming within its purview.

The principal undesirable effect of identification is that it prevents the organized individual from making correct decisions in cases where the restricted area of values with which he identifies himself must be weighed against other values outside that area. The organization structure must be designed, and decisions allocated within it, so as to minimize the decisional bias arising from this cause. Two important applications may be mentioned. To avoid biases of identification, budget decisions must be made at a point in the organization where they will be viewed from a standpoint of efficiency rather than adequacy—that is, where the real alternatives of cost as well as value are posed. Likewise, the success of functional specialization will depend, in part, on the absence of value-consequences that lie outside the area of functional identification, for the presence of such consequences will introduce serious biases into decision.

If identification is highly useful in depersonalizing choice within an organization and enforcing social responsibility, it may be equally harmful if it colors and distorts the decisions that precede the establishment of the organizational structure itself. The construction of socially useful organizations requires an unprejudiced assessment of all the values involved. Prejudice is bound to enter if the assessor's judgment is warped by his identifications. Hence, the personal loyalty to organizational values which is generally so useful an aspect of behavior in an organization may be correspondingly harmful when encountered in the fields of invention and promotion, that is, in the tastes of the administrator at the higher levels of the hierarchy.

LOYALTIES AND ORGANIZATIONAL IDENTIFICATION

PSYCHOLOGICAL ROOTS OF ORGANIZATIONAL IDENTIFICATION

CHAPTER X DISCUSSES BRIEFLY (pages 287–289) the psychological bases for organizational identifications. Our knowledge today of organizational behavior allows us to make an even stronger case for the strength of these identifications than is made in the chapter. On the cognitive side, perhaps too little emphasis is placed in Chapter X on the limits of rationality as an explanation for subgoal formation and loyalties to subgoals; and as a result the close dependence of this chapter upon Chapter V is obscured. The first section of this commentary will seek to redress the balance.

At the same time, a new analysis of the psychological bases of altruism shows, on the motivational side, a strong connection between altruism and organizational identification and new reasons for supposing that organizational loyalties can be exceedingly strong independently of personal gains attached to the attainment of organizational goals. A second section of this commentary will discuss this tie between altruism and organizational loyalty.

COGNITIVE BASES FOR IDENTIFICATION[22]

The cognitive component of the mechanism of identification discussed in Chapter X can be described thus:

(1) As we saw in Chapter IX, high-level goals often provide little guide for action because it is difficult to measure their attainment and difficult to measure the effects of concrete actions upon them. The broad goals (e.g., "long-term profit," "public welfare," and so on) are thus not

---

[22]This section, co-authored with DeWitt C. Dearborn, is taken, with minor revisions, from *Sociometry*, 21:140–144 (1958), reprinted with permission.

operative, nor do they provide the common numerator discussed in Chapter IX as essential to efficient choice among alternatives.

(2) Decisions tend to be made, consequently, in terms of the highest-level goals that are operative—the most general goals to which specific activities can be related in a fairly definite way and those that provide some basis for assessing accomplishment. The operative goals provide the seed around which the decision-maker's simplified model of the world crystallizes. Decision-makers tend to take into account those matters that are reasonably directly related to these goals and discount or ignore others.

(3) Not only do their subgoals cause decision-makers to attend selectively to their environments, but the administrative structures and communication channels they erect to attain these goals expose them to particular kinds of information and shield them from others. Yet, because of the complexity of the information that does reach them, even this selected information is analyzed only partially and incompletely.

An important result of these conditions, which make perception very selective, is that decision-makers acquire a representation of the situation in which they are working that focuses upon the operative goals and interprets these in terms of the very partial information that is attended to. In this way, decision-makers in an organization unit can identify strongly with a set of goals and a "world view" that may be quite different from those held by members of other units in the same organization.

These phenomena are frequently prominent in the anecdotes of executives and observers of organizations, but little evidence of a systematic kind vouching for their reality has been available. It is the purpose of this section to supply some such evidence.

The proposition we are considering is not peculiarly organizational. It is simply an application to organizational phenomena of a generalization that is central to any explanation of selective perception: Presented with a complex stimulus, a person perceives in it what he or she is "ready" to perceive; the more complex or ambiguous the stimulus, the more the perception is determined by what is already "in" the subject and the less by what is "in" the stimulus.[23]

EVIDENCE FOR COGNITIVE MECHANISMS IN IDENTIFICATION

Motivational and cognitive mechanisms mingle in the selection process, and it may be of some use to assess their relative contributions. We might

[23]J. S. Bruner, "On Perceptual Readiness," *Psychological Review*, 64:123–152 (1957).

suppose either: (1) selective attention to a part of a stimulus reflects a deliberate ignoring of the remainder as irrelevant to the subject's goals and motives, or (2) selective attention is a learned response stemming from some past history of exposure to particular information. In the latter case we might still be at some pains to determine what kinds of information will be learned. But by creating a situation from which any immediate motivation for selectivity is removed, we should be able to separate the second mechanism from the first. The situation in which we obtained our evidence meets this condition, and hence our data provide evidence for internalization of the selective processes.

The Experiment

A group of twenty-three executives, all employed by a single large manufacturing concern and enrolled in a company-sponsored executive training program, were asked to read a standard case that is widely used in instruction in business policy in business schools. The case, Castengo Steel Company, described the organization and activities of a company of moderate size specializing in the manufacture of seamless steel tubes, as of the end of World War II. The case, which is about 10,000 words in length, contains a wealth of descriptive material about the company and its industry and the recent history of both (up to 1945), but little evaluation. It is deliberately written to hold closely to concrete facts and to leave as much as possible of the burden of interpretation to the reader.

When the executives appeared at a class session to discuss the case, but before they had discussed it, they were asked by the instructor to write a brief statement of what they considered to be the most important problem facing the Castengo Steel Company—the problem a new company president should deal with first. Prior to this session, the group had discussed other cases, being reminded from time to time by the instructor that they were to assume the role of the top executive of the company in considering its problems.

The executives were a relatively homogeneous group in terms of status, being drawn from perhaps three levels of the company organization. They were in the range usually called "middle management," representing such positions as superintendent of a department in a large factory, product manager responsible for profitability of one of the ten product groups manufactured by the company, and works physician for a large factory. In terms of departmental affiliation, they fell in four groups:

Sales (6): Five product managers or assistant product managers, and one field sales supervisor.

Production (5): Three department superintendents, one assistant factory manager, and one construction engineer.

Accounting (4): An assistant chief accountant, and three accounting supervisors—for a budget division and two factory departments.

Miscellaneous (8): Two members of the legal department, two in research and development, and one each from public relations, industrial relations, medical, and purchasing.

The Data

Since the statements these executives wrote are relatively brief, they are reproduced in full in the appendix to this chapter. We tested our hypothesis by determining whether there was a significant relation between the "most important problem" mentioned and the departmental affiliation of the mentioner. In the cases of executives who cited more than one problem, we counted all those they listed. We compared (1) the executives who mentioned "sales," "marketing," or "distribution" with those who did not; (2) the executives who mentioned "clarifying the organization" or some equivalent with those who did not; (3) the executives who mentioned "human relations," "employee relations," or "team work" with those who did not. The findings are summarized in Table 1.

The difference between the percentages of sales executives (83 per cent) and other executives (29 per cent) who mentioned sales as the most important problem is significant at the 5 per cent level. Three of the five non-sales executives, moreover, who mentioned sales were in the accounting department, and all of these were in positions that involved analysis of product profitability. This accounting activity was, in fact, receiving considerable emphasis in the company at the time of the case

Table 1
Judgments of Most Important Problem, by Department of Judge

Department	Total number of executives	Number who mentioned		
		Sales	Clarify organization	Human relations
Sales	6	5	1	0
Production	5	1	4	0
Accounting	4	3	0	0
Miscellaneous	8	1	3	3
Totals	23	10	8	3

discussion, and the accounting executives had frequent and close contacts with the product managers in the sales department. If we combine sales and accounting executives, we find that eight out of ten of these mentioned sales as the most important problem; while only two of the remaining thirteen executives did.

Organization problems (other than marketing organization) were mentioned by four out of five production executives, the two executives in research and development, and the factory physician, but by only one sales executive and no accounting executives. The difference between the percentage for production executives (80 per cent) and other executives (22 per cent) is also significant at the 5 per cent level. Examination of the Castengo case shows that the main issue discussed in the case that relates to manufacturing is the problem of poorly defined relations among the factory manager, the metallurgist, and the company president. The presence of the metallurgist in the situation may help to explain the sensitivity of the two research and development executives (both of whom were concerned with metallurgy) to this particular problem area.

It is easy to conjecture why the public relations, industrial relations, and medical executives should all have mentioned some aspect of human relations, and why one of the two legal department executives should have mentioned the board of directors.

Conclusion

We have presented data on the selective perceptions of industrial executives exposed to case material that support the hypothesis that each executive will perceive those aspects of a situation that relate specifically to the activities and goals of his department. Since the situation is one in which the executives were motivated to look at the problem from a company-wide rather than a departmental viewpoint, the data indicate further that the criteria of selection have become internalized. Finally, the method for obtaining data that we have used holds considerable promise as a projective device for eliciting the attitudes and perceptions of executives.

EXECUTIVES' RESPONSES

Executive	SALES
4	Apparent need for direct knowledge of their sales potential; apparent need for exploitation of their technical potential to achieve a broader market and higher priced market; apparent need for unit and operation cost data.
5	How to best organize the company so as to be able to take

full advantage of the specialized market available.

6   Appointment of Production Manager familiar with business; Analysis of market conditions with regard to expansion in plastics market.

12   Develop a sales organization which would include market research.

20   Lack of organization to plan and cope with postwar manufacturing and sales problems.

25   The President's choice of executive officers.

PRODUCTION

1   Policy pertaining to distribution of product should be reviewed with more emphasis on new customers and concern for old.

15   Lack of clear-cut lines of responsibility.

16   Determine who the top executive was to be and have this information passed on to subordinate executives.

18   Review the organization. Why so many changes in some of the offices such as works manager.

24   Absence of policy—should be set forth by company head.

ACCOUNTING

7   Standards brought up to date and related to incentives. (Incentives evidently do not exist.)

9   Future of the company as to marketability of products—product specification—growth or containment or retirement (i.e., from product).

10   Distribution problems. Not necessarily their present problems in distribution, but those that undoubtedly will arise in the near future—plastics, larger companies, etc.

11   Reorganization of the company to save its lost market for its product and to look for an additional market is the prime problem.

OTHER

3   (Legal) Manufacture of one product which (a) competes against many larger manufacturers with greater facilities in competitive market, and (b) is perhaps due to lose to a related product much of its market.

14   (Legal) Board of directors.

8   (Public relations) The handling of employee relations—particularly the company-union relationship.

17   (Industrial relations) Can we get the various departments together to form a team in communications and cooperation.

19   (Medical) Reorganization of corporate structure; lines of authority and command; personnel relations.

21   (Purchasing) We should start to think and organize for our peacetime economy.

22   (Research and development) Overcentralized control by the president.

23   (Research and development) No formal organization with duties defined.

ALTRUISM IN ORGANIZATIONAL BEHAVIOR[24]

Contemporary evolutionary theory has cautioned us against attributing altruistic motives to people. In standard models of natural selection, nice guys generally aren't fit—they don't multiply as rapidly as their more selfish brethren. This argument has often been used to fill the utility function with selfish personal economic goals. But the argument is incorrect; models of natural selection that take bounded rationality into account actually provide strong support for the idea that most people will be strongly motivated by organizational loyalty, even when they can expect no "selfish" rewards from it.

How Natural Selection Sustains Altruism

First, what natural selection increases is fitness, the number of progeny of the successful competitor. But in modern society, the attainment of wealth or other selfish rewards is not directly connected to number of progeny. However, let us waive this point and suppose that attainment of the goals usually described as selfish contributes to evolutionary fitness.

We come then to the second point: each human being depends for survival on the immediate and broader surrounding society. Human beings are not independent windowless Leibnitzian monads. Society provides the matrix in which we survive and mature. Families and the rest of society provide nutrition, shelter, and safety during childhood and youth, and then the knowledge and skills for adult performance. Society can react to a person's activities at every stage of life, either facilitating them

[24]This section is based upon H. A. Simon, "A Mechanism for Social Selection and Successful Altruism," *Science*, 250:1665–1668 (1990), and "Organizations and Markets," *Journal of Economic Perspectives*, vol. 5, no. 2, 25–44 (Spring, 1991). The reader will find in the former the technical details of the model of altruism, in the latter, additional discussion of the implications of altruism for organizational loyalty.

or severely impeding them. It has enormous powers to enhance or reduce a person's evolutionary fitness.

What kinds of traits, in addition to personal strength and intelligence, would contribute to the fitness of this socially dependent creature? One such trait, or combination of traits, might be called docility. To be docile is to be tractable, and above all, teachable. Docile people tend to adapt their behavior to the norms and pressures of the society. "Docility" perhaps conveys too much a sense of passivity, but I know of no better word.

The argument is not that people are totally docile, nor that they are totally selfish, but that fitness calls for a measured but substantial responsiveness to social influence. In some contexts, this responsiveness implies motivation to learn or imitate; in other contexts, willingness to obey or conform. From an evolutionary standpoint, having a considerable measure of docility is not altruism but enlightened selfishness.

According to evolutionary theory, to survive as a trait, docility must contribute on average to the fitness of the individual who possesses it. Yet it may still lead, as a result of social influences, to self-injurious behavior in particular cases. Thus, docile individuals may do better than others at earning a living, but loyalty to their nation may lead them to sacrifice their lives in wartime. Once docility is present, society may exploit it by teaching values that benefit the society but are truly altruistic for the individual who accepts them: that is, that contribute to the society's fitness but not to the individual's. The only requirement is that on *balance* and on average the docile individual must be fitter than the one who is not docile.

Let me sketch the algebra that underlies these statements and guarantees their logical soundness. Let k be the average number of offspring of an individual in the absence of docility; d the gross increase in offspring due to docility; c the cost to a docile person, in offspring, of the socially induced altruistic behavior; p the percentage of people who are docile and hence altruistic; and b the number of offspring added to the population by an individual's altruistic behavior. Then it is easy to see that the difference between the net fitness of altruists and non-altruists (non-docile individuals), respectively, will equal $d - c$. Hence, provided that d is larger than c, altruists will be fitter than non-altruists. Moreover, a society will grow more rapidly the greater the fraction of altruists, and the increase in average fitness in the society will be $(d - c + b)\, p$.

Ample empirical evidence shows that most human beings have a considerable measure of docility. The purpose of the present argument is to show that this docility and the altruism it induces are wholly consistent with the premise of selection of the fittest. In fact, by the argument given above, natural selection strongly predicts the appearance of docility and altruism in social animals.

Altruism and Identification

One use of docility for enhancing the survivability and fitness of a social system, organization or other, is to inculcate individuals with group pride and loyalty. These motives are based upon a discrimination between a "we" and a "they." Identification with the "we," which may be a family, a company, a city, a nation, or the local baseball team, allows individuals to experience satisfactions from successes of the unit thus selected. In this way, organizational identification becomes a motive, which exists side by side with material rewards and the cognitive component already discussed, for employees to work actively for organizational goals.

To show, as has just been done, that natural selection provides a powerful base for socially induced identifications with groups is not to pronounce a moral judgment on the desirability of such identifications. We are all too familiar with the devastating group conflicts that identification with national, religious, and ethnic groups have induced among mankind on innumerable occasions in the past and in many parts of the world today. Our present concern is not to evaluate, but to explain the existence of group loyalties and the important role they play (for better or for worse) in promoting the effectiveness of organizations.

CHAPTER XI

The Anatomy of Organization

IT IS TIME NOW to draw the threads of discussion together, and to see whether they weave any pattern for administrative organization. The reader may wish, first of all, to review Chapter I, which gives something of an overview of the topics that have been taken up thus far.

In the present chapter, as in previous ones, no attempt will be made to offer advice as to how organizations *should* be constructed and operated. The reader has been warned before that this volume deals with the anatomy and physiology of organization and does not attempt to prescribe for the ills of organization. Its field is organizational biology, rather than medicine; and its only claim of contribution to the practical problems of administration is that sound medical practice can only be founded on thorough knowledge of the biology of the organism. Any prescriptions for administrative practice will be only incidental to the main purpose of description and analysis.

The central theme around which the analysis has been developed is that organization behavior is a complex network of decisional processes, all pointed toward their influence upon the behaviors of the operatives—those who do the actual "physical" work of the organization. The anatomy of the organization is to be found in the distribution and allocation of decision-making functions. The physiology of the organization is to be found in the processes whereby the organization influences the decisions of each of its members—supplying these decisions with their premises.

THE PROCESS OF COMPOSITE DECISION

It should be perfectly apparent that almost no decision made in an organization is the task of a single individual. Even though the final responsibility for taking a particular action rests with some definite person, we shall always find, in studying the manner in which this decision was reached, that its various components can be traced through the formal and informal channels of communication to many individuals who have participated in forming its premises. When all of these components have been identified, it may appear that the contribution of the individual who made the formal decision was a minor one, indeed.[1]

> We may see the treasurer of a corporation affix his signature to a contract whereby the corporation borrows a sum of money to finance a particular project. The treasurer evidently has authority to make this decision for the organization and to commit the organization to it; but what steps preceded his decision? Perhaps the chief engineer (acting, no doubt, on information and analyses communicated to him by his subordinates) decides that for the adequate operation of a technological system there should be a particular structure that his department has designed at an anticipated cost of five hundred thousand dollars. The general manager to whom he reports does not object to the proposal from the technological standpoint, but doubts that its value is sufficient to justify so large an expenditure; but before making a decision he consults the president or some members of the board as to their willingness to approve the risk of additional investment, as to the feasibility of financing, and as to the time of financing. This results in a decision to ask for a revision and curtailment of the proposal, and plans are redrafted in the engineering department to reduce the cost to four hundred thousand dollars. The proposal is then formally drawn up, approved by the chief engineer and the officers, and presented to the board. The questions then are: should the project be approved, and how should it be financed? It is approved, but it is suggested that in view of the danger of error of estimate, financing to the amount of four hundred fifty thousand dollars should be sought because otherwise the financial position of the company would be embarrassed if the cost should exceed four hundred thousand. Then, after much discussion, it is decided to finance by means of a mortgage loan at an interest rate not exceeding a certain amount, preferably placed with Company X, and the officers are authorized by the board of directors to proceed. Company X, however, when consulted is not interested in the proposal at the interest rate suggested and on examination of the plans thinks the engineering aspects call for revision. The matter goes through the same process again, and so on.

In the end, the officer making the final negotiation or signing the contract, though appearing to decide at least the major questions, is reduced almost to performing a ministerial function. The major decisions

---

[1] I am indebted to Mr. Barnard, through correspondence, both for the term "composite decision" and for the particular example of composite decision that is given here. The reader can undoubtedly supply many comparable examples from his own organizational experience.

were made neither by the board nor by any officer, nor formally by any group; they evolved through the interaction of many decisions both of individuals and by committees and boards. No one man is likely to be aware of all the decisions entering into the process or of who made them, or of the interaction through a period of time that modified decisions at one point and another. That decision is almost always a composite process of this sort will be illustrated further in a later section of this chapter that deals with the planning process.

From the standpoint of process, it is useful to view composite decision from the standpoint of the individual who makes a decision, in order· to see (a) how much discretion is actually left him, and (b) what methods the organization uses to influence the decisional premises he selects.

The Degrees of Influence

Influence is exercised in its most complete form when a decision promulgated by one person governs every aspect of the behavior of another. On the parade ground, the marching soldier is permitted no discretion whatsoever. His every step, his bearing, the length of his pace are all governed by authority. Frederick the Great is reported to have found the parade-ground deportment of his Guards perfect—with one flaw. "They breathe," he complained. Few other examples could be cited, however, of the exercise of influence in unlimited form.

Most often, influence places only partial limits upon the exercise of discretion. A subordinate may be told *what* to do, but given considerable leeway as to *how* he will carry out the task. The "what" is, of course, a matter of degree, and may be specified within narrower or broader limits. A charter which states in general terms the function of a city fire department places much less severe limits upon the discretion of the fire chief than the commands of a captain at the scene of a conflagration place on the discretion of the firemen.

A realistic analysis of influence in general and authority in particular must recognize that influence can be exercised with all degrees of specificity. To determine the scope of influence or authority which is exercised in any concrete case, it is necessary to dissect the decisions of the subordinate into their component parts, and then determine which of these parts are determined by the superior and which are left to the subordinate's discretion.

In Chapter III it was shown that a rational decision can be viewed as a conclusion reached from premises of two different kinds: value premises and factual premises. Given a complete set of value and factual premises, there is only one decision which is consistent with rationality. That is, with a given system of values, and a specified set of alternatives, there is one alternative that is preferable to the others.

The behavior of a rational person can be controlled, therefore, if the value and factual premises upon which he bases his decisions are specified for him. This control can be complete or partial—all the premises can be specified, or some can be left to his discretion. Influence, then, is exercised through control over the premises of decision. It is required that the decisions of the subordinate shall be consistent with premises selected for him by his superior. The scope of authority, and conversely the scope of discretion, are determined by the number and importance of the premises which are specified, and the number and importance of those which are left unspecified.

As pointed out previously, discretion over value premises has a different logical status from discretion over factual premises. The latter can always be evaluated as "right" or "wrong" in an objective, empirical sense. To the former, the terms "right" and "wrong" do not apply. Hence, if only factual premises are left to the subordinate's discretion, there is, under the given circumstances, only one decision which he can "correctly" reach. On the other hand, if value premises are left to the subordinate's discretion, the "correctness" of a decision will depend upon the value premises he has selected, and there is no criterion of right or wrong which can be applied to his selection.

When it is admitted that authority need extend to only a few of the premises of decision, it follows that more than one order can govern a given decision, provided that no two orders extend to the same premise. An analysis of almost any decision of a member of a formal organization would reveal that the decision is responsive to a very complex structure of influence.

Military organization affords an excellent illustration of this. In ancient warfare, the battlefield was not unlike the parade ground. An entire army was often commanded by a single man, and his authority extended in a very complete form to the lowest man in the ranks. This was possible because the entire battlefield was within range of a man's voice and vision, and because tactics were for the most part executed by the entire army in unison.

The modern battlefield presents a very different picture. Authority is exercised through a complex hierarchy of command. Each level of the hierarchy leaves an extensive area of discretion to the level below, and even the private soldier, under combat conditions, exercises a considerable measure of discretion.

Under these circumstances, how does the authority of the commander extend to the soldiers in the ranks? How does he limit and guide their behavior? He does this by specifying the general mission and objective of each unit on the next level below, and by determining such elements of time and place as will assure a proper coordination among units. The colonel assigns to each battalion in his regiment its task; the major, to each company in his battalion; the captain, to each platoon in his company. Beyond this, the officer does not ordinarily go. The internal arrangements of Army Field Service Regulations specify that "an order should not trespass upon the province of a subordinate. It should contain everything beyond the independent authority of the subordinate, but nothing more."[2]

So far as field orders go, then, the discretion of an officer is limited only by the specification of the objective of his unit, and its general schedule. He proceeds to narrow further the discretion of his subordinates so far as is necessary to specify what part each subunit is to play in accomplishing the task of the unit.

Does this mean that the discretion of the officer is limited only by his objective or mission? Not at all. To be sure, the field order does not go beyond this point. It specifies the *what* of his action. But the officer is also governed by the tactical doctrine and general orders of the army which specify in some detail the *how*. When the captain receives field orders to deploy his company for an attack, he is expected to carry out the deployment in accordance with the accepted tactical principles in the army. In leading his unit, he will be held accountable for the *how* as well as the *what*.

When we turn our attention, finally, to the man who carries out the army's task—the private soldier—we see that a great mass of influences bear upon the decisions which he makes. The decision that he will participate in an attack may have been made by a divisional, or even a corps, commander. His precise geographical location and place in the attack will be determined with ever increasing degrees of specificity by general, colonel, major, captain, lieutenant, sergeant in turn. But that is not all. The plan of attack which the captain determines upon will be a result not only of the field orders he receives, but also of the tactical training he has received, and his intelligence of the disposition of the enemy. So also the private, as he moves forward to the attack in the skirmish line, must thenceforth rely more and more upon the influences of his training and indoctrination.

To understand the process of decision in an organization, it is necessary to go far beyond the on-the-spot orders that are given by superior to subordinate. It is necessary to discover how the subordinate is influenced

[2]*U.S. Army Field Service Regulations*, 1923, p. 7.

by standing orders, by training, and by review of his actions. It is necessary to study the channels of communication in the organization in order
to determine what information reaches him which may be relevant to his
decisions. The broader the sphere of discretion left to the subordinate,
the more important become those types of influence which do not
depend upon the exercise of formal authority.

The Modes of Influence

The ways in which the organization brings its influence to bear on the
decisions of the individual have been enumerated in Chapter I. The
"external" influences include authority, advice and information, and
training. The "internal" influences include the criterion of efficiency and
organizational identifications. Each of these has been discussed at length
in preceding chapters, and that discussion does not need repetition here.

It is a fundamental problem of organization to determine the extent
to which, and the manner in which, each of these forms of influence is to
be employed. To a very great extent, these various forms of influence are
interchangeable, a fact that is far more often appreciated in small than in
large organizations.

The simplest example of this is the gradual increase in discretion
that can be permitted to an employee as he becomes familiar with his
job. A secretary learns to draft routine correspondence; a statistical clerk
learns to lay out his own calculations. In each case training has taken the
place of authority in guiding the employee's decisions.

"Functional supervision" often takes the form of advice rather than
authority. This substitution of advice for authority may prove necessary
in many situations in order to prevent conflicts of authority between line
officers, organized on a geographical basis, and experts organized on a
functional basis.

To the extent to which these forms of influence supplement, or are
substituted for, authority, the problem of influence becomes one of internal education and public relations. Following is an example of this kind
of influence:

> To the administration of a big department, the staff of the department
> themselves constitute a kind of inner "public," the right orientation of
> whose attitudes to each other in their mutual office contacts, in the
> inevitable absence of the direct personal touch which secures it in a
> small organization, would seem *prima facie* to call for just the same kind
> of attention, the same "practical psychology" or "salesmanship," as their
> attitude to members of the outside public. . . .

Consider, for example, the machinery for preparing official instructions to the staff. . . . Do not official instructions tend to be drafted too rationalistically? Is not the draftsman's attention often concentrated too exclusively on framing a logical statement setting accurately and comprehensively what *ought* to be done? . . . But after all, the primary object of an instruction is not to be admired by critical specialists in the same office; an instruction is intended to be acted on, and that by people who are as a rule neither critical, nor specialists, nor in the same office—in other words, to produce such an impression on the *ultimate* recipient that on receiving it, he *will* forthwith proceed to do what is required of him.[3]

Administrators have increasingly recognized in recent years that authority, unless buttressed by other forms of influence, is relatively impotent to control decision in any but a negative way. The elements entering into all but the most routine decisions are so numerous and so complex that it is impossible to control positively more than a few. Unless the subordinate is himself able to supply most of the premises of decision, and to synthesize them adequately, the task of supervision becomes hopelessly burdensome.

When viewed from this standpoint, the problem of organization becomes inextricably interwoven with the problem of recruitment. For the system of influence which can effectively be used in the organization will depend directly upon the training and competence of the employees at the various levels of the hierarchy. If a welfare agency can secure trained social workers as interviewers and case workers, broad discretion can be permitted them in determining eligibility, subject only to a sampling review, and a review of particularly difficult cases.

If trained workers can be obtained only for supervisory positions, then the supervisors will need to exercise a much more complete supervision over their subordinates, perhaps reviewing each decision, and issuing frequent instructions. The supervisory problem will be correspondingly more burdensome than in the first example, and the effective span of control of supervisors correspondingly narrower.

Likewise, when an organization unit is large enough to retain within its own boundaries the specialized expertise that is required for some of its decisions, the need for functional supervision from other portions of the organization becomes correspondingly less. When a department can secure its own legal, medical, or other expert assistance, the problems of

[3]H. Townshend, "'Practical Psychology' in Departmental Organization," *Journal of Public Administration*, 12:66.

functional organization become correspondingly simpler, and the lines of direct authority over the department need less supplementation by advisory and informational services.

Hence, problems of organization cannot be considered apart from the specifications of the employees who are to fill the positions established by the organization. The whole subject of job classification needs to be brought into much closer coordination with the theory of organization. The optimum organizational structure is a variable, depending for its form upon the staffing of the agency. Conversely, the classification of a position is a variable, depending upon the degree of centralization or decentralization which is desired or anticipated in the operation of the organizational form.

PLANNING AND REVIEW IN THE PROCESS OF COMPOSITE DECISION

There are two administrative techniques that are of key importance in the process of composite decision and in bringing to bear on a single decision a multiplicity of influences. Reference has already been made to them from time to time, but they deserve more systematic discussion as a part of the over-all decisional structure of the organization. The first of these is planning—a technique whereby the skills of a variety of specialists can be brought to bear on a problem before the formal stage of decision-making is reached. The second is review—a technique whereby the individual can be held accountable for the "internal" as well as the "external" premises that determine his decision.

The Planning Process

Plans and schedules are perhaps not strictly distinguishable from commands, since they usually derive their authority from an order. None the less, they are of special interest as devices for influencing decisions because of the immense amount of detail which it is possible to include in them, and because of the broad participation that can be secured, when desirable, in their formulation. Let us consider the last point first. An example is given by Sir Oswyn Murray:

> There is very little that is haphazard or disconnected about the array of Admiralty Departments. The noteworthy thing about them is not their number or variety, so much as their close inter-connection and the manner in which they combine to serve those administrative ends which I mentioned at the beginning of my paper. Perhaps I can best

illustrate this by describing briefly the procedure followed in the design and production of a new battleship, which always seems to me to be the very romance of cooperation.

We start with the First Sea Lord and his Assistant Chief of Naval Staff laying down in general terms the features that they desire to see embodied in the new design—the speed, the radius of action, the offensive qualities, the armour protection. Thereupon the Director of Naval Construction, acting under and in consultation with the Controller, formulates provisional schemes outlining the kind of ship desired, together with forecasts of the size and cost involved by the different arrangements. To do this he and his officers must have a good general knowledge—in itself only attainable by close relations with those in charge of these matters—of the latest developments and ideas in regard to a great range of subjects—gunnery, torpedo, engineering, armour, fire-control, navigation, signalling, accommodation, and so on—in order to be reasonably sure that the provision included in his schemes is such as is likely to satisfy the experts in all these subjects when the time for active cooperation arrives.

With these alternative schemes before them, the Sea Lords agree on the general lines of the new ship, which done, the actual preparation of the actual designs begins. The dimensions and shape of the ship are drawn out approximately by the naval constructors. Then the Engineer-in-Chief and his Department are called in to agree upon the arrangement of the propelling machinery, the positions of shafts, propellers, bunkers, funnels, etc., and at the same time the cooperation of the Director of Naval Ordnance is required to settle the positions of the guns with their barbettes, and magazines and shell rooms and the means of supplying ammunition to the guns in action.

An understanding between these three main departments enables further progress to be made. The cooperation of the Director of Torpedoes and the Director of Electrical Engineering is now called for to settle the arrangements for torpedo armament, electric generating machinery, electric lighting, etc. So the design progresses and is elaborated from the lower portions upwards, and presently the Director of Naval Construction is able to consult the Director of Naval Equipment as to the proposed arrangements in regard to the sizes and stowage of the motor boats, steamboats, rowing and sailing boats to be carried, as well as of the anchors and cables; the Director of the Signal Department as to the wireless telegraphy arrangements; the Director of Navigation as to the arrangements for navigating the ship, and so on. In this way the scheme goes on growing in a tentative manner, its progress always being dependent on the efficiency of different parts, until ultimately a more or less complete whole is arrived at in the shape of drawings and specifications provisionally embodying all the agreements. This really is the most difficult and interesting stage, for generally it becomes apparent at this point that requirements overlap, and that the best possible cannot be achieved in regard to numbers of points within the limit set to the contractors. These difficulties are cleared up by discussion at round-table conferences, where the compromises which will least impair the value of the ship are agreed upon, and the completed design is then finally submitted for the Board's approval. Some fourteen departments are concerned in the settlement of the final detailed arrangements.[4]

The point which is so clearly illustrated here is that the planning procedure permits expertise of every kind to be drawn into the decision without any difficulties being imposed by the lines of authority in the organization. The final design undoubtedly received authoritative approval; but, during the entire process of formulation, suggestions and recommendations flowed freely from all parts of the organization without raising the problem of "unity of command." It follows from this that to the extent to which planning procedures are used in reaching decisions, the formal organization has relevance only in the final stages of the whole process. So long as the appropriate experts are consulted, their exact location in the hierarchy of authority need not much affect the decision.

This statement must be qualified by one important reservation. Organizational factors are apt to take on considerable importance if the decision requires a compromise among a number of competing values which are somewhat incompatible with one another. In such a case, the focus of attention and the identification of the person who actually makes the decision are apt to affect the degree to which advice offered him by persons elsewhere in the organization actually influences him. This factor is present in the example of the warship just cited.

This same illustration throws in relief the other aspect of the planning procedure which was mentioned above—that the plan may control, down to minute details, a whole complex pattern of behavior. The completed plan of the battleship will specify the design of the ship down to the last rivet. The task of the construction crew is minutely specified by this design.

The Process of Review

Review enables those who are in a position of authority in the administrative hierarchy to determine what actually is being done by their subordinates.

---

[4]Sir Oswyn A. R. Murray, "The Administration of a Fighting Service," *Journal of Public Administration*, 1:216–217 (July, 1923).

Methods of Review. Review may extend to the *results* of the subordinates' activities, measured in terms of their objectives; the tangible *products*, if there are such, of their activities; or the method of their *performance*.

When authority is exercised through the specification of the objective of the organizational unit, then a primary method of review is to ascertain the degree to which the organizational objective is attained— its results. A city manager, for instance, may use measurements of results as a principal means of reviewing city departments. He may evaluate the fire department in terms of fire losses, the police department in terms of crime and accident rates, the public works department in terms of the condition of streets and the frequency of refuse collection.

A second very important method of review is one which examines the piece of completed work to see whether it meets the requirements of quantity and quality. This method assumes that the reviewing officer is able to judge the quality and quantity of the completed work with a certain degree of competence. Thus, a superior may review all outgoing letters written by his subordinates, or the work of typists may be checked by a chief clerk, or the work of a street repair crew may be examined by a superintendent.

It has not often enough been recognized that in many cases the review of work can just as well be confined to a randomly selected sample of the work as extended to all that is produced. A highly developed example of such a sampling procedure is found in the personnel administration of the Farm Credit Administration. This organization carries out its personnel functions on an almost completely decentralized basis, except for a small central staff which lays down standards and procedures. As a means of assuring that local practices follow these standards, field supervisors inspect the work of the local agencies, and in the case of certain personnel procedures, such as classification, the setting of compensation scales, and the development of testing materials, assure themselves of the quality of the work by an actual inspection of a sample. The same type of procedure is usually followed by state boards of equalization which review local assessments. Finally, welfare agencies in California, New York, and perhaps other states have developed an auditing procedure on a sampling basis, in order to review the work of local welfare agencies.

The third, and perhaps simplest, method of review is to watch the employee at work, either to see that he puts in the required number of hours, or to see that he is engaging in certain movements which if continued will result in the completion of the work. In this case, the review extends to procedures and techniques, rather than product or results. It is the prevalent form of review at the foremanship level.

Functions of Review. To determine what method of review should be employed in any concrete administrative situation, it is necessary to be quite clear as to what this particular review process is to accomplish. There are at least four different functions that a review process may perform: diagnosis of the quality of decisions being made by subordinates, modification through influence on subsequent decisions, the correction of incorrect decisions that have already been made, and enforcement of sanctions against subordinates so that they will accept authority in making their decisions.[5]

In the first place, review is the means whereby the administrative hierarchy learns whether decisions are being made correctly or incorrectly, whether work is being done well or badly at the lower levels of the hierarchy. It is a fundamental source of information, then, upon which the higher levels of the hierarchy must rely heavily for their decisions. With the help of this information, improvements can be introduced into the decision-making process.

This leads to the second function of review—to influence subsequent decisions. This is achieved in a variety of ways. Orders may be issued covering particular points on which incorrect decisions have been made, or laying down new policies to govern decisions. Employees may be given training or retraining with regard to those aspects of their work which review has proved faulty. Information may be supplied to them, the lack of which has led to incorrect decisions. In brief, change may be brought about in any of the several ways in which decisions can be influenced.

Third, review may perform an appellate function. If the individual decision has grave consequences, it may be reviewed by a higher authority, to make certain that it is correct. This review may be a matter of course, or it may occur only on appeal by a party at interest. The justifications of such a process of review are that (1) it permits the decision to be weighed twice, and (2) the appellate review requires less time per decision than the original decision, and hence conserves the time of better trained personnel for the more difficult decisions. The appellate review may, to use the language of administrative law, consist in a consideration *de novo,* or may merely review the original decision for substantial conformity to important rules of policy.

Fourth, review is often essential to the effective exercise of authority. As we have seen in Chapter VII, authority depends, to a certain extent, upon the availability of sanctions to give it force. Sanctions can be

---

[5]A somewhat similar, but not identical, analysis of the function of review can be found in Sir H. N. Bunbury's paper, "Efficiency as an Alternative to Control," *Journal of Public Administration,* 6:97–98 (Apr., 1928).

applied only if there is some means of ascertaining when authority has been respected, and when it has been disobeyed. Review supplies the person in authority with this information.

When we recall the "rule of anticipated reactions," we see that the anticipation of review and the invocation of sanctions secures conformity to authority of the decision made prior to review. It is for this reason that review can influence a prior decision.

CENTRALIZATION AND DECENTRALIZATION

Our examination of the process of composite decision, and particularly of the methods and functions of review in an organization, casts considerable light on the way in which decisional processes can best be distributed through the organization, and on the relative advantages and disadvantages in centralizing the processes of decision.

What has already been said with respect to this issue? In Chapter VII it was pointed out that the specialization and centralization of decision-making serves three purposes: it secures coordination, expertise, and responsibility. In Chapter III some pragmatic tests were suggested for arriving at a division of function between legislator and administrator. In Chapter VIII, the relation between centralization of decisions and the problems of communication was explored. In Chapter X, it was seen that a need for centralization sometimes arises from the faulty institutional identifications of the members of an organization. In the present chapter, it was urged that the capabilities of the members of an organization would be one determinant of the possible degree of decentralization. Are there additional considerations, beyond those already mentioned, that should carry weight in the allocation of decisions?

At the outset, one important distinction must be clearly understood. There are two very different aspects to centralization. On the one hand, decision-making powers may be centralized by using general rules to limit the discretion of the subordinate. On the other hand, decision-making powers may be centralized by taking out of the hands of the subordinate the actual decision-making function. Both processes may be designated as "centralization" because their result is to take out of the hands of the subordinate the actual weighing of competing considerations and to require that he accept the conclusions reached by other members of the organization.

The very close relationship between the manner in which the function of review is exercised, and the degree of centralization or decentralization should also be pointed out. Review influences decisions by evaluating them, and thereby subjecting the subordinate to discipline and control. Review is sometimes conceived as a means of detecting wrong decisions and correcting them. This concept may be very useful as applied to those very important decisions where an appellate procedure is necessary to conserve individual rights or democratic responsibility. Under ordinary circumstances, however, the function of correcting the *decisional processes* of the subordinate which lead to wrong decisions is more important than the function of correcting *wrong decisions*. As the resources of the subordinate for making correct decisions are strengthened, decentralization becomes increasingly possible. Hence, review can have three consequences: (1) if it is used to correct individual decisions, it leads to centralization, and an actual transfer of the decision-making function; (2) if it is used to discover where the subordinate needs additional guidance, it leads to centralization through the promulgation of more and more complete rules and regulations limiting the subordinate's discretion; (3) if it is used to discover where the subordinate's own resources need to be strengthened, it leads to decentralization. All three elements can be, and usually are, combined, in varying proportions.

But why should administration aim at decentralization? All of our analysis to this point has emphasized the important functions which the centralization of decision-making performs. Nevertheless, we are warned against a naïve acceptance of the advantages of centralization by the distrust which careful students of administration express for it. Sir Charles Harris, for example, has this to say:

> If I appear before you as a thoroughgoing advocate of decentralization, it is as a convert to the faith in middle age. . . . At the beginning of my service I was greatly impressed by the lack of general knowledge and grasp of central principle displayed in the local decisions and actions that came under my notice. For years the conviction grew upon me that a larger measure of active control from the centre would conduce to both efficiency and economy of administration; and today, if I were to confine my view to particular details and to immediate results, I should still feel on that point no possible doubt whatever. It is when one falls back to Capability Brown's view-point, and tries to see the wood as well as the trees, that the certainty disappears.
>
> . . . Simple centralization drives up the functions of decision and authorization to the top centre, it leaves action, when decided upon, to be carried out by the subordinate authority.
>
> Don't cut down the discretion of the man below, or his class, by requiring submission to higher authority in the future, because he has made a mistake. Teach him and try him again; but if he is unteachable, shunt him.[6]

---

[6]Sir Charles Harris, "Decentralization," *Journal of Public Administration*, 3:117–133 (Apr., 1925).

Almost any person, unless he recognizes the long-term consequences, feels "safer" if he makes decisions himself instead of delegating them to a subordinate. The superior rationalizes this centralization on a variety of grounds: he is more highly skilled or trained than the subordinate; if he makes the decision, he can be certain that it is decided as he would want it. What he does not always realize is that by concentrating the entire function of decision in himself, he is multiplying his work, and making the subordinate superfluous.

There are two principal reasons for decentralizing decisions even in cases where the superior is more highly trained than the subordinate. The first harks back to the distinction in Chapter IX between efficiency and adequacy. It is not enough to take into consideration the accuracy of the decision; its cost must be weighed as well. The superior is presumably a higher paid individual than the subordinate. His time must be conserved for the more important aspects of the work of the organization. If it is necessary, in order that he may make a particular decision, that he sacrifice time which should be devoted to more important decisions, the greater accuracy secured for the former may be bought at too high a price.

The second reason why decentralization is often preferable to centralization is that the referral of a decision upward in the hierarchy introduces new money and time costs into the decision-making process. Against any advantages of accuracy when the decision is made at the center must be balanced the cost of duplicating the decisional process, together with the cost of communicating the decisions.

To emphasize the costs of uneconomic standards of review, we cannot do better than quote an example cited by Ian Hamilton from his personal experience:

In 1896 I was Deputy Quartermaster-General at Simla; then, perhaps still, one of the hardest worked billets in Asia. After a long office day I used to get back home to dinner pursued by a pile of files three to four feet high. The Quartermaster-General, my boss, was a clever, delightful work-glutton. So we sweated and ran together for a while a neck and neck race with our piles of files, but I was the younger and he was the first to be ordered off by the doctors to Europe. Then I, at the age of forty-three, stepped into the shoes and became officiating Quartermaster-General in India. Unluckily, the Government at that moment was in a very stingy mood. They refused to provide pay to fill the post I was vacating and Sir George White, the Commander-in-Chief, asked me to duplicate myself and do the double work. My heart sank, but there was nothing for it but to have a try. The day came; the Quartermaster-General went home and with him went the whole of his share of the work. As for my own share, the hard twelve hours' task melted by some magic into the Socialist's dream of a six hours' day. How was that? Because, when a question came up from one of the Departments I had formerly been forced to compose a long minute upon it, explaining the case, putting my own views, and endeavoring to persuade the Quartermaster-General to accept them. He was a highly conscientious man and if he differed from me he liked to put on record his reasons—several pages of reasons. Or, if he agreed with me, still he liked to agree in his own words and to "put them on record." Now, when I became Quartermaster-General and Deputy-Quartermaster General rolled into one I studied the case as formerly, but there my work ended: I had not to persuade my own subordinates: I had no superior except the Commander-in-Chief, who was delighted to be left alone: I just gave an order—quite a simple matter unless a man's afraid: "Yes," I said, or "No!"[7]

There is an additional objection to centralization that goes beyond those already considered. It has been assumed thus far that, given ample time, the superior could make more accurate decisions than the subordinate. This will be true, however, only if the information upon which the decision is to be based is equally accessible to both. When decisions must be made against a deadline, or when the organization is characterized by geographical dispersion, this may be far from the case. The "facts of the case" may be directly present to the subordinate, but highly difficult to communicate to the superior. The insulation of the higher levels of the administrative hierarchy from the world of fact known at first hand by the lower levels is a familiar administrative phenomenon.

Centralization is sometimes urged as a necessary concomitant of the specialization of work. If work is specialized, then procedures must be introduced to secure coordination among the members of the group; and among the most powerful of coordinative procedures is the centralization of decisions. This is true; but in accepting this conclusion we must not blind ourselves to the very real disadvantages and costs that accompany specialization.

Interpersonal coordination involves communication of a plan. Complex and powerful as are the devices which can be used for such coordination, their effectiveness is in no way comparable to the coordinating power of the individual human nervous system. When the elements of the plan can be reduced to diagrams and maps, as in the case of a design for a ship or a bridge, interpersonal coordination can reach even minute detail. But the coordinative mechanisms of a skilled pianist, or of an engineer bringing all his skill and knowledge to bear on a problem of design, are far more intricate.

[7]Sir Ian Hamilton, *The Soul and Body of an Army* (London: E. Arnold & Co., 1921), pp. 235–236.

Successful use of the device of specialization to increase efficiency implies either that no coordination is required among the specialized segments of the complete task, or that this coordination can be achieved with the available techniques of interpersonal coordination. If neither of these conditions is fulfilled, then specialization must be sacrificed in order to retain the use of the individual brain as the coordinating mechanism. It is not very easy to thread a needle if one person holds the thread and another the needle. Here the task is to get thread and needle to the *same* place, and interpersonal coordination accomplishes this much less successfully than the coordination of the movements of the two hands by the human nervous system.

The quotation in which the procedure for designing a battleship was described[8] is another case in point. A careful analysis of the procedure reveals that there were involved in it not only the experts on various aspects of battleship design, but also a group of functionaries who might be described as "expert jacks-of-all-trades in battleship design." The Director of Naval Construction, and not the functional experts, lays down the general lines of the ship. To repeat:

> Thereupon the Director of Naval Construction, acting under and in consultation with the Controller, formulates provisional schemes outlining the kind of ship desired, together with forecasts of the size and cost involved by the different arrangements. To do this he and his officers must have a good general knowledge—in itself only attainable by close relations with those in charge of these matters—of the latest developments and ideas in regard to a great range of subjects—gunnery, torpedo, engineering, armour, fire-control, navigation, signalling, accommodation, and so on—in order to be reasonably sure that the provision included in his schemes is such as is likely to satisfy the experts in all these subjects, when the time for active cooperation arrives.[9]

Only after the "jack-of-all-trades" has done his job are the experts called in for their suggestions. Next, a technique of interpersonal coordination, the conference, is used to reconcile the competing claims of experts. Finally, the plan is turned over again to the non-specialist for authorization.

We may conclude, then, that some measure of centralization is indispensable to secure the advantages of organization: coordination, expertise, and responsibility. On the other hand, the costs of centralization must not be forgotten. It may place in the hands of highly paid personnel

---

[8]See pp. 312–314, *supra.*

[9]Sir Oswyn A. R. Murray, *loc. cit.*

decisions which do not deserve their attention. It may lead to a duplication of function which makes the subordinate superfluous. Facilities for communication must be available, sometimes at considerable cost. The information needed for a correct decision may be available only to the subordinate. Finally, centralization leaves idle and unused the powerful coordinative capacity of the human nervous system, and substitutes for it an interpersonal coordinative mechanism. These are the considerations which must be weighed in determining the degree to which decisions should be centralized or decentralized.

LESSONS FOR ADMINISTRATIVE THEORY

In Chapter II the position was taken that the currently accepted "principles of administration" are little more than ambiguous and mutually contradictory proverbs, and that a new approach was needed to establish a consistent and useful administrative theory. This is a fact that is beginning to be recognized in the literature of administration. If we study the chain of publications extending from Mooney and Reiley through Gulick, the President's Committee controversy, to Schuyler Wallace and Benson, we see a steady shift of emphasis from the "principles of administration" themselves to a study of the *conditions* under which competing principles are respectively applicable. We no longer say that organization should be by purpose, but rather that under such and such conditions purpose organization is desirable, but under such and such other conditions, process organization is desirable. It is the central thesis of this study that an understanding of these underlying conditions for the applicability of administrative principles is to be obtained from an analysis of the administrative process in terms of decisions.

If this approach be taken, the rationality of decisions—that is, their appropriateness for the accomplishment of specified goals—becomes the central concern of administrative theory. As was pointed out, however, in Chapter II, if there were no limits to human rationality administrative theory would be barren. It would consist of the single precept: Always select that alternative, among those available, which will lead to the most complete achievement of your goals. The need for an administrative theory resides in the fact that there *are* practical limits to human rationality, and that these limits are not static, but depend upon the organizational environment in which the individual's decision takes place. The task of administration is so to design this environment that the individual will approach as close as practicable to rationality (judged in terms of the organization's goals) in his decisions.

The Area of Rationality

As has also been explained in Chapter II, when the limits to rationality are viewed from the individual's standpoint, they fall into three categories: he is limited by his unconscious skills, habits, and reflexes; he is limited by his values and conceptions of purpose, which may diverge from the organization goals; he is limited by the extent of his knowledge and information. The individual can be rational in terms of the organization's goals only to the extent that he is *able* to pursue a particular course of action, he has a correct conception of the *goal* of the action, and he is correctly *informed* about the conditions surrounding his action. Within the boundaries laid down by these factors his choices are rational—goal-oriented.

Rationality, then, does not determine behavior. Within the area of rationality behavior is perfectly flexible and adaptable to abilities, goals, and knowledge. Instead, behavior is determined by the irrational and nonrational elements that bound the area of rationality. The area of rationality is the area of adaptability to these nonrational elements. Two persons, given the same possible alternatives, the same values, the same knowledge, can rationally reach only the same decision. Hence, administrative theory must be concerned with the limits of rationality, and the manner in which organization affects these limits for the person making a decision. The theory must determine—as suggested in Chapter X—how institutionalized decision can be made to conform to values developed within a broader organizational structure. The theory must be a critique of the effect (judged from the point of view of the whole organization) of the organizational structure upon the decisions of its component parts and its individual members.

Perhaps an example of the way in which the organization can alter each of the three types of limits enumerated above will make the problem more concrete:

Limited Alternatives. Suppose a bricklayer is unable to work at an acceptable speed. There may be no lack of rationality in his behavior. The fact may be that his skills are not sufficiently developed to enable him to lay bricks rapidly. However, if attention were to be given to the skills themselves, if he were given instruction and training in proper methods, the impossible might readily become possible. Skills are examples of behavior patterns that in the short run limit the sphere of adaptability or rationality, but in the long run may, by training, open up entirely new behavior possibilities.

Reorientation of Values. Sometimes rationality is limited by the individual's failure to identify himself correctly with the goals of the whole organization. In certain situations, at least, it is possible to reorient an individual from identification with a subgoal of the organization to identification with a broader and more inclusive goal. The writer has had occasion in another context to point to this method for reorienting the behavior of a "rational person" by altering his framework of values. The problem dealt with in that situation was to control and modify the motivation of a group of social workers who were participating in an administrative experiment:

> To the worker, the experiment might seem inconsistent with the objectives he was trying to attain in his daily job. The cooperation of such a worker could be obtained only by interpreting the study in terms of his more fundamental values and by showing him that these broader values would be benefited by a temporary sacrifice of some of his immediate objectives and attitudes. In this way his attention might be detached from the narrower frame of reference—the conditioned reflexes, so to speak—forced on him by his regular daily schedule of work.[10]

Limits of Knowledge. Where a particular item of knowledge is needed repeatedly in decision, the organization can anticipate this need and, by providing the individual with this knowledge prior to decision, can extend his area of rationality. This is particularly important when there are time limits on decision. Thus, a policeman is trained in methods of making arrests, handling unruly prisoners and the like, so that he will not have to figure these things out on the spot when occasion requires.

Individual and Group Rationality

A decision is rational from the standpoint of the individual (subjectively rational) if it is consistent with the values, the alternatives, and the information which he weighed in reaching it. A decision is rational from the standpoint of the group (objectively rational) if it is consistent with the values governing the group, and the information that the group possesses relevant to the decision. Hence, the organization must be so constructed that a decision which is (subjectively) rational from the standpoint of the deciding individual, will remain rational when reassessed from the standpoint of the group.

Suppose that an officer orders a soldier under his command to capture a particular hill. Rationality (subjective) demands of him that he combine this objective, or value, with the skills he possesses for approaching hostile positions, and with the information his senses provide him regarding his situation.

---

[10]Simon and Divine, *op. cit.*, p. 487.

On the other hand, rationality requires of the officer that the objective he assigns the soldier shall contribute to the broader objective of his unit (which usually implies that the soldier's objective must have a reasonable possibility of successful attainment), and that he provide the soldier with all available information that may assist him in his task. To say that the officer is rational means that the soldier's behavior continues to appear rational when evaluated from the broader viewpoint which the officer's position affords him.

This is the basic task of administration—to provide each "operative" employee with an environment of decision of such a kind that behavior which is rational from the standpoint of this environment is also rational from the standpoint of the group values and the group situation. Moreover, it must be taken into consideration that the establishment of an environment of decision for the individual involves problems of communication for the organization. These then are the basic elements from which a theory of organization can be constructed: (1) a decision made above the operative level must be communicated; (2) wherever a decision is made, its quality will depend on the environment that bounds the area of rationality of the person making the decision. With respect to the first element, the technology of communication (in the very broadest sense) is the limiting factor; with respect to the second, the limiting factors are the very factors that limit the area of individual rationality.

Importance of Organizational Location

Since administrative theory is concerned with control of the nonrational, it follows that, the larger the area of rationality, the less important is the administrative organization. For example, the function of plan preparation, or design, if it results in a written plan that can be communicated interpersonally without difficulty, can be located almost anywhere in the organization without affecting results. All that is needed is a procedure whereby the plan can be given authoritative status; and that can be provided in a number of ways. A discussion, then, of the proper location for a planning or designing unit is apt to be highly inconclusive, and may hinge on the personalities in the organization and their relative enthusiasm, or lack of it, toward the planning function.[11]

On the other hand, when factors of communication or identification

---

[11]See, for instance, Robert A. Walker, *The Planning Function in Urban Government* (Chicago: University of Chicago Press, 1941), pp. 166–175. Walker makes out a case for attaching the planning agency to the chief executive. But he rests his entire case on the rather slender reed that "as long as the planning agency is outside the governmental structure, however, planning will tend to encounter resistance from public officials as an invasion of their responsibility and jurisdiction." The verb "will" seems entirely too strong for the facts of the case.

are crucial to the making of a decision, the location of the decision in the organization is of great importance. The method of allocating decisions in the army, for instance, automatically (and "theoretically," I hasten to add) provides, at least in the period prior to the actual battle, that each decision will be made where the knowledge is available for coordinating it with other decisions. Similarly, we may note that final decisions regarding budget allowances are always entrusted to administrators who are not identified with the particular items to be allowed, but must weigh these items against alternative items.

THE ROLE OF THE ADMINISTRATOR

It may be appropriate to conclude this volume with a brief statement about the role and training of administrators. It has been suggested earlier that the decisions which might be uniquely designated as "administrative" decisions are those which are concerned with the decision-making process itself. That is, such decisions do not determine the content of the organization's work, but rather how the decision-making function is to be allocated and influenced in that particular organization.

But to say that in any organization certain "administrative" decisions have to be made, is not to say that the person who happens to be designated an "administrator" in that organization makes, or should make, only administrative decisions. Whether or not it is desirable that there *should* be functionaries whose tasks are confined within these limits, it is certainly not an accurate description of administrative organizations as they exist today to define the administrator's task in those terms.

In almost all organizations he has a responsibility not only to establish and maintain the organizational structure, but also to make some of the broader and more important decisions regarding the content of the organization's work. To mention only one of these decisions, the higher administrator ordinarily has a considerable responsibility for budget decisions—that is, decisions as to the directions in which the organization's efforts should be applied. Further, to him falls the responsibility, within the limits of his discretion, of formulating organizational objectives—that is, the values that will guide decisions at all lower levels of the organization.

The statement, then, that as we proceed upward in the hierarchy "administrative" duties come to occupy more and more of the administrator's time, and "technical" duties less, must be interpreted with considerable caution. It is not true if the term "administrative duties" is taken to refer only to the organization-determining functions. It is true, if the broader decisional functions which fall to the administrator are considered as "administrative duties."

What is the difference between these latter functions and the "technical" functions at the lower levels of the hierarchy? Simply that the content decisions of the higher administrator deal with more ultimate purposes and more general processes than the decisions of the lower administrator. We might say that the lower administrator's purposes are the upper administrator's processes.

The stenographer's rationality is exercised in translating a piece of copy, whatever its content, into a typewritten manuscript. Her employer's rationality is exercised in determining the content of the copy, taking for granted the very element with which the stenographer is concerned—its translation into typewritten form.

If the Chief Engineer's decisions are less concerned with engineering technology than those of his designing engineers, with what are they concerned? If the Health Officer's decisions do not involve the minutiae of medical knowledge, what do they involve? They involve the application of the criterion of efficiency to the broader purposes of the organization. Since the broader purposes of governmental organizations (and, to a lesser extent, commercial organizations) are predominantly social, and the larger problems of means are principally economic and fiscal, this means that the decisions of the higher administrators involve social science principles and economic calculations.

One further point should be noted that applies even to those decisions which deal with the organization structure itself. If, as has been suggested, administrative theory cannot be entirely freed from concern with the content of the organization's work, it follows that sound organizational decisions require also a knowledge of that content.

We see, then, that the work of the administrator, as organizations are now constituted, involves (1) decisions about the organization structure, and (2) the broader decisions as to the content of the organization's work. Decisions of neither type can rest entirely, or even primarily, upon a knowledge of or facility with administrative theory. The former must be firmly grounded in the organization's technology. The latter must be grounded in the organization's technology and requires in addition (a) a thorough appreciation of the theory of efficiency, and (b) a knowledge of those aspects of the social sciences which are relevant to the broader purposes of the organization.

If this analysis is correct, it has direct implications for the training of an "administrative class," that is, for the training of persons who are skilled in higher administration. In the first place, it casts grave doubts on the possibility of developing administrative ability apart from subject-matter competence except at the very highest levels of the hierarchy. In the second place, it indicates that the proper training of "administrators" lies not in the narrow field of administrative theory, but in the broader field of the social sciences generally.

CONCLUSION

Our study has not led us to any definitive administrative principles. It has, however, provided us with a framework for the analysis and description of administrative situations, and with a set of factors that must be weighed in arriving at any valid proposal for administrative organization. It has shown us, further, that currently accepted "principles" of administration suffer from internal ambiguity and mutual contradiction.

What are the next steps that research must take? First, it must develop adequate case studies of existing administrative situations. It will do well to initiate these on a small scale—dealing in minute detail with organizational units of moderate size. Only in this way can superficiality be avoided.

Second, techniques must be developed and improved for measuring the success of particular administrative arrangements. Specifically, the assumption so often made in administrative studies, that an arrangement is effective because it exists, is a circular argument of the worst sort. Students of administration are possessed of no occult vision which permits them, by simply observing an administrative organization, to determine whether it is "working" or not. The only procedure of evaluation that can possibly be valid is the comparison of alternative administrative schemes in terms of their objective results.

Finally, the valuable investigations already initiated of the "conditions" under which different administrative principles are validly applicable might well be extended with the use of the "decisional" framework described in this study.

THE ANATOMY OF ORGANIZATION

As Chapter XI brings together and summarizes the main themes in the chapters that precede it, there is no need to summarize Chapter XI. Instead, this commentary will undertake two tasks: first, to offer some brief comments on the developments in administrative theory that have taken place since the first edition of *Administrative Behavior* was published; second, to provide two additional examples of organizations' interactions with their environments. The two examples concern organizations in which I have personally been involved, one at the crucial moment of its birth, the other both at birth and for the succeeding 47 years. In both cases, the central issue is representation (or, if you prefer, organizational culture): how an organization views itself and the contingency of its structure on its environment.

A HALF CENTURY OF GROWTH IN ORGANIZATION THEORY

The commentaries on the preceding chapters of *Administrative Behavior* mainly examined the important new ideas that have been injected into organization theory by the half century of research and observation since the book was first published. The purpose of these final comments is to observe how these ideas are related to the text that antedates them.

In the course of the discussion it will become evident that I see strong continuity extending from the writings on "classical" organizational theory right down to the present time. Sometimes this continuity is obscured in the literature by talk of "schools" of management,[12] sometimes by the invention of new terminology when particular ideas attract the attention of researchers and are expanded (and renamed in the process). I hope that the emphasis on continuity will not encourage the

---

[12]My reasons for thinking it profitless or harmful to analyze the management literature in terms of "schools of management" are stated at length in "Approaching the Theory of Management," in H. Koontz, ed., *Toward a Unified Theory of Management* (New York: McGraw-Hill, 1964).

false idea that "it was all there already in 1947." On the contrary, there has been massive and continuous progress in management theory, which I hope is reflected in these commentaries. But the new knowledge amplifies rather than deconstructs what we knew earlier.

Human Relations

The so-called human relations movement in management, whose origins antedated by about two decades the appearance of *Administrative Behavior*, shows its influence in the book's treatment of authority and identification, and generally in its emphasis upon psychological mechanisms in management in general. The earliest human relations theme was worker participation in decision-making; which spawned a great deal of research about the effects of participation on morale and the relation between employee morale and productivity.[13]

The participation theme subsequently provided some of the groundwork for the more general attacks on authority and hierarchy that began to appear in the 1960s and '70s, and the concerns with self-actualization of human beings in the workplace. These developments have been discussed, in relation to the balance of inducements and contributions, in the commentary to Chapter VI; and in relation to authority, in the commentary to Chapter VII.[14]

Rationality and Intuition

Because of its emphasis on motivation and the emotions, the human relations research also played a part in generating objections to what was regarded as the excessively rational stance of other management models. But perhaps even more important than human relations for raising the rational-versus-intuitive issue was a reaction of skeptics to the enthusiasm for the quantitative tools of operations research, management science, and economic analysis that appeared after World War II.

[13]Kurt Levin was a key figure in the launching of this work. See his *Selected Papers on Group Dynamics, 1935–1946* (New York; Harper, 1948). It was also stimulated by the Western Electric studies, reported by Roethlisberger and Dixon in *Management and the Worker* (Cambridge, Mass.: Harvard University Press, 1939). For more recent reviews of the Western Electric evidence, see R. H. Franke, "The Hawthorne Experiments: First Statistical Interpretation," *American Sociological Review*, 43: 623–643 (1978), and "Worker Productivity at Hawthorne," *American Sociological Review*, 45:1006–1027 (1980).

[14]This whole range of topics is dealt with in V. H. Vroom, *The New Leadership: Managing Participation in Organizations* (Englewood Cliffs, N.J.: Prentice-Hall, 1988); K. E. Weick, *The Social Psychology of Organizing* (Reading, Mass.: Addison-Wesley, 2nd ed., 1979); and H. J. Leavitt and Homa Bahrami, *Managerial Psychology: Managing Behavior in Organizations* (Chicago: University of Chicago Press, 1988).

Administrative Behavior found itself in an interesting position in the middle of this controversy, and like most occupants of the middle, it was sometimes attacked from both sides. On the one side, classical economists resisted the adjective in the phrase "bounded rationality," and have only recently shown any willingness to depart from a strict utility-maximizing model. On the other side, non-quantitative students of management resisted the noun "rational," believing that it left too little room for the intuitive component of human thinking. Both issues were addressed at some length in the commentary to Chapter V.

As conventional wisdom insists that in such controversies truth seldom lies at the extremes, I take comfort from the position of *Administrative Behavior* somewhere close to the middle. While challenging the adherence of most economic analysis to unlimited rationality, this book also shows how "intuitive" thinking can be analyzed as a (boundedly) rational process which needs no veil of mystery.

Intuition enables the expert's rapid recognition of and response to situations that are marked by familiar cues, and thereby give access to large bodies of knowledge assembled through training and experience. This indexed encyclopedia in expert heads provides the basic mechanism for expert behavior and organizational routine.

Contingency Theory

The idea that different tasks and different environments call for different organization structures, an idea generally called "contingency theory," comes straight out of the challenge in Chapter II to the proverbs of administration as universal principles of structure. The commentary to that chapter describes the relation between the critique of the proverbs and contingency, illustrating it by examples of accounting organization and the organization of product development. Two additional and more elaborate examples are presented at the end of the present commentary.

Authority Relations

One of the proverbs challenged by *Administrative Behavior* was the principle of unity of command, which was replaced by Barnard's more sophisticated theory of the authority relation. While there now seems to be considerable consensus about the nature of authority and the way it actually operates, there is much less consensus about how authority should be exercised in organizations and how much of it, if any, is desirable. These issues are discussed in the commentaries to Chapters VI and VII.

Computers and Communications

The new electronic technologies that began to emerge just as the first edition of this book was published have attracted, as they should, enormous attention, and have already had a large impact on organizations, especially in automating much routine clerical work as well as most engineering computation. Effects on the structure of organizations are less easy to define, but the possibilities of major future changes should not be dismissed. These issues are discussed, with what I hope is the appropriate degree of tentativeness, in the commentary to Chapter VIII.

Identification and Organizational Loyalty

It has become steadily clearer over the years that identification strengthens enormously the motivations provided by tangible rewards and the employment contract to work toward organizational goals. Meanwhile, a great deal has been learned about the psychological bases for identification: both the cognitive bases that derive from bounded rationality and selective attention to the environment, and the emotional bases that arise out of the exploitation by organizations of human altruism—the latter explained, in turn, by the interaction of bounded rationality with docility. These matters are discussed in Chapter X and brought up to date in the commentary to that chapter.

Organizational Culture

The rather new interest in organizational culture appears to be identical, except for the language that is used, with the long-established interest in the ways in which organization members characterize their environments and organizations. Hence, it has a close connection with contingency theory and with goals and representations, topics that are discussed in Chapters V and X and their commentaries, the commentary to Chapter II, and the remainder of this commentary.

THE BIRTH OF AN ORGANIZATION[15]

We hear a good deal these days about an organization's need for a "vision statement" and a "mission statement." Many of the manifestos produced in response to this supposed need appear to contain little more

---

[15]This section draws heavily upon an article of the same title, published in the *Public Administration Review*, 13:227–236 (1953), and used with permission.

than apple pie and motherhood. A proclamation that a company is going to make high quality products, give its customers what they want and need, treat its employees fairly and generously, and provide the greatest possible returns to its stockholders is not likely to have any noticeable effect upon decision-making or other corporate behavior. The sentiments expressed are laudable, but they don't even hint at what to do.

But cynicism about the effectiveness of platitudes should not cause us to dismiss as unimportant the sharing, by both executives and non-managerial employees, of a common conception of an organization's goals: of the particular strengths and comparative advantages it can best employ to establish and maintain a competitive niche, and the "style" and strategies best designed to exploit and enhance these strengths and advantages. In previous chapters I have used the term "representation" to speak of the ways in which an organization characterizes itself. Finding an appropriate representation is especially important to the achievement of effective cooperation in new and growing organizations, and making sure that such a representation is conceived and then promulgated until it permeates the decision processes of the organization is an important leadership responsibility.

I can best illustrate both the nature of an effective representation and effective methods for diffusing it by developing more fully an example that has already been mentioned briefly in the commentary on Chapter II: the Economic Cooperation Administration.

Creation of the Economic Cooperation Administration

On April 3, 1948, the United States Congress approved the Economic Cooperation Act, implementing the so-called "Marshall Plan" to help restore the weak economies of European countries after World War II. By the end of July, the Economic Cooperation Administration was a going concern, and had already accumulated considerable experience in administrating its foreign aid program.

The following account reports some of the stages in the creation of the ECA. My knowledge of these events was gained largely from the vantage point of a position in the Organization and Management Division of the agency. While I had some small opportunity to check my observations with persons in other parts of the agency, they never saw exactly the same things that I saw, nor do I have any reason to believe that what I saw was the "reality." Indeed, one moral of the story is that initially the organization consisted largely of different pictures in the minds of different people. As these several representations of the organization were far from congruent, organizing required arriving at a single picture that was held more or less in common.[16]

Birth Pains

A good deal of the history of the agency during its period of mushroom growth can be read in the phone directories that were revised almost daily. The first directory, issued about April 13, lists fifteen names. As it does not include clerical personnel, the total number of persons who arrived on the scene in the first week and a half was probably about thirty. By April 22, the list contained 138 names including clerical personnel; by July 26, it contained 741 names, and the period of rapid growth was over.

The growth process was one of cell-splitting. Within a few days after his appointment as administrator, Paul Hoffman had appointed, in addition to two personal assistants, a director of operations, Wayne C. Taylor; an acting controller, soon replaced by E. L. Kohler as controller; and a director of administration, Donald C. Stone. Hoffman also brought in three economists to review for him the substantive programs that had been developed before the agency was formally created. The senior member of this group was Richard H. Bissell, who had served as executive secretary to the President's Committee on Foreign Aid.

On the program side of the agency the cell-splitting process was very slow; on the side of the machinery of organization, it was very rapid. There are two reasons for this discrepancy. First, there was already in the State Department an "interim aid" unit that was administering earlier assistance funds granted to Austria, France, Greece, Italy, and Trieste, that kept the supply pipeline filled in the early period, and that was soon absorbed as a Procurement Transactions unit in ECA.[17]

Second, questions of mechanics were much clearer than questions of substance. The agency would need rooms, telephone service, and other housekeeping services, and would have to hire many employees. Even the press relations function was not overlooked. It was much less clear how the agency would administer foreign aid.

---

[16]The principal sources are: PCFA—President's Committee on Foreign Aid (Harriman Committee), European Recovery and American Aid, November 7, 1947; HSC—80th Congress, Second Session, House Select Committee on Foreign Aid (Herter Committee), Final Report H.R. 1845, May 1, 1948; ECA1—Economic Cooperation Administration, First Report to Congress, for the Quarter Ended June 30, 1948; ECA2—Economic Cooperation Administration, Second Report to Congress, for the Quarter Ended September 30, 1948. These reports will be referred to by the initials indicated. The first two relate to the period prior to the enactment of the act, the second two to the first six months of ECA's existence.

[17]For a description of the interim aid organization, see HSC, pp. 758–763.

By the middle of April the director of administration had appointed a budget director, an organization and methods director, a personnel director, and an office services director. By the third week in April, 63 per cent of the personnel were in these units and another 13 per cent in the Controller's Office, leaving 24 per cent for all the activities associated with the substantive program. By July 26 the personnel in the program units had increased from one-quarter of the total staff of the Washington office to one-half.

In mid-April, ECA resembled nothing so much as a manufacturing concern without a factory. An office desk or a telephone could be obtained in a matter of hours. In the new, partially finished building the agency occupied, interior partitions were erected with amazing rapidity. But whatever product was emerging was being produced by the State Department group, which was operating with a minimum of contact and almost no direction from the new agency. This course of events is completely understandable. As Washington had a clear conception of what an administrative agency looked like, the framework could be erected. But since no consensus existed about a program, the skeleton was not yet ready to be covered with flesh, blood, and nerves.

Alternative Representations

How then, did the program of the ECA and the organization to implement it emerge? One can identify at least six approaches to the organization of ECA. The early administrative history of the agency can be written in terms of the rise and fall of these approaches and of the administrative units with which they were associated. Since they are not wholly incompatible, and since no single one was clearly espoused by the statute creating ECA, the final structure that emerged made room for several of them.

Commodity Screening. Considerable experience had been gained in the administration of foreign assistance through wartime aid programs and postwar interim-aid programs. The chief repositories of administrative memory were the export licensing unit in the Commerce Department and the interim-aid group in the State Department. Some persons in the Departments of Agriculture and Interior had also participated in these earlier programs.

The conception of foreign assistance of this group was to determine specific commodity needs of countries and approve or disapprove individual shipments of commodities. The decisions amounted to screening these transactions against the need of the country for the commodity for defense or nutrition and the availability of scarce commodities.[18] The screening process called for two kinds of specialized knowledge: of needs, and of availabilities. The former suggested some combination of commodity and area specialization; the latter pointed toward commodity specialization.

The Balance of Trade Approach. The enactment of the Marshall Plan had been preceded by economic research on the magnitude of Europe's needs for assistance. The Committee of European Economic Cooperation (CEEC) had drawn up an estimate in the fall of 1947 of the goods that would have to be imported to maintain acceptable consumption levels, and of the balance of payments that would result from the import program. The "dollar gap" thus arrived at provided a basis for the amount of assistance requested. These estimates, after revision, guided the ECA legislation and the subsequent appropriations.[19]

In this picture of the program, individual commodity purchases played a subordinate role. Once the aggregate figure for aid to each country was set, it was unimportant whether a particular import was financed with ECA dollars or with dollars bought with exports. The notion that the foreign assistance problem was one of making up a "dollar deficit" follows from the balance of payments concept that has been central to international trade theory. From an organizational point of view, this suggested arriving by economic analysis at overall decisions on dollar amounts of foreign assistance to individual countries.

The European Cooperation Approach. Another set of preconceptions was aimed at bringing about more international trade, economic cooperation, and rationalization of industry in Western Europe. This approach was an essential element in the studies already mentioned and an integral part of State Department and congressional policy.[20] Its implications were: first, that the initiative for programming should rest with the European countries acting cooperatively; second, that our relations with them under the program should be multilateral rather than bilateral, and should be channeled primarily through the Paris rather than the Washington office of ECA.

The Bilateral Pledge Approach. A somewhat different idea was that assistance should be conditioned on bilateral pledges between the individual

[18]Concepts of commodity screening for export control are discussed in HSC, pp. 638–643, 646–687.

[19]The estimating procedures of PCFA and HSC are based squarely on the balance-of-trade approach.

[20]HSC, pp. 21–56, 603–604; PCFA, pp. 4–6, 31–32.

participating countries and the United States.[21] As one element in the required agreement was the willingness of the participating country to cooperate with the other countries, the two views were not in direct contradiction. Nevertheless, the bilateral agreements required direct negotiation through the State Department with individual countries, and thereby weakened CEEC and the Paris office of ECA as the primary channels of contact. The bilateral agreements also emphasized certain specifically American goals such as the continued availability of strategic materials.

The Investment Bank Approach. The Act specifically provided that, of the $5.3 billion in first-year aid, $1 billion be in the form of loans, with the Export-Import Bank as the lending agency. This suggested that it was necessary to determine whether individual projects for plant construction or other capital improvements were economically sound. The Congress itself was ambiguous (and probably intentionally so) in stating the criteria for approval of loans. Both the earning power of the investment and the ability of the country to repay were to be considered.[22] The facts that the Congress included the earning power criterion, and that Mr. Taylor, the director of operations appointed by Mr. Hoffman, came to ECA from the Export-Import Bank, had important consequences for the organization of ECA during the first months.

The Policy-Administration Approach. The Budget Bureau had constructed tentative plans for the internal organization of the agency. Because there was no clear conception of the program, these plans resembled the organization that began to develop early in April—great emphasis on machinery and little on production. Provision was made for a bureau of policy coordination, a program bureau, a bureau of operations, and a controller. The first would be concerned with the broader aspects of European recovery, the second with the review of commodities lists, the third with actual procurement, and the fourth with documentation and accounting for funds.

It is a familiar idea that one should deal with a complex problem—any problem—by first making broad decisions, then implementing these with more specific decisions, and then implementing these in turn. This plan mistook a description of the governmental process for a list of the administrative units needed to carry out a program. Certain elements that later emerged in the ECA organization can be identified with the

[21]HSC, pp. 869–877; PCFA, pp. 108, 273–277; ECA1, Appendix I.
[22]HSC, pp. 634–636, 718–719.

units proposed by the Budget Bureau. But except for the controller, this was a matter of coincidence and not planning. As the organization was modified by gradual adaptation, the unit corresponding to policy coordination absorbed more and more of the functions of the program bureau, and the program bureau absorbed completely the bureau of operations. The reasons will perhaps become clear in the sequel.

The Development of Program Organization

As the process of cell division continued, each of the program conceptions we have described found a concrete embodiment in one or more of the emerging organizational units. The fate that each unit suffered tended to depend upon two things. It depended, first, upon how easily its conception of the program could actually be implemented. Each program conception had to be spelled out in terms of concrete administrative activities, and a workable allocation of decision-making responsibilities. A program conception could not be regarded as workable unless it could be elaborated into a decision-making process for allocating $5 billion among the Western European nations and for translating these allocations into authorizations for the purchase of specific goods and services. Not all the approaches were capable of being implemented in this sense.

A unit's fate depended, second, on the natural alliances it found with powerful Washington agencies surrounding the ECA that shared its conception of the agency program.[23] Such alliances might decide the outcome as between competing approaches that were both workable.

In the ensuing power struggle, ideas—in particular the conception of the program—played a major role both as weapons and as motives for empire building. The conceptions were weapons that could be used to advance the claims of units to a larger place in the program. They were motives for empire-building because these units saw the broadening of their functions as the principal means for implementing their conceptions of the program. This kind of struggle was not peculiar to ECA; analysis of empire-building in government and in business would show that these elements are always present and very often of central importance. It is easier to identify them in the early history of ECA than in an agency that has already gone through a process of natural selection.

The commodity screening view of ECA's program prevailed in the Procurement Transactions Division (the new name of the State Department interim-aid group) and in two program units that were set up on a

23HSC, pp. 698–730, 755–778; ECA1, pp. 42–45.

commodity basis: the Foods Division and the Industry Division. The Foods Division was largely under Agriculture Department influence, and all three of the units had close working relations with the Office of International Trade in the Department of Commerce. Commodity screening was also the prevalent conception in the ECA Controller's Office.

The workability of the commodity screening approach rested largely on several provisions of the act itself. One of these required that the aid should not impair the fulfillment of vital needs of the American people. Crude oil was to be purchased, as far as possible, outside the United States; no meat was to be purchased in this country except horsemeat, and there were other clauses for the protection of the American economy. Private trade channels were to be used as far as possible in the procurement of supplies, and at least half the goods were to be shipped in American bottoms. The effect of all these provisions was to require scrutiny of individual transactions.

Paradoxically, these provisions also created a basic weakness in the commodity screening approach. The crucial decision in screening scarce commodities was not whether their purchase was financed from ECA funds, but whether they were to be exported from the United States. Hence, quotas of total shipments of each commodity had to be established, and these quotas had to be enforced through export licenses rather than through the approval of financing. As a consequence, the main licensing responsibility had to devolve upon the Commerce and Agriculture Departments rather than ECA.[24]

The same weakness undermined the more naïve, but strongly held, conception that the purpose of screening individual transactions was to conserve the American taxpayer's money by making sure that the European nations were using the funds only for "needed" items. Since 50 per cent of total European export dollars was being earned by regular international trade and only 50 per cent was provided by ECA, if a transaction were disapproved, the particular item in question could be procured instead with earned dollars and another item substituted on the ECA list.

In the end the ECA organization had to adapt itself to the facts (1) that export licensing, not procurement transaction screening, was the effective means for controlling individual transactions, and (2) that screening could not control the overall European import program. The Controller's Office, with its auditing responsibilities, remained the only center of power for the commodity screening approach, which gradually disappeared from the conceptions of the programming divisions.

[24]PCFA, p. 113; HSC, pp. 672–686; ECA1, pp. 14–18, 44.

The balance of trade conception found its base—at first a very unstable base—among the economists who were brought into the agency, largely by Bissell on a consulting basis. Mr. Hoffman and most of the senior personnel immediately associated with him were preoccupied in the early days with external problems. They had to work out relations with the State Department and negotiate the bilateral agreements; they had to develop instructions for the Paris office that was just coming into existence; and they had to prepare for the appropriations hearings on the Hill.

This left the task of developing the programming procedures and of reviewing the second- and third-quarter programs of foreign assistance to the economists. The actual program revision was the work of a few able, energetic, very young, and very inconspicuous professionals who had participated in the interdepartmental committees reviewing the original CEEC proposal and who were now operating under Bissell, perhaps not more than a half dozen persons.

The European cooperation approach was easier to describe than to implement.[25] It required strengthening the OEEC through plans made by the European nations themselves. Because the Paris office was clearly the appropriate unit for dealing with OEEC, and because the cooperation goals had little relevance for programming and financing assistance, this approach never had a strong organizational embodiment in the Washington office; the center of gravity was in Paris.

The cooperation approach had, however, a negative implication that influenced thinking about the Washington office. There was great temptation to establish "country desks" in the program bureau, which was to be a replica of the WWII Foreign Economic Administration (FEA) organization—with an "areas" division and a "commodities" division. This conception, however, would foster bilateral relations with the individual countries rather than cooperation among them. These objections prevented country desks from sprouting as rapidly as they might have. They were not altogether prevented from developing in units where knowledge of the individual countries was needed for programming and arriving at balance of trade estimates.

Negotiation of the bilateral agreements required by the Act was a high-level matter involving State Department leadership. In the ECA Washington office, only the Office of the General Counsel was deeply involved. Once the pledges had been signed, their implementation of necessity devolved largely on the Paris office and the ECA Special Missions in the cooperating countries. Hence the agreements never exerted an important influence upon the organization of the Washington office.

[25]ECA1, pp. 6–13, 46.

The investment bank approach found its main internal support in the Director of Operations, Taylor, and its external support in the Export-Import Bank. The conception was applicable, if at all, only to a small part of the total program. Taylor's unit soon became isolated from the flow of day-to-day transactions in the agency and gradually withered on the vine. The rapid decline of this unit was easily visible in terms of size of staff, changes in titles (Taylor became "the assistant to the administrator"), and office locations.

The unit early established its claim as the loan-approving authority, but a growing conflict developed between the investment criteria and the balance of payments criteria for loans. A crisis in the fall of 1948, when a large proportion of the loan funds were still uncommitted, gave convincing evidence of the unworkability of the investment bank approach and led to a resolution of the conflict in favor of the balance of trade approach.

The result is that during the first two or even three months the entire operating portion of ECA consisted of three groups. The first, comprised of Mr. Hoffman and a few high-level aides, conducted the external relations of the agency with the Congress, the State Department, other federal departments, and the participating nations. They negotiated the bilateral agreements and saw the appropriation bill through the Congress. A second group, in Bissell's office, worked up a quarterly aid program and shaped up the programming procedures that were later accepted. A third group, inherited from the State Department, actually processed the requests for aid and kept the pipelines full. These three groups, together with their clerical support, could not have consisted of more than seventy-five persons, and probably fewer. During this period the rest of the agency was not so much "doing" as getting ready to do.

The Organization and Management Division

The ECA organization acquired a reasonably coherent form without apparently ever having been planned. What was the Organization and Management Division doing during this period? During the early days one could get only a fragmentary picture of what was going on. The operating personnel, each conceiving that he or she had a job to do and little time to do it, did not want to spend time talking to procedures specialists or reading organizational announcements. Although the O&M Division made a valiant effort to find out what the procedures actually were, and to record them, any influence it had on the form of the organization was achieved in more informal ways.

A small staff brought into the division early in April to make organizational plans spent two feverish weeks trying to arrive at its own conceptions of the program and their organizational implications. For better or worse, the two representations that found greatest acceptance in the division were the balance of trade approach and the European cooperation approach. In order to influence the organization toward implementing these notions, a mimeographed memorandum—"Basic Principles of ECA Organization"—was circulated in draft form by the division on April 30. This memorandum largely ignored the proposed Budget Bureau plan, emphasized the balance of trade approach, and pointed to the weaknesses in the commodity screening and investment bank approaches. It stressed the need for strengthening the Paris office in order to foster multilateral rather than bilateral negotiations and warned against "country desks."

No formal approval was sought for the memorandum, thus avoiding a tedious and probably interminable process. The memorandum was formulated as a set of underlying assumptions and their organizational implications (a "mission statement"?), rather than as an organizational blueprint. It was thought that a relatively brief draft memorandum of some two thousand words might actually be read by a few influential people, and that a few of the central concepts might be absorbed and influence future thinking about organization. The document clearly did not pass unobserved, but it would be impossible to assess precisely what influence it had.

At about the same time, the O&M Division had to provide the Personnel Division with descriptions of positions so that jobs could be classified and appointments authorized in the various units. This put the Division in a strategic position to influence the growth of the units. Until a unit could describe its functions to O&M and get acceptance of its role in the structure, it met a wall of red tape when seeking approval of its appointments. Personnel could be retained by a determined unit chief on a consulting basis, but the lack of a table of organization made a unit's position very uncertain and exercised a check on expansion. This procedure made possible an effective delaying action against the establishment of country desks and the multiplication of statistical units.

The unit that fared worst was that under the director of operations, for the O&M analysts found themselves unable to reconcile Taylor's conception of his task with the overall pattern that was emerging in the agency. Although the fate of that unit would probably have been the same in the long run, the halt in its expansion in the early weeks gave Bissell and his assistants time to organize their activities into a coherent pattern.

A happy accident gave the O&M Division its third tool. In the appropriations hearings Mr. Hoffman, when asked how many persons he would need in the Washington office, replied almost at random, "six hundred." Having stated the number, he had to live with it; he also now had a means for countering the requests of the Washington units for more and more personnel as the cell-splitting process went on.

When, early in June, the personnel "needs" of individual units were added up, the total exceeded six hundred by a considerable margin, and the deputy administrator turned to the O&M Division for help in arriving at a balanced table of organization in hearings with the heads of individual units. Of course in the end the ceiling had to bulge. By the end of July, the Washington staff exceeded seven hundred. But the agency remained for years spectacularly smaller than any federal agency carrying out a task of comparable magnitude, and the sudden reduction in its rate of growth by the end of July can only be attributed to the ceilings.

On July 26 the first official organization chart of the Washington office of the ECA was reproduced. The chart did not create new organizational arrangements but ratified and gave solidity to the patterns that had tentatively emerged. From the beginning of August, it provided a set of historical boundaries in terms of which new claims for territory had to be argued.

It should be reasonably clear from the recital of these events that the O&M Division was by no means the predominant influence on the final form of the ECA organization. Although that form embodied most of the views expressed in the "Basic Principles" memorandum circulated on April 30, the relation was in only small part causal. The memorandum represented less an influence on organization than a rather accurate forecast of the mold into which the organization would be forced by the requirements of its tasks and goals—the conditions of "workability."

The Aftermath

An organization chart depicting the structure of the Washington office on December 1, 1948,[26] shows the focus of program activities lying in the office of the assistant deputy administrator for program, Mr. Bissell. Under him, the balance of trade approach was implemented by the Program Coordination Division, assisted by the Foods, Industry, and Fiscal and Trade Policy Divisions. Provisions of the law unrelated to the central programming functions were being handled by other divisions. The Office of the Controller was performing auditing functions, and a Statistics and Reports Division was "auditing" the effect of the program on the Euro-

[26]ECA2, p. 85; also, ECA1, pp. 37–42.

pean economy. The other important boxes on the chart correspond to the usual housekeeping units—administrative services, personnel, O&M, budget, security, and information. Mr. Taylor had become assistant to the administrator, with a small staff. The Procurement Transactions Division had dwindled to a small Program Methods Control Staff attached to Bissell's office. A total of 770 persons was employed in the Washington office, 290 in the Paris office, and 1,127 in the country missions.

In less than four months, by July 26, the agency had attained virtually its final form, a form dictated by: (1) the relative political support for differing conceptions of the agency task; (2) the identifications and conceptions of the other government agencies surrounding ECA; and (3) the appropriateness of the structure for implementing that conception of the agency's task which prevailed. But while the form was somewhat predictable it was certainly not planned. The processes of cell multiplication and the power struggles within and around the agency were the main processes through which this rapid adaptation and evolution of an effective organization took place. The organization that evolved represented an oversimplification of the agency's task—an overemphasis of certain of its aspects, a relative neglect of others. But it did encompass the central features of the task and the requisite political emphases, and did so relatively effectively.

In this sense, the organization structure of ECA can be regarded as a reflection of the way in which the foreign assistance problem was structured by human minds endeavoring to grapple with its complexity. Each organizational unit can be roughly equated with some identifiable element in one of the competing conceptualizations of the problem.

When we observe organizational change in the short run, and particularly at a moment of large and rapid shift, we see environmental forces molding organizations through the mediation of human minds. We see a learning process in which growing insights and successive restructurings of the problem as it appears to the humans dealing with it reflect themselves in the structural elements of the organization itself. This view has important implications for reorganization. First, it implies that reorganization can seldom affect efficiency without altering program goals. When we change the organization, we change the picture of the concrete tasks to be done and the concrete goals to be achieved—the representation of the program. When we change the concept of the program, we change the relative importance of the several parts of the complex whole, we alter allocations of resources and priorities among goals.

Second, this view casts some light on the significance of formal organization. Plans of organization affect behavior in at least two ways. First, when they are officially approved, they draw force from the motivations of legitimacy—employees feel that they ought to observe the plans because they accept the system of authority that approved them. Second, plans may influence behavior because they provide employees with a conceptual scheme of the agency's program, a scheme that serves as a framework for decision and action. If the scheme translates the agency's complex problem into terms that are clear and understandable to the persons who have to solve it, if it leads to a relatively simple division of activities and is helpful as a guide to decision—then its workability will be a powerful force toward its acceptance.

THE BUSINESS SCHOOL: A PROBLEM IN ORGANIZATIONAL DESIGN[27]

In 1949 I came to Carnegie Institute of Technology to assist in the organization of a new business school, the Graduate School of Industrial Administration (GSIA). Its central educational mission was to offer a master's degree in Industrial Administration for persons wishing to prepare for a career in management, but the plans also called for Ph.D. programs in both business and economics and a strong emphasis upon research.

None of the senior members of the new faculty came from business school backgrounds, and it quickly became their avowed purpose to change business school education to resemble, more closely than was then customary, professional training in engineering and medical science. In the latter two fields there was a strong current at this time toward increased emphasis on the sciences, physical and biological, respectively, that provided the fundamental knowledge base for the profession.

Research in a business school may, of course, cover a wide spectrum from studies aimed at advancing fundamental knowledge about human behavior, economics, and even mathematics to studies aimed rather directly at improving business practice. Regardless of where the research lies on the spectrum, the fact that it is carried on in the environment of a business school presumably means that it has some relevance, direct or indirect, for business. Later, I will discuss the criteria of relevance.

The Information Base of the Professional School

The objectives of all professional schools—engineering, medicine, law, education, business, architecture, or what not—can be stated as (1) education and training for prospective or present practitioners in the profes-

---

[27]The account in this section is drawn from a paper bearing the same title, published in the *Journal of Management Studies*, 4:1–16 (1967).

sion and (2) for persons wanting to do research in the professional school, to advance knowledge relevant to the practice of the profession. We should expect, therefore, that at an appropriate level of generality, the organizational design problems of all professional schools will be essentially the same.[28]

Information[29] relevant to the accomplishment of a professional school's teaching and research goals comes from two main sources. First, it comes from the world of practice: its institutional environment and the skills and techniques for handling professional problems. Second, the professional school must provide access to information and skills within the sciences that are relevant to the improvement of professional practice. In the case of the business school, these sciences include economics, psychology, sociology, applied mathematics, and computing science. The business school (that is, its faculty, collectively) must understand such things as the principle of marginalism, human motivation, political processes, linear programming, problem-oriented computer languages, and probability theory.

In one-to-one correspondence with the two main bodies of information and skill the professional schools need to possess are two sets of social systems that possess the knowledge: the social system of practitioners, and the social systems of scientists in the relevant disciplines. These systems themselves have elaborate institutions and procedures for storing, transmitting, developing, and applying knowledge. In business, the institutions are business firms, trade associations, and professional management societies. In the sciences, the institutions are graduate schools, research institutes, and professional societies. The main way for an organization to get access to the information and skill that are stored and transmitted by a social system is to participate in the system. Hence, the business school must participate effectively in the social system of business, on the one hand, and in the social systems of the relevant sciences, on the other.

Liberal and Professional Education

We must not confuse the distinction between knowledge from the disciplines and knowledge from the profession with the distinction that is

---

[28]N. B. Henry, ed., *Education for the Professions*, First Yearbook of the National Society for the Study of Education, Part II (Chicago: University of Chicago Press, 1962). *Education for Professional Responsibility*, Proceedings of the Inter-Professions Conference on Education for Professional Responsibility, Buck Hill Falls, April 12–14, 1948 (Pittsburgh: Carnegie Press, 1948).

[29]For brevity, I will often use "information" and "knowledge" to refer not simply to "knowledge about" (i.e., facts and principles) but also "knowledge how" to produce results, conduct inquiry, solve problems, and so on. These kinds of skills constitute a large part of the knowledge relevant to any profession.

often made between "liberal" and "utilitarian" knowledge. Pierson, in his study of American business education, speaks of universities as being "the product of two distinct and sometimes conflicting traditions. According to the first . . . , knowledge is pursued for its own sake. . . . Most proponents of this view . . . would regard direct preparation for particular careers as basically alien to the purpose of academic work. . . . The other great tradition . . . would leave ample room for those students desiring to prepare for particular careers. According to this tradition, the search for truth is not impugned because it proves useful.[30]

Those responsible for organizing the Graduate School of Industrial Administration assumed that the goals of a university include both the pursuit of knowledge for its own sake and the application of knowledge to practical pursuits. They saw no reason why knowledge about physics or history should be useless; and no more reason why knowledge about inventory control or organization structure should not be intellectually and aesthetically challenging. They viewed the idea that utility is the only touchstone of relevance in the professional school, and *in*utility the only touchstone in the disciplines as a mischievous doctrine causing untold harm to education in both domains. Education cannot go on satisfactorily without intellectual challenge and excitement. The professional school must be vigorous in research as well as teaching and must provide a solid intellectual core to the professional as well as the disciplinary portion of its concerns.

Knowledge Requirements for Research

Invention calls on two quite different kinds of knowledge: knowledge about needs to be filled and knowledge about things that can be done (i.e., about the laws of nature and what they make possible). Invention is easiest when it can operate at one extreme or the other of the range from end-use requirements to laws of nature. The effective sales engineer and product engineer, on one end of the range, immerse themselves in information from the end-use environment, trying to discover what products customers would like to have, and what improvements in existing products. Then they apply known technology to provide the new or improved products.

At the other end of the range, scientists immerse themselves in knowledge of natural science, determining what questions about natural phenomena have not been answered and applying available research techniques (or inventing new ones) to answer these questions.

---

[30]F. C. Pierson, *The Education of American Businessmen* (New York: McGraw-Hill, 1959), pp. 16–17.

Research becomes more difficult when its undertakes to extend farther along the entire range. Product engineering becomes more difficult when, going beyond the needs reported by customers, it tries to conceive what needs customers would have if only they knew they had them! One way to do this is to turn to the environment of scientific knowledge, asking what uses the materials and processes located there might have. Similarly, pure science becomes more difficult when it goes beyond the environment of science itself and looks to areas of application for unanswered questions; then seeks to apply the methods of science to answer them. Improving nails and improving hammers, each separately, is easier but generally of less value than designing powerful new combinations of nails and hammers that are especially suited to each other.

Many of the very good problems in pure science have been posed from outside. Industrial chemistry provided much of the impetus for basic research in biochemistry, and electronic computing and communication devices for basic research in solid state physics. The contacts during World War II of economics with military operating problems led to operations research and a revolution in the theory of the firm. The need to understand and deal with the Great Depression launched Keynesian economics. Necessity is indeed the mother of important inventions, including many that are important to the basic sciences.

These alternative ways of doing science disclose a whole range of opportunities for the business school. The business school is not simply a place where researchers with strong applied interests can use known principles of economics or psychology, or known statistical methods, to solve practical business problems. It can be a productive and challenging environment for basic researchers who understand and can exploit the advantages of having access to the "real world" as a generator of basic research problems and a source of data. The business school must be made attractive to such scientists if it is to do its job.

Fundamental Research in Other Professional Schools

Everything said above about basic research in business schools could be said equally of schools of engineering and medicine. Leading engineering schools, especially in the decades just after World War II, might almost better be described as schools of science than schools of engineering. Most of the research topics they pursued would be appropriate to physics, chemistry, or mathematics departments. Relatively little research was aimed at engineering design. Similarly, research in leading medical schools has in many ways closer connections with biology and biochemistry than with medical practice. Much of the fundamental work in bio-chemistry in the past half century was carried on in medical schools.

In fact, the pure science emphasis in both strong engineering schools and strong medical schools created serious concern about whether the needs of the practicing professions were being met. In engineering schools today, there has been a substantial growth in research on engineering design. This development was made possible by basic research on artificial intelligence and human cognition that provided a foundation for inquiring into and understanding the design process as a process of thought and decision-making.

Access to the Knowledge Base: Business

How can business schools participate effectively in the business system? Historically, the schools have tried to do this in several ways. They have sought faculty members with management experience, encouraged faculty consulting practice and offered consulting and applied research services to business, brought in businessmen as occasional lecturers and adjunct professors, and offered mid-career courses as another way to bring managers within their walls. How well have these methods worked?

Faculty with Business Experience. Seeking faculty members with management experience has provided a number of outstanding successes and innumerable failures and mediocre outcomes. The problem lies in attracting away from their business careers the kinds of managers who can perform well in these roles. A low-level manager with modest prospects for further rise in business is unlikely to shine more brightly in the one environment than the other. What such managers bring to the business school is ability, not business experience, for they have operated at too low levels for their experience to have much value in instruction.

Managers approaching retirement sometimes view the business school as a less stressful environment than business. Of course there is no evidence that the desire for semi-retirement produces professorial excellence. These experienced managers may also suffer from the dangerous illusion that good business teaching consists in "telling the students how I did it."

Managers who are looking for a new range of experience, have an affinity for things intellectual, and catch the excitement of a first-rate university environment are the rare birds who must be netted at all costs. And after they have been netted, the school must provide the challenge they were looking for, and help them to interact fruitfully with the more long-haired among their colleagues.

Typical business school faculty members, however, even on the applied end of the curriculum, will not have had much or any experience as managers. The school must provide ways for those who have followed academic careers to get access to the business environment. (It must provide these ways even for those who have had business experience, for that experience will recede rapidly into the past.)

Consulting Practice and Field Research. While consulting practice is potentially an excellent route of access to the business environment, its potential will be realized only if there is a strong institutional tradition of non-routine consulting at a high professional level, and against routine consulting. The practice must also remain within reasonable limits of time—an average of one day a week is a rule of thumb that many schools have found practical.

Research that brings faculty members inside the business firm for many hours—gathering data by observation and interview or collaborating in research with management personnel—is probably at least as valuable as consulting. There need be no sharp line between the two, except: (1) the faculty member and the firm should both be crystal clear as to when they are doing the one, and when the other; (2) the faculty member should receive payment for consulting, not for research; (3) the research agreement should not promise valuable results to the firm, although such results should be welcomed if they appear; (4) research calls for an agreement between the school and the firm, consulting on a direct relation between the professor and the firm.

Research plays an especially important role in gaining access to the business environment for junior faculty and those farthest from the applied end of the curriculum. Whether the research is "applied" or "basic" is irrelevant. What is critical is that conduct of the research bring about massive exposure of faculty members to actual behavior inside the business firm.

Access to the Knowledge Base: The Sciences

Some business school faculty members will be recruited from the scientific disciplines that are relevant to business. Provided that certain rather difficult conditions are met, this group will provide access to the bodies of scientific knowledge that are associated with their disciplines. Of course quality is the first concern. We should not suppose that first-rate scientists will have the urge to join a business school faculty much more often than first-rate managers will. In the value structures of most scientific disciplines, the word "basic" carries positive connotations and the word "applied" negative connotations. High status is associated with basic research.

This is a fact that business schools must take into account in their faculty planning. The school must provide the conditions that will convince talented scientists that they can do significant, fundamental work in the business school environment, and do it *more* effectively there than in a traditional department in their discipline. High salaries will help in the persuasion, but will not do the job unaided.

The most convincing argument for the business school as a superior research environment for scientists is that it will expose them to problems of end use, arising from the business environment, that they can transform into exciting, non-routine problems of fundamental research. Nearly a half century of success with this strategy at a number of business schools makes the argument more persuasive than it was a generation ago. But even today, it will appeal mostly to the adventuresome, to the mavericks.

The business school will not recruit or retain many first-rate scientists if it insists that all research done within its walls must have direct relevance to business. It can demonstrate its respect for basic research by valuing among its faculty at least some members whose work does not have obvious business relevance but does command high respect in its discipline. Equally important, it is essential that tests of relevance, when applied, take account of the tortuous many-step process by which basic knowledge may gradually be brought to bear on problems of practice.

It has been demonstrated that it is possible to recruit good scientists to professional school faculties and to create an environment where they will be productive. It has been done by respecting scientists' desires for identification with, and approval by, their scientific disciplines. An economist who is not respected by economists is unlikely to achieve self-respect from contributions to management science. A certain part of the activity of such faculty members will result simply in good science, not particularly relevant to business. If *all* their activity is of this kind, then the point of their being in the business school has been lost.

The Professional School in the University

There is no single answer to the question of how far the professional school should depend on other departments in the university for teaching in the disciplines, or how far it should be self-contained. However, a strong case can be made for not excluding the disciplines entirely from the professional school faculty. At a minimum, each of the relevant disciplines should have an effective beachhead within the professional school: in the business school, some social or organizational psychologists, some applied mathematicians and statisticians, some economists. It needs them whether or not those disciplines are represented elsewhere on the university faculty.

The business school must have effective communication with members of the departments representing the relevant disciplines; and joint appointments, with the "jointness" more than nominal, are almost essential to maintaining such communication. Joint appointees can perform their function only if they are *more* than minimally acceptable to their disciplinary colleagues. Second-class citizens cannot do the job. Some of the faculty with joint appointments need to be sufficiently strongly identified with their business school functions to take a vigorous role in staff and curriculum planning in the school.

One way in which the professional school can strengthen its ties with the disciplines is to provide funds for fundamental research in areas *broadly* relevant to its mission, and to make those funds available to appropriate scientists in the disciplines, particularly to groups who link the school with the disciplines.

The Knowledge Base: Synthesis

The business school envisaged in these pages would include one faculty cohort drawn from the scientific disciplines and a second, more "applied" cohort trained in business subjects. The barrier between these two sets of social systems must not be allowed to transfer itself from the outside world to the interior of the school itself. A social system left to itself gravitates toward equilibrium—maximum entropy, so to speak. The position of maximum entropy for a professional school is the one in which the faculty trained in the profession is absorbed in the culture of the profession, whereas the faculty trained in an underlying discipline is absorbed in the culture of that discipline, leaving a deep gulf between them.

This position of equilibrium does not permit the business school to perform its teaching and research functions effectively. The "practical" segment of the faculty becomes dependent on the world of business as its sole source of knowledge, and is likely to become a slightly out-of-date purveyor of almost-current business practice. Similarly, under equilibrium, the discipline-oriented segment of the professional school faculty becomes dependent on its disciplines of origin for goals, values, and approval. Sealed off from the practitioner's environment, that environment becomes inaccessible and irrelevant as a source of data, research problems, or development and application of innovations. Soon, the members of each discipline in the school demand increasing autonomy so that they can pursue disciplinary goals without regard to the "irrelevant" professional goals. At the same time, the professional school environment loses its attraction as a locus for research and teaching, and it becomes harder and harder to attract and retain first-class scientists.

Some of these dynamics can be seen in the historical development of American business schools. Originally spawned, in most cases, within economics departments, they gradually moved toward the business environment until the "pure" economists constituted minority enclaves. This led the economists, in turn, to seek separation from the business school.[31] Similar histories can be traced in the relation of psychology departments to schools of education and science departments to engineering schools.

A professional school administration has an unceasing task of preventing the system from moving toward the equilibrium it would otherwise seek, an equilibrium that means mediocrity for the professional school and inability to fulfill its special functions. All efforts to avoid this state of death must aim at lowering the barriers that impede communication between the discipline-oriented and the profession-oriented wings of the faculty. The specific measures that will best achieve this end range from the simple and concrete to the sophisticated and subtle. Such a "trivial" matter as office locations may be important. Homogeneous office grouping of faculty—almost guaranteeing homogeneous luncheon groups and the restriction of casual conversation to homogeneous clusters—is the worst possible arrangement; but it will normally emerge unless it is deliberately avoided.

Departmental structures must not be allowed to develop within the professional school, or, if they are unavoidable, their importance must be minimized. It may be necessary to give specialized subgroups some particular responsibilities for the recruitment and evaluation of faculty within their specialties—but not autonomy. Curricular planning, too, can best be done by groups that cut across disciplinary boundaries. Marketing is an important function in business institutions, but influence processes are an important topic in social psychology, and consumer choice a topic in economics. As they are all concerned with the same human behavior, they need to be brought together, not separated, in the curriculum. Almost every curricular area can be organized so that practical management problems are rubbed up against economic and psychological theories and mathematical techniques—and conversely.

Parallel opportunities for communication across boundaries can be sought in research. There is no guaranteed magic in interdisciplinary research, but if faculty members from different disciplines find them-

[31]F. C. Pierson, *op. cit.*, chap. 3.

selves in frequent contact, a pair or triad will occasionally discover an area of common interest where they want to undertake joint work. The task of the school's administration is not to establish sterile formal plans for interdisciplinary work but to encourage contacts that will cause projects to develop spontaneously. Encouragement of doctoral theses that require the student to work with faculty members from several disciplines often acquaints faculty with each other's work.

These examples do not exhaust the possibilities for lowering the barriers to communication between disciplines. These and others will be found if the administration of the professional school takes the lowering of barriers as a major goal of its policy. To do this, the organization must be willing to expend energy continually to oppose the social forces that would otherwise push it toward equilibrium with its disciplinary environment.

Art and Science

A deep source of communication difficulty between the discipline-oriented and the practice-oriented members of a professional school faculty stems from the difference between science and art, between analysis and synthesis, between explanation and design. The pure scientist wishes to explain phenomena in nature; the practitioner wishes to devise actions or processes or physical structures that serve some specified purpose.

Analysis leading to explanation is generally thought to be itself susceptible of analysis and systemization, hence to be teachable. Synthesis aimed at design is generally thought to be intuitive, judgmental, not fully explicit, hence an art. Medicine, engineering, management, teaching are arts.

A full solution of the organizational problem of the professional schools hinges on developing an explicit, abstract, intellectual *theory* of the processes of synthesis and design; a theory that can be analyzed and taught in the same way that the laws of chemistry, physiology, and economics can be analyzed and taught. As I mentioned earlier, considerable progress has been made toward this development because the decision-making process underlying design is now sufficiently well understood so that computer programs can automate it and simulate it in significant instances.

Our increasing ability to approach synthesis and design as rigorous intellectual disciplines supplies a missing component for the construction of an effective professional school organization. For these new disciplines provide a focus for the profession-oriented part of the faculty, and a set of tasks more challenging than merely monitoring and interpreting the information system of the business environment, or even applying existing knowledge to business problems. They thereby give us means for increasing the intellectual attractiveness of the school's practitioner-oriented concerns, and making it easier to establish meaningful communication between the discipline-oriented and business-oriented members of the faculty.

A Parallel Problem: Research and Development

I have emphasized throughout that the same organizational problem is shared by all the professional schools: the problem of bridging the gap between the social system that produces scientific knowledge and the social system where professional practice takes place. But this problem is also present in all kinds of research and development organizations. I have already discussed R&D organization in these terms in the last part of the commentary on Chapter II.

Conclusion

The central thesis of this section is that organizing a professional school or an R&D department is much like mixing oil with water. It is easy to describe the intended product, less easy to produce it. And the task is not finished when the goal has been achieved. Left to themselves, the oil and water will separate again. So also will the disciplines and the professions. Organizing, in these situations, is not a once-and-for-all activity. It is a continuing administrative responsibility, vital for the sustained success of the enterprise.

What Is an Administrative Science?

THE DISTINCTION MADE IN CHAPTER III between the ethical and the factual helps to explain the nature of administrative science. Scientific propositions, it was said in that chapter, are statements about the observable world and the way in which it operates. Ethical propositions, on the other hand, are expressions of preferences. Do principles of administration qualify, under this definition, as scientific propositions, or do they contain an ethical element?

THEORETICAL AND PRACTICAL SCIENCES

Sciences may be of two kinds: theoretical and practical. Thus, scientific propositions may be considered practical if they are stated in some such form as: "In order to produce such and such a state of affairs, such and such must be done." But for any such sentence, an exactly equivalent theoretical proposition with the same conditions of verification can be stated in a purely descriptive form: "Such and such a state of affairs is invariably accompanied by such and such conditions." Since the two propositions have the same factual meaning, their difference must lie in the ethical realm. More precisely, the difference lies in the fact that the first sentence possesses an imperative quality which the second lacks. The first sentence can be said to be "true" or "false" only if this imperative aspect is ignored.

This situation is strictly analogous to that which we found to hold with respect to decisions. In so far as decisions can be said to be "correct," they can be translated into factual propositions. Their ethical element must be eliminated before the terms "true" and "false" can be applied to them. Similarly, the propositions of a practical science must be put in hypothetical form in order to eliminate the ethical element.

When factual propositions are selected primarily for their usefulness in deriving one imperative from another, they may be considered practical. In other cases, they are *theoretical*. It is clear that they differ from each other only with respect to the motives of the persons who employ them.

From the foregoing discussion, two definite conclusions may be drawn:

First, science is interested in sentences only with regard to their verification. Hence, science is concerned with the factual aspects of meaning, but not with the ethical.

Second, practical sciences differ from theoretical sciences, as those terms have been used here, only in their ethical aspects.

Propositions of an Administrative Science[1]

Propositions about administrative processes will be scientific in so far as truth and falsehood, in the factual sense, can be predicated of them. Conversely, if truth or falsehood can be predicated of a proposition concerning administrative processes, then that proposition is scientific.

It is sometimes thought that, since the words "good" and "bad" often occur in sentences written by students of administration, the science of administration contains an essential ethical element. If this were true, a science of administration would be impossible, for it is impossible to choose, on an empirical basis, between ethical alternatives. Fortunately, it is not true. The terms "good" and "bad" when they occur in a study on administration are seldom employed in a purely ethical sense. Procedures are termed "good" when they are conducive to the attainment of specified objectives, "bad" when they are not conducive to such attainment. That they are, or are not, so conducive is purely a matter of fact, and it is this factual element which makes up the real substance of an administrative science. To illustrate: In the realm of economics, the proposition "Alternative A is *good*" may be translated into two propositions, one of them ethical, the other factual:

"Alternative A will lead to maximum profit."

"To maximize profit is good."

The first of these two sentences has no ethical content, and is a sentence of the practical science of business. The second sentence is an ethical imperative, and has no place in any science.

Science cannot tell whether we *ought* to maximize profit. It can merely tell us under what conditions this maximization will occur, and what the consequences of maximization will be.

If this analysis be correct, then there are no *logical* differences which distinguish the sentences of one science from those of another. Whatever differences exist must arise from the subject matter of the several sciences, rather than from the intrinsic nature of their sentences.

---

[1]Luther Gulick has set forth substantially this same view with respect to the nature of administrative science. See "Science, Values, and Public Administration," in Gulick and Urwick, eds., *op. cit.*, pp. 191–193.

THE NATURAL AND THE SOCIAL SCIENCES

The discussion thus far leads to the solution of one issue which has been debated by methodologists of the social sciences. It has often been argued that the social sciences involve ethical norms, and therefore lack the objectivity of the natural sciences. A recent statement of this view may be found in Robert S. Lynd's *Knowledge for What?*[2] Since it is clear that truth or falsehood cannot be predicated of ought-sentences, this distinction cannot be valid. If there are fundamental differences between the natural and the social sciences, they must lie in some other direction.

Another group of distinctions, although valid, must be dismissed as superficial. First, social phenomena are probably far more complex than the data with which the natural sciences are concerned. Consequently the task of discovering regularities underlying social phenomena might be expected to be more difficult. Second, experiments cannot be carried on in the social sciences without regard to the consequences for the objects of experimentation. The doctor in *Arrowsmith* had an unequaled opportunity to experiment with vaccine under controlled conditions; but his human values got the best of him, and he found himself unable to deprive his control subjects of the benefits of treatment. The validity of both of these distinctions may be granted, but they can hardly be considered fundamental. Complexity is a matter of degree, and it may well be questioned whether some of the more involved phenomena which have been dealt with in the physical sciences are not as complex as some of the simpler social phenomena. Experimentation, too, can hardly be the real distinction, for astronomy, the first developed of the natural sciences, has never had the advantages of the laboratory in discovering its laws.

Expectations as Factors in Social Behavior

If there is a fundamental difference between the social and the natural sciences, it derives from the fact that the social sciences deal with conscious human beings whose behavior is influenced by knowledge, memory, and expectation. Consequently, knowledge by the human beings themselves of the forces which mold their behavior may (but need not) alter that behavior. It is apparent today, for example, that public awareness of the uses to which propaganda was put in an earlier world war affected to some degree public reaction to propaganda in the Second World War.

[2]Robert S. Lynd, *Knowledge for What? The Place of Social Science in American Culture* (Princeton: Princeton University Press, 1939). A somewhat more sophisticated variant of this viewpoint runs through the writings of Frank H. Knight. See especially his review of "Bertrand Russell on Power," *International Journal of Ethics*, 49:253–285 (Apr., 1939), and the Preface to the reissue of his *Risk, Uncertainty and Profit*, pp. xv–xvi.

This does not mean that it is impossible to state valid laws of human behavior. It simply means that one of the variables to be included in the statement of social laws is the state of knowledge and experience of the persons whose behavior the law purports to describe.[3] The more deliberate the behavior which forms the subject matter of a science, the more important the role played by knowledge and experience.

This characteristic of purposive behavior, that is, its dependence on belief or expectation, has further consequences in the social field when group behavior is involved. The decision of each member of the group may depend on his expectation of the behavior of the other members of the group; that is, A's decision may depend on his expectation of B's behavior, while B's decision may depend on his expectation of A's behavior. In this way a certain indeterminacy may arise, as indeed it does in such social institutions as the stock market, where successful behavior involves outguessing other participants in the market with regard to these expectations.[4]

It is a fundamental characteristic of social institutions that their stability and even their existence depend on expectations of this sort. In so far as behavior of another person can be accurately predicted, it forms a portion of the objective environment, identical in its nature with the nonhuman portions of that environment.

Applying these considerations to the field of administration, we see first of all that the administrative organization implies purposive behavior on the part of its participants. Hence the expectations of these participants will be a factor in determining their behavior. Further, part of their expectations will involve expectations as to the behavior of other members of the administrative organization.

In this sense administration is not unlike play-acting. The task of the good actor is to know and play his role, although different roles may differ greatly in content. The effectiveness of the performance will depend

[3]A careful search for discussions of this point in the literature of social science methodology revealed a brief but clear statement of the proposition in a paper by W. Edwin Van de Walle, "A Fundamental Difference Between the Natural and Social Sciences," *Journal of Philosophy*, 29:542–550 (Sept. 29, 1932). The distinction is closely allied to the differentiation between the artificial and the natural which was introduced into the field of sociology by Lester F. Ward, *Dynamic Sociology* (New York: D. Appleton, 2nd ed., 1926). Cf. Joseph Mayer, "Scientific Method and Social Science," *Philosophy of Science*, 1:338–350 (July, 1934). But both in the writings of Ward and in Frank Knight's discussion of the same issue (*Risk, Uncertainty and Profit*, pp. xv–xxxii) the view is apparently taken that the "artificiality" of society implies that a science of sociology inevitably involves ethical assumptions. In the present study, the contrary view is taken.

[4]Frank Knight's fundamental thesis is that this "outguessing" is the explanatory mechanism for profit in a competitive economic system (*Risk, Uncertainty and Profit*, pp. 35–37, 333–335). See also analyses of the economic problem of duopoly, where the phenomenon of outguessing shows up to an extreme degree, in R. G. D. Allen, *Mathematical Analysis for Economists* (London: Macmillan, 1938), pp. 200–204, 345–347, and references cited therein.

on the effectiveness of the play and the effectiveness with which it is played. The effectiveness of the administrative process will vary with the effectiveness of the organization and the effectiveness with which its members play their parts.

THE NATURE OF ADMINISTRATIVE PRINCIPLES

We may summarize the conclusions we have reached with respect to a science of administration. In the first place, an administrative science, like any science, is concerned purely with factual statements. There is no place for ethical assertions in the body of a science. Whenever ethical statements do occur, they can be separated into two parts, one factual and one ethical; and only the former has any relevance to science.

Using the terms "theoretical" and "practical" as they have been defined in this section, an administrative science may take either of these two modes. On the one hand, propositions about administration may be descriptions—with reference either to a particular organization or to organizations in general—of the way in which human beings behave in organized groups. This might be called a sociology of administration.

On the other hand, a practical science of administration consists of propositions as to how men would behave if they wished their activity to result in the greatest attainment of administrative objectives with scarce means.[5]

These two alternative forms of administrative science are exactly analogous to the two forms which economic science takes. First economic theory and institutional economics are generalized descriptions of the behavior of men in the market. Second, business theory states those conditions of business behavior which will result in the maximization of profit.

This treatise has included discussions of both the sociology of administration and the practical science of administration. Chapters IV, VI, VIII, and X have been concerned primarily with the former, and Chapters III, IX, and XI primarily with the latter.

---

[5]For a fuller discussion of the distinction between a sociology and a practical science of administration, see Richard A. Musgrave, "The Planning Approach in Public Economy: A Reply," *Quarterly Journal of Economics*, Feb., 1941, p. 324, and Herbert A. Simon, "The Planning Approach in Public Economy: Further Comment," *ibid.*, p. 329. For an example of the misconceptions which result from a failure to make this distinction, see the recommendations for research in administration set forth in V. O. Key, "The Lack of a Budgetary Theory," *American Political Science Review*, 34: 1143 f. (Dec., 1940).

INDEX